Process Improvement Essentials

James R. Persse

O'REILLY®

Beijing • Cambridge • Farnham • Köln • Paris • Sebastopol • Taipei • Tokyo

Copyright © 2006 O'Reilly Media, Inc. All rights reserved. Printed in the United States of America.

Published by O'Reilly Media, Inc. 1005 Gravenstein Highway North, Sebastopol, CA 95472

O'Reilly books may be purchased for educational, business, or sales promotional use. Online editions are also available for most titles (*safari.oreilly.com*). For more information, contact our corporate/institutional sales department: (800) 998-9938 or *corporate@oreilly.com*.

Editors: Mary O'Brien and Tatiana Apandi	**Cover Designer:** Mike Kohnke
Production Editor: Sanders Kleinfeld	**Interior Designer:** Marcia Friedman
Copyeditor: Linley Dolby	**Illustrators:** Robert Romano and
Indexer: Reg Aubry	Jessamyn Read

Printing History:

September 2006: First Edition.

RepKover™ This book uses RepKover™, a durable and flexible lay-flat binding.
ISBN-10: 0-596-10217-8
ISBN-13: 978-0-596-10217-3
[C]

To Laura Chodosh Allen,
and to Winifred Persse and Patricia Persse

CONTENTS

Preface

THIS BOOK IS NOT INTENDED AS A COMPREHENSIVE LOOK AT THE ART AND TECHNIQUE OF PROCESS improvement, nor is it intended to give you a complete look at ISO 9001:2000, CMMI, or Six Sigma. Those types of books are already out there. The weighty thing about them is that they *are* comprehensive, filled with good information, depth, and a lot of material. Sometimes they contain more than what you might be looking for initially.

Because I work in the field of process improvement, it is not uncommon for people to come up to me at trade shows or after seminars or at organizational meetings and ask my opinion about one of these three well-known programs.

They *want* an answer that's less than comprehensive. (In fact, they often want an answer that's less than useful.) Two or three sentences to the query: Which program should we adopt? Or, what's the difference between these three? Or, what would it cost to get certified? Those are questions none of us can answer in a three-minute conversation. But I've tried to come close to that in this slim volume.

The chief purpose of this book is to help people who are new to process improvement get a basic understanding of the purpose, aim, and structure of this growing field and to help them understand how ISO 9000, CMMI, and Six Sigma relate to the industry and to one another. It's also designed to help set beginners on the way to making an informed decision, should they wish to move into deeper exploration along more specific lines.

In Part 1 of this book, I'll begin by taking a general look at the intent of process improvement. Today's technologies industries are becoming more and more quality-conscious, especially as IT budgets grow and represent bigger and bigger expenditures within corporations. Waste, inefficiencies, and compromised quality can have a dramatic impact on a company's competitive position and its success in the marketplace. So technology managers are more and more attuned to the business nature of their missions. And they realize that there are very real business advantages to process management.

Next, in Part 2, I'll look at the 9001:2000 Quality Management Standard from the ISO, the International Organization for Standardization based in Geneva. The ISO is a large network of organizations that work to establish a large variety of standards. The ISO 9001:2000 standard focuses on quality management for manufacturing industries. While the standard can be applied at canning companies, automobile factories, and so on, many technology companies find it suits their own needs quite well. I've worked with a large software development organization in Ottawa, Canada, called Systems House Limited. SHL is an ISO shop, and their ISO program helps them manage their projects and engagements very successfully. I'll review the framework of ISO 9001:2000, with special focus on sections 4 through 8, the sections that describe each component of the quality program.

After I look at ISO, I'll look at the Capability Maturity Model from the Software Engineering Institute, a foundation based out of Carnegie Mellon University in Pittsburgh. (The latest release of this program is actually named CMMI-Dev, Version 1.2, with the "I" standing for Integration and the "Dev" standing for Development—an integrated model intended for development organizations.) CMMI integrates quality recommendations for systems engineering, software engineering, and integrated product and process development. You'll notice that's a more constrained focus than ISO 9001:2000. ISO is shaped for any manufacturing enterprise. CMMI is specially designed for technology companies, especially those that deal in some form or fashion with the design and development of software. CMMI is structured differently from ISO. It's shaped as a collection of Process Areas, each with a series of goals and practices designed to help you reach those goals. I'll look at each Process Area in CMMI and then look at ways an organization can implement the Process Areas to reach its own quality goals.

I'll also take a look at Six Sigma. Six Sigma is a quality program that's been used to great extent and with great success at companies such as Honeywell, Motorola, and (most famously) General Electric. Six Sigma is a way to measure quality by measuring a company's ability to meet the needs of its customers through process refinement and process improvement. It's highly customer focused and highly data-centric. One of its core philosophies is that decisions should not be made on gut instinct alone. Instead, decisions should be made based on hard data, and that data should be collected from sources that support the needs of the customers. Unlike ISO and CMMI, Six Sigma is not published or regulated by a central body. It is a free-floating program, but as its user community increases, more and more support for its application is coming into the market. I'll look at the intention and philosophy of Six Sigma and then delve into its methodology, DMAIC. Then I'll look at some basic statistical tools that can help support a Six Sigma program.

The Audience for This Book

This book is intended for people who are new to process improvement. It is written for people who want to know more about process improvement and about the process improvement programs most popular today.

Most technology companies can benefit from some kind of process management focus. This became painfully apparent when the dot-com bubble burst around 2000. At that time, it seemed the software industry was going haywire and the venture capital industry was on for the ride. Hundreds of millions of dollars were being pumped into the most superfluous of concepts. Companies funded to the teeth literally appeared overnight: frenzied operations racing toward some ill-defined finish line. Amazingly, the management at a large portion of these start-ups was incredibly naive. They paid little attention to integrated design, to team organization, to product requirements, to even the most basic of business school management fundamentals.

Today the industry is becoming wiser. The fact that there is increased interest in ISO, CMMI, and Six Sigma is an indicator of that. This is a good trend, but it has not yet matured.

While more and more companies are looking at the potential benefits of process management and process improvement, they have a tendency to appoint internal people to carry the torch for them, people who have a vested interest in the outcome but who have little or no formal training in process improvement or much exposure to the facets of the field.

This book is intended for those people who would like to get a starting foundation in process improvement. For the focus of this book, these people typically fall into two general groups.

Process Managers

The term *process manager* is pretty softly defined in the industry right now. Scott Brenner is an IT director, but his company singled him out to lead its process charge. From my practice, this is the way I have seen more and more companies get into formal process improvement. They appoint an insider to shape the new capability. They may plan to fund it appropriately and to give it the kinds of experienced resources those kinds of teams need. They may even move to suggest what the program of choice will be. But early on, the process manager is typically left to take the first steps into uncharted territory and to do it somewhat alone.

People in this position are usually appointed for several reasons. They typically know their organizations, they know the ins and outs of their IT operations, they know their people and the culture, and they know a lot about the current problems and issues. But they probably don't know a lot about process improvement.

This book provides these types of managers with a high-level overview of the purpose of process improvement: What's the case for such an undertaking and what benefits might it bring to an organization? They can also look to this book to get a general approach for establishing a process program: steps they can coordinate to define a program, implement it, and then manage to realize sustained benefits from it.

These managers can also use this book to garner a working knowledge of the three leading process/quality programs: ISO 9001:2000, CMMI, and Six Sigma. It's very helpful to have at least a basic understanding of what these programs are about.

Executive Managers

The executive management is the other audience for this book. I am currently working on a major quality-program refresh initiative for a large credit card processing company. The CEO and CIO caught on that this might be a good idea when the board of directors asked them to audit their internal systems for SOX compliance. (SOX regulations directly impact business systems that touch accounting or financial reporting operations.) When they looked to see if their people were managing these systems with the expected controls in place (sign-offs, reviews and approvals, documented technical approaches), they were unpleasantly surprised. Less than 10 percent of the projects used any of the controls a SOX auditor might expect to see. My job was to embed SOX compliance procedures into all the company's systems and software management activities.

I was actually the third party they rushed in to address this problem. The first was Price Waterhouse. The second was the third floor of the city's most prestigious law firm. In the wake of scandals, such as Enron and WorldCom, and the subsequent introduction of the Sarbanes-Oxley Act, executive management is becoming increasingly aware of the need for reliability, dependability, consistency, and visibility in their operations. Quality programs deliver these kinds of benefits. They lower risk by raising predictability. On top of that, they help maximize efficiencies, bringing real benefit to the bottom line. Understanding how the discipline of process improvement can protect data integrity, ensure statutory and regulatory requirements, and improve business accountability can arm management with additional horsepower they can use to meet their strategic and tactical goals.

Executive management probably should not be burdened with needing to know the ins and outs of process improvement. So heavy books on the topic are probably not the ticket. But a lighter overview can certainly help. From this, management can acquire a general understanding of the scope and purpose of process improvement, and can gain a strategic appreciation for the very tangible value it can bring to the business enterprise.

Everyone Else

From a broader perspective, a general overview of process improvement can probably benefit just about any member of your organization. Some will need to know a lot about the specific path you choose; they are the folks who will make the program work. Some may need to know only a little, just enough to work effectively within the program.

But before I move into the next section of this book (an overview of how to design and manage a process improvement program), I'll take a brief look at what types of organizations—or situations within organizations—might have to work through some foundational issues before they can take full advantage of a process improvement program. That's an odd statement to make, especially in a book such as this that endorses and heartily recommends such programs. But the fact is, there are conditions that can derail even the best of intentions to set a process improvement program in place.

Safari® Enabled

When you see a Safari® Enabled icon on the cover of your favorite technology book, that means the book is available online through the O'Reilly Network Safari Bookshelf.

Safari offers a solution that's better than e-books. It's a virtual library that lets you easily search thousands of top tech books, cut and paste code samples, download chapters, and find quick answers when you need the most accurate, current information. Try it for free at *http://safari.oreilly.com*.

How to Contact Us

We have tested and verified the information in this book to the best of our ability, but you may find that features have changed (or even that we have made a few mistakes!) Please let us know about any errors you find, as well as your suggestions for future editions, by writing to:

O'Reilly Media, Inc.
1005 Gravenstein Highway North
Sebastopol, CA 95472
800-998-9938 (in the U.S. or Canada)
707-829-0515 (international/local)
707-829-0104 (fax)

We have a web page for this book, where we list errata, examples, and any additional information. You can access this page at:

http://www.oreilly.com/catalog/artofsoftware/

To comment or ask technical questions about this book, send email to:

bookquestions@oreilly.com

For more information about our books, conferences, Resource Centers, and the O'Reilly Network, see our web site at:

http://www.oreilly.com

Acknowledgments

For help in the production of this book I'd like to thank my editor at O'Reilly Media, Mary O'Brien, and my copyeditor, Linley Dolby, who polished the manuscript from start to finish.

I would also like to thank the executives who allowed to me to feature their professional insights in the "Views from the Top" segments of the book: Jim Ditmore of Wachovia Banks, Guy Bevente of SBC, Bruce Brown of T-Mobile, Linda Butler of BellSouth, Shailesh Grover of Cingular Wireless, and Ken Raybun of T-Mobile.

PART ONE

Process and Process Improvement

In this section, I look at considerations you may want to entertain when you set out to introduce concepts of process and process improvement to your IT organization.

Topics I look at in this section include:

- The importance of process improvement
- Myths of process improvement
- Benefits of process improvement
- Techniques for establishing a process improvement program
- Tips for sustaining process improvement across the organization

CHAPTER ONE

Introduction

A FEW YEARS AGO, I ATTENDED AN **IBM** RATIONAL UNIFIED PROCESS TRADE SHOW, HELD AT A CONVENTION center somewhere just outside Dallas. The center was a sprawling complex—hotels, restaurants, convention halls—anchored by an enormous indoor arboretum, a five-story glass-domed cathedral landscaped with palmetto and live oak, featuring, on its west wall, an exact replica of the Alamo, only at about twice the size.

Naturally it was a Disneyland-clean version of the Alamo. And the stone pathways, trickling canals, and set-aside grottos were all exquisitely manicured to reflect a kind of comfortable glow balanced between true life and cartoon. The theme of the show was something like, "Achieving Your Quality Goals." As I looked around, I knew this place was the perfect choice for that. Whoever had taken on this landscape project had not let up until every blade of grass had been trimmed to shape, oiled green, and shellacked properly into place.

This was Wednesday evening, after the show's opening, and the sponsors were hosting a huge cocktail reception in this arboretum. So after an afternoon of moving in and out of sessions and giving a brief talk on tailoring CMMI to organizational size, I found myself in a packed crowd in front of the Alamo, standing just under St. Jerome, at the best bar in the place. That's where Scott Brenner introduced himself.*

Scott was a senior IT director for a major health-claims processing company, one of the largest in the nation, and he wanted my thoughts on how he might improve the way his people managed IT projects. It seems that he and the company had had a "pretty rough" year last year getting his folks marching along productive lines. Scott didn't know a lot about process improvement, but his company used a lot of the Rational products and, given his role in the organization, management thought he'd be a good choice to send out into the field to collect some ideas. We chatted for a few minutes about the size of the organization, how it was structured, and what kinds of work its people engaged in. From Scott's answers, it seemed like a pretty typical Fortune 100–type shop. Then I asked him if he had any ideas about what specifically he might want to improve.

"I guess," he said, "it'd be our drop rate."

I'd never heard of that. "What's a drop rate?"

"That's the return revenue we lose when our systems misapply or misdirect a payment claim."

I liked that. That was a tangible metric. And I liked the fact that Scott seemed to have a handle on it. This seemed like a pretty good start toward a meaningful improvement target.

"Do you know what your drop rate was last year," I asked.

Scott took a club soda from the bartender. "Maybe three hundred million."

I knew I heard him right because the shooting didn't start until just after that. In fact, I'm pretty sure the "three hundred million" may have been what started it. But whatever it was, Santa Anna's men were suddenly swarming all around us, musket balls whizzing through the air, the glint of fixed bayonets throwing off slivers of hard light. I could sense The Defenders somewhere above us, stalwart shadows moving against the wash of cannon smoke, firing bravely over the crest of the chapel. And here we were, right out front. How did we manage this? Had they forgotten us? Could we ever hope to make the wall? Or were we lost? Were we doomed? Was it all a futile…

"James?"

I blinked. Scott was back in front of me, making a slight gesture with his club soda. The ice clinked against the glass.

---

* The name has been changed. Throughout this book, I'll be citing stories and case histories that illustrate many facets of process improvement. Most of the names and companies I cite are real. You'll probably recognize them. But when an event might be embarrassing or the individuals involved have specifically requested I not use real names, I use pseudonyms. The details, however, are all as accurate as I know them to be.

"Right," I said. "Absolutely. Project management. Yeah. Well, there are certainly things. Several things, actually. And things for drop rates...." And I can't really remember what else I said. But I'm reasonably sure it made little contribution to the industry's overall body of knowledge. I was stuck on that $300 million figure. To me, that's a fantastic amount of money to misapply or misdirect. And to make things more fantastic, I knew this company. I owned its stock. A good bit of it actually. And I hadn't heard of any such debacle. Not in the papers. Not from the analysts. In fact, when I checked later, I found that for that "pretty rough" year he was talking about, the stock had actually gone *up* two percent.

I knew this kind of thing happened, but I had never been this close to it happening in such a big way. Another technological pothole—this one about the size of the Astrodome— cloistered behind the walls of American IT.

As a rule, corporations like to keep their troubles quiet. They prefer to keep their problems from showing up on the street. It can be embarrassing. And it takes a lot of explanation to a lot of people who probably aren't prepared to appreciate that these things happen. Nobody's perfect. Defects happen.

Meat packers and car manufacturers probably have it the worst. The defects that enter their products are often miniscule in size: a bit of bacteria here, a missing shim there. And so they can be hard to spot. Often it's not until the consumers themselves stumble on it (a case of food poisoning, a crushed bumper) that the problem emerges. When that kind of failure goes public, an organization will scramble to locate the source of the problem. The company will divert all kinds of energy to tracking down the problem's cause and determining how much of the defective product got out. The course of last resort—when the milk's really been spilt—is usually to set a recall into action. Take your ground beef back to the supermarket; return to your dealership. Recalls are usually massive undertakings, and they can cost millions and millions of dollars. But by the time the error's in the public eye, the company has no real choice. Public failure is always expensive.

But sometimes it's also purging.

Take the Chevrolet Venture for example. This popular minivan ran into something of a quality problem in the late 1990s. At issue was the questionable design of its passenger seat latch. The company received data that indicated maybe the latch had an operational defect. After some study, Chevrolet determined that a general recall of the 1997 Venture was in order. Here is an excerpt from the text of that recall notice: "RECALL NOTICE (1997 Chevrolet Venture): Passenger's fingers could be severed by latch mechanism that moves seat fore and aft (Consumer Reports 2005)."

Now, as a general rule, severed fingers should not be a part of anyone's driving experience. What manufacturer would want that picture etched into the brand image of their minivans? Chevrolet no doubt brought its forces to bear. That latch was probably redesigned and remanufactured against the highest standards, with inordinate attention to detail: test after test, exhausting verification runs, complete assurance of unquestionable integrity. It wouldn't surprise me if that latch today—almost 10 years later—stands as the world-class epitome of efficiency and safety in seat latch technology.

That same call to quality came to poultry processor Pilgrim's Pride in April of 2002. In the largest meat recall in U.S. history, the company pulled back 27.4 million pounds of cooked sandwich meat after internal tests came back positive for potential listeria contamination. The discovery followed outbreaks of listeria in eight Northeast states that caused at least 120 illnesses.

Pilgrim's Pride, with encouragement from the FDA, left no tile unturned in its quest to remove even an amoeba's chance of impurities finding home in its food sources. There was simply too much riding on the outcome. Today, the company has one of the most stringent processes for meat inspection, meat processing, and meat packing in its industry.

Chevrolet and Pilgrim's Pride are both companies with established reputations. They have not grown to who they are by ignoring issues of product integrity, product performance, and quality. However, the complex nature of their businesses means things will not always go as planned. But with each misstep comes improvement: things get better, and then a little better. In these cases, the companies followed, but the public led. The public, when it's all said and done, may be the most effective quality-control system anyone could have.

That brings us to one focus of this book: performance improvement in technology companies.

No one screamed at Scott Brenner's company, because no one outside knew about the fault points of its claims systems.

From my experience, technology industries—corporate software, systems development, and operations—have been somewhat immune from the cleansing light of public failure. It's common in this industry that users—used to less-than-perfect technology products—will often put up with buggy software. They learn to work around the problems or to find substitute solutions while the issues are being fixed.

Most of the major missteps that occur on technology projects are discovered long before the end product ever sees real-world deployment. People internal to the organization observe that the new payroll system is printing security-sensitive data on checks. State taxes are being calculated at erroneous rates. Systems slow down to a crawl when new functionality is plugged in. The lights go out. Maybe we should back up a step.

In a way, that's fortunate: some of these potentially disastrous production problems are avoided. But by another way of thinking, it might also be unfortunate. When a project goes up in smoke, no one outside a core group may learn the details. These failures—often by publicly held companies—are all too often discreetly swept under the rug, or quietly navigated back to the starting gate with a no-harm-no-foul attitude. Often millions of dollars have been spent by the time the plug is pulled. Millions of dollars down the drain, with little to show for it.

And then there are the potentially disastrous production problems that do get through. Some folks might say, "Sure, but we aren't talking road safety here, or botulism." But given the prevalence of technology today, we just might be. Anyway, the issues certainly belong in the same ballpark.

The general feeling, as I have gathered it firsthand in the technology field, is that these miscalculations, false starts, and first shots are simply part of the cost of doing business. These situations (I have seen my share of them) are often further rationalized with a slew of caveats: we were never given the right resources, the timeline was always unrealistic, the specs were never clear. And because many corporate managers outside of IT assume that what goes on inside IT must be techno-mystery, the level of questioning that might penetrate these veils is seldom undertaken.

As a consultant, I have seen this happen in big ways and in small ways at MCI/WorldCom, Home Depot, GTE, Public Health Software Systems, ALLTEL, and many others. Ten years ago, the Standish Group released what is now famously known as "The Chaos Report." This was a study of software projects undertaken by Fortune 500 companies—the big players in the game. The results showed that the average project managed by these guys ran 222 percent over schedule and 189 percent over budget, with over 30 percent of planned functionality missing in the final product. Those were 1994 figures. About three years ago, Standish updated its Chaos Study, and though the numbers had improved somewhat, the deficits were still considerable.

I doubt there was a public recall in the bunch.

A Path of Quality

Of course the fault does not lie solely within corporate IT. Those numbers just cited are symptoms of multiple conditions: constrained resources, disconnected business objectives, changing market forces, new statutory and regulatory climates, finicky boards, and so on. But while that might help explain the result, it doesn't change the result. If that's the sea IT must sail on, it's better to adapt practices to make the sailing as smooth as possible.

The point I'd like to put forward here is that the poor technology performance that produces unusable software, severely compromised systems, or delayed business objectives has a real corporate cost no matter how often it is resettled into new projects or new initiatives. The failures may go away, but their impacts don't.

Today, technology has become too much a part of overall corporate success for its effectiveness to be left to chance. The stakes are too high. Fortunately, more and more companies are beginning to embrace this idea. The idea of "quality management" is being reinvigorated. Recognized and proven quality programs, such as ISO 9001:2000, the Capability Maturity Model, and Six Sigma, are rising in popularity. More and more technology managers are looking for ways to help remove degrees of risk and uncertainty from their business equations, and to introduce methods of predictability that better ensure success. But before I move into that topic, let's look at why it's even relevant. Let's look briefly at how the worlds of business and technology can no longer be considered separate, or complementary. They are not even two sides of the same coin. They are the same side of a one-sided coin.

The Innovation/Chaos Paradox

Today's IT is big business for sure.

According to the Gartner Group's Worldwide IT spending report of 2004, the amount of money being funneled into this field will grow 5.5 percent a year for 2006, 2007, and 2008 until it reaches nearly $3 trillion. Gartner Dataquest's Software Support Portfolio Review looked at current revenues for the worldwide software support services market. That market alone is worth $52.3 billion.

Those numbers tend to separate IT from the business operations they support. That's simply a convenient separation. Today's IT *is* the business. IT has become woven into the fabric of every business transaction. Remove cell phones from the picture today, and what adjustments would businesses have to make? Take away email. Take away word processors. What would become of the deal?

People in technology—the people who plan, design, develop, install, maintain, monitor— are as key as any other component to the success of business enterprises. And at the macro level, the success story stands out. But the focus of the discussions in this book is not on the macro level but on the micro level. To begin focusing toward that point, I'll take a step back.

Data processing has been around in American business since the late 1950s. The computers then weren't what we would recognize today as powerful. But by the early 1970s, these machines had become entrenched as core business tools. They were especially big in transaction-intensive industries. Banks, insurance companies, utilities, and reservation systems all found computing to be an effective way to process and manage mountains of data. Data-processing centers back then were somewhat removed from the daily bustle of the business. They were set off in climate-controlled rooms, set on raised floors. Access to these resources was strictly controlled. And those people who did have their fingers on terminal keyboards or worked the centers were either highly trained engineers or mathematicians, or they were working along rigidly codified lines. And the tool set was quite small: MVS, tape storage, COBOL and JCL, dumb terminals. These were the ubiquitous elements of just about any data center. And even though things did not always run as they should have, the centralization helped in the management of any problems that did crop up.

That was 30-plus years ago. Things began to change in the late 70s and early 80s, with the introduction of the personal computer and the runaway success of microtechnology. In fact, by 1990, data processing was gone. Information processing had replaced it. Walk into any American company today, and PCs are everywhere, bounded by mini and midrange systems. More than that, software is everywhere. And nearly everyone is using all this technology, using it everyday, automatically, without giving it so much as a thought. We now operate in the field of Information Technology Management. What are we managing?

We're managing servers and server farms, networks, routers, gateways, databases, spreadsheets, security profiles, email, word processors. And the developmental tool sets now available have grown so diverse as to be almost impossible to keep up with. What was *en vogue* seven years ago is *passé* today. The pace of change in IT is relentless. Innovation has become a fixed characteristic of this discipline, and that has pushed it more and more away from the bounds of discipline.

Back in the 70s, maybe a handful of people in an organization were devoted to data management. Today, everyone has a voice in it. The capabilities have become so flexible that applications have the potential to be cranked out in incredibly short spans of time. The process-centric approach that was required to manage a data shop in 1975 has been displaced through innovation. I am not a programmer, but using a tool like Microsoft Access, I can build a database system that tracks project risks, and I can have a working prototype of it ready to look at before lunchtime. That innovation has shaped a technology field that many describe as weakly linked, reactive rather than proactive, and poorly focused. DataQuest reports that 70 percent of today's IT workers are between 22 and 37 years old. The average length of experience is 11 years. All those people—talented as they probably are—were raised in environments of click, fast, flash, and cash.

So that's how it is. What's the answer? Do we return to glass-walled rooms? I don't know anyone who would advocate that. But the paradox lies not with the click or the fast or the flash. It lies with the cash. We've already mentioned the size of the IT industry: trillions of dollars as a single enterprise. And most of that money is public money, channeled into companies through stockholders, through investors. Most of them know nothing about how the dollars allocated to IT are being spent. On top of that, I have seen that even top management has little clue as to how well those dollars are being spent. The core issue is that the dollars are in all likelihood being spent less than efficiently, with little control, with little insight into best practice, with little knowledge of crossover or hidden failures.

Philip Crosby, one of the leading process improvement pioneers, says in his famous book *Quality Is Free* (McGraw-Hill) that it's cheaper to do things right the first time, that it always costs more to have to go back and fix something. And process improvement is all about getting it right the first time.

The theme I want to put forward in this book is that process—the process that was born with this industry—can make a difference in today's technology organizations. The thoughtful implementation of a considered process improvement program can help a technology shop operate more effectively, with increased focus, with reduced waste, with a better bead on its mission and the overall goals of the company.

More and more IT managers are adopting this mode of thought. I am not a John crying in the wilderness. Today a renewed interest in management through process has arisen. In the last decade, process programs have become more and more prevalent. And out of all the available options, three have moved to the top of the chain. These three are as follows:

- The 9001:2000 Quality Management Standard from the International Organization for Standardization
- The Capability Maturity Model Integration from the Software Engineering Institute
- Six Sigma, a methodology for improvement shaped by companies such as Motorola, Honeywell, and General Electric

These programs are not esoteric philosophies; they are not whiteboard theories. They offer practical, tangible guidelines. And they aren't fads either. Over time, each has proven itself in measurable, quantitative ways. They have been shown to visibility open the production process, to heighten management effectiveness—not through increased control but through commonly designed and measured controls. And, ultimately, they have been shown to increase the quality of the products you produce, not only external products (those you ship) but internal products as well.

Marshal Extra Forces If...

As I mentioned earlier, this book if not designed as a full treatise on process improvement, ISO, CMMI, or Six Sigma. It is designed to give you a working orientation to what the field is about. What I have found is that people who know they need some kind of quality solution or approach for their organizations want to get a feel for what's involved in such a move. They would like to get a taste of each of the three popular programs they've been hearing so much about so that they can begin to direct more concentrated efforts along focused lines.

But just because you want to implement a quality program in your company (and in my book—this book actually—you should be commended for that), there are real conditions that can derail even the best of intentions. Take a look at what I have found to be the five most potent situations responsible for quality-program disruption. If you're faced with one or more of these, you might want to work with your management to see if you can minimize their impact.

Someone Somewhere Upstairs Said Do It

This is probably the most common reason why quality programs fail to take hold in companies. Someone—usually a high-level executive, and usually responding to lagging sales, a falling reputation, or some other pain point—mandates the solution. She may have read about ISO, or CMMI, or Six Sigma, about how these programs have been runaway successes for other companies that adopted them. Maybe she worked somewhere previously that used one of these programs, and she remembers that place working pretty well. Whatever the cause, the executive mandate is made.

I have been consulting in the field of process improvement for about 20 years, and it's amazing to me how many programs get started this way. One major telecommunications infrastructure company brought me in because some distant senior vice president released a directive that the entire 6,000 person IT organization would be ISO 9001:2000 compliant within nine months. In spirit, that may have been an honorable objective, but in reality, it was outrageous. Maybe 60 people of those 6,000 even knew what ISO was. Maybe 20 of those 60 thought it was a good idea. The requirements of 9001:2000 aside, just the basic logistics of moving that mass of people down that kind of change path over such a compressed span of time was in itself just about impossible.

In a smaller organization, it might have been done. I have done just that in smaller organizations. But where I succeeded, an additional dynamic was present: the organization as a whole—large or small—wanted the quality program. That is the biggest success factor with any quality initiative. When you think about it, that makes sense. Any process improvement program is made up of a series of planned activities, and it takes people to carry out those activities. Line workers, supervisors, managers: all have a part in the program's operation. If these people—the heart of any organization—do not have their hearts in the program, the program's in trouble. If you don't believe in something, if you think it's superfluous, if you think it just makes your job more complex or cumbersome, you probably won't do it, or you'll do the barest minimum to get by.

Often with these kinds of mandates, passive resistance is what kills them off. People just ignore the thing. They let it wither on the vine. And because there's no active champion for the program (that senior VP is off solving other problems), it quickly dissipates. Soon, like the amoeba that cannot fossilize, no evidence of it even remains.

You Want It Now—Tomorrow at the Latest

Just outside of Arlington, Virginia, there is a large systems-integration company that has been doing business with the U.S. Department of Defense for over 25 years. The company has been very successful. But over the last eight or nine years, senior management had been noticing an emerging DoD trend. The Department is, more and more frequently, requiring that vendors wishing to bid on prime contracts—the multiyear, multimillion dollar contracts—have to be recognized as CMMI Level 3 organizations.

Senior management queried down-line management. How many of these restricted contracts did we have to walk away from last year? The answer came back: nine. Nine contracts worth a total of $412 million. The company had the contacts; it had the experience and the expertise. It even had the political pull. But without the "seal" (as the company considered it), it couldn't even bid.

There was no question of commitment here. Everyone agreed. The company *had* to be Level 3, and it had to be Level 3 *now*.

I would guess that 50 percent of my business comes from situations like this. Companies realize that without a recognized quality program in place, their chances of being trusted with large, top-dollar projects dwindle down to, at best, long shots. So there's an economic imperative to transform overnight. Every day in the old way is seen as fiscal degeneration. The problem is that process improvement is not a quick-fix hit. It is not low-hanging fruit.

For a program to be designed, documented, rolled out, and used enough so that its benefits begin to emerge—that takes time. How much time depends on many things: the type of program, its scope, the size of the organization, the number of available resources, the range of expertise in-house, and so on. But the bottom-line rule is that you simply can't rush it. By its very nature, process improvement is a long-term commitment. Those who want it now—who want to *be* it without *becoming* it—almost invariably sprint down the same dead-end path. They reallocate resources (often inexperienced resources), they may bring in high-end consultants, they establish deadlines they euphemistically label as "aggressive." They then set this uncoordinated machine into motion, cranking out processes for the sake of process, rarely matching them up with identified needs or considering their fit into the culture of the company. After an expanded burst of energy, a program emerges: flowcharts, procedures, policies, forms. But there has been no real foresight guiding the implementation. And so these artifacts are pressed upon teams that are usually pressed already. They are employed halfheartedly. No synchronization methods are in place. The burden of using these unwelcomed processes is exaggerated by their unfamiliarity.

Ironically, the end of this path usually sees an organization worse off than before. Morale has been dealt a blow. Faith in the value of process, if it existed at all, may have been permanently crushed. The quality program sits on a shelf collecting dust. The company's competitive position has not improved.

Insisting that it materialize *now* may be the surest way to make any quality program vanish.

You Have Bigger Fish to Fry

Not to catch. To fry. In oil. In other words, the organization is in trouble.

There's a well-known marketing story about the Sunkist Company. This was back in the 60s. Sales of Sunkist's boxed prunes had regularly trended slightly upward from year to year, but now they were going nowhere. So management hired the famous advertising consultant Stan Freberg to see if he could help them out of this jam. He took a look at their marketing strategy and saw the problem right away. Sunkist was promoting the product mainly by putting prune recipes on the back of the boxes. Things like prune pies, prune breads, and prune pudding.

Freeman said, in so many words, "Look guys, get rid of the recipes—before anybody's going to go for prune pudding they've got to go for prunes." So he engineered a now classic television spot with a stuffy Englishman noting that the prunes were awfully wrinkled but still awfully good. Maybe they could do something about the wrinkles. The strategy worked. Prune sales were regular again.

Sunkist didn't have a quality problem; it had a marketing problem, and so it's likely that no quality program would have stimulated prune sales. Today, even if an organization does have a quality problem, it might be symptomatic of other more systemic problems. I've seen this often enough that now I look for it at the start of any process improvement engagement. If you're in trouble because for some reason the market doesn't want your product, delay the quality program. Work first to change the product. If your management is at one another's throats, there's every reason the product may be falling apart, but a quality program won't fix it. If your CFO is cooking the books, or your cigarette lighters have a penchant to explode, or you've got the lowest staff retention rate in your industry, maybe it'd better to focus your efforts there.

This is not always an easy call to make. An organization is a dynamic entity. Its parts exist in symbiosis, so cause and effect is not always easy to determine. The point to remember is that a quality program is in place to enhance an organization, to help make it better. But in order for the program to work, the organization as a whole must at least be ready to move down the success path. If your organization is rife with these other factors that impede not only quality but the company's viability as well, you'd be better served by first removing (or minimizing) those obstacles so that your quality program will have the best chance of achieving its goals.

It's Just About the Money

To be blunt, businesses don't exist to produce quality. They don't even exist to produce. They exist to invoice, to bring in money. If they could make money by making nothing, plenty would do so. If they could make money by producing garbage, plenty would do so. (Plenty *do* do so.) Fortunately the pattern that's emerged is that quality and profitability tend to go hand in hand. The companies that do well tend to do what they do well. But not always.

This past autumn, I advised the board of directors at a young company. The company, Sector Inc., designed software that could prowl the perimeters of any computer network and set off alarms when an approaching intruder was detected. The unique quality of the software was that the alarms would go off before the intruder had breeched any portion of the network. By using heuristic profiles, the software could pinpoint *likely* intruders and shine a spotlight on them while they were still a safe distance away.*

The CEO, Sherrie Kinkaid, wanted to know my thoughts on process programs and the business advantages of implementing quality controls. She had a sincere desire to grow her enterprise as a quality-conscious company from the ground up. After all, the product—even though it was still in an alpha form—was beginning to attract a lot of attention, mainly from major credit card companies, banks, and insurance outfits. So, in her view, quality from the outset was essential.

Two weeks later, she had changed her mind. In the span of six days, her sales people had closed deals with seven major commercial enterprises, all worried about security, all willing

---

* I've made the company name up. And the CEO's as well. I'll be doing that again throughout this book. While all of the anecdotes I relate are true, as a practicing process consultant, I am often allowed to look deeper into a company than management would want the general public to see. So I want to stay clear of airing anyone's errors, missteps, or poor decisions. Especially because in many cases I was not privy to all the facts myself. For this reason, then, all names of people and companies mentioned in these chapters—unless specifically noted—have been changed.

to take on this new product even in its early stages. There was no time to create a new quality initiative within the company. All energies had to be focused on getting the product ready for the field—patched in any way that would hold it together.

The venture capitalists were not far behind. They saw a bright future for Sector Inc. That future was one filled with expanded programming teams, enhanced product features, a beefed-up marketing organization, and a speed-to-market philosophy that left little room for anything as esoteric as quality. Finally, $58 million in upfront funding with incentives for a series of three more infusions sealed the deal.

Now Sector Inc. was a solid company. And its product was the best in the industry. The advertising said so. And Sherrie Kinkaid agreed. After all, she had Alexander Hamilton, Thomas Jefferson, Ulysses S. Grant, and Benjamin Franklin to vouch for her.

Companies that are doing well are rarely motivated to initiate process improvement programs or quality initiatives. They tend to equate "doing well" with cash flow. If the money's coming in, why change anything? In my view, that's false security. Many organizations that appear to be firing away on all cylinders are burning fuel at a wasteful rate. Once you got past the new marbled foyer, Sector Inc. was a rodeo on fire. People wore either cowboy hats or fireman hats, galloping off into new directions or putting out fires. Planning was dismal. Rework was constant. The company (and this is an estimate I got simply from internal comment) was spending about 93¢ to earn $1. In the software industry as a whole, that figure should be closer to 61¢. In that sector of the software industry where process is embraced, the figure falls to around 49¢.

The issue is, why believe me? As a process advocate, I can't guarantee those numbers; I can only promise improvement. And it's hard to persuade a company to invest in improvement when things appear to be going according to game plan.

Then there are the companies at the other end of the Sector spectrum. These are the ones with fish to catch. Not fry. Catch. They are those small technology shops that can't afford to turn down any business. They are in it for the money, and in the types of jobs they get, their clients typically don't care about the company's quality initiatives or process improvement goals. They are hired to crank out code. Or test product. Or design solutions. Any way they can do it. Period.

Your Teams Are Matrixed Away

A final major reason why quality programs suffer short lives and then die is because there's no one to control them. Programmers control the keyboard, so code gets generated. Project managers control the schedule, so dates get adjusted. But if no one controls the processes, the processes are going to stagnate.

What many organizations fail to understand is that process improvement requires action on the part of most of the organization—certainly most of the members of the project teams. Instead, they feel that if they can hire a process analyst or two, the program should be able to run itself. That's a point I try to bring up early on in any initiative. A lot of people are going to have to be onboard. They are going to have to get involved. But that's often difficult in today's organizational environment.

A very common trend today is the matrixed environment. Technology organizations here are segmented into functional units, not focused teams. For example, there may be a Project Management Office that farms out project managers to new projects. There may be an Engineering Division that farms out architects and programmers. There may a Creative Services Division that supplies the UI and graphic designers. The same could be true with the technical writers, the testers, and the business analysts. All of these groups report to their own supervisors.

There are valid organizational design reasons for matrix structures. But the structure requires a firmer degree of commitment to a quality program. If your teams are essentially matrixed away from your control, you may find it difficult to negotiate the processes they follow. You may find that they feel no obligation to comply with your methods or to support your procedures. This may be further complicated when there is competition between these stovepipes. As immature as it sounds, managers often choose not to cooperate with fellow managers.

Cooperation, then, is yet another success factor for any process improvement program. As you'll see later on, programs such as ISO 9000, CMMI, and Six Sigma are able to reach across broad areas of organizational structure. Because of this, support of the program will need to come from all corners of the organizations—especially where the corner offices are. That unity is important because any kind of improvement effort requires harmony along three lines: 1) the participants are working toward a shared vision, 2) there is an appreciation among parties as to the value each party brings to the table, and 3) there is a common understanding of what the ultimate destination is and belief in the map that's been designed to get there.

If these elements are missing, the program is at risk to be torn apart from the inside.

So, examine your own organization if:

- You've been given a blind mandate to implement a process improvement program, realize you're probably going to have an uphill struggle.

- Your organization needs a program so desperately that it will cut corners and shave edges just to bring it in, understand that it may very well fail to live up to expectations.

- Your organization is suffering from troubles that come from areas other than product quality, you might want to improve those areas first.

- You realize that, ultimately, quality is not a core value in your organization (at least not at this time), maybe you should plan the effort for a later time.

- You want a quality program, but management in your organization is not positioned to provide you the backup and cooperation needed for its success, you might decide to scale back its scope or delay the initiative altogether.

Moving Forward

Every day we can see how process helps businesses build business. Successful banks balance their portfolios of risky loans and secured loans using proven processes, ones that mitigate risk, provide for flexibility, and, in the end, average out in the plus column. Builders of tract homes rely on what they call "packages": highly reliable inventories of what goes into entry and mid-priced houses. The Big Mac you get at a McDonald's in Knoxville tastes exactly like the one you'd get in San Diego. That's because McDonald's has worked out a stable process for putting Big Macs together. You can purchase a Dodge Neon—a machine that consists of over 12,000 integrated components—for under $12,000 and expect to drive it for over 100,000 miles. Daimler Chrysler has meticulously engineered a detailed process that can bring those 12,000 components together in a highly predictable way.

Process works. And process can work in your technology organization, too. You'll find that with process—even light, malleable process—your planning becomes more accurate, your estimates are more dependable, and your expectations tend to remain aligned with those of your client. There are many other benefits in implementing process, and I'll take a look at these in Chapter 2.

You have taken a smart step in moving forward. The processes contained in programs like ISO 9001:2000, CMMI, and Six Sigma are proven to deliver distinct benefits, whether you're designing software, integrating systems, building components, or architecting solutions. Acquiring a good, beginning understanding of process improvement and of these three widely recognized programs will help you establish a process program in your organization that moves you toward your goals of quality, predictability, efficiency, and success.

Summary

- The business of IT has evolved to mesh more and more closely with business itself. Today IT supports the business more than it ever has before.

- Corporate IT shops are annually accountable for billions of dollars in spending, shaping projects that will guide the futures of many companies. Yet many struggle to embrace or implement basic project and process controls.

- The use of process—shaped to the needs of the organization—can raise accountability, increase efficiencies, and improve quality.

- This book presents a primer in topics on process improvement by looking at fundamentals of process programs, then presenting overviews of the ISO 9001:2000 Standard, the Capability Maturity Model Integration, and Six Sigma.

CHAPTER TWO

The Case for Process

MANY READERS OF THIS BOOK WILL BE LOOKING INTO THE DISCIPLINE OF PROCESS IMPROVEMENT FOR the first time. But even if this area is new to them, most readers should be pretty much experts in more than one realm of information technology, perhaps programming, project management, or quality control; maybe architecture, design, or implementation; or, still yet, management, strategic planning, or performance analysis. Those kinds of backgrounds are invaluable when it comes to understanding the roles process improvement can play in organizational success. And they are essential for making the case for process improvement.

In fact, if you are what might be called the "typical" reader of this book, you may well understand more about the potential for process in your organization than most. The reason is simple. Process improvement is about improving the way the organization works. When it comes to that work, you're a pro.

Process is not (or should not be) about adopting new "things" blindly and then hoping that those things do whatever it is they're supposed to do. It should not be a series of new practices that represent what the "industry" says you should be doing. That is the antithesis of the process improvement philosophy. Process is about taking your approach to work and formalizing it into a program others can follow.

At its heart, process improvement is about four basic activities:

1. Looking at what you do

2. Focusing in on the things you do well (or want to do well)

3. Setting tools in place to help everyone do it similarly well

4. Keeping an eye open for ways to make that approach better over time

Those four steps are about as basic as you can get, but they bring me to an important point. Your expertise as a programmer, a manager, an analyst—these are all keys to the success of your organization's process improvement efforts. Your knowledge, experience, and insight should be the crucial components that will form the foundation of your improvement program. Without those, the program has nothing to stand on. And in their absence, even the most recognized of programs—like ISO 9001, CMMI, and Six Sigma— are just words on paper.

Those who do not seek to take advantage of what the organization already does well (its habits, knowledge, experience, and insight)—those people who prefer to wipe the slate clean—are missing a critical element to process improvement success.

Given that, I can now take a first step toward making the case for process in any technology organization. And the first point toward that goal is that *you* are the process.

An American Success Story

In a book like this, it can be tempting to focus solely on what's wrong with the technology industry. After all, there are lots of tools we can use to make IT more effective. So why not point out all the holes that need to be filled? Any serious observer would agree that there are lots of things wrong with how we structure, manage, and execute IT in this country. Plenty. But in my view, that's looking at bent nails. It's handy, but it doesn't tell you much that's helpful.

A better view—the more informative view—is to focus on what the industry does right, to remember that American IT is a story of unparalleled success. In the span of only 30 years or so, it has achieved a level of saturation and sophistication no other industry in history can match. In fact, the main reason we are able to spot so many issues with IT is because of its runaway success. It's taken off in all directions. Look at these 2005 numbers:

- Global IT industry spending: $1.3 trillion

- Revenue of the U.S. Software 500: $311 billion

- Number of electronic cash cards in circulation: 40+ million

- Number of MRI scans: 20+ million

- Dollar volume of online shopping: $38.3 billion

- Number of global Internet users: 1,022,863,307

- Number of wireless cell phone subscribers: 194,500,000

- Number of iPods in use: 10+ million

- Number of cities that went berserk at 12:01 a.m., January 1, 2000: 0

- Number of emails you really didn't get that your cohorts insist they sent you: _____

And if a picture is worth a thousand statistics, Figure 2-1 is a great picture for you.

FIGURE 2-1. Technology is an unparalleled American success story. Not only are cell phones, email, and laptops de facto ways of life, IBM scientists have been able to harness the attractive properties of atoms to line them up in an impressive, albeit tiny, billboard.

Figure 2-1 is not a promotion for International Business Machines. It's a picture of the result IBM scientists got when they trained a bunch of atoms to line up in a row. And not only were they able to get them to line up, they were able to build a camera sensitive enough to take a picture of it. So any way you look at it, the success story is there.

The idea behind process improvement then is to capitalize on that success, to institutionalize as much if it as we can.

In the previous section, I mentioned that a good first step in making the case for process is to remember that *you* are the process. Here's what I mean by that. Most IT professionals know what they are doing. They follow a general routine when they work. They have a process, even if it's a personal process.

The real issue then, the Big Issue, is not about personal competence; the talent pool in American IT is pretty competent. The issue is more about coordination, consistency, synchronicity, and predictability within and across groups. An organization is not an individual. So for an organization to operate efficiently, it helps for the groups that make up the organization to work along similar lines, to approach the issues of business in a consistent way. When the organization can do this regularly and predictably, it can synchronize its energies in a focused way. Not only that, it can now begin to observe the way it works so that it can improve the way it works.

The Conscious Organization

All organizations use process. Many times they are not well defined. Many times they are just embedded in the culture. Often they are the wrong processes. Management may not even be aware of what they really are. But if you look closely to see what these processes are, you can learn a lot about what's important to a company.

Process reveals an organization's values, priorities, and preferences. They naturally emerge from the actions an organization employs to see its work through.

I once worked with a software company that regularly, always around release time, scheduled marathon testing and defect-correction sessions: 12-hour days, weekends included. It was an all-hands-on-deck routine. The company's values, priorities, and preferences were just about all focused on market perception and competitive position. But not so much on planning. And less so on its people.

One of the early benefits of implementing a formal process program is that these values begin to visibly emerge. In the example above, management probably would have balked had it been asked to document the marathon sessions as a matter of company policy. I think if they were asked to consciously commit such descriptions to paper, they would have naturally realized that such routines are not very commendable. Weak management can hide behind a lack of formalized process. But when a company is committed to growth—committed to catalyzing its own growth—the visibility of formal process becomes a welcome opportunity.

Many, maybe even most, IT shops are what I would call unconscious. They are not concretely aware of how they do things. They can't describe their mode of operations. They're not conscious of the processes at work within their groups, the procedures that drive them to be who they are. And so, they are not adept at learning from their performances. The organization has no viewpoint from which to watch itself. It has no outer perspective. That makes things tough on management and line workers alike. Environments of this kind tend to be reactive. They tend to be driven by heroes: people who can thrive in chaos. There is a lot of firefighting going on, a lot of backtracking. And there's a dearth of hard information as to how things really are proceeding at the micro level. There's little consensus of status.

This is not only a tough way of doing business, it's an expensive one. This tenuous grasp on consistency and predictability carries with it major drawbacks and risks. Here are some recent numbers:

- Seventy percent of all corporate software solutions were delivered late.
- Fifty-four percent of major, business-critical projects came in over budget, many by as much as 222 percent.
- Sixty-six percent of what IT delivered was considered unsuccessful when the systems were installed.
- Thirty percent of projects were simply cancelled.

Those numbers come from a 2004 study by the Standish Group, in an extension of their now famous 1994 Chaos Study. Standish studied the performance of Fortune 500 IT shops—the big boys—and those are the figures they came out with.

In the 1994 report, the numbers were eye-opening. The 2004 report showed some improvement, but the overall performance indicators shed light on a still-present problem. Corporate IT is wrestling with its ability to manage technology development and deployment in a consistent and predictable fashion.

Here's another number: a 2002 ANSI report puts the cost of American IT failure for the year at just under $60 billion.

What might it be in 2008?

Of course, all these numbers are not the problem; they are symptoms. And we need to acknowledge that IT is not the lone contributor to these results. Here are some other likely contributors:

- Lack of adequate funding for IT
- Limited IT resources
- Shifting executive mandates
- Conflicting objectives between marketing and IT
- Competing customer demands
- Unrealistic turnaround expectations
- Complex architectural and system constraints

Very little of those factors are under the direct control of IT. Yet they have enormous potential to impact IT performance.

But if we recognize the above factors to be true, doesn't that promote the case for process even more? If we recognize that we are indeed in a business that's going to be pressured often by changing or unrealistic demands, shouldn't we respond in part by getting internal operations running as well as we can?

I'm not trying to paint all corporate IT departments as underperformers. They are not. As mentioned above, American technology, and the reign business has on technology development and management, is unparalleled. The industry can deliver, and it does deliver.

But still there is that $60 billion. It's not missing money. It didn't vanish. Nobody dropped it. It went mainly to people who had to do things over. They had to go back to the customers and ask them what it was they really wanted. They had to add in new design components or redesign existing components. They had to reprogram things they thought they had programmed just fine in the first place. They had to retest, retrain, and reinstall. They had to buy the kinds of parts they should have bought when they first went shopping. They had to replan and recoordinate, bump new things out of the way, renegotiate and revisit. And somewhere in here came the big change: the shop went from balancing to juggling.

Process won't solve all of IT's problems. No one should promote that line. But it can help almost all IT shops in three very distinct ways:

- Provide tools to proactively plan, manage, and integrate work.

- Set into place methods and controls to maximize internal efficiencies.

- Establish mechanisms to regularly assess, report on, and improve performance.

And with those abilities in place, the organization can better anticipate risks and constraints, and so can manage their impacts; it can plan for and coordinate the effective uses of its resources; and it can better manage its position in the overall environment to better meet its goals and objectives. And those are all marks of a conscious entity.

The Business of Technology Is Business

This is a book about process improvement, about the benefits of process improvement, about techniques for process management, and about the structures of three of the industry's leading process management programs. The premise of this book is that American IT needs process, that it should embrace process more because as a whole it has not embraced it enough.

There are pockets of stellar performances out there, companies that know how to use process to make their business practices stronger and more profitable. Divisions in organizations like GE, Lockheed Martin, Honeywell, and Texas Instruments could show us enough about process management to convince even the most hesitant adopters.

In this chapter, I want to begin to build the business case for process improvement, to identify why process can be used in small IT shops as well as large IT shops to conduct and manage business along predictable, successful, and profitable lines. The financial numbers above tell a story, but I'm not chalking those figures up solely to illustrate the lack of process. There are other dynamics certainly at play: shifting management roles, evolving market conditions, internal politics.

But we do know that most of the IT shops that drive corporate America do not operate under any kind of distinct or managed process program. They depend on the talent of their people. They rely on the individual processes at work. Many of these shops are either unfamiliar with the rudiments of process application, unexposed to the purpose of process improvement, or adverse to the disciplines of quality management. Whatever the case, these organizations may be heading in the directions they want to move, getting to their goals, but at what cost? How much time might they spend traveling off course before they are able to veer back on?

Calvin Coolidge is famous for his saying in the 1920s, "The business of America is business." The same could be said today about American IT. The business of technology is business. Technology is not analogous to a game. It is not a different spin on war. It is not an adventure. It's a business, and it should probably be run like a business.

And so a good way to begin the case for process improvement is to begin by addressing it in the same way a business would.

Some Number Stories

Most of the IT managers and executives I know have an intuitive appreciation for process, at least in general. What they most often ask me when I am making the case for them to formalize a process program in their shops is, "What's the return?" They want to know what kind of ROI they can expect from the investment they know they'll have to make. And it's not that they need proof. It's that the people around them—perhaps a CEO or a CFO—are trained to support decisions built around those kinds of concrete terms.

The fact is most of us in the process improvement field can't guarantee an ROI figure. We can anticipate a positive ROI. We know how to shape a program to generate an ROI. But each IT shop is different. Each has its own focus, its own culture, its own specialties, its own distinct customer base. All those variables make it tough to predict an ROI.

Most of this chapter will focus on what I call the qualitative benefits of process. And by qualitative, I don't mean "soft." Power steering gives you better control of an automobile, but how much more over manual depends on the driver. Likewise, process can give you better control over projects. That's a safe assumption. How much depends on what you build.

John Brodman once conducted an empirical study of the qualitative traits of process improvement and noted that many soft benefits were often overlooked. These included improved morale by the developers, less need for overtime, smoother day-to-day operations and communications, and increased respect from the customer base (Brodman 1995).

But I do appreciate the need to link process with hard improvement data. The best way I know to do this is by reference. Let's take a look at some companies that have made the commitment to process improvement, studied what they were doing, and then reported their results.

I think the best understanding to take away from these brief cases is that process improvement does have a track history of delivering tangible benefits. And these benefits have a very strong potential to deliver impressive returns for the organization that undertakes the effort seriously.

Schlumberger

Process improvement at Schlumberger helped the company meet its on-time delivery goals. At program inception, the company was meeting schedule dates about 50 percent of the time. Less than three years after implementing a program that focused on process definition, project planning, and project tracking, on-time delivery rose to 99 percent. Extensions to the program then helped the company reduce post-release defect rates from 25 percent of all defects down to 10 percent. Schlumberger also reported productivity increases between 2X and 3X, and noted an ROI value for the program of 6:1 (Curtis 1995).

- Pre-program on-time delivery rate: 50 percent
- Post-program on-time delivery rate: 99 percent
- Pre-program post-release defects: 25 percent
- Post-program post-release defects: 10 percent
- ROI: 6:1

Raytheon

Raytheon has had similar success with its process management program. Its goal was, in part, to reduce the amount of rework it had to deal with in its projects. Before the program, rework typically accounted for up to 41 percent of a project's budget. Raytheon invested about half a million dollars in a program to address this issue, and in the first full year of its use, realized a savings on rework of $4.48 million, along with a 2X productivity increase (as might be expected). After just under five years, the savings were documented at $15.8 million, and rework accounted for only about 11 percent of the project budget (Dion 1993).

- Investment: $580,000
- Productivity increase: 2X
- Savings on rework (one year): $4.48 million
- Savings on rework (five years): $15.8 million
- ROI: 7.7:1

Tenzer-Spring Dynamics

Tenzer initiated a process program to help the company better manage its development costs. Hard costs of internal projects were slimming the company's profit margins. Net margins that were anticipated in the range of 12 to 19 percent were being realized at closer to 9-to-14 percent levels. The company invested about $400,000 into an enterprise program to define processes around project planning, project monitoring, and requirements control. After two years of implementation, the company documented a reduction in project overruns of just under $3 million. Development costs dropped by 55 percent, cycle time dropped by 38 percent, and post-release defects dropped by 74 percent (Lildman 2001).

- Software development cost reduction: 55 percent
- Cycle time reduction: 38 percent
- Post-release defect reduction: 74 percent
- ROI: 6.35:1

Behrben International

Behrben directed its process improvements at a very specific issue: requirements validation. The company was dealing with two issues. First the lack of precision in requirements
definition was resulting in many iterative cycles of validation. The effort of these cycles
had a cascading effect on project schedules. Schedule slippage was endemic across project
groups. After Behrben standardized a methodology for requirements definition and control, activities began to improve. Validation cycles dropped from an average of 34 to 17, a
50 percent reduction. As a result, delivery dates began to improve also. On-time delivery
of software increased from 51 percent of the projects to 94 percent in less than 19 months.

- Pre-program on-time delivery: 51 percent

- Post-program on-time delivery: 94 percent

- Pre-program validation cycles: 34

- Post-program validation cycles: 17 (50 percent reduction)

Hughes Aircraft

Hughes Aircraft invested in a process initiative that focused on project and team support
areas: training, peer reviews, Process Group formation, and quality assurance. Hughes also
implemented quantitative measures to track how well these areas impacted overall operations. From an investment of $445,000, the company reported savings of $2 million annually. Managers also reported softer benefits realized from the program: improved quality of
work life in the business environment, fewer overtime hours, and increased retention.
Additionally, management attributed this program, in part, to a rise in the company's
marketplace image (Humphrey 1993).

- Improved quality of work life

- Fewer overtime hours

- Increased staff retention

- Annual savings: $2 million

- ROI: 4.2:1

Boeing Space Transportation Systems

Boeing Space Transportation Systems focused one aspect of its process improvement
efforts on cycle time and defect detection, two interrelated productivity gates. The company addressed this with a formalized peer-review program. Initially, about 70 percent of
defects were discovered during verification activities, with an additional 19 percent being
found in validation. After the peer reviews began, a significant number of the defects were
eliminated before even reaching verification. This improved the cycle times by 50 percent
and dropped the amount of rework that needed to be done by 31 percent. The reviews
also had the added benefit of increasing design effort efficiencies by 25 percent (4 percent

of total development). This 4 percent increase in overall project efficiency provided for the 31 percent reduction in rework (Yamamura and Wigle 1997).

- Design efficiency: +25 percent
- Cycle time reduction: 50 percent
- Rework reduction: 31 percent
- ROI: 7.65:1

Hewlett-Packard

Hewlett-Packard worked with two of its divisions to focus process improvement around the benefits of reuse. The company calculated that its ability to identify and reuse proven systems code and components was crucial to achieving productivity and quality objectives. After the reuse program went into effect, one group experienced a 51 percent reduction in code defects with a 57 percent increase in productivity. The other group experienced a 24 percent defect reduction, with a 40 percent increase in productivity. One group within HP that had been committed to reuse for 10 years reported gross (period) program costs of about $1 million with a savings of $4.1 million. Another group, involved in reuse for eight years, reported gross program costs at $2.6 million with savings of $5.6 million (Lim 1994).

- Defect reduction (code): 51 percent
- Productivity increase: 57 percent
- Cycle time reduction: 42 percent
- ROI: 216–419 percent

An SEI Study

Finally, Carnegie Mellon University studied a group of technology companies that had been committed to process improvement an average of three years. The results showed a range of positive indicators. Project costs were reduced from 5 percent to as much as 83 percent. On-time delivery was improved from 15 percent to as high as 95 percent. Productivity increases were realized from 11 percent to 60 percent. And all companies showed a positive return on investment. ROIs ranged from 2:1 to 13:1.

- Cost reduction: 5–83 percent
- Improvements in meeting schedules: 15–95 percent
- Productivity increases: 11–60 percent
- ROI: 2:1–13:1

These are all success stories. And one of the reasons they have been publicly released is no doubt because they are success stories.

As compelling as these cases are, they don't seal the case for process improvement and process programs. But they go a long way to helping us see what kinds of tangible and measurable improvements well-designed processes can bring to an IT organization.

The error at the other extreme would be to ignore those numbers, to treat them as belonging to a different industry set. People might say, "That's fine for Boeing, but we are not Boeing; we're a small shop." Or "Schlumberger's industry is totally different from ours—what works in that industry won't work in ours." And so on.

Often I get those responses from the same people who asked me to provide the ROI data in the first place. I think that attitude goes back to one of orientation. Many IT managers are not adverse to process. They just lack the appreciation for how it can be implemented in almost any shop.

Along that line, I've noticed six pretty common myths that are often cited as reasons why managers choose not to consider making process improvement a focus in their shops. We'll take a look at these in the next section.

Six Common Myths

The way to manage technology business more effectively is to define what it is the business does. Once you have defined that, you can begin to operate the business based on that definition. And once you begin to move down that path, you begin to know the path, and you can start to refine the shape of the path. That is the basis for nearly all process improvement initiatives. It seems logical, even intuitive. So why is it that management will often steer away from implanting process, from adopting process improvement as a goal?

The reason could be that management is often not educated as to what process is about. Or they may have been exposed to only poor examples of the discipline in the past. They may have preconceived notions of what process demands or what process requires, and these may not match up well with what it's really all about. Dealing with this, I've noticed six myths that are pretty common to the field of process improvement. They are often identified as reasons why people don't want to bother with process.

Let's take a brief look at the six.

Myth 1: Everything's Fine

There's a company in South Carolina that is one of the nation's largest processors of Medicare health claims. I'll call them MetaCare. Annually, they pay out about $20 billion. They have an impressive corporate campus, a solid service reputation, and—for these days—an amazingly low staff turnover rate.

They also serve a very mature and stabilized industry. The management and processing of Medicare claims depends more on compliance with established regulations than on innovation. The company contacted me about helping them develop an internal process program for their IT groups. But what I noticed when I got there was that they already had a program. It just wasn't highly visible to them. The program was embedded in the contracts they won from Centralized Medicare Services. These contracts dictated how projects would be run, what service levels were expected, how changes would be managed, what communication channels would be honored, who could do this, who could do that. You can probably understand that. A federal agency that is going to hand you the combination to $20-something billion in tax funds is wise to attach some strings.

In my mind, they didn't need another process program. They were doing pretty well.

How many MetaCares are out there? No doubt a few. But in the field of information technology, market stability, fixed revenue streams, and heavy structural dictates are not the norm. The opposite is more often the case.

I spent a few years in the late 1990s consulting with MCI WorldCom. I was with their Local Number Portability group. I was helping them set up a project management team to roll out a new service that would let customers come into the MCI family while keeping their old phone numbers.

Naturally this service hit a lot of MCI's networking systems. The project management teams were going to need a pretty solid methodology to run projects in and out of this new technological infrastructure. When I proposed setting some fixed processes into place, the director of the group balked. Actually it was probably less than a balk. She simply dismissed the idea as if it were one among a full series of possible choices. The culture at MCI, at the time I was there, was not one based on procedural guidelines or well-defined roles and responsibilities. People did whatever they had to do to get the job done. Speed-to-market took precedence over all else. The phrase, "We'll fix it in production" was routinely expressed. In the director's mind, and the minds of most of the people around her, the organization did not need a process program. All it needed was way to move a Bell-South TN into MCI's TN database. Quickly. So that MCI could quickly begin to bill.

From my experience, that's the way many IT shops can be primed to think. "We don't need a process program," may not echo in heads of most CIOs, but I bet that's because the phrase hasn't been invited inside.

Today's technology businesses operate in a hectic environment. Demand is up; users are savvy. And now that technology has become so capital-intensive, it has also become political. Technical solutions are constantly changing; innovation has displaced stability. Maybe it's no wonder that technology management has a hard time focusing on the big picture. There's so much happening at the detail level it can be difficult to pull away.

If yours is a tiny start-up, struggling to simply define and build a product, maybe the organization really isn't ready for process. Or if yours is a mature company, operating in a solidly stable environment, maybe you're already there. But chances are that's not the way it is.

Chances are, the IT organization at hand is moving to the currents of technological flux and change. And part of the reason that this flux and change is pulling management down to the detail is that the organization, in the absence of process, lacks a predictive way of dealing with dynamics.

Process can be viewed in this light as a viewing tool. Once in place, it reflects the way the company operates at both a strategic level as well as a tactical level. This feature may be what causes many executives to avoid the topic. Because to implement a process program, you have to work to define not only who your organization is, but what you want it to become. And that takes work. It takes leadership. It takes a certain amount of vision. Perhaps in such a dynamic industry, those requirements are hard to meet. Perhaps the more expedient route is to simply back up the position that this organization—our organization—does not need process.

Views from the Top

BUSINESS OBJECTIVES DRIVE PROCESS VALUE

"The focus of process in technology management should be no different from any other business program. It's important to remember that IT processes are business processes in the same way that accounting processes are business processes.

"The key to implementing effective process—in any environment—is to shape the activities so they address the business needs of the organization. When you do this, the 'Value Proposition' of process becomes clear. Your people will more readily embrace the program because they can see its visible link to business objectives, and therefore to their jobs. Also, you end up with a benchmark to measure how well the processes are working to help achieve the objectives."

—Linda Butler, Director IT, Corporate Services CIO, BellSouth Telecommunications

"Key to realizing the benefits of a process program is the ability to tie the program's design to the business objectives of the broader organization. In order to do this effectively, you must implement the tools that trace and measure the performance of the program across your enterprise. For example, at an executive level an organization may set a broad goal to 'reduce the cost of IT.' This can be supported at the mid-level by the introduction of a quality and process program designed to 'reduce rework.' This can be further decomposed to the front line IT employees where individual goals are focused at 'reducing the number of production defects.' Using this approach, you introduce tangible objectives that can be measured at the varied levels to assess the overall success of the program and drive accountability down to the employees.

"This method of tying process design to business goals clearly moves forward the agenda of the enterprise and lets people at all levels in the organization understand the purpose and value of the process program."

—Guy Bevente, AVP, Information Technology National Data, SBC

Myth 2: What We Do Is Too Unique for Process

The "We don't need process" idea is, fortunately, an idea on the wane. In recent years—due in no insignificant part to the dot-com bubble burst—the industry is more and more turning on to the ideas of accountability and discipline. More and more, companies are hearing about process, about programs like ISO 9001, the Capability Maturity Model, and Six Sigma. About Sarbanes-Oxley.

Initiatives are under way across corporate America to introduce, at least at some level, some degree of recognized best practices. In fact, it's almost become fashionable now to tout the benefits of process improvement, to show that the concepts are appreciated and the benefits understood. And to herald that overall it's a good thing for the IT world. But when you get this level of constrained enthusiasm, it's not uncommon to hear it followed by, "Yes, but it's not for us. What we do is too unique." I'd almost rather hear the we-don't-need-it line.

I know plenty of managers who say they don't want anything to do with process. They believe it, too. And I know managers who sincerely feel that they aren't in a position to focus on process. But whenever I hear that what an organization does is too unique for process, there's always something in the voice that says, "And that's my final word." I think it's a defensive response. In fact, it's rhetorically backward. If what an organization does really is so unique, I would say that there is even a greater need for process, to formally define that tricky thing it does.

Then there is the Rule of Averages, the maxim that says there's very little that is really uniquely displaced in the technology enterprise. No matter what our product focus is or how we direct our services, we share more in common than those elements that set us apart. We all have to deal with customer requirements in one form or another. We have to work against schedules and within budgets. We need estimates and plans. We need to produce documents and work products, and they need to be controlled. We need to keep track of our project teams and the work they are doing. We have to keep our customers informed as to how we are doing. We need to keep management up-to-date. And we need to gather regular metrics to know where we stand at various steps of the way.

Is there any technology organization that doesn't need to do any of those things? You can even remove the concept of technology, and the activities still retain their integrity. They represent basic business fundamentals.

The people who say that what they do is too unique for process are probably trying to skirt the issue. They may prefer to do business in a hectic, reactive environment, one that's dynamic and unpredictable. Many people find that that's a fun way to work. I can see it as being fun, too. As long as there's not too much at stake.

But if people are building products that other people rely on to be right—maybe the people in marketing, the shipping clerks, the sales force, or the facilities management folks—then maybe there is an obligation to work under some structure.

If they're dealing with stockholder monies and impacting the future value of a company, then perhaps they have a fiduciary responsibility to operate under some form of process. If they are building something that they want the marketplace to embrace *en masse*, then what's their obligation to the public?

Usually the "too unique" phrase is a mask for a preference to operate on the fly. Business is easier when you don't have to plan, or forecast, or track, or inform. But then it becomes less like business and more like play. I think all technology businesses need process: the more unique, the stronger the recommendation. When people play at business—when they play at technology development—they usually prove before too long that they don't play very well.

Myth 3: Process Will Cramp Our Style

People in technology tend to understand and appreciate concepts of flexibility and adaptability. That's the nature of our business. When you work in technology for a time, you might begin to think that the people who really make things happen are, among others, the cowboys and the gunslingers. It's cool to see someone shoot from the hip and hit the target dead-on. In an environment of cowboys and gunslingers, firefighters and artistes, individuals and lone wolves, gurus and magicians, the idea of process might be a bit threatening.

People who don't work in process-centric environments can easily perceive process as a series of roadblocks. They might think that process will constrain them to the point of immobility. That it will rob them of their freedom of expression, of their unique approaches to problem solving. Of the imprint of their personal identity.

Is that the goal of process? Of course not. Process well-defined, well-considered, and geared to driving business objectives is not a roadblock. It's a fence line. If you run the fence line, you're free to move in and out. But as long as you keep the fence line in view, you'll always know where you are and where you're going.

On the other hand, there are certainly circumstances in which process will cramp style, and thank goodness for that. I have been in shops where I would have liked nothing better than to see a heavy dose of process descend from on high and cramp as much runaway style as possible. In fact, the best example I can think of is a company I once ran.

In the mid-90s, I owned a software company called Public Health Software Systems. We developed and deployed software that helped public health departments track and manage the delivery of immunizations to young children. We were a young bunch, energetic and enthusiastic, and we liked the idea of our niche. The problem we faced turned out to be success. In those years, President Bill Clinton was working on his own immunization initiative, and he was pumping hundreds of millions of dollars into the public health sectors, providing funding for health departments to better manage their immunization programs. With this funding influx, health departments could now afford to automate their record-keeping systems. Counties from all across the nation came to our door, ready to buy our product. Thing was, we weren't exactly ready for broad market appeal. We had no real business identify. My partner and I were known simply as the "two guys who do computers."

Actually, we were 19 people with energy and knowledge but no business approach, no insight into market expectations. And no real approach to product engineering. We had a good base product, but in hindsight, there's nothing more I would have liked to have had than a good dose of development process. We were so loose, we needed boundaries. Fortunately, a much larger corporation wanted in on the immunization trend, and they purchased our company, folding it under an anonymous corporate umbrella.

However, the better view to take might be that process, properly applied, does not cramp style. It liberates style. In a process managed environment, people don't have to figure out how to do the routine jobs. That figuring out has been done already. People don't have to feel their way through business flows. That map has been drawn. They don't have to invent how to integrate or how to verify or how to report. When they are freed from that routine, they are then free to innovate, to create, to think, and to apply their technical skills in innovative and focused ways.

Myth 4: We Can't Afford the Overhead

When people are working full steam to get a product out, or when they are trying to marshal the troops to get an organization organized, there can be a tendency to want to cut out everything seen as superfluous. To get down to core essence, back to basics. And when people aren't versed in process or maybe have little background in organizational design, they can tend to see lots of things as being superfluous.

I once advised management at a software company in Atlanta that was going through rough times. Their product had slipped from a competitive position in the marketplace. Management was scrambling to get back on track. They brought in a host of new contract programmers to crank out new code. They had their testers working 12-hour shifts, seven days a week. And here's another smart thing they did: they cancelled the plant-watering service. They decided they couldn't afford the overhead of watering the plants.

The advice they were looking to get from me was how to sequence these hectic activities into some semblance of a production line. I mapped out a very light framework of milestone definitions, team goals, communication avenues, and peer reviews. I wasn't entirely satisfied with it. It didn't seem accountable enough. And for the amount of money that was going into this scramble, I didn't like to see so many potential side-door openings. But it was, I thought, a beginning.

Management, however, was not going to buy it. They thought I was going to recommend some kind of automated tool set, something they could plug in and turn on. When they saw I wanted to change the way work was being done, they balked. They told me they didn't have time to reorder the group dynamics. They needed these people to go after the problem full bore. The overhead of process was simply too much. So the process recommendation died first. And then the plants. The company was not far behind. It didn't die, but its parent sold it for a quick price to another player and got quietly out of that particular industry.

Process, early on, will indeed add some overhead. After all, you have to introduce something new into the organization. You are attempting to change the organization. This will require a degree of people, resources, energy, and investment. But the focus of well-done process is to reduce inefficiencies, to minimize waste. And when a process program is built that way, overhead should fall. It is when the organization is unguided and unfocused that the lines between product cost and overhead blur. It may even appear that overhead is thin because product costs have crept into an area in which they do not belong. Process has taken over funding that should have been reserved for other priorities.

Like the plants.

Myth 5: Process Is Heavy

This may be the biggest myth surrounding process improvement: that any process program is by necessity heavy, that it will weigh down or confuse the organization, that it can have no real organic place in the daily life of a company.

I have heard this even from CEOs and CIOs who believe in process. Their mark of wisdom is to advocate selective use of programs like ISO 9001:2000, CMMI, and Six Sigma. They recommend borrowing those elements that fit your specific needs.

By and large, that's good advice. I offer it up, too. It is a good idea to use the established models and frameworks as *sources* of best-practice advice. But the implication here is a little misleading. The subtext says, use the pieces because the full sets are too much. They *are* too heavy.

Throughout this book, I'll be stating and then reinforcing the difference between light process and heavy process. Process is not by nature heavy. If you choose to implement ISO 9001:2000, you can implement it in a light way. If you elect to achieve CMMI Maturity Level 3—maybe 21 Process Areas—you can do so in a light way. If you want to use Six Sigma with a deep set of statistics, you can do so in a light way. The reason that people think process is a heavy thing is because people often turn it into a heavy thing.

When people begin to develop processes for their organizations (and I'm assuming here that they are qualified and have been prepped to do it properly), they soon discover that they can map out basic activities very efficiently. And then they discern that they can take that a step deeper, and so they do. And then they discover more activities that can be logically supported by process, and so they take on those. The heaviness that ensues is not a product of process. It's a product of people's success with process. It represents the enthusiasm of a solution discovered to be readily applicable. But maybe premature.

The need is simply for discipline, for a definition in direction so that just the right amount of process is applied. Lay it on light. Use it in that form until it is habit in the group. Then expand it to further serve the organization.

But avoid the trap that process is heavy. If you print out the core essence of the ISO 9001 Standard, or the goals of CMMI, or the DMAIC framework of Six Sigma, each would tip the scales at less than four ounces.

That's about as heavy as process starts. Where you take it from there is up to you and the needs of your people.

Myth 6: That's Just Another Flavor of the Month

There's not a lot about the discipline of process improvement that I take personally anymore. Twelve years ago I was a novice. Ten years ago I was an enthusiast. A little later I was an evangelist. Now, after a dozen years of working process in corporate America, I have moved to the position of being an observer.

I like helping companies design and implement process programs. I like seeing them succeed in this arena. But when I run up against resistance, especially at executive and management levels, I don't feel compelled to convince anymore. I'll help educate if that's requested. But I don't really feel the need to prove the wisdom I have found in process programs, process improvement, and process management. However, there is one attitude that I sometimes feel obligated to discuss. That's the attitude that process in general—or a particular process program (ISO, CMMI, Six Sigma)—is just another flavor of the month, just another trendy solution put forth to solve a well-established problem.

But anyone who has seen a well-designed ISO 9001 program in active use would be hard pressed to dismiss it as a flavor of the month. The same for CMMI. And companies like GE and Motorola have presented a wealth of documented evidence as to the effectiveness of Six Sigma.

Often the people who tend to label these kinds of programs as flavors of the month are actually expressing their own limitations to commit to the regimen and discipline of process improvement. The term "flavor of the month" means basically that you try something for a month and then, if it doesn't taste quite right, you throw out the recipe and start all over. If that mix doesn't do it, you toss it out, too. And on and on and on. In other words, there's no time to get the mix right. Quick results are the only proof.

There are a host of reasons why process programs can go awry, and just as many reasons why process programs might fail to live up to their potentials. But it's rarely because the flavor is wrong. What's lacking is the full appreciation that process improvement takes time.

Benefits of Process

The word "quality" means different things to different people. For some, it's a sign of endurance. For others, it's a measure of innovation. But just about everyone agrees that, in the end, the concept of quality has to do with expectations, usually the expectations of the customer.

When you build something that performs in a way the customer wants or needs, you'll typically be credited with delivering quality. If you miss the mark—no matter how well put-together the thing is—its quality quotient will come into question. In the business of technology, then, it's important that organizations arrive at a definition of quality. The value in this bit of advice becomes clear when you think about process.

Process is about inputs and outputs. It is a way to shape inputs in order to generate desired outputs. In any production system, the ultimate output is a viable product. "Quality" then will be imbedded in the thing you've created. And so any process is dependent on first understanding what the output has to be.

The phrase "quality culture" describes an organization that has designed the pattern of its activities to deliver a product (or service) that carries within it the corporate definition of quality. Very few IT organizations would admit to having a weak understanding of what their customers want. And even fewer would admit to having no real way of getting there. But more than a few studies indicate that definitions of quality and the production processes that help ensure quality are absent in many, many IT shops.

Many American technology companies have been slow to embrace quality cultures. I think I know the reasons why; it's a blend of issues. When I have sat with CIOs and other senior IT managers, I hear pretty much a common theme. They listen politely to me and then say, "That's great, James. We really see the value in that. But right now we've got other priorities to wrangle with. This just isn't a good time for us." What can you say to that? If management is focused on pressing issues outside this realm, there's probably little that will change that focus somewhere else. The best follow-up may be to schedule another visit.

Another reason for the hesitance is that U.S. technology shops have traditionally been held pretty much unaccountable for the specifics of their operations. At the macro level, they need to hit a certain operating budget, and they need to solve general problems, but what goes on inside the black box is not readily scrutinized. I touched on this in the introduction. External managers still think in large part that technology is a mystery, that it's complex engineering, that it's a specialty realm best judged by those on the inside. As long as what comes out of the box works, it almost doesn't matter what it took inside the box to make it happen. In these environments, building it right the first time and fixing it 12 times prior to release are the same things.

And then there's the simple question of education. To my surprise, I've discovered that many of the managers running the $350 billion technology industry in America have almost no knowledge of quality management. When they think of terms like "quality assurance" or "quality control," they automatically think testing. They know a few of the rules—"you can't test quality in"—but they don't move much farther from there. It may be that the renewed push to quality is a recent thing (what with Sarbanes-Oxley and all). And it may be that few if any of these managers ever received any training in the fundamentals of quality management. By and large, IT managers move up in their organizations through a technical or engineering path. They just haven't had exposure to this body of knowledge. Those that have acquired it typically do so through their own initiative.

What I am convinced of is that once people understand the benefits of implementing a quality program, the reasons not to do so pretty much evaporate. And there are plenty of reasons. Some as we have noted are esoteric and qualitative, but many are tangible and concrete, and translate directly into improved performance.

The benefits of process management, process focus, and process improvement are real. They are not abstractions or reductions. They are not derivatives of some other result. Process works. And not because it is a revolutionary innovation. The opposite is true. It works because time has shown that all production is a process. If an organization employs weak or misdirected processes, its products will be produced in a weak, unpredictable fashion. If an organization employs sound processes, its production environments will operate in smoother, more controlled fashions. In that way it *is* rocket science. Rocket scientists use some of the most efficient and proven processes ever put to work.

We looked earlier at some of the more empirical, quantitative benefits of process—such as ROI numbers from Boeing and Schlumberger.

But here are some just-as-real benefits of process, of a more qualitative nature but providing the same significance of impact.

Operational Stability

I was in Manhattan not too long ago visiting a friend. Shelly's a financial analyst for one of the larger brokerage houses. One evening she took me uptown to a restaurant off East 52nd street to meet some of her work associates. I expected an evening filled with talk of P/E ratios, leverage points, and acquisition targets. But I was surprised at the interest Shelly's friends had in what I do. They seemed to know quite a bit about it. They were quite familiar with how Jack Welch used Six Sigma to get a real handle on defect reduction at GE. And they knew how Motorola has used it to boost pager production. They talked about CMMI at Lockheed Martin and Northrop Grumman, and the government's growing insistence on the use of quality systems by its major vendors.

"When did you guys get into process?" I asked Shelly.

She tapped her finger on the solid surface of the table. "James," she said, "stability is an asset."

That was the first time I had heard it put that way. But Shelly was right. And her analyst friends had picked up on an intuitive insight. They were beginning to add process into the mix of elements they used to value companies. It made perfect sense. Stability certainly is a corporate asset. And process is a way to add stability into an organization. A process program can help set boundaries for operations and for production. It can establish paths of activities that your work teams can follow in a consistent and repeatable manner. It introduces predictability into work flows. It helps you forecast and plan. And it does this in a way that is visible to everyone in the organization, from management on down. Further, it provides a mechanism for the public to see this stability as well. And that can go a long way to enhancing the image of an organization.

LAUNCHING INTO STABILITY

"You can delineate organizational growth into two broad categories: launch mode and operational mode. The way you manage quality is very different in each. In launch mode, the organization is by necessity short-sighted. The driving push is to get the product out in a way that meets basic market demands. But in operational mode the organization begins to look long-term. The strategy moves away from product to process, to refining the best way to do business. Here you can begin to plan quality.

"Launch mode and operational mode also require different kinds of people. Launch mode takes a high energy, entrepreneurial spirit. There is not much focus on efficiency or analysis. Goals are typically near-term and very cut-and-dry. When an organization moves from launch mode to operational mode, you'll often see that its people change. The entrepreneurs give way to long-vision leaders, focused management, and strategic analysts. There is a deep emphasis on efficiencies, on driving costs out, on managing cash flow. And energies are focused on sustainability, embedded success, and growth."

—Bruce A. Brown, Senior Vice President and CIO, T-Mobile USA

Cultural Identity

There's a technology company in Pasadena called Tenzer-Spring Dynamics. In its 12th year of business, the company of about 100 people found itself in a somewhat common position.

Over the years, it had grown its software development services in fits and starts. Between the ups, it focused on staff augmentation, farming contractors out to other companies for a cut of the hourly rate. So it did some contract development and some contract placement. Then, because it did have some pretty senior technical folks in-house, it began to find revenues in doing architectural assessments for other software development companies, sometimes its competitors. Then it found some luck putting together and farming out Test Teams. After a dozen years of business, Tenzer found itself in about half a dozen lines of business.

The problem it faced was that it had no real identity. Tenzer was whatever it was that could bring Tenzer revenue. Naturally there was very little staff cohesion, little strategic focus, and almost no loyalty. Tenzer turned into a marriage of convenience among 100 or so partners.

I don't know if some form of process early on could have helped Tenzer. But the case illustrates well the importance of identity. Process is one way to help an organization establish its identity.

You can see this—almost without looking—at very successful process companies. There is an indisputable way of doing business at Coca-Cola. It is the Coke way. The same holds true at Apple Computer. Apple's way of doing business was not born out of its marketing image; its image was born out of its business processes. Think of Kentucky Fried Chicken. Or NASA. When you embrace a process program, you embrace a set of practices that evolve over time into a set of cultural behaviors and values. Those things that your processes emphasize and promote become the culture.

Think of the phrase, "There's the right way, the wrong way, and the Army way." That's a process-driven mantra. Corporate identity may be just as important an asset as operational stability. Identity is what keeps a collection of individuals (the basis of any company) together. It is what helps move them forward in a common direction. Process can make a significant contribution to establishing this identity. It takes what can be an invisible, intangible attribute and, through action, makes it visible throughout the whole organization.

Sharper Focus

Quality management programs save money several ways: by reducing costs, by streamlining operations, by helping shrink waste. But these actions not only save money; they sharpen the focus of an organization.

Every organization—every functioning group—has a culture, and that culture dictates how the company works. Some cultures are open and free-moving. Others are structured and carefully balanced. But either way, the culture is impacted by how the company is focused. You'll find that a quality management system is an effective tool for focusing the energies, work direction, and activities of your company. Let's look at an example.

Burger King has a quality management system. That's why a Whopper ordered in Tucson tastes exactly like a Whopper ordered in Jacksonville. Thirty years ago, Burger King figured out how to make Whoppers, and by and large, they've stuck to that successful formula. Burger King's employees and managers don't have to figure it out anymore. The inventing part is done. Now they are free to focus their energies on other things: new sandwiches, new promotions, the future. The burger-making issue—aside from occasional refinements—has been taken care of. The formula is established.

That's what a quality management system can do for just about any organization: bring it operational unity.

Operational unity is a desirable trait because it sharpens focus. An organization has only so much energy it can expend to meet its goals. If the energy is dispersed, like in a soft light bulb, the light can only travel so far before it dissipates. If the energy is concentrated, like in a laser beam, the distance greatly increases.

Through an effective quality management program, you can sharpen the focus of your organization. Your people don't have to continually figure out effective ways of doing business—you've already found those and documented them in processes. Instead, your people are more free to innovate, to move the company forward toward its goals.

The organizational unity that comes from a sharper focus has another advantage: it solidifies the organizational culture.

If you look at hyper-successful companies like Mars, Johnson & Johnson, or Apple Computer, you'll find that they each have a very distinct culture. Were you to work there, you would know that you were working there. There's a feeling about each place, and that feeling comes from their way of dong business.

Mars, Johnson & Johnson, and Apple Computer have worked hard to establish cultures that reflect their values and goals and their ways of doing business. When you think about it, a quality management system helps you do the same thing. It formalizes—externalizes through its processes—your goals. As a consequence, when you're working in an organization with a defined process program, you'll find that it's easier to know what is expected of you, to know what contributions you are there to make, and to know how to work effectively with other people and other groups.

There is a popular management exercise called JET, Job Expectation Technique. The idea behind JET is that members of a group can't work effectively as a team until they understand four fundamental things: the mission of the group, their job within the group, what contributions they are expected to make toward the mission, and how to communicate with other members of the group. Once a person understands his place in the group—and the value he brings to the group—he can become an active participant in that group.

A Higher Performance Bar

In any organization, you get a mix of talent. There are strong performers. There are weak performers. The committed and the coasting. Thinkers and tinkers. That's the mix of human nature. Management's job is to bring together the different people that make up an organization and harness their different degrees of talent toward a common purpose. To a degree, that mission exists with or without a quality management system or a process program. But when looked at from a best-practices viewpoint, a quality management system can play a complementary role in that mission—and not a passive role, an active one.

By definition, a quality management system is a collection of processes selected for suitability and designed for effectiveness. The processes are best when they are built (at least in part) on the best practices of your strongest people. The chief quality, then, of a proven process—one proven to facilitate a desired result—is that, if you follow it, it should deliver predictable results. In other words, if your best employee follows it, it should produce pretty acceptable results. And if your weakest employee follows it, your chances are strong that you'll at least get something similar. Organizations that create effective process programs almost always look to their strongest performers for input, guidance, and feedback. The program then ultimately reflects how those guys, in large part, work.

When you set a quality management system into place this way, the program begins to lift the performance bar for the whole organization. It gives workers discrete accountability standards for their own work. At the same time, the internal success secrets possessed by the talented and the committed become externalized and available to all. The process program you build as a tool to manage quality becomes in use an organizational educational tool. Its theme—once you have sharpened it through use—is "This is the way that our organization works." Your program begins by setting a work path for all your people; it allows them a predictable route on which to practice their talents. Further, it provides the resources and training for all team players to become effective contributors. Redundant explorations and repetitive seek-and-find are greatly reduced.

Through a quality management program, you'll find that your super-talented people are free to spend their time on innovation, on creativity, on pushing the company forward. Dan Payne, a senior IT project manager in the telecommunications industry, specializes in helping IT organizations use process to free their best folks to focus on innovation. Dan works chiefly with CMMI, and in these implementations, he reports that, in addition to freeing the best, you can take once-mediocre performers and give them the structure and the guides they may need to become valuable players. At this point, the core talent of the organization is no longer embedded invisibly in its people. Your quality management system exists, in large part, as a success program everyone can follow. When you design your program to reflect successful practices, when you school your people to follow these practices, and when you conscientiously commit the organization to the path, you provide a real service to your people. You raise the bar for everybody. And you help them clear it. Performance rises.

Reduced Costs

The process prophet Philip Crosby coined the phrase, "Quality is Free." If there is one misconception about quality that I encounter more than any other, it's that quality costs. To many, implementing a quality program means adding overhead to an organization. It's seen as an expense with a questionable return. Maybe you know people who think this way. I don't mind this opinion too much because it is easy to overcome.

Here's one illustration:

Around 1980, Art Sundry and Bill Smith were in engineering at Motorola, making pagers for the company. They were working on the issue of defect management because the company had been struggling with a quality problem for some time. They were looking at the pager production line to see if they could learn anything about how to make things better. They followed pager assembly down its many steps. Once a pager was put together, it went through a pretty comprehensive final field-ready check. If it passed the check, it was packaged and shipped. If the test hit an error, the error was noted and the pager was sent to repair. Once the pager was repaired, it was repackaged to be shipped.

Sundry and Smith began to keep their eyes on these early trouble pagers. What they found was these pagers carried their troubles with them. Pagers that were flagged to go

THE CHALLENGE OF IT INTEGRATION

"The importance of technology management has grown as the IT profession has become more complicated, both for the practitioner and the business. All the choices that we have today exist to make things easier but they really add to the overall complexity.

"The relationship between choice and complexity becomes clear when you look at IT shops today. The trend is to not spend lots of time and resources developing new solutions. Solutions can be acquired, efficiently acquired. That's good for the business but it introduces a host of new integration and interface issues. A major job of IT now is to facilitate the putting together of this solutions puzzle, piece by piece, and the most reliable way to accomplish that is through a delivery life-cycle process.

"Many IT shops have found a hidden advantage in acquiring third party solutions. Products like SAP and Seibel deliver defined functionality to an established business need but they also—by default—operate a certain way. There's a built-in process there. And so when you adopt these kinds of products you may find that you are also beginning to introduce process into the organization, processes you can extend further or that you can use to refine other processes."

—Ken Rabun, Vice President of IT Quality, T-Mobile USA

---

through the repair process turned out to have significantly more problems in the field than pagers that passed. Put aside the issue of testing thoroughness or flagging procedures right now. The point is that the products that left the shop in a quality state retained their quality state in the field, well into life. The products that showed early signs of problems kept on evidencing problems, even when the original ones were corrected. Fundamentally, quality products required less attention than defective products.

In fact, many additional production steps were required to ship a product flagged as defective:

1. The defect had to be identified and noted.
2. The product had to be moved to the repair team.
3. The repairs had to be queued and then made.
4. The product had to be retested.
5. The product could then be repackaged and shipped.

And that's just five basic steps. The procedure at Motorola was no doubt more complex.

What was this repair route costing Motorola? In labor, in inventory, in time, in market reputation? There were all kinds of possible ways to address this problem. Open more field repair centers to reduce customer downtime. Subcontract out for ready-assembled components. Farm all defect repairs out to a centralized operating group.

But Sundry and Smith, early pioneers of Six Sigma, knew that the best solution—the right solution for Motorola—was to get to the source of the issue, to reduce defects, to produce pagers that passed their initial quality test and thus promised reliable performance in the field. The way to cut costs and save money at Motorola *while strengthening its market position* was to raise quality.

Here's another illustration. I'm back now at MCI in the late 1990s, helping the company design a software system to "port" customer phone numbers from carrier to carrier.

The complexities of moving phone numbers from, say, AT&T over to BellSouth were enormous and involved questions of reprovisioning, new switch addresses, node transfers, and on and on. And so we contracted a company out of Ottawa, Systems House Limited (SHL), to code the system as we designed it. SHL had a great deal of telephony experience and was very familiar with the demands of such number-sensitive operations. What we didn't anticipate was SHL's meticulous approach to managing this project.

SHL was an ISO 9002 registered shop (a direct antecedent to ISO 9001:2000), and they had every intention of following their quality management system for the life of this contract. We balked at first (and I was one of the balkers). SHL wanted to do a lot of planning. They wanted to spend a lot of time validating the design materials we gave them. They asked a lot of questions and got their teams (and us) together often to drive down to detail. They had a great reputation as a coding shop, but it often looked like the last thing they wanted to do was code.

We worried because Local Number Portability was a federally mandated service. Telecommunications companies had to offer this free market service to its customers by a certain date or face major fines. Between now and the due date, we had to make a lot of smaller deadlines: industry review meetings, the exchange of coordination plans, pilot runs of data transactions, etc. We didn't want a lot of additional "management activity" that might slow us down and potentially make MCI look less than competent to its rivals. But SHL insisted, and we went along, more or less because by that point we had no choice.

But then we began to notice something. The cross-industry design meetings began going very smoothly. Our teams seemed to have a deeper grasp on the issues and a clearer vision of how things should flow through the system. Our designs became stronger, and the picture of the whole system with all its interrelationships began to take solid shape. When SHL began to code, the components worked just about how we had all anticipated. There were some backtracks and some redos, but by and large the construction phase was remarkably uneventful.

Two months later, the government pushed the deadline back because most of the other phone companies weren't making our kind of progress. That just gave us more time to fine-tune our solution. When it came time for integration testing, the system proved to be in solid shape. When we did system testing, it was even tighter. When it came time for acceptance testing and production dress rehearsal, MCI was able to forgo bringing in a large support staff. It had planned to hire upward of 70 contractors for a final blitz, but there was no need to blitz. A team of about one-half that size proved adequate.

A little over two years later, MCI WorldCom would go down in a blaze of flames, but in that project MCI led the industry in readiness, innovation, response, and quality. And there's no way to estimate how much they saved in hard costs, aggravation, and industry stature by working with a company like SHL, a company that insisted on doing things the way they knew was right.

The Project Is the Process

This may be one of the strongest benefits that process can deliver into a technology development organization. The full breadth of this benefit didn't really hit me until I had been in the business for about six years. But what I began to see was this: IT shops that had used process for quite a while seemed to be able to very confidently and consistently predict budgets, schedules, activities, contingencies, and variances. They seemed to have a good grip on things that at first, to me, appeared transparent. I was impressed that these places could visualize a project, with its different dimensions and demands, very early on in the formulation period. But after a while I saw the trick. Only it wasn't a trick. It was a technique. And a pretty reliable technique.

The people in these organizations had begun to place the concept of The Project behind that of The Process. In these shops, process superseded the project. When I looked at their processes, it was clear why they were taking this approach. Their processes had been well tested over time, so much so that these people could rely on them and depend on them. And when you looked closer, you could see that they had a process for every major phase in technology development. There were processes for requirements management, requirements development, technical design, peer reviews, defect handling, verification, product integration, validation, and delivery.

When these shops acquired new project work, they began by assembling all the processes they would need to get the work done. Once the right process set was in place, the full set told the project story. For all processes, there were inputs and outputs. These were planned as work products. For all processes, there were steps. These were planned as activities. Resources were assigned to support these activities. Timelines were set into place. Budgets were allocated to cover the costs.

By the time the process assembly was completed, the project itself had taken full shape. With a process program in place, your organization can count on the same kind of advanced step-ahead. Your way of doing business becomes encapsulated in your processes, and so you can more readily predict the shape of your projects by the processes you put to work on them.

Better Quality

Sure, why not. Seems obvious. But it's worth setting out explicitly because while many of the benefits of a quality program are by-products of the program, better quality is the *primary* product. And better quality has such a radiating effect that it can almost be said to be its own reward.

CONFIRMING QUALITY, ASSURING STANDARDS

"Programs like ISO 9001 and CMMI are often thought of solely as mechanisms to produce process programs. But another helpful way to use them is as a benchmark for program success. These models all contain what have been recognized in the industry as the common best-practices for IT development. Because of this you can use them as a basis of comparison, as a way to look at your process program and see where it is strong, where it might be improved, and where it might be extended to further your business goals."

—Susan Goldman, Chief Process Officer, AXON Strategic Management

"In any production stream—manufacturing, technology, whatever—quality protects the process; the process protects delivery.

"CMMI (or ISO 9001) can be thought of as a 'quality confirmation' tool. It's a program of best-practices that professional technology shops should be practicing anyway. CMMI simply gives the set a framework to operate from. In light of this, one should think of something like CMMI compliance not as a goal but as a tool. The idea is that, if you're in a state where your quality goals can be more readily achieved, you're probably already close to compliance.

"The concept of process improvement is action in pursuit of quality, with a continuous view into how you are doing. It's an ongoing activity."

—Shailesh Grover, Senior Director, IT Methods, Processes, and Tools, Cingular Wireless

We discussed the question of what quality is earlier in this section. Once you define what it is and how it should be realized in what you produce, and then work to realize that, your company almost automatically becomes stronger.

Quality enhances your company's reputation. Quality has a tendency to motivate the work force, inspire innovation and creativity, and bring out best efforts. Quality leads in the marketplace. It promotes sales, builds customer satisfaction, and fosters brand loyalty. It establishes competitive standards. In many ways, for many industries, it defines success. It's the benchmark for achievement.

The old adage "nothing succeeds like success" is true. And it's a derivative of delivering quality.

The art of process improvement revolves around three concepts: establishing a process program, using the program, and evolving the program's effectiveness over time. Each of these requires its own approach and its own set of considerations. The first—planning the scope of the program—appears to most people to be the most daunting. In the following chapter, I'll show some of the factors you might consider when setting out to develop an internal process improvement program.

Summary

- The American IT business is a $350 billion annual enterprise. Yet every year IT failures negatively impact that figure by $60 billion.

- The business of American IT is not technology; it's business. American IT shops should run their business like a business.

- There are many myths that hinder organizations from adopting process. Among these are that process is too heavy, process will cramp their style, and process is just another flavor of the month.

- Any production environment requires some degree of order and sequence. IT shops are no different. Process is a way to help order the work of technology development.

- There are real benefits to implementing process. Some of these are operational stability, organizational identity, cost reduction, and quality assurance.

CHAPTER THREE

Establishing Your Process Program

ISO 9001:2000, THE CAPABILITY MATURITY MODEL INTEGRATION, AND SIX SIGMA ARE NOT REALLY process programs, though many people think of them in that way. The better description is to say they are frameworks you can use to create your process program. ISO, CMMI, and Six Sigma wrap a series of practices, areas of focus, and methods into an approach that can support definition, control, and improvement of your technology projects. They are a great foundation, taken alone or in combination with one another. But creating a process program—a big one or a small one—is an effort that requires more than adopting a model or a standard. It requires customization. In fact, one could say it is an effort that *relies* on customization.

Successful process programs are typically ones that have been carefully tailored to the needs of an organization. They are based on the way the organization works—or knows how it should work. And they capitalize on what it is the organization does well. It may be tempting at times to introduce something "fresh" from the outside, something that may look to hold the promise of addressing many of the issues the IT shops deals with. That may help, but real success rarely lies in something outside the organization. A tool like Photoshop might help someone be a better artist, but it probably won't make them a good artist to begin with. It's the same with ISO 9001, CMMI, and Six Sigma. You can use these tools to make your process program as effective as it can be, but you'll need to set the right foundation in place. If you haven't even tailored your program to specialties of your shop, even the most promising of programs will rattle and roll.

In this chapter, I'll look at some tips and techniques you can use to help establish a process program in your organization, one that fits well with what your shop is and what it does.

I'll look at a series of recommendations that you can use to right-size a process program. Here's a brief up-front look at what I'll cover:

Building through executive sponsorship

Executive commitment is an essential ingredient to any process program. In fact, one could argue that it is the single most essential ingredient. Executive sponsorship will provide you with the charter, the authority, and the resources you need to shape your program and then roll it out into the organization. Without this commitment, a program can easily dissipate over time, or never take hold in the first place. So as you begin your process efforts, make sure you're able to count on executive support.

Capitalizing on your strengths

Chances are your IT shop is doing a lot of things very well already. You should want to identify those traits and incorporate them into your process program: take your proven practices and formalize them. This will position your program from the start to align with current habits, and so give it the best chance to take deep root in the organization.

Understanding what you'd like to do better

The new process elements you introduce into your shop will spring from this recommendation. Here you work with your people to understand what it is the organization would like to do better, what its pain points are, what business objectives might need to be better supported. Linking your processes to these needs is another crucial success element. When you can begin to show that your process program is directly addressing tangible business needs, you'll find that the organization will be willing to embrace it as a logical way to conduct business.

Focusing on targeted improvements

The idea here is to target improvement opportunities that will promote business success, but to do so in a way that is manageable. In other words, don't feel obligated to address every performance issue you and your shop can identify. Target what you want to initially tackle. It's OK to start small; it's probably preferable (at least early on) to start small. You can grow from there.

Borrowing from the industry

Study what the IT industry has learned and then adopt those elements that appear to be beneficial to your focus and that seem to fit your needs. Review the recommendations of ISO 9001, CMMI, and Six Sigma (and maybe even ITIL, CobiT, Theory of Constraints, or any of the other models available). There are many sources of best practices available. Chances are others have had to solve problems similar to the ones you are faced with. So look at what the industry has adopted, and incorporate those proven ideas that help move you toward your goals.

Building from the inside

When you begin to build your process program, make sure to build it from the inside. That is, get the people in your shop to help you create your processes, procedures, forms, templates, etc. If they have an active hand here, they will help you produce components that are usable by the culture, components that will reflect the way your people work. And by seeking their input, your people will feel a degree of ownership over the program they help create.

Building to grow

Build your process program with the flexibility it will need to grow over time and adapt to changes as your business evolves. To do this you will need to find the right balance between detail and control, between standardization and customization. Naturally this balance will depend on the needs of your shop. As a general rule, newer programs take best when they are built with less detail and more flexibility. More mature programs can move toward greater levels of granularity and control.

Training your people

Next to executive commitment, this may be the strongest success factor for any process program. The benefit of training should not be undervalued. It's one thing to create a process program; it's another to use it to its full potential. By training your people on the smooth use of the program, you'll bring them a long way toward adopting it for the long term. Make this an early consideration in your design efforts. Plan for the right level of training your people will need, plan for the types of training you can deliver, and then work to deliver it to the right people.

Providing support

Any organization that manages its activities around processes will need to provide ongoing support for its program. This can include a range of components: coaching for people just moving into the program; documentation, guidelines, and other program materials; and templates, forms, and checklists. In short, your organization should provide the type of support materials that your people will need to use the program on a daily and ongoing basis.

Patience, not perfection

Process management and process improvement require a commitment over time. The full benefits of your program will not be realized until the organization has had the chance to institutionalize the program across its culture. This will take time. And so the program's success should be measured in gradual improvements, as a trend line that is steadily moving in the direction you want. Patience is important here. Consistent, incremental progress will add up over time to make significant contributions to quality and performance across the organization.

I'll cover these 10 recommendations in more detail in the following sections, but first let's take a look at an industry-recognized general approach to establishing a process program.

Using IDEAL

The ideas that drive introducing process are pretty standard. People want to help make the workplace more predictable, help it become more stable, shape it for better control—in short, help the environment as a whole focus on its potential. And so it's a good idea to follow something of a predictable path when you want to establish a process program: a method that will help shape the program as smoothly as possible, in an orderly and manageable way. One approach to this can be found in the IDEAL model: Initiate, Diagnose, Establish, Act, and Learn. IDEAL is a general approach to process improvement. You may find it helpful as an approach to your own process efforts. Let's take a look at IDEAL.

IDEAL can be thought of as an umbrella philosophy covering process improvement. In many ways IDEAL is a formulation of the famous Plan-Do-Act-Check mantra. IDEAL isn't a process itself; it's a model designed to help you manage your process management activities. Here is a brief breakdown of how IDEAL is structured (see Figure 3-1).

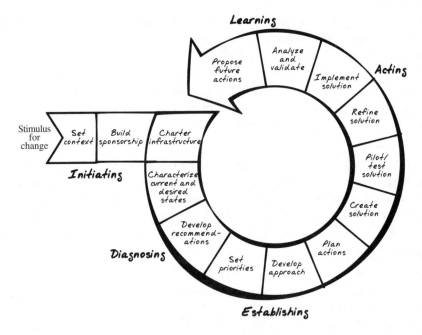

FIGURE 3-1. The concept of IDEAL is to Initiate, Diagnose, Establish, Act, and Learn. Its circular nature has an important implication. The process is ongoing. Process improvement programs are long-term commitments to evaluation and measurement.

An important aspect to IDEAL is its shape. It is circular, and the meaning of that shape is clear: you cycle through a series of activities, and when you close out the last step, you repeat, either in the same area for continuous improvement or in new areas for fresh improvement. Just about any improvement program can be managed following the concepts of IDEAL. Let's look at each phase of IDEAL:

Phase 1: Initiate

This first stage is one of realization, decision, and then dedication. In the Initiate phase, an organization typically reaches the understanding that it has operational issues that need to be addressed. This realization is often predicated by some symptomatic imbalance within the organization: falling sales, rising costs, increased complaints, low morale, or even the appreciation for general improvement, for strengthening the organization's current position. It can be many things, but it's always a trigger for action.

Out of this realization, the organization makes a conscious decision to initiate action, to act on its needs. This decision is then followed by the critical impetus of dedication—dedication to act.*

The Initiate phase is typically the point at which you acquire executive sponsorship and begin to formulate the scope of what you want to address in your process program.

Phase 2: Diagnose

I used the word "symptomatic" earlier. The value of any symptom is its visibility—or, maybe, its distracting presence. But the symptom is rarely the cause, and in the field of improvement the trick is not to remove the symptom but to identify and isolate the cause. This is often easier said than done, given the complexities of technology and software development. But it is an essential and high-value activity: diagnosing what the organization should change, where it should focus its improvement activities. Many process managers would argue that this is the stage where you should devote most of your energy, most of your creative thinking. The better the diagnosis, the better the chance for a highly successful solution.

In the Diagnose phase, you typically determine the organization's current quality and process positions, its strengths and weaknesses, and what areas for improvement should be addressed by this effort.

Phase 3: Establish

Here, the organization establishes the solution to the problem (or the enhancements to its strengths). It's important that this solution carry a trio of trademarks, and so careful design during this step becomes very important. First, the solution should show "goodness-of-fit." It should be designed with organizational use in mind. That is, you should be pretty certain that if you implement it, it will work. Next, the solution should be designed not to impact the integrity of any up-line or down-line activity. You don't want to cause other problems by fixing one. And finally, the solution should be in some way measurable. The best way to test if any solution works is to measure its activity. (This use of the measurement data comes into play during the Learn portion of IDEAL.)

---

* Few people familiar with process would argue that the single most common reason that process improvement programs fail to deliver on their promises is that the organization's dedication to seeing the programs through fizzles over time.

In the Establish phase, you typically create your process components or refine existing ones. The key to successful establishment (as we'll see in following sections) is to create solutions that reflect the way your people work, solutions that possess a strong goodness-of-fit to the culture of the organization.

Phase 4: Act

This may be the most straightforward step of them all. Here, you implement the solutions you designed. Act may require a series of support steps, such as training or documentation preparation, but the real goal here is to *act* on your design: put it effectively into place, monitor its use, and then move to the final step, Learn.

Act is the phase during which you typically train your people, provide them with program support materials, and then implement the program in the organization.

Phase 5: Learn

Process improvement is all about learning. That's a core trait of the discipline: it's a cultural commitment to continued learning. Learning, however, takes time, and it takes data, and you'll find that there should be an extended observation period between acting and learning. What that observation period largely depends on is the nature of your environment and the solutions you've added into the environment. But keep in mind two things. First, give the solution time to prove its viability. Second, as early as practical, begin measuring the performance of the solution. Time and data will give you the factual base you need to determine the success of your efforts and may also point you to new opportunities for strengthening the system.

You may find that IDEAL is a good path to follow as you build a process program for your shop. But whatever path you take, it's helpful to think through a series of considerations that are generally accounted for in any process program. It's a good idea to address each of these, at least on the surface. These considerations (and the recommendations they contain) can be used to guide you through a series of activities that help ensure an orderly and accountable approach to program preparation, design, and deployment, one that is focused, well-communicated, supported by management, and keyed to deliver specific benefits to the groups using it.

Though I present them in a sequential order, the following sections should not be viewed as a set of prescribed steps. Rather, read them as a set of common considerations, each one accounting for an organizational aspect that can help your program take root, grow, and prosper. The points you elect to use will naturally depend upon a set of conditions: the current state of your organization; its size, culture, and temperament; the style of management; the industries you serve; and other environmental traits.

The first recommendation falls under the IDEAL domain Initiate. It is designed to help you take your process initiative from being a basic idea for improvement to ascertaining what degree of improvement might be right for the moment. A key starting point here involves obtaining executive sponsorship for your initiative.

Let's look at this topic in more detail.

COMPONENTS OF A PROCESS

When you build a process program, the only real requirement is to build a program that fits the working style of your people. After that, you're free to go in any direction you see as best. But one thing you will need, in some form or another, is a set of documented processes. What goes into a good process? Here are some traditional components you might want to include:

Purpose description
> Provide a brief description of the purpose and use of the process.

Entry criteria
> Describe the entry criteria. These are previous activities or preconditions that may need to have occurred in order for the activities of this process to be successfully carried out.

Inputs
> Describe any work products that may be required as inputs into the process. This may include any documents or plans that are needed in order to conduct the activities described in the process.

Actors
> Here you describe the roles that people will undertake in order to carry out the process activities. Primary actors are typically the people who execute the process. Secondary actors are typically people who support the process or who may be impacted by the process.

Activities
> This is the heart of the process description. Here you describe the steps that are taken to see the process through. These can be expressed as numbered steps, as a narrative description, or in any manner suitable to the actors who will use them.

Outputs
> Most processes are in place to produce something or to refine something already in existence. And so it's beneficial to identify what outputs should appears as a result of the process activities.

Exit criteria
> Describe the exit criteria. These are results that should be in place in order to conclude that the process has been successfully run through and that its responsibilities have been properly accounted for.

Measures
> Finally, you can define the measures that you will collect for this process. These should be selected so that they provide insight into how well the process performs for your teams.

COMPONENTS OF A PROCESS PROGRAM

A process program can contain any set of elements that you deem fit for it. The key is to furnish it with those assets and components that will help you set up your program effectively, in a way that will give your people the tools they need to carry it out as intended:

Processes
These are the overall processes that will be used to help govern and manage project activities.

Procedures
These are supporting subprocesses that may be used to help carry out the processes.

Templates
These are outlines and guides that help you create documents in a consistent manner.

Forms and checklists
These are process aids that help you plan and follow task completion and help you document activity progress and progression.

Guidelines
These are instructions that your people can use to properly execute the program and its components.

Repositories
These are the locations where you store your program elements for use by your project teams.

Training materials
These are the materials you develop to ensure that your people are able to use program elements in an informed and directed manner.

Establishing Executive Sponsorship

Establishing executive sponsorship is an activity that is typically cited as a key success factor in the fields of process improvement and quality management. It is specially emphasized in ISO 9001:2000, the Capability Maturity Model Integration, and Six Sigma. These kinds of programs thrive when the broad workforce adopts them and backs them up, but they can only get to that point through a top-down organizational commitment.

Most corporate and IT initiatives work through executive sponsorship. The team that's charged with selecting a new automated test tool will usually answer to some type of sponsor. Committees put together to explore new market potentials or new product lines will usually operate through the guidance of a sponsor. The people who help promote the annual blood drive do so with the help of an executive sponsor. If there's a need for a special effort, if it's going to cost money, if it's going to require dedicated resources, the company will probably want to manage that, and that is typically done by appointing an executive sponsor. The same holds true for process improvement programs.

The executive sponsor is the arm of management that steps up to the plate to shepherd the program into the organization, to give the program the backing and the visibility it needs, and to intervene when necessary to make sure that the program's design and implementation activities are progressing along acceptable lines.

You could make a logical argument that those responsibilities could be handled by someone less senior in the organization. And, logically, that might be right. But the appointment of an executive to the job adds an element of clout that's hard to replicate in any other way. So when you begin down the path of process improvement, ensure that you have executive sponsorship on your side.

The Need for Executive Sponsorship

Executive sponsorship works best when the executive occupies a position of deep authority in the company. The sponsor should probably not occupy a block on the org chart that has a crowded view of the sky. If you are able to influence this decision, try to promote sponsorship at as high a level as you can communicate. Seek out a sponsor with broad authority, a track record with the IT group, and an ability to bring off strategic initiatives. Capable, empowered sponsorship is essential for three clear (but often unappreciated) reasons:

- First, executive sponsorship demonstrates that the organization's leadership sees the importance and value that a quality program will bring to the company. Through sponsorship, it shows that it has adopted this vision and is now moving to share it with the rest of the company. This may be a subtle point, but it's one that runs below the surface, influencing the climate of the culture. Process management and quality can sometimes become set-aside concepts, overshadowed by deadlines, competitive pressures, or strained resources. When the executive arm of the organization raises the importance of quality to a level visible to all, the focus sharpens and appreciation for its value rises. An active sponsor, committed to the cause, is able to push this vision in a way that makes the vision tangible.

- Second, executive sponsorship shows commitment to the nuts and bolts of your emerging process program. The value here is that sponsorship is able to communicate to the organization that the executive level is backing this initiative with confidence. With proper commitment, the program will less likely be viewed as a trial, a test, or a proof-of-concept (unless you intentionally shape it to be that); it will promote endorsement for the concept of quality, and for the company's ability to master its quality goals. That's a message that travels well. The executive sponsor should not only demonstrate belief in the principles of quality management, but should be seen to visibly move to make those principles part of the organizational culture.

- Third, executive sponsorship will be required to govern the resources required to plan, design, create, and implement the program. This may be the single most important role of the sponsor. Your process initiative is going to need an independent existence within the organization, and it's going to need to be well integrated at the same time. This will require people (full-time or part-time) who will conduct program activities; money for payroll, computers, and tools; facilities; and time to carry the job through. The scope of your program will shape the type of resources you'll need, but you are going to need the backing of executive management to release those resources toward your goal.

All three of these reasons demonstrate the importance of having an executive sponsor to back your program.

A Leadership Assignment

In my work, I'm often called on to help organizations shape process programs that are starting from the ground up. These kinds of clean-slate assignments carry a lot of appeal because they can be carefully shaped with the foundation for long-term success. And one of things I like to contribute here is a sense of what executive sponsorship will mean to the program, what kind of person in the organization might be best suited to this role. Sometimes it takes a bit of reminding to management that this is not a toss-off job. Its purpose is not simply to connect a line up the organizational chart. In fact, together with the decision to move forward on a process improvement initiative, it may be the most important decision management will make regarding the program.

Last fall, I was working with Guy Bevente, an AVP of Information Technology at SBC who's done some impressive process work over the course of his career. He mentioned the importance of executive sponsorship and the criticality of executive involvement.

His point was that the issue of executive sponsorship, vital as it is to the success of a process initiative, should be seen as management making the choice to move the program forward. It becomes one of the first demonstrations of management's commitment to the vision. "It's a leadership function," Guy said. "The program sponsor is going to need a level of authority and visibility to shepherd the program through. More than that, though, the sponsor is going to have to possess the expertise to be the 'voice' of the initiative; and that requires the ability to live the commitment in the eyes of the organization."

For many, especially those new to process improvement programs, that's not an intuitive understanding. And so Guy made a recommendation to me that was obvious once I heard it: for someone engaged in a new process initiative and seeking the right kind of sponsorship, try creating a job description for the executive sponsor. Put this description down on paper and introduce it to management as early into the program as possible.

I like that idea. And I have found that management, even if they don't adopt the description *in toto*, more often than not uses it as starting point for appointing a sponsor.

You might want to try creating a job description for the kind of sponsor you think your program will need.

There is no generic template for this job. The description will need to reflect the specific needs of your program and your organization. But there is a general set of capabilities that may help you shape such a job description. I describe these next.

EXECUTIVE SPONSOR TRAITS

Guy Bevente, AVP of Information Technology at SBC, talked about the importance of executive sponsorship for any process program. And because the appointment of the right person to the job can be a crucial move in program success, he recommends creating a basic job description of the role. Following are some of the traits you might want the sponsor to possess:

Stand as a leader

Executive sponsorship demonstrates organizational commitment to the process program at the highest levels of management. In light of this, executive sponsorship is a leadership role. The sponsor needs to be an individual with the visibility, authority, and respect to move the vision forward. This is not a sideline job. It's not a backroom assignment. It requires active participation, an ability to communicate effectively up and down the chain, and talent for articulating the mission, goals, and values of the program.

Know the value

Another desirable trait is for the sponsor to possess knowledge of the field of process improvement. Effective sponsors understand the principles of continuous improvement and quality management. As an added plus, they might have a walking knowledge of popular programs like ISO 9001, CMMI, and Six Sigma. It's not critical that the sponsor be an expert in this field (the right staff will take care of that). But this understanding is clearly a plus when you consider that sponsors may well be called on to explain the programs in the field, what they're based on, and how they can help the business.

Carry the weight

Your process program represents an investment in the quality capabilities of your organization. And all investments require an allocation of resources. The executive sponsor needs to be that person who can carry this weight, someone with the authority and budgetary reach to deliver the funding, tools, and facilities you'll need to see your plans through. The sponsor should also be the kind of person who can carry a different sort of weight: the weight of progress. As we've mentioned before, process programs don't gel into success stories overnight. They take time and commitment to mature. The sponsor will need to be able to keep the organization focused on the long-term vision for this program, to help navigate over bumps in the road, and to keep the momentum of the process team moving forward.

Walk the walk

Executive sponsorship should not be a benign appointment. Sponsors should be the type who can walk the walk of the program. They should know the detail of where the program stands; they should have a finger on the pulse of how the program is affecting impacted work groups. They should follow progress closely so they can promote early successes and be prepared for any course corrections that might be approaching.

Aligning with Business Objectives

Another good, early consideration when you're working to establish a process program is to align the initiative up front with the organization's business objectives. This may seem obvious, maybe even a given, yet it's one that can be easily overlooked. There can be a number of reasons for this. Often the champions that are striving to create the program simply assume that any process will further the business goals. Likewise, management may assume that the team chartered with program development is naturally keyed into the strategic business objectives.

But for an improvement program to be successful, it must not only fit the organization well, it must serve the organization well. It should be designed so that it finds its natural place in the order of the business. To do that, you should work with management to consciously tie the program to the company's business objectives.

And to do that, it's helpful to understand where the organization stands in terms of its strategic and tactical performance goals. You can use this positioning to derive the high-level process needs of the organization and then shape an approach to address these needs. Two activities are helpful here:

1. Elicit the business objectives of your organization.

2. Use these to shape the goals and scope of your process program.

Elicit the Business Objectives of the Organization

Most successful process improvement programs share at least one thing in common: their processes are aligned with the business objectives of the organization. Business objectives—explicit, conscientiously designed, and carefully articulated—are a key component to how any organization operates. Business objectives define the organization. Your IT shop (whether it's a group, a department, or a division) exists with a specific purpose. It has a defined job, and the outcome of that job should promote the goals of the IT organization as a whole. The business objectives encapsulate this purpose. These business objectives then should serve as the foundation of the process program you create.*

Usually management owns the business objectives. And so it's a good idea as you set off on this initiative to work with management to collect and document the business objectives that your program can help promote. Study the objectives. Analyze them. Once you know what is important to the organization, you'll be better positioned to create a relevant process program.

---

* If the business objectives aren't available to you (if they are for "executive eyes only") or if they simply don't exist, you'll know very early on that you have something more than a process problem. You've got a very basic business management problem. If your organization is not operating under a set of fundamental, well-documented, and well-communicated business objectives, then the likelihood of that organization performing to any level of predictability, consistency, or quality is seriously compromised.

Look at these examples of business objectives:

- Obtain on-time delivery for 90 percent of all IT projects.
- Achieve 97 percent uptime for all network elements.
- Increase project cycle activity by 25 percent.

These sample objectives can deliver tips that will help you shape an effective program. First, they tell you that management is concerned about on-time delivery. So maybe your program should set into place some tools to support on-time delivery. Network uptime is also important, with a goal of 97 percent. So, maybe your program could include some measurement and reporting techniques to monitor uptime. And management would like to see project activity increase. So maybe your program could include a set of project management components designed to better control project activities.

Understanding the business objectives will take you a long way toward shaping a sound process program. And if you are able to show over time that your process program really is addressing management priorities, then management will probably provide the support you need to see the program continue and grow.

(On the other hand, I have been in situations where management hasn't taken time to document or think through its business objectives. If you find yourself in this situation, if the objectives are not readily available, then work with management, even in a casual way, to determine what the program should accomplish from a business perspective. Treat these as the beginning objectives and incorporate them into your plans.)

Map Process Goals to the Objectives

The operational activities you'll formalize in the process program should be constructed to further the goals of the enterprise at large. And so the objectives defined for your group—and reflected in the design of your process program—should be shaped to support those of the enterprise. That's why it's important to use the objectives you identified earlier as a basis to build the process program. You will be able to show that you have a successful process program in place when you are able to show that it both furthers the goals of your group and furthers the overall mission of the enterprise.

At this point, your initiative should be working against a commonly shared description of the business mission of your organization. It is now positioned to reflect what contributions your group is expected to make to the enterprise, and it can tie these expectations to the progress the enterprise hopes to achieve. The strength of this linking activity is that it establishes a common description. The word "common" here is important. Once you have set it into place, everyone in your organization should be able to acknowledge it, accept it at face value, and share the same understanding of it. You should now have a solid base on which to build your program.

Identifying Improvement Opportunities

If you're new to process improvement, or if you're creating a new program for your organization, remember that the discipline of process improvement promotes the idea of starting small and growing over time. You don't have to tackle every opportunity at once. There's wisdom in carefully targeting your first improvement steps, shaping a program around those, implementing them, and then, as they take hold in the company, adding to them over time.

Naturally, the scope and push of your initiative will depend on multiple factors: management expectations, your current process position, and the resources made available to you.

But as you begin to identify improvement opportunities, keep these three considerations in mind:

1. Capitalize on your strengths.

2. Understand what you want to do better.

3. Target improvement opportunities with promise.

Capitalize on Your Strengths

People are often tempted to move into process improvement with an eraser in one hand and a new pen in the other. They feel an obligation to start everyone off on a clean slate, with a fresh start. That's not usually the best approach, at least not for an organization that's been around for a while. A better place to start is to look at what your organization does well. Process initiatives can easily focus solely on the problems that trouble an IT shop. But it's important to remember that what the shop does well is really the best place to start on a program.

There are three reasons for this:

- First, the organization already understands those things that it does well. Somehow, no matter what the reason, those effective and beneficial activities have taken hold in the company. Your job might be as straightforward as documenting what these activities are and how they usually progress in your shop. By documenting these, you capture the best practices for new members while formalizing the behavior across your working groups.

- Second, it's safe to assume that what the shop does particularly well probably ties to the organization's business objectives. If these practices were not in line with the objectives, they probably wouldn't have been around long enough to become efficient. So as you look at what your teams do well, keep in mind that what these practices will show you are very likely avenues that can be enhanced to further the needs of the business.

- Third, by capitalizing on what your teams do well and by formalizing those things into your program, you'll begin with a program that is already, in many ways, familiar to the people who will be called on to use it. This familiarity is a big plus. If you build your program based on already successful work habits, your people will embrace it more readily, and it can then serve as a base for the development of new program extensions.

As you begin your process initiative, look at what your shop does well with a view to its business objectives and to the areas that you may want to improve (see the next section). Do this by moving out into the organization and talking to its members. Find out what management thinks are areas of strength. Talk to members of the various teams. This is a great opportunity to get a consensus of opinion of best practices, to identify sources of best practice data and activities, and to share the purpose and goals of the process program with members of the organization.

Once you have solicited this information, you should come away with a pretty good idea of the existing practices you will want to integrate into the new program. On top of that, you should come away with a sense of the areas of weakness in the organization: potential targets for focused process improvement.

Understand What You'd Like to Do Better

If you work to define the organization's business objectives and then examine your shop to identify those things it does well, you'll be in a good position to identify areas where things could be done better: potential targets for process improvement activities. Look to document these in your shop. Keep your focus on the business objectives you want to achieve. Then begin to look down to the activity level; look to the business activities that realize performance.

For example, one of the shop's objectives may be to improve IT's ability to meet scheduled release timelines. Stakeholder comments may have indicated that schedules are difficult to honor due to high levels of continuous change. Looking at this, you might see opportunities for improvement in at least two activities. The degree of change, you may decide, might be better managed, and so a good target for improvement might be to review and refine your change control procedures. Another side of this could involve requirements management. You might conclude that the volume of change indicates that the requirements aren't being properly reviewed, that they are arriving in an incomplete manner, or that they are not being tracked well. So here you may see an opportunity to improve your procedures for analyzing, understanding, and committing to customer requirements.

Third, remember the importance of stakeholder participation, especially when it comes to improvement targets. To work to their full potential and promise, all process programs need the support and backup of key stakeholders, particularly the members of your shop. So as you review potential targets, seek a degree of consensus concerning the opportunities. This will hopefully result in improvement choices that ring true with many of the people in the organization.

Of course, here you may have to strike something of balance between want and need. You and management may see an important need for improvement in one area of the business, while the working teams may show a concern for another area. Here you'll need to weigh the appropriate target: tackle an improvement opportunity with a large need, or target an opportunity that, while not as pressing, shows broad support for change. There's not a clear answer here. You'll have to make that call in line with the culture and makeup of your organization. But as long as you keep both views in mind, you'll stand a better chance of making a choice that works to make a difference.

Finally, after you've looked closely at your shop, settle on a range of targets that you and your team can effectively evaluate. Depending on the size, ability, and experience of your team, these may be a few opportunities or they may be a good many. The thing to avoid is lining up too many opportunities, ones that sit on the shelf apparently ignored, or a large set of others that overwhelms your team. The goal here is to realize a core set of key opportunities and then begin a visible campaign to shape organizational activities around those opportunities.

Target Opportunities with Promise

Your process program will begin to take solid shape once you are able to target specifically what it is you want the program to address, what it is you want to improve. If you have a handle on your business objectives, if you understand those things your shop does particularly well, and if you've had an opportunity to discuss the program with members of your various IT teams, then you should be able to identify many potential improvement opportunities.

You might have a chance to extend an already successful activity. You might see an opportunity to support a relatively weak activity with some new tools. You might see big opportunities and small ones, complex ones and simple ones. It's a good idea to keep a list of these, but naturally you can't take on all of them at once.

When it comes to introducing new elements into you program, it's best to be selective, to choose strategically. You probably have limited resources. You may have limited time. You may be chartered with making a set amount of progress. So, if it's best to choose a few select opportunities, then look at the ones that hold the most promise for strong returns.

Here are a few tips to help you do this. They are not presented in any order but are simply considerations that can help you focus on targets with the potential for visible rewards.

A good way to select the strongest opportunities is to begin by looking again at the goals of your company (operating unit or work group). Which ones might your process program be able to influence, to support? If you can be successful at furthering these business objectives, there is no doubt that your process program will be a success. So examine the business goals with this in mind and select those that you are sure you can impact, that you have a pretty good idea of how to impact, and that you are comfortable you have a way to measure and report on.

AIMING FOR THE RIGHT SIZE

The purpose of the activities discussed so far has been to focus the scope of your process program along lines that support the business goals of your organization. The scope you begin to establish here will shape the rest of your process program activities. Sometimes people want their programs to have a broad scope, touching on many areas of IT operations. Other people prefer to start off with a very constrained focus, perhaps seeking to standardize only a few operational traits. Sometimes you may not even be in control of the scope of your program.

But you'll need to address the questions of when to aim low and when to aim high at some point, and it's usually best to think this through early on. There's no clear-cut answer here, but here are some tips you can consider when thinking through what's best for your organization.

Times when it's better to aim low include the following:

Soft commitment

> Many shops realize that they need process, but they aren't deeply informed about what it takes to implement a process program. Consequently, they may be looking for quick benefits and fast returns before they are willing to invest in it properly. When you are faced with this type of soft commitment, it's best to begin with small, targeted efforts. Select one or two areas you can use as a proof-of-concept in order to demonstrate the value of process improvement to management.

Unfocused work groups

> We mentioned this earlier. If the organization as a whole is unfocused—if it lacks any common idea of where it needs to improve or what its overall objectives are—then your program should begin small. It should serve as a candle that lights the way for future, more solid improvement. Select an opportunity or two that will be visible to all groups, work these through, and then see if this helps align the organization for extended efforts.

Cultural resistance

> It's possible that your process initiative will reveal a degree of cultural resistance. Some resistance is always to be expected, but if it shows itself as dominant, you should avoid a large program that could be seen as intrusive. Often you'll find that resistance begins to soften when you're able to show progress in small ways. By aiming low, you can target a few areas specially selected because of their impacts on work loads, workplace fluidity, or quality. When these solutions have been implemented and begin working well, people once cool to the idea of process improvement may begin to change their minds and become open for broader implementation.

Soft benefits

> Even when people know they need process, they may not know exactly what they need it for. They don't yet have a clear idea of the benefits they want to see from a program. And without a good fix on the benefits you're aiming for, you won't be able to readily measure the program's success. So it's best to aim low when the benefits are soft. Start with a couple areas of improvement, work those through, and carefully measure the advantages they deliver.

Times when it's better to aim high include:

Big business

If your IT shop is an enterprise dealing with major clients and large projects, you may find that you have to aim high because your clients require it. This is becoming more and more common. And it's understandable. If a company is going to allocate tens of millions of dollars and a piece of its future to your shop, they should very well want to know that you're operating against some kind of established process or quality program. Ten years ago, you hardly ever heard of this requirement. As a result, billions were scattered to the wind in the dot-com bust, much of it due to cowboy management and charge-up-the-hill business strategies. But the industry has gotten smarter now. Big business now knows that big projects require mature management, most often through the full use of recognized process management programs.

Big risks

Jail time and ankle bracelets have done a lot for the process improvement industry in the last five years. The Sarbanes-Oxley Act, legislated in the wake of corporate scandals like Enron, Worldcom, and Qwest Communications, established standards for controlling, accessing, managing, and reporting on corporate data. Process programs like ISO, Six Sigma, and CMMI happen to address the same kinds of concerns for IT operations. As a result, corporate IT shops are being pressed on by CEOs and CFOs to implement recognized quality controls that build data protection into their business systems.

Big stakes

If you want to do business in certain sectors of the IT industry, you will be required to operate through a recognized quality program. Many major companies in Europe will not grant IT contracts to any shop that is not registered as ISO 9001-compliant. In the U.S., large federal agencies like the Department of Defense and the Department of Housing and Urban Development are requiring that their major IT contractors demonstrate compliance with CMMI. And in the commercial space, companies like GE are requiring their vendors to demonstrate levels of quality control and oversight that reflect the standards of Six Sigma. When you wish to participate in these high revenue markets, you'll need to aim high with your process program.

Now you're ready to look at the organization. Once you know the business objectives that you'd like your program to address, look for "accessible" business activities to build your program on. I put quotes around "accessible" for a reason: accessibility here holds several meanings. One is that you'll need to obtain access to work groups that will exercise your program. They will need to be willing to take on the learning and discovery curve and invest in the time and resources needed to get your program into its initial, workable form. Another is that you'll need access to the kinds of business activities that tie back to the business goals you've selected. Even if a group is willing, if it turns out that their business domain does not impact the goals you've selected, they may not be the best choice. So accessibility requires relevance as well. Another consideration is access in terms of authority. In other words, will the organization grant you the authority to potentially reshape operational processes that might be critical to business success? Try to lock down your domain of influence early on here; know where you are allowed to move and with whom you are allowed to work. With access, relevance, and authority duly considered, you should be able to select proper business activities to assess and report on.

Now that you know the business goals you want to support, and you know the work groups that impact the goals and will partner with you on the program, you can zero in on specific opportunities to target. If you're selective about this choice, you'll end up with a finite yet focused approach to build out your program, one that links directly to business objectives, one that capitalizes on those you do well, and one that extends your capability into new realms of quality management and control.

> ## NOTE
> *Reminder on controlling scope:* Process improvement enthusiasts often reach a little farther than their grasps allow when they set out on an improvement initiative. By its very nature, business is full of processes—documented, undocumented, well done, poorly done. Designing a program that fits well with your IT shop requires focus, time, and attention to detail. You'll want to do it properly—that is, you'll want to do it well. So at first, don't try to do too much at once. Don't try to manage too much or address too many issues. If you keep the scope of the program sized to the capabilities of your team, you're probably scoping to the right level.

Establishing the Process Team

You may need a process team to help carry out your initiative. Or you may not. It all depends on the scope of your program, on what you're trying to achieve. In this section, I'll present a generic look at what you might typically see in a traditional process team. You can establish the process improvement team by either appointing people within the organization or hiring from the outside. But either way, the job of the process team will (in general) encompass a threefold responsibility:

- Interact with organizational stakeholders to shape a set of processes and procedures into a formal process program.
- Set the program into place within the organization.
- Monitor its long-term use throughout the organization.

All three of these are important jobs. They'll require that you put together a team composed of people with the process management skills required to get the jobs done and who have the ability to work together as an effective team.

NOTE

Because I'm presenting the considerations in this chapter sequentially, you might be wondering about a slight chicken-or-egg question at this point. The activities I've described earlier may benefit from the use of a team. On the other hand, you may not find need for a team until your organization is further along into the process. For some organizations, it may not be until more work is completed that you'll know the scope of you program and therefore the kinds of people you'll need long-term on your team. On the other hand, if you don't bring someone onboard earlier, you may not have resources to apply to the original design and scoping.

The point is to not take the sequencing a rule. Rather, use the descriptions I provide of the team as a way to understand what kinds of people you may require to further your initiative, and then make a judgment as to when is the best time to bring them onboard.

When it comes to putting the team together, there are not a lot of fixed rules. In the field of process improvement, there are no specialized titles you must represent on the team. There is no set team size. There is no single proven structure. The size, makeup, and structure of your team is going to depend on several very qualitative traits, including the scope of your quality program, the resources that have been allocated to the team, and the current process maturity of your shop. There are, however, some guidelines you might follow.

It's helpful to remember that creating a process program is not administrative work. That's not to disparage administrators. But on more than a few occasions, I have been in situations where management moves to assign this work to office administrators. The best that I can think is that these people are looking at the process program from the outside in: as a stack of paper to be filled in and maybe sorted—a forms-based task. This most recently happened to me at a company called IdeaMall.* The head of the project management office—there was even a PMI on his business card—suggested to our design team that the group's administrative assistants be given process development duties as an "off-peak" job assignment. The administrative assistants I work with are typically tossed a lot of odd jobs in an organization, and most of them catch pretty well. But creating a quality program is not an odd job or an off-peak assignment. It is a specialized effort, and so it requires a specialized team. I still can't figure out why this misstep is so common, but I want to mention it here because it is so prevalent.

When you begin to form your process team, you don't have to take on certified process engineers (but that's not a bad idea), and you don't have to bring in high-end consultants. But you do need to assign people who demonstrate an aptitude for the task at hand. They should show an interest in process improvement, have some working knowledge of process

---

* The name of this company and the names of the people associated with it have been changed.

development, and know generally how the organization works. It's also a plus if those you select have sound writing and organizational abilities and can communicate well with other people.

The second guideline is this: there's a valid temptation in all organizations to first make the process team assignments part-time. That approach is easy to understand. I have been in a lot of IT shops, and just about all of them are as busy as they've ever been. They would like to avoid staff fluctuations as much as possible. So there's always an effort up front to see if the work can be handled by existing resources.

Many times, membership on the process team can be a part-time job. That's the smart path to take. It can work well that way. But before you make the assignments part-time, make a sincere effort to make sure the job is part-time. Naturally, you'll need to use your judgment here. If you plan to begin with a very targeted and limited process program, you may be able to take it on as a part-time project. If your goals or needs are more ambitious, then recognize that the team will probably need a full-time focus for its tasks. Without that focus, the team and its efforts could easily evaporate in deference to other duties.

Team Roles

Here's a calculation you may run across in mature configuration-management shops: you need 1 system administrator for every 100 or so programmers. There's a similar yardstick for web-centric test teams: for a normal test cycle, 1 tester for every 25 screens. I don't know how useful those formulas prove to be, but I do know that we don't have any guides like that yet for process initiatives. That begs the question, what size team do we need? And, what *kind* of team do we assemble?

Those aren't questions anyone can answer straightaway. There are too many variables attached to a specific answer. I can offer some advice. Your process initiative should be treated, by and large, like almost any technology project. And so you'll need to account for some well-defined roles. Let's take a look—a very brief look—at what these key ones might be.

Job roles and titles vary greatly across organizations. Even seemingly standardized job types like "Java developer" or "software designer" don't mean much outside a specific work environment. This is especially true with process improvement jobs. Job titles, and the subsequent job descriptions that go along with them, haven't really become standardized. At the same time, when you begin to staff your process team, you'll need to assemble something of a hierarchy of talent to ensure that the right blend of skills and the right capabilities are in place to carry your program forward. To help with this, here is a basic list of some traditional process-team job roles, together with a general description of typical skills and experience.

The following descriptions are presented to give you a feeling for the kinds of jobs that can be accounted for on a process team. If you find them helpful, use them. But don't think that you are required to explicitly assign these roles to your process team. Bottom line, look for people with good communication skills (especially writing skills), good analytical skills, and the ability to work well in a team.

Process architect

This is a senior position on the process team, a technical one that requires both strategic and tactical abilities. Process architects are the people who will design the form and function of your process program. If you are creating a program to fit a certain model—like ISO 9001, CMMI, or Six Sigma—the architects will need to be well versed in the model's components, requirements, and implementation methods. Process architects also need to work with a solid understanding of the current business environment, as the program they design will need to exist within that environment. Additionally, process architects should posses the attributes of any good strategist: solid communication skills, sound analysis and synthesis abilities, good management and planning skills, and the ability to work with varied levels of management.

Process engineer

The job of a process engineer is to take the program design and turn it into a series of discrete yet integrated program components. This requires an understanding of the architecture at large; an understanding of the goals, objectives, and scope of the process initiative; and the ability to assign a series of clearly identified assets and artifacts needed to realize the goals and objectives. Process engineers need the ability to work well with focused teams, interface with a variety of stakeholders, and manage activities across independent work groups.

Process analyst

A process analyst usually deals with delineating the detailed steps required to effectively execute processes and procedures, and then turning these into effective process tools via descriptions, flowcharts, forms, templates, etc. Operating under the direction of a process engineer, the analyst will manage a set of process activities, work with organizational stakeholders and users to elicit needs, formulate the data into initial artifacts, and then review these artifacts for refinement and (ultimately) approval and acceptance.

Technical writer

Many people make the mistake of thinking that creating a process program is a documentation job. As we'll see later on in this chapter, that's something of a narrow view. However, the job of documentation is an important one. The success of your process program will rely heavily on the quality of the documentation you create to realize it and support it. Appointing technical writers to your team can help you manage the documentation you'll need to publish. This can take three general forms: paper-based manuals, templates, and forms; electronic reference material; and training, overview, and presentation materials.

A good technical writer will show developed written communications skills, good investigative abilities combined with interpersonal skills, a sense of layout and design, and proficiency in a set of publishing, presentation, and support tools.

Defining an Improvement Charter

When organizations set up a process improvement initiative, I like to see management officially define the project through some type of charter. A charter is a document that formally establishes the mission, makeup, and purpose of the project. In my opinion, all focused group activities in a company should be guided by a charter. Charters can be helpful for several reasons, which I outline next:

It is an agreement between you and management

A charter will help you understand the mission of the process initiative from management's perspective. In many ways, it can be seen as a contract between you and management. And because the charter is in writing, it is an agreement that can be commonly understood by both you and management. This is a real advantage. If you begin an initiative with only a verbal understanding of the task, there is a strong chance that as the mission progresses over time, understandings can drift apart. If the charter is there for both parties to reference and fall back on, you and management will likely be able to stay in sync as the project evolves.

It defines the boundaries and goals of your mission

One of the main benefits of a charter is that it can define the purpose of the initiative, establishing the boundaries of your activities and the goals you are expected to achieve. In other words, the charter can help you define what success will mean for your initiative, and what resources will be committed to help you achieve that success. This is especially helpful in a process initiative because progress early on can be somewhat intangible, hard to pin down. Without the benefit of a fixed focus, process efforts can be prone to shift in both scope and purpose. A charter will help you fix that focus to everyone's mutual agreement.

It serves as an official authorization mechanism

The best value of the charter may be in its power to serve as official authorization for your process initiative. You may be asked to create the charter for your project, but management will ultimately need to endorse it. And this endorsement makes the project "real" to everybody in your shop. In the absence of this endorsement, the project may float about the company as an idea, or it may roll through the organization as a potential, but it probably won't have the traction it needs to really get rolling. The charter can give it the traction it needs.

For your process program, you might find that a charter is good way to demonstrably fix what it is you want your initiative to achieve, and how you plan to achieve it. So consider working with management to define a charter for your process program initiative.

Charters should not be complex documents. In fact, it's better if they are brief and to the point. You can format your improvement charter using some points usually found in typical business charters. Consider defining the following for your project:

Purpose

The purpose statement should reflect the general strategic intention of your program. The scope statement (see next) can be more tactical. A purpose statement might read something like, "The purpose of the QED Process Initiative is to improve the organization's ability to meet regulatory deadlines, promote consistency across planning and release cycles, and provide mechanisms for measuring project performance across IT working units." That kind of statement is focused on the benefits the program is designed to deliver, and by tying these benefits to larger business objectives, the program becomes integrated into core business activities of the organization.

Scope

The purpose and scope statements you create for the charter may be closely related. In the scope statement, you might define the scope of the improvement program using a tactical description of the reach of the project. An example could be, "The scope of the QED Process Initiative is to design and implement procedures, tools, and controls to manage requirements definition, change control, and project planning activities in the IT Services organization." That's a pretty targeted statement, yet it allows for specific refinement at a later date. At this point in your program development, you'll probably have a similar idea of where you'd like to focus your program. Shape the statement around this expectation; you can refine it with greater detail at a later date if you choose as the project evolves.

Sponsor

Identifying the sponsor for the improvement charter is an important institutionalization step. So, consider documenting two sponsor traits here. First, attach an organizational position to the sponsor role. This might be something like Chief Process Officer, V.P. Quality Delivery, or Director of New Initiatives. Whatever is, the role links sponsorship to the organizational chain; it gives it a place within the structure of the organization. Second, and you might see this as being optional, you can identify the name of the executive holding the sponsorship position. This puts a known face to the role, and even though sponsors may change over time, it helps to give a sense of personality and ownership to your program.

Resources

You might also call this section "organization." Here in the charter, you describe how this initiative will be organized. Without going into great detail, you might describe the resources planned to support the program: team size, general team roles, and any special facilities needed. Describing the resources helps solidify executive commitment to the program. Without a firm commitment to allocating resources to the improvement program, the program might never materialize past the charter stage.

Effective dates

The improvement charter should not be thought of as a one-time, fixed document. The work it reflects is too evolutionary. So assign the charter an effective operational range: a start date and an expiration date. The expiration date will establish a benchmark for reviewing the charter and refining it as necessary.

A charter that contains the kinds of details described above will help solidify the initiative in the minds of management, you, and other members in the organization.

As mentioned earlier, you will probably be the one asked to come up with the charter if you think it's important for your project and your team. If so here are some general steps you can follow to instantiate it in your IT shop:

1. Work with your sponsor and executive management to define the details of the initiative (see the charter points described earlier).

2. Create a draft of the charter.

3. Review this draft with management and revise as necessary.

4. Seek official management approval of the charter.

5. Make the charter available to the organization at large.

6. Use the charter as a benchmark for ongoing project work.

At this point in establishing your process program, I've discussed key activities that can work to set the initiative on its way. I've discussed assessing the organization's current quality position and business objectives, as well as targeting potential improvement opportunities. Within this scope, I've discussed obtaining executive sponsorship for the program and, by implication, receiving corporate buy-in. I've looked at some typical process team roles you may want to accommodate as you formulate a process team. And now I've looked at a way to formally shape the program through an authorized organizational charter.

The improvement charter will help set in place the infrastructure you'll need to make your program a going concern in the enterprise. Just as important, it positions you to begin to take real improvement steps: sending your people out into the organization to assess targeted process capabilities.

Choose Your Model (or Not)

"Choose your model" means now is a good time to select one of the existing process models (preferably one of the proven ones) upon which you can structure the process program you're about to build. For most people in the field of technology development, this means ISO 9001:2000, Capability Maturity Model Integration, or Six Sigma. In coming activities, you and your team members are going to begin looking at the organization from a process design perspective: looking at what process areas to address, deciding what process components to build, and choosing how to build them. If you know a model that will work for you, you'll want to begin tailoring your decisions to that framework so that it and what you build will fit well together. That's the gist of "Choose your model."

Of course, you don't have to choose a process model at all. You don't need to look at ISO, CMMI, Six Sigma, or any of the others in order to create a good process program for your shop. You might decide to create a purely customized process approach, one you build based solely on internal parameters. If that's the course you'd like to go with, go right ahead.

I don't mean that facetiously. I am a firm believer in the three programs I present in this book, and I am a vocal advocate of their use in technology shops of all kinds. But I'm also the first to say that a big part of process success comes from the program's ability to serve your organization well. And if a purely custom approach gets you there, then you've met the spirit of process improvement embedded in ISO, CMMI, and Six Sigma.

Most people working in process improvement today, usually working on highly visible process initiatives, are likely to draw on one of these three established models. But there's a Fire-Ready-Aim issue here I'd like to mention here, and it comes not with how the choice is made, but rather when it's made.

Choosing a process model can be the step where many people *begin* their process programs. I attend a lot of trade shows, seminars, and symposiums on quality management and process improvement, and invariably I'm approached by someone who says, "We know we need a program, but we're torn between Six Sigma and ISO 9000. Which one do you think is right for us?" Or, "Our systems managers say CMMI is the right way to go, but we've got a couple people in-house now who have already used ISO at previous jobs. So doesn't it make sense to go with a known quantity?" I also hear this, "The CIO says we have to be CMMI Level 2 by next year or no performance bonuses."

It's ironic, but in the world of technology development—a discipline that requires deep planning, strategic positioning, and the capability for abstract thought—I hear lots of statements like those. The topics of process improvement and quality management are cool these days, and discussions of the three leading programs buzz around conventions and process gatherings. People have *heard* of ISO 9001:2000; they *know about* Capability Maturity Model Integration, and they've *read* all the success stories concerning Six Sigma. But somewhere along the line, the popular concepts of these programs have blurred. They've begun to merge together. They've fallen into a common category labeled "process solutions," as if the answer lay in simply deciding which one to pick off the shelf.*

The original title for this book was *ISO 9001, CMMI, Six Sigma: Which Is Right for You?*. I wanted to write a general guide that would help clear up this homogenous misconception,

---

* ISO 9001, CMMI, and Six Sigma are the dominant process improvement methodologies for use in technology development organizations, but there are other process models for use in different realms of IT and technology management. These other frameworks include programs like ITIL, OPM3, and CobiT.

to help people understand what these approaches have in common, how they are different, and even how they might best be used together. I wanted to show people how they could use these programs—together or in parts—to further their process goals.

The point is that, in the realm of process improvement, it's important to move into operational management and control with a comfortable degree of management and control working on your side. As you begin a process initiative, you may not have all the detail in mind, but you're likely to have the big picture in place. The problem with moving before you're ready, with selecting a solution to an unknown equation, is that you're likely to end up bending the equation to fit the answer. But in process improvement (in fact, in any model-based work), the solution does not lie in the model; it lies in the way you use the model to link process to business. So it's best to understand the basic shape of the business problem before you move on to the solution.

> ### NOTE
> Part 2 of this book presents general summaries of the ISO 9001:2000 Standard, Capability Maturity Model Integration, and the methodologies behind Six Sigma. These descriptions are designed to give you a high-level understanding of each of these programs, or at least an understanding that's adequate for evaluating their structures, strengths, requirements, and potentials for use. (It's also a way to give you a core of knowledge without having to buy three more books.) However, this book is not designed to replace publications dedicated to in-depth explanations of ISO 9001, CMMI, or Six Sigma.

When you set about choosing a model, treat the effort not so much as a hunt for the Grail; treat it more like a piece of investigative journalism. Be prepared to devote time to fact finding—read, talk to people, get in touch with experts—then assimilate your understanding in light of your business objectives. Finally, you can formulate an answer that, even if not perfect, will probably take you in the direction you want to go.

Let's briefly look at three tips to keep in mind when you set about choosing a model that may work for you.

Study Alternatives

You don't have to be a process model expert to shape a successful process program. But it pays to know what's out there, what programs have worked for other people, and what the industry as a whole has found to be successful. The main alternatives focused on in this book are ISO 9001:2000, CMMI, and Six Sigma. For the business of technology development, these three are the most widely used models. And each has established the kinds of track records to show they can work very well. Given that, there are lots of other models available. So take time at this point in your process initiative to look at what's out there.

You can find lots of books that describe the ISO 9001:2000 Standard. You can purchase the Standard itself from the ISO web site. The same holds true for CMMI. There's a good selection of books and articles on implementing this framework. As an added plus, the official CMMI specification is available for free download at the web site for the Software Engineering Institute, the governing body for CMMI. You'll find that there's a wealth of free CMMI information at this site: white papers, proposals, studies, techniques, and so on.

There may be more information available on Six Sigma than on the other models. That may be because Six Sigma is not managed by a central governing body. Anyone can write about it and promote it. Because of Six Sigma's "openness," you need to be a little careful about what sources of data you plug into. Two that are naturally very reliable are the web sites for Motorola and General Electric. Motorola and GE are the two companies most responsible for developing the concepts embedded in Six Sigma. They offer a lot of information about this model.

Another good way to get a feel for what's available in these alternatives is to talk to people in your industry. I have found in my own experience that the professionals who work in process improvement are usually very willing to take time to discuss what they've learned, offer advice, and provide general counsel. The good ones rarely seek to promote a specific agenda. The same holds true for people who work under these process programs. In fact, they may be the best source of ideas, advice, and information.

Focus on Function, not Form

Most process models have a form—a paradigm—built into them. ISO 9001 organizes its requirements into a series of distinct sections: Quality Manual, Management Responsibility, Product and Service Provisioning, and so on. CMMI is a collection of 25 Process Areas and, in its staged representation, organizes them along five Maturity Levels. Six Sigma employs a methodology called DMAIC: Define, Measure, Analyze, Improve, Control. All of these implementation modes are valid; they provide a handy framework for you to hang your efforts on. But when you're initially looking at these programs, don't concentrate too much on these formats. It's convenient to be able to say, "We're going to be operating at Level 2 in nine months," but it's more crucial to know exactly what that means.

When evaluating potential models, look to function instead of form. The strength of each of these models is that they are built upon a series of sound practices that have proven themselves over time in the technology industry (and in other industries as well). These practices represent the core activities you'll be shaping for your process team and for the organization's working groups. And it's through understanding these practices that you'll be able to select the model that is most appropriate for their needs.

You'll find that ISO 9001, CMMI, and Six Sigma are distinctly different in form, but they share a lot of similarities in function. For example, all three support configuration management. They all define requirements for measuring performance. All three call for detailed planning. But they tackle these topics in different ways, from different perspectives, giving different weights to each. Look to the focus of these programs, how they define and emphasize their functionalities, and see which provides the closest match to your view of process improvement and the needs of your organization. By focusing on function instead of form, you'll be able to identify the key components of these models that translate into effective process improvement actions.

Borrow at Will

When you choose a model, when you find one that seems to fit your approach to process improvement, you shouldn't feel that you have to discard other choices. You're not wed to a single option. It's actually a good idea—sound and valid—to select one model's framework and then fill it with practices that you've found from other sources. So feel free to borrow at will. Bruce A. Brown, the CIO at T-Mobile, reminded me of this not too long ago when we were talking about the general wealth of knowledge floating around in the process improvement industry. Bruce communicates to his people the value in interpreting, selecting, and internalizing those portions of CMMI, ISO, and Six Sigma that line up with the needs of his different divisions. The key, he tells them, is to take those selected parts and then shape them to fit the organization. That's good advice.

Another executive I know, Linda Butler, Director of Telco IT Delivery for BellSouth Telecommunications, echoes that thought:

> The advantage of process models like ISO 9001 and CMMI is that they can be referenced as a set of proven best practices, tried and true over time. They give you the benefit of what other people have learned. But it's important to take them simply as tools. They are there to help you build your program. They are not the program itself. The smart approach is to look at one, determine how it can help you, and then borrow from it those elements you find useful.

This idea of free association among models is actually endorsed by most of the sponsors of these models. I have personally worked with people heavily involved in the evolutions of CMMI and Six Sigma, and all of them have said to me that the idea behind these process improvement programs is process improvement, not program allegiance. So borrow away in the best way it helps you.

> **NOTE**
>
> The idea of setting yourself free to borrow assumes one freedom we should briefly address: the freedom to shape your process program the way you want to. In my consulting practice, that's the way I like to promote. That way almost always ties more closely to the business objectives of your organization than the formal, regimented ways. But in the real world of business, we don't always have that freedom.
>
> Often you'll find that the industry you're in dictates which model you need to implement, and even how you ought to implement it. Or you may have an important client who will do business with you only if you follow a certain methodology. Or maybe your management has already made the model decision for you.
>
> When you find yourself in this situation (and it's all to common), you probably will have to select one model, implement it in full scope, and tailor it as you go so it fits well in the organization.

CROSS-FUNCTIONAL MATURITY

"In organizational development you'll typically see a hierarchy of quality. Early on, processes will be developed within working groups, designed to address specific jobs with a specific focus. At this stage the groups are learning how to do their jobs. Later on, as the organization becomes more mature, you'll find that working groups develop processes to help coordinate how different teams work together. By this time the teams know how to perform their individual jobs. Now they are focusing on mid-level integration and coordination. Finally, with high maturity, the whole organization is able to operate against a common set of standards, one that steers the full enterprise. At this point the enterprise is operating cross-functionally."

—Bruce A. Brown, Senior Vice President and CIO, T-Mobile USA

Developing Process Program Components

This step represents the bulk of the work you'll undertake in creating your quality program. As its name suggests, this cycle is an iterative process. But it begins with a period of extended observation, questioning, and knowledge acquisition. The objective here is to learn the business. You and your team will be working to build standards, processes, and procedures to improve the business, but this can't be undertaken in a vacuum. You need to first learn how activities are being conducted, delve as deeply as you can into the rationale behind the activities, and then evaluate them for improvement opportunities.

Engage Relevant Work Groups

I find that a SWOT analysis is usually helpful here. SWOT stands for Strengths, Weaknesses, Opportunities, and Threats. Just about any business strategy, situation, or activity can benefit from a SWOT analysis. In this case, you and your team look for what strengths lay in the current processes—that is, what is working well in terms of management, accountability, and control. Next you identify what appears to be working less well: what might be only partially fulfilling its purpose, what might be lacking structure, what might be missing altogether. Then you can analyze these strengths and weaknesses. You look and determine where you see potential opportunities for improvement. This may become clear with weaknesses, but bear in mind that you can make improvements to strengths, too. It's helpful to list these opportunities, and even prioritize them a number of ways: perhaps by difficulty or effort, perhaps by business criticality, maybe by organizational impact.

Once you have identified opportunities for improvement, you can then assign threats. You can think of a threat as a potential cost to the organization should the opportunity not be addressed. There can be all kinds of threats: internal and external. Some inside threats might be impaired communications, risk of data loss, misalignment, increased costs, or extended correction time. External threats might be regulatory fines, potential loss of market share, or reduced customer satisfaction.

By thoroughly analyzing targeted business practices with SWOT, your team and the partner groups will acquire a common understanding of the current structure of the organization, which is a good foundation for moving on to improvements. You can now work with the groups to identify areas to work on. You'll probably have plenty to choose from, so you'll need to facilitate this step carefully. It's generally a good idea to select processes that will strengthen the groups that helped you uncover them. At the same time, you need to weigh the overall needs of the organization. Once you've selected processes to work on, your team can begin design activities.

This is not yet the time to formulate the entire solution. Here is where the cycle begins to turn. In your first design effort, keep the solution at a somewhat high level. Then take this back to your partner groups for review, feedback, and maybe even a tryout. Then take their input and drive the solution to a deeper level. Depending on the business activity and the process you are defining, this cycle might go through several iterations. The key, however, is to develop it in manageable steps, ensuring that you, your team, and the partner groups remain in sync, with a common understanding, each step of the way. The resulting solution should be one that you are comfortable with, one that addresses a specific business need, and one that can exist in harmony with other related business activities.

Follow the observation-design cycle until you have created acceptable trial processes for each of the targeted business activities.

Build from the Inside

A "collaborative design" approach works best for creating a process program within an organization. This approach is particularly effective when an organization is already following loose or undocumented processes, or has a fixed business path already set into place. The collaborative nature of the approach requires two teams working in tandem along a six-step axis of activity.

The first team is made up of selected organizational stakeholders. These stakeholders are those people within the organization that possess depth of knowledge concerning business activities, contracts, clients, applications, and other elements that may be impacted by process management. Often these people are called SMEs: subject matter experts. They should be selected as design contacts based on three criteria:

- They need to have the business knowledge required to direct and shape processes designed along effective and proper lines.

- They need to be available to the process team during the design process. If they can only dedicate a limited amount of attention to the effort, or they are susceptible to being pulled away at any given time, it might be best to select someone else.

- Finally, they need to have some appreciation of process. Ideally, they will embrace the idea of process and want to work to establish it within their teams.

Carefully consider the stakeholders you select to participate in the design process. They will have considerable impact on the success of this effort.

The second team is made up of process design consultants: usually the members of your process team. This team consists of process professionals who have deep familiarity with the structure, requirements, and recommendations embedded in your process model. These members will work with the appointed stakeholders to design, document, and validate the process and artifact components of the new program. Together, these people will work to design the program components using a collaborative approach.

The six-step collaborative design approach includes the following:

Identification

The process team consultants (PTCs) work with the subject matter experts (SMEs) to identify the inventory of elements needed to be pulled, formalized, created, or adapted in order to realize a fully compliant business process program. This is accomplished through formal and informal discussions and work sessions. The baseline for these discussions is the focus of your process program. Using this framework (perhaps based on ISO 9001, CMMI, or Six Sigma), you begin to target those processes, procedures, and artifacts that the complete program will need.

Elicitation

PTCs then work with the SMEs to design and develop the templates, processes, forms, and artifacts required to support the program. The emphasis at this step is on tracing the current flow of business activity, examining and reusing existing business support materials, and reviewing descriptions of activities already in place in the organization. These elicitation activities seek first to use what exists, incorporating things into the program that give it familiarity. Once the value of existing materials has been identified, the two teams can work to identify missing elements that will need to be jointly created to fill the model.

Documentation

The PTCs and SMEs will work together to document the processes and artifacts that represent the process program, establish a central repository to house and control these elements, and then prepare the components for organizational review. This activity probably represents the bulk of observation-design work. It is very much a shared activity, and very much iterative in nature. It is typically carried out as a series of short work cycles: gathering and understanding business flows, mapping to framework needs, analyzing procedures, documenting, reviewing, and revising for wider release. With several of these teams working at once, you'll soon begin to amass a set of process documentation that will begin to fit together into a cohesive, comprehensive program.

As this material begins to appear and take more and more solid form, you'll want to begin presenting it for broad organizational review and potential refinement.

Review/revision

To the extent deemed appropriate by the organization, the key stakeholders review and analyze the documented program components and share them with other relevant stakeholders. This step serves as a socializing verification and validation step. Here, components can be adjusted and tailored to reflect specific needs of the various project teams, and to accommodate differing degrees of focus among similar teams.

(Trial)

This is an optional step the organization may elect to use for certain program components. This is actually an activity that mini-pilots the program components on a trial application or for a trial project. This step is an extension of the review/revision step and serves as proof-of-concept and real-world test opportunities for the program components and for use by project teams. This trial method can be valuable if you're dealing with complex processes or if you're building components that need to be verified by multiple working groups.

Publication

In this final step, the program is judged ready for adoption by the organization and is instituted as a managed tool set. A central repository is established, and the program components are published into the repository.

Views from the Top

TOOLS FOR FORWARD MOTION

"The advantage of process models like Six Sigma, ISO 9001, and CMMI is that they can be referenced as a set of proven best practices, tried and true over time. They give you the benefit of what other people have learned. But it's important to understand that these models are simply tools; they are frameworks that help you build your program. They are not the program itself. And so you should never look at any of these models as gospel, as a set of mandates you have to implement. The right approach is to pick one, determine how it can help you, and then borrow from it those elements you find useful.

"Your management will appreciate such a process program because it can be shown to help further business objectives. Your people will appreciate the program because, when it's designed right, it makes their jobs more productive."

—Linda Butler, Director IT, Corporate Services CIO, BellSouth Telecommunications

---

Training

In the phase shown previously, you and your team took the time to create an initial version of your process program. Because you did this through tight interaction with the partner groups, you should all share something of a common understanding of the program. This understanding is good, but it's probably not enough to ensure smooth, wide use of the program. In the next phase, you are actually going to run the program through a pilot, and pretty soon, you're going to roll out the program to the whole enterprise. And so it's very important that you think about providing some degree of training and education in the use of the program. If you have been working on a finely targeted program with a small group of support players, then your training needs may be somewhat contained. If you have been working on a large program, with many contributing groups, you will undoubtedly face a larger training challenge.

But be careful not to skimp on training. The lack of training may well be one of the chief reasons process programs fail. It's not that people don't want to follow the program; it may be that they don't know how to follow the program. To figure it out on their own may seem like too much extra work. That's why adequate training is so important. It gives people the background and the tools they need to use a new program. And it gives them a chance to become familiar with the program and with how it will impact, and hopefully improve, their jobs.

The success of your process program will rest largely on the relationship your people have with it along three lines:

- Understanding
- Accessibility
- Comfort

First of all, your people are going to have to understand the program. They are going to need to know its contents, appreciate what parts apply to them, and understand how to use these parts. Next they are going to need direct and unfettered accessibility to the program. This aids understanding. Especially in the early stages, people will be moving through your process components a lot, finding their way through tools and forms, learning where things are, and establishing paths of common access. For this reason, accessibility needs to be focused on ease and speed. If you put up barriers to getting to the program, you'll quickly find that people stop trying to get there. The final trait is comfort. There's a parallel relationship between the success of your process program and the degree of comfort your people have with it. The more comfortable they are with the program, the more they will take advantage of it.

Training will help ensure that all these elements come together for your people.

You may consider training in two phases. Right now you may be focused solely on the pilot. The extent of training at this point may not need to be overly intensive. The scope of the pilot and the number of people involved may only require a less formal and more personal approach to training. More in-depth training will be required later.

But whatever your approach, keep a strong focus on training. Begin to develop materials early on. Plan for the delivery of training and training needs like facility space, hand-out materials, and support materials.

Training will usually take one of three general forms in a technology organization. Let's briefly take a look at these three now.

Formal Training and Instruction

Formal training using takes the form of classroom training or some type of computer-based training. When carefully designed and competently delivered, it proves to be a highly productive way to disseminate knowledge.

Just about any process program will benefit from the support of formal training. Keep a few things in mind when you plan for formal training:

- Provide for general, high-level, orientation-type classes as well as detailed, nuts-and-bolts classes.

- Target the audiences for the classes and plan course material based on that. Not everyone will need to go through full program training. Understand who will be working in what areas and plan training to accommodate the needs of these different groups.

- Make sure that training sessions are scheduled well in advance to coordinate with people's schedules and that times are varied and flexible to allow for maximum participation.

- Spend time developing good course materials. The better your materials, and the more you make them generally available to people, the more effective they will be.

TBWA

A great complement to formal training is TBWA, "training by walking around." That borrows from MBWA, "management by walking around." MBWA is based on the idea that you can learn the most about how your people work by walking around and watching them work. Sitting in your office, waiting for things to come to you, is a pretty poor substitute. It's the same with learning. For your process program, you may have developed some very good and comprehensive class materials. And you may have succeeded in delivering a very beneficial series of courses. Training by walking around can be a very effective follow-up to this. By walking around and observing, by sitting in during process activities, by being available to lend a helping hand, you can gauge quite well how much of the training has sunk it, where people are working well, and where they might need some extra help.

In programs I help design, I try to build in the capability for TBWA. I do this by assigning project quality analysts (PQAs) onto project teams.* The PQAs serve a general process-audit and compliance role, but they serve as regular coaches for project teams. By being assigned to a team, the PQA is generally on hand to provide advice and guidance about how parts of the program should be used.

TBWA is also a good way to determine what kinds of additional learning folks may need and what kinds of training may need to be added to the formal training program.

Program Rollout

The activities you have engaged in so far (and I have certainly condensed them here) have brought you to the point of having a quality management system in place, backed up by a supporting process program. You have entered into the project with executive support and have chartered a process team. You have focused your efforts along very distinct lines, and then you and your team have built a program with the active help of the people who will ultimately use it. Then you piloted the program and fine-tuned it based on the results of the pilot. Now you are ready to roll out the program into the day-to-day business of the organization.

Program rollout is not so much about sprinting out of the blocks as it is about preparing the organization to move with you. To do this, you need to make sure you have a sound implementation plan in place. The implementation plan is a roadmap you can use to integrate the process program into the company's way of doing business. Such a plan typically includes the following:

- A description of the scope and contents of the process program
- An identification of the impacted groups and managers the program will touch
- An identification of any additional training or coaching set into place to support the rollout
- A description of the support team (the process team) that will shepherd rollout activities
- A schedule for the rollout of program components across the groups
- A description of process support materials available to the groups
- A description of the milestones and target dates used to define a successful rollout

As early as a draft is available, the implementation plan should be reviewed by executive management, by the partner groups, and by any potentially impacted parties. The plan is a significant change agent within the organization and thus needs the blessing of all these groups.

---

* The role of project quality analyst is used in the three leading quality programs, though with varying emphasis and focus. You'll find this role described in Part Two of this book in Chapters 5, 6, and 7.

When you've developed the plan and it's been approved, it should be implemented with the same discipline you'd apply to any project within the organization. The program should be tracked according to its budget and schedule, its milestones and deliverables, and you should regularly monitor its progress.

Depending on the nature of your program and the scope of its reach, the rollout may last from a few to many weeks. The key here is to keep it under your guidance and control until you are sure it has been firmly cemented into place—that is, that it is being used how it should be used by the people who should use it, with only general mentoring and guidance by your team.

Here's a brief look at some considerations to help make program rollout a smooth process.

Views from the Top

LEADERSHIP LEADS

"Leadership is critical in implementing an improvement program. Organizational conduct always follows leadership activity. Despite what kind of program is set into place, if leadership does not visibly demonstrate its commitment to it, the organization will drift from the program."

—Linda Butler, Director IT, Corporate Services CIO, BellSouth Telecommunications

"Executive commitment—sponsorship—is vital to the success of a process initiative. But it must be appointed appropriately and thoughtfully. True leadership is required. The program sponsor must have the authority and the visibility to shepherd the program through. More than that, though, the sponsor must posses a sound understanding of the subject matter to be the 'voice' of the process initiative; he must live the commitment in the eyes of the organization. You have to be passionate about this subject; you can't fake it."

—Guy Bevente, AVP, Information Technology National Data, SBC

Identify Impacted Groups

You and your process team may be charged with creating the process program, with caring for it, with managing and maintaining it, but you're not really the owners. The owners are the groups impacted by the program, those who will adopt the program for their own use, who will rely on it to help them carry out their business activities. That's why it's important to identify these work groups as part of the rollout. By this point, you have worked closely with these groups, so there's no doubt now as to who they are. But it helps to document the relationship. It serves as an organizational link between the groups, your process team, and the process program.

Identify the Support Team

At this point in the evolution of the organizational process program, your role and the role of your team will begin to change. Up until now, you've been focusing on strategic activities. You've assembled the team, targeted improvement opportunities, and assessed the organization. With your team, you've developed a process program that fits with organizational business objectives. You'll continue with these strategic activities: process improvement is about their ongoing application. But now you'll need to begin focusing on more tactical activities. Your process team now moves from development into implementation. The team members are now going to need to work to help support the use of the program throughout the designated work groups.

It's important to identify your team members as taking on this support role. It serves as a show of executive commitment to the program's success. It also allies your team, in a public way, with the members of the work groups who'll be using the program. This support role is essential to your program's success. It might be the single most essential element.

Especially early on in program adoption, the work groups will rely heavily upon the support that your team provides. There will be a lot of hand-holding, a lot of very active participation from your team. And so it's important that the work groups know explicitly who they can call on for help, who will be available for guidance and assistance, and who will shepherd through the new activities they may be called on to perform.

Define Program Support Materials

The work groups that will be adopting the process program are naturally going to need access to it. As we saw earlier in this chapter, a process program can be made up of many elements: processes, procedures, templates, forms, checklists. Usually these will be managed from some form of repository. The work groups will need access to the material in this repository, but this will probably not be enough. In "Formal Training and Instruction," earlier in this chapter, I looked at the necessity of providing the work groups with the training they need in order to follow the program conscientiously. In much the same way, the groups will also need access to the kinds of support materials that will complement the training and provide an ongoing reference as work unfolds.

This typically includes items like guidelines, instructions, even sample artifacts. It can also include points of contact for coaches and mentors. And in sophisticated scenarios, it might include workflow management systems, hyperlinked manuals, or forms of e-learning and content management systems. The success of your program rollout will be greatly benefited by ensuring that this support material is identified and made available to the work groups.

Schedule the Rollout

You'll need a well-thought-out schedule to successfully implement the process program in the organization. The schedule will be used by you to manage the various implementation activities. It will be used by your process team as a way to guide delivery of their tasks and measure progress. And it will be used by the partner work groups to coordinate interactions while still managing daily business duties. Management may also use it as a way to monitor progress.

Keep two things in mind when developing the implementation schedule:

- First, create a schedule that is realistic, one that comfortably accommodates all the various activities you'll need to account for in order to introduce the various process components into the organization. Often people are tempted to push forward an aggressive schedule, with the idea that it's better to show fast action here after so much planning and preparation. But this approach is rarely effective. Instead, carefully consider the scope of your program, the type of groups that will be using it, and the resources of your process team to put a schedule in place that reflects the true organizational environment.

- Second, imbed a priority into the schedule. Focus early on implementing major program components, those elements that are critical to overall success or that support major business practices. Then you can allow later on for a focus on the smaller or tangential components of the program. If you imbed this kind of priority, you can be assured of implementing the parts of the program that will mean the most to the organization as a whole.

Establish Milestones and Target Dates

Plan the rollout of the process program as a series of distinct, measurable goals. If you create a schedule that accounts for the numerous and varied implementation activities, and you imbed into this schedule an implementation priority, you should have a structure that supports the identification of progress milestones, with target dates attached to them. These milestones—and how you identify them—should be geared to a single purpose: to chart the way for your teams to move through implementation activities. Defining these milestones is a way to introduce a logical order into the sequence of implementation activities.

It is also a way to segment activities into a series of mini-projects. Depending on the scope of your program, the overall implementation schedule may be large, and it may involve multiple teams, each with separate parts to play. Defining milestones—and linking them to specific deliverables—provides a way to break down tasks and responsibilities into manageable chunks. Your process team can then use this segmented schedule as a way to manage time, direct focus, and coordinate work. The work groups can use it as a way to plan when their resources will be needed, and what these resources will need to be. And, of course, you will use it as a way to manage overall project activity and report status to the process team, the work groups, and upper management.

Institutionalization

A final consideration to think through for your process program is institutionalization. Institutionalization is a word you'll encounter a lot in the field of process improvement.

The word implies a way of conduct that becomes firmly ingrained in the culture of the organization. Institutionalization is the hallmark of organizational commitment. It is the ultimate goal of any quality management program.

Naturally, institutionalization takes time. It is not an automatic process. And it can be a temptation, sometimes after a series of initial successes, to announce "mission accomplished." A quality program, however, needs the continued and ongoing focus of management. It should be seen as one of the foundations on which the company operates.

Institutionalization may be the hardest implementation step to accomplish, simply because it does take time and there's no checkered flag to let you know when you've gotten there. But once you've achieved this mark, your program will be integrated within the whole organization, able to function at peak efficiency.

It's your people who will accomplish the work of institutionalization. And in the next chapter, we'll look at some techniques and tips you can use to support your process program and to help it take hold in your organization. But the focus shouldn't veer too far from your people.

In fact, you might want to take a look at who you'll be turning the program over to once you have it designed, in place, and ready to use. More than likely, it will be one or more managers in the organization. The approach used to nurture the program once it's been deployed will have a large impact on how well and how soon the program becomes institutionalized.

Let's look at five general categories of the kinds of managers usually called on to institutionalize a process program.

The Blind Victor

This type of person represents the least effective way to institutionalize a process program. We've probably all seen examples of the Blind Victor through the course of our careers. These types are initiative-driven. They need a specific project with a specific shape to it in order to feel that they are being productive. They are called "blind" because they cannot see beyond the initiative. To them, the project is everything. They are tactical, go-do-it types. They are not as good at strategic thinking or long-term forecasting. And they are called "victors" because their myopia causes them to declare victory as soon as the final project deliverable materializes. Blind Victors often lack the ability to appreciate the depth of organizational change, are unable to appreciate the need to shore up an initiative with support, or simply lack the capability to appreciate the multifaceted aspects of change.

Process improvement programs have had to suffer through more than a few Blind Victors. These folks will devote their time and energies—and that of their staffs—to thinking through, creating, and shaping a process program. And what they end up with may in fact be very good. But that's when the Blind Victor declares victory. Everybody shakes one another's hand and then goes off looking for the next problem to solve. Very little thought or commitment is given to the issue of implementation, long-term support, or institutionalization.

As a result, the classic failure of process programs typically occurs: the program, probably collected together as a series of binders, is placed on a shelf, consigned to gathering dust. The work groups may sigh and roll their eyes, another of management's brilliant ideas unrealized. And work goes on as usual, the only difference being that now the idea of process improvement may very well have become something of a company joke.

Blind Victors can be effective at program creation, but don't count on them to follow through with implementation. Here are some tips:

- Work to provide the organization with implementation support.

- Account for active and continued management participation.

- Consider the appointment of dedicated implementers or process program owners.

The Thankful Patron

A rung up from the Blind Victor is the Thankful Patron. Often you'll these two working together (or at least working in sequence). The Blind Victor will slap the solution in place and then leave the Thankful Patron to make it materialize. The problem with Thankful Patrons is that they have not been involved in creating the process program. They may not even have that much of a handle on what the program's been designed to do. They may manage the group that's supposed to use it, but that's about as much as they know.

Thankful Patrons know they lack the knowledge to push the program through. But, already busy in their "real" jobs, they usually feel too pressured to take time to acquire the needed information. As a result, they rely on their working teams to adopt and use the program in an appropriate manner. And because they aren't equipped to link the program to their business operations, they tend to view the processes as supplementary activities, tasks that aren't—when it comes down to it—absolutely necessary to operations. The process program becomes a "nice to have," and Thankful Patrons are disinclined to force it on anyone. They don't want to rock the boat.

Thankful Patrons are grateful that anybody uses any part of the program at all. If they see even a bit of it in use, they consider that to be successful enough.

Process programs under the care of Thankful Patrons may be tinkered with, tried out, or fiddled with. But in the end, they are neither promoted, managed, or monitored. And when their elements begin to disappear from the environment, the common excuse cited is that the program must not have fit in well. If it had, the convenient thinking goes, it would have been successful.

Thankful Patrons may need education and training sessions to help them feel comfortable with the program their people will be using. Here are some tips:

- Consider working with them to develop a general implementation plan that will incorporate new activities with existing activities.

- Set concrete yet achievable implementation and adoption objectives.

The Gentle Shepherd

Now we begin to step into the realm of program commitment. The popular view of shepherds is that they take care of sheep. But they really don't take care of sheep. The sheep pretty much take care of themselves. They know when to eat, when to sleep, and so on. Shepherds herd sheep. They walk them to the fields, prod them back to the pens, and keep the wolves at bay.

In process program management, Gentle Shepherds take on pretty much the same role. Shepherding is not a fast-paced business. They work to slowly move their groups into process adoption, taking on a little at a time. Like Thankful Patrons, Gentle Shepherds usually don't like to rock the boat. They view their role as protecting their people, taking care of them. They are insulators.

At the same time, Gentle Shepherds are pretty willing to take on the new ways of the process program. They just want the integration to go as smoothly as possible, and because their emphasis is on smoothness, they usually move slowly. There are lots of people I know who promote the Gentle Shepherd as the most effective of all these implementation types. When it comes to learning and absorbing information, and to employing new job techniques, this approach of slow and steady can work very well. However, nice as that maybe from a social systems perspective, it might not work well for the organization. If we assume that the process program was designed and built to address specific business needs, then its adoption and full use might not be best left to personal preference. The slow way might work well for some people, but it might not be the best way for the business. Persistent problems might remain too persistent to long.

Gentle Shepherds will rarely abandon the process program or let it sit unattended. But they may not come with the natural inclination or gumption that can prove handy to bringing it into the business and making it a part of operations in a way that quickly realizes its designed benefits.

Here are some tips:

- Provide a strategic approach that promotes the role of the program with its importance.
- Support institutionalization with a schedule to guide implementation activities.
- Consider using process auditors from your process team to provide ongoing coaching and mentoring for the working groups.

The Personal Trainer

Personal Trainers can be a great process program asset. They are like a coach and a mentor rolled into one, with a few extra characteristics. They want to be well versed in process, they want to know the ins and outs of your process program, and they want to know the business activities that the working groups will engage in. All of that makes for a great asset, especially when you consider that Trainers typically work side by side with the work teams. They not only provide advice, support, and guidance, they can also help show the teams how to do things in the new way.

The trick to Personal Trainers is finding them. It's not always easy to hire them from the outside because chances are they will not know your process program and may not know the particulars about how the work teams do their jobs. And it's not always easy to find them on the inside either: the folks you already work with will either be strong in current business practices or strong in your processes, but not often both. Or not often inclined to both.

A viable option is to consciously take one or more members from your identified work teams and integrate them early on into your process team. That way, you take business knowledge and shape it with process knowledge. Those folks, when chosen well, will then make very good personal trainers. Of course, I'm implying here that you have the luxury of pulling someone off one team, training them for what might be an extended period in another discipline, and then putting them back. As a technique, it's very effective, but it may not be very practical for you or your organization.

Another consideration is one of authority. If you have a solid, strong manager looking over the work group, then you won't have much of a problem. But if not, you might find that the expertise and dynamics of a good Personal Trainer can begin to overshadow the influence of the manager. The people in the work groups may begin to look to the Trainers for business solutions and guidance over the manager. And there is the potential that this may cause perception problems—or even real problems—over time. If you are able to go the route of Personal Trainers, you'll probably have to take time to match as carefully as you can the Trainers to the managers, or find people who can fill both roles.

Developing Personal Trainers takes commitment, time, and money, and the focused allocation of resources to get the teams into shape process-wise.

Here are some tips:

- Plan to develop internal Personal Trainers early on in your program.
- Set aside resources (time and money) to develop your Trainers, ensuring that job duties are adequately accounted for and covered.
- Create job descriptions that detail how Trainers and managers can interface effectively to accomplish a common purpose.

The Drill Sergeant

Personal Trainers tend to have a personal association with the groups they work with in an organization. They may even work side by side with the people, showing them the way, rooting them on. Drill Sergeants are a different type. They are usually brought in—or appointed—when management notices the potential for significant resistance to process adoption or requires that adoption be condensed into a tight time frame.

Like the Trainers, the Drill Sergeants know process and the organization's process program, but they don't necessarily have to know the business practices, and there's probably no way they're going to pitch in and help. These guys are here to push the program through, to set the performance bar and then train the people to make that bar. They'll

SUCCESS SAILS ON COMMITMENT

"Business success in any form requires commitment, a belief in what you're doing, confidence that you know how to get there. Effective process management requires the same thing. Any talented group can create a sound process program. But without the commitment to seeing it through, the program will pay few dividends."

—William H. Wiltshire, CIO, The Ballston Group

"Commitment to quality is not a project or a one time event. It does not have start and end dates. It needs to be a way of doing business for an organization, and so it's an ongoing, evolving journey. As such, the quality attitude in an organization is just as important as the quality program, maybe more so. The cultural commitment to becoming a better, more efficient workplace is vital to the path of process improvement in an organization."

—Guy Bevente, AVP, Information Technology National Data, SBC

arrive on the scene with special blessings from management. There will be no question from anyone as to whether it's their way or the highway.

Drill Sergeants typically take on an implementation with a three-prong approach: supply, discipline, and motivation.

You can't train anyone without the right supplies, and so Sergeants are going to make sure that everything necessary to make the process program run smoothly is in place. That includes good documentation, forms, guidelines, preparatory training, and so on. If the team is short on supplies, you (as CO in this analogy) will have to make sure supplies are provisioned. If you can accommodate that, great. If not, you might consider postponing rollout until the supply chain is in place.

Next is discipline. Drill Sergeants are going to select a targeted group, and for a set period of time, they are going to work the process program through that business unit, looking over the shoulders of the working teams until the teams demonstrate that they have the right practices down pat. If things go smoothly, the Sergeants won't interfere. If there's fumbling or doubt or lack of effort, they'll be on top of it.

Finally there is motivation. Here, that's probably best seen as "incentive." Business often works well when performance is tied to a series of concrete objectives. Follow the program, and Drill Sergeants have the authority to send rewards your way. Ignore it, and they have the authority to remind you that, while you might not be right for this IT shop, there are no doubt plenty of opportunities for a person like you in any of the food service industries.

All of this makes the role of the Drill Sergeant somewhat prone to complexity. It is probably best to employ that role only when it is truly necessary, when a core factor of your business depends on successful program adoption or when process program underperformance might reflect so poorly on the company that its long-term value may fall into question.

You'll need to give Drill Sergeants lots of responsibility, but remember, with that comes authority. Be prepared to cede it. Here are some tips:

- Give them the time they need to shape up their troops. And make sure that line management is aware of this focus.

- Ensure that the Sergeants don't become too carried away with their charge.

- Feel free to make it clear that the Sergeants report up the chain, too, and so results are in the line in which company goals are expected.

The Assassin

The job of the Assassin is very clear: achieve commitment to the process program. By any means necessary. Failure is not an option. Compromise is for wimps. Sure, there are going to be casualties, but this is business, not recess, so get over it.

When the Assassins appear, their first move is going to be to confirm that the program really is in place: that the pieces are all there and it's ready to go. If not, you've brought them in too early, and that's no good for Assassins. They're not afraid of command and they're not afraid of carnage, but even Assassins appreciate that without a workable end-game, command and carnage—fun though they might be—don't get anyone anywhere by themselves.

When they're sure the program's there, the Assassins step in and set the performance bar, right at the level they want it to be. And they make sure this level is obvious to everyone, that there are no questions about it. Assassins leave no room for excuses. And when they're sure that that's understood, they start the clock ticking. From this moment, the business is going to conduct business following the business processes. Period.

And then the Assassins will leave you alone, for a while. But they're not really gone. They're coming back. Management has given them *carte blanche*, and pretty soon they'll be wheeling that carte down your hallway.

They begin performing process audits. Everywhere. Regularly. And when they find anything or anyone out of step, their idea of process improvement is very simple: you're out of step; you've got one chance to get back in step and stay in step.

Meanwhile, the Assassins are running help-wanted ads all over the place, for just about any job position touched by the process program. There's a common phrase in all these postings: "Must work well in a process-managed environment."

The Assassins were hired to bring order, and so they move through the branches of the process program and look at compliance, and then—methodically, with a portfolio full of resumes—they weed out the cowboys, the know-it-alls, the firemen, the martyrs, the loners, the prima donnas, and the artistes.

You know Sandra, that renegade designer who built the search engine that handles a million hits a minute? History. Key card blanked. And Eric, the programmer with the attitude? His lunch may be at his desk, but he's not. And your manager, Steven? You remember that innovative plan he was talking about yesterday? Forget about it.

The Assassins replace them all with fresh talent, talent that comes onboard ready to embrace process, ready to honor the company's program, ready to do things the company way.

Here's a tip: Do not—under any circumstance—get in an Assassin's way.

The Element of Change

The roles above cover a range of process management types that you'll typically find in an organization. Most of them can help you implement your process program. How you do it will depend on the fit between their style and your needs.

But remember that you should probably not leave the picture. You should remain an important part of the success equation. And so for this reason, it's important to appreciate an additional characteristic of your process program, and that is *change*.

You are changing how work groups work. You are giving them new references, new expectations. And as is probably true of many things, change can be uncomfortable. It can be difficult. That's why you'll need to monitor the progress of your program over time. As it moves closer and closer to the people who will ultimately be working through it, you should continue to consider the best way to introduce change into the organization.

Effective change management is an important ingredient to establishing any process program.

Helpful Change Agent Skills

Process improvement at its most fundamental is about organizational change. And the application and management of change, as a major consideration in the business world, is more essential than ever. Today, technologies and technological capabilities are evolving at such a rapid, pervasive rate that businesses, even those not labeled as technology companies, have to continually deal with the choices, challenges, and strategy shifts that constant change brings. The considerations that revolve around change management have been pressed to stay up with the speed of the change in business environments. Change management and change agency are now more than ever seen as strategic considerations in many companies. And since process improvement begins with change, the same considerations might well be recognized when you begin such an initiative.

As with all change, when you begin to introduce process into a group, you may face varying degrees of resistance, frustration, insecurity, doubt—a host of reactions. To help minimize these and make the way smoother for your program's acceptance and adoption, here are some tips to help you usher in change.

Professional Readiness

Effective change management begins with professional readiness. Whenever you introduce something new into an organization, it is, by default, unproven and so it is usually open to wide scrutiny. In the technology field, where the "latest and greatest" is all too often overhyped, this can be especially true. And so you should not move prematurely to introduce your new process program. It's important to make sure that it is professionally ready to go. That's not to say it has to be perfect from the outset (no one should expect it to be). But it does need to be in a solid state, ready to be used to the extent it was purposed for.

To begin, it's important to check that your program components are in place, that they are complete (even in an early form), and that they are well-organized. These components will likely be the first elements that the various groups experience about your program. So they need to show that they have been carefully considered, and from a presentation perspective, they should appear polished. Resist sending them out into the world if the components are incomplete, if they might appear to look thrown together, or if they contain errors or omissions (even slight ones) that might confuse users or give the impression they have yet to be finalized.

Look for the same level of readiness for your process support teams. At this stage, they will probably know the program components well enough, but they still need to be well versed in the plan to roll the program out into the organization. You can start here by making sure the rollout plan is in place and that you and the teams have thoroughly reviewed it. Then check that the individual team members each understand their different jobs, that they are ready to work with the various groups in a supportive way, and that they have the resources they need to carry out their jobs.

Finally, professional readiness extends to overall organizational readiness. It's important that this rollout go as smoothly as possible. To support this, double-check that the schedule and the implementation activities have been communicated to the right people and that they are indeed expecting the rollout as planned.

If you can demonstrate this level of readiness, your process program will communicate a valuable sense of professional preparedness, helping it to make a good first impression in the organization and giving it the weight it needs to take hold and make a lasting contribution.

Open Communications

At its most fundamental, effective change management is all about communications, communications that are as open and full. Ironic as it may seem, it's easy to talk about open communications; it's more difficult to practice it. But when it comes to change, nothing can replace good communications. It is essential that you and your management are able to communicate the purpose, reach, and scope of your process initiative with the organization. By the time the program is being rolled out, you'll want the various impacted groups in your shop to be cognizant of what changes are coming. There are several ways to help bring this about.

As your program is taking shape, you can arrange to host high-level orientations and use these to introduce the program to various working groups. You might also make arrangements to host smaller, less formal sessions, maybe even one-on-one, with some of your team members who are then able to move about the organization, educating folks as they go.

You might also publish information about the program through established corporate communication vehicles, like an intranet site, newsletter, or even break-room bulletin boards.

If you can create an open-door environment around your program—one that emphasizes access, attention, and management support—people will typically show a degree of deference to your efforts.

An Ear for Feedback

Change can sometimes be interpreted as negative even when it delivers positive outcomes in the workplace. This reversal of fortune usually occurs when change movement is one-sided—that is, when change is pushed into the organization one way with little regard for the groups being pushed on. That's why effective change agents actively seek out feedback when introducing change elements.

Perhaps even more important is the attitude that what you're introducing might not be in its final, best form. Having such an open ear to feedback is a valuable technique for successfully introducing change. When you introduce your process program, understand that people will naturally want to question it, comment on it, probably even adjust it. When the response to this is frustration or (worse) silence, channels of communication may quickly shut down. That can set up a hurdle that could be hard to get over, especially if it's not well mitigated.

So as you roll out your program, do it in a way that invites feedback. Listen to the people who will be using the program. Take comments from the field seriously. Acknowledge that the people on the front line, actively engaged in the daily business activities, may know quite a bit about how things might work best. Allow time to analyze and develop this feedback and incorporate what you practically can into the new program. This will help instill a sense of authorship and ownership for the program throughout the organization.

Active Participation

The process program you build for your organization will likely reach into multiple areas of the organization. And whether it's a large or small program, it will touch many people's jobs. These people will be required to use the program, to shape it over time, to ultimately shepherd its benefits into fruition. But this can't happen simply by turning the program over to its intended audience. Audience adoption, while a primary and essential ingredient for any successful program, takes time to develop, and one of the best ways for that adoption to percolate up is for you and your process teams to actively participate in the institutional use of the program from the time its introduced until that time comes when the targeted groups have come to own it completely (and then you should still be around as support to help these groups refine the program).

The active participation of the process group across program implementation serves to show that the organization is committed to the program, that the idea is not a one-off or a toss-off but is strategically backed by management, funded by management, and seen as an ongoing component of business operations.

This participation delivers two distinct benefits. First, it's a very effective way to socialize the program within the organization through the individuals that make up your team. That way, the program becomes, in a very real way, a people program, not a paper program. On top of that, it establishes an open avenue for feedback and improvement ideas; it builds a channel not only for supportive adoption but for refinement as well.

Coaching and Mentoring

Another important trait of effective change management is change support. Introducing well-designed, professional change into an organization is only one objective of a larger mission. Another one, just as important, is to provide the support that change needs in order for it to become the norm. In line with this, you might consider providing coaching and mentoring services for your process program. The various work groups that will initially be adopting your program will probably need to adjust (to some degree) their way of doing business. Business as usual may not be as usual anymore. There will be questions. People may need prompting and reminders. They'll probably welcome as much help as you can give them.

If you can show that you support these teams, chances are they'll adopt the new ways much more readily than if they had little or no support. Many organizations forget the importance of this. Once they put a program "out there" (as if "out there" were someplace else), they assume it's the group's responsibility to take it on. That might be technically true, but it's not very amenable to effective change.

A better course is to back up the rollout with the same kind of technical support you would employ when rolling out any other technology solution. For process programs, two ways to do this are with coaching and mentoring.

Coaching is usually positioned as a support oversight role. A good coach will need to be pretty much an expert on your process program, or at least expert in specialized areas. She should know the playbook and should be able to provide guidance on the program, how it works, and how to use it. Coaches usually serve something of an off-field role. They should be available when groups are getting ready to embark on process activities, helping them prepare for and plan these activities. They should help point the groups in the right direction and ensure that the groups feel comfortable with what they have to do and how they have to do it. The coaches should strive to be accessible, and when called on, they should provide ready and supportive assistance.

Mentoring is more of an on-field support role, not oversight as much as it is foresight. Coaches are available and ready to lend a hand, and all along they can be observing how the play is going. Mentors are typically actively engaged in the progress of the program. They are assigned to working groups so that the members of the groups can learn by following the lead of one already proficient in the tasks at hand. The fourfold role of the mentor is very similar to that of the coach, but in each activity, it is applied in a more direct way.

Your mentors will usually be selected from inside of the working groups. Their level of knowledge about the business and about the process program needs to be just as strong and just as thorough as that of the coaches, but the mentors will need to be positioned to take an active role in carrying out the jobs. In this light, they provide guidance to the use of the process program not simply by explaining the program but by moving through the activities of the program with the groups. Mentoring is coaching by showing, coaching by doing. Because of this, most organizations find that mentoring is a highly effective way of transferring knowledge. It provides hands-on experience for the junior parties, bolstering on-the-job training with senior-level knowledge and experience.

The mentors should not only educate by example but should also provide a constant and reliable sounding board for members of the working groups, ready to offer assistance and advice either in groups or one-on-one. And finally, as with the coaches, the mentors—and perhaps especially the mentors—should provide feedback to the working groups and the process program teams on the effectiveness of the program.

Combined together, coaching and mentoring help smooth the transition in an organization from one state to another. That makes it an activity that is supported and coordinated through inside involvement, in-depth knowledge, and recognized leadership.

Visible Executive Interest

Earlier in this chapter, I discussed the scope and importance of establishing executive sponsorship for your process program. Executive sponsorship provides the leadership, authority, resources, and visibility needed for the program's success. All of these are important, but in terms of effective change agency, visibility may be the key.

Change can sometimes feel like a lonely thing. When you're working for an organization doing your day-to-day job and a host of new objectives, expectations, and procedures seem to descend upon you, you can feel a bit isolated. You might start looking around for support. If that support is not there, you might decide just to stay with the familiar day-to-day stuff. So part of management's job is to understand this aspect of change and to make itself visible as active change agents.

This need for visibility applies to your process program, too. Throughout the course of its development—through its planning, design, and on to its rollout—you, as the program champion, and your executive sponsor should place yourselves squarely in the open, moving the program always into the light.

The success of your program, especially its acceptance during its introduction, will rely heavily on your visibility, moving with the program as it moves into the organization. Take this as an opportunity to spread your knowledge of process and its advantages into new domains. Use it to promote the ability of the program to enhance business objectives. Link it to future growth and development. If you have built the program to tie closely with the needs of the business and to reflect and complement the way your people work, the program should almost certainly be successful.

Patience Not Perfection

A central tenet of process management is that improvement should come gradually, over time, with acquired knowledge and experience.C That's a good approach to take with any type of change. Trying to do too much too soon may result in achieving little or nothing at all. Too much change at one time can tend to overwhelm people; in the midst of other duties they may not be able to properly absorb new information or new expectations. Effective change agents understand this, and so they put a particular emphasis on patience. It's not practical to assume that a new program, any new program, will enjoy seamless integration into an organization. And so it's better to begin slowly, to take on a change mission as series of discrete objectives. Small steps toward success will over time lead to full success. This is helpful to remember for your own process program.

Keep the long-term advantages of your program always in mind, but don't strive for perfection right out of the gate. Introduce new elements gradually, giving people the chance to absorb, practice, and grow comfortable with new ways. Measure progress in incremental steps. Your patience here sends two supportive signals. First, it tells the people that you're aware of the energy required to integrate change and that you're going to manage that as effectively as you can. You don't want to overburden anyone. Second, it shows that you'll be patient with gradual progress, that your expectations are realistic, and that management will be satisfied with progress, even if it's gradual as long as it's steady.

Change management should always be considered when introducing a process program into any organization. Awareness of the principle of change management will provide you and your teams with, at the very least, the kinds of considerations you should take into account when you wish to modify the business activities in a business environment. When it comes down to basic assumptions, you can safely bet that your process program is going to change how people work. Hopefully this change will be for the better: people's jobs will become more productive, more streamlined, maybe even easier. To get to that point, however, you should keep the human factor always in mind. You'll find, as with everything, that the best way to make change for people is to make change with people.

Summary

- Establishing a process program should begin a strategic activity in the organization, one that involves working through a series of managed considerations.

- Establish executive sponsorship: obtain formal commitment from executive management for the design and development of a process improvement program.

- Establish a process team: formulate a team to begin the work of structuring the process group and planning process program components.

- Program design cycle: observe how the organization conducts select business activities, help detail how activities can be enhanced, and then reflect those practices in documented processes.

- Train the organization: prepare the organization to begin effectively using the program and its components in an informed and capable manner.

- Roll out: carry the program out into the IT community at large and establish it as an organizational standard.

- Refine: periodically adjust the program and its components to reflect lessons learned.

- Institutionalize: encourage full use of the program across relevant IT groups so that it becomes ingrained in the culture over time.

CHAPTER FOUR

Sustaining Process Improvement

GIVEN SOME GOOD PEOPLE, THE RIGHT RESOURCES, AND TIME, YOU CAN PROBABLY BUILD A PRETTY good quality program. If you follow some of the recommendations and guidelines discussed in the last chapter, chances are you'll create a program built to add real value to your business, and one that fits well with your business to boot.

But in the field of process improvement, it's important to understand that building the program is just the beginning. When the program is complete, you've achieved a major milestone. And by all rights you should be proud. But the real work is not finished. It's only about to begin. If you've designed your process program the right way, then you've designed it to successfully improve your business. And as is true with most significant factors in the business world, the measure of that improvement—its degree of success—takes time. The term *continuous process improvement* holds the key. The trick to the success of your program will not come from merely *building* something good, it will come from *using* it: using it over time, refining it, making it better and better, and allowing it to become a permanent part of your organization's business approach.

The key to successful process improvement is sustaining process improvement.

Most quality programs get through their design and construction phases pretty well. Where they begin to falter is typically in the first six months of implementation. There are some general reasons why this is so.

Sometimes those first months of implementation are seen as anticlimactic. The building phase may have been full of enthusiasm and anticipation. A lot of creative energy was probably energetically spent. Then when it comes to rolling out the program—to broadly disseminating it—the daily rhythm of the business routine may take over, dulling the shine of the new initiative and perhaps weighting it down under long-standing day-to-day concerns.

Sometimes the program suffers because of a simple yet all-too-common oversight: the people in the organization were not properly prepped to use it. Training (as discussed in the last chapter) is a critical ingredient in establishing your process program. It's an equally important ingredient in sustaining the effectiveness of your program. Perhaps it's often overlooked because training can easily be perceived as an add-on or extra (supplemental) activity: something nice to have but maybe not essential. But when this is skipped, for whatever reason, you run the risk of alienating your people from the process. If the process appears dense or intense, cumbersome or confusing, irrelevant or irrational, people will not adopt it. They'll ignore it as best they can. They'll implement it in the lightest way possible. That being the situation, even the best of programs will evaporate over time.

Sometimes process programs fall short because the commitment to their success wanes. This is usually a management issue. During the design phase, management may not have truly realized—despite all the floating wisdom—that a process program is primarily a management program. Only in a secondary sense is it a worker tool. And so for it to be successful, management must back the program as an essential business practice.

But what often happens is that program adoption and use is viewed as a down-line responsibility, something that should rightly filter up from the organization, or that once implemented should naturally take hold across work teams. This laissez-faire approach is rarely successful. It communicates an air of indifference. In that kind of atmosphere, no process program can prosper, much less realize its benefits.

And then there are other common problems, all the result either of weak interpretation, misdirection, or speculative inaction. For example, once the program is in place, management might decide that the resources that brought it into the organization can now be directed elsewhere. Or if resistance is encountered (as it always will be to some extent), no official effort is made to mitigate it. And then, as tends to happen in immature organizations, once the heat gets turned up on a project or on a business initiative, the first thing that gets jettisoned over the side is the process program.

In this chapter, I'll discuss some tips and techniques for sustaining process improvement in your organization to avoid the kinds of situations described above. But when it comes to success, there are really no formulas for process program management. And as far as rules go, there are only two:

1. Use the program.
2. Follow rule #1.

But the following series of considerations should be helpful to those starting out on a process improvement initiative, and they are points that I have used successfully and have seen used successfully to help root a process program in place so that it stands the best chance of growing to its potential.

In brief, these 12 considerations are as follows:

1. Remember what you do (and do it well).
2. Weld business success to program success.
3. Participate in the life of your program.
4. Train your people.
5. Encourage compliance.
6. Seek feedback.
7. Provide performance incentives.
8. Measure, measure.
9. Celebrate success.
10. Publish progress.
11. Reassess periodically.
12. Appreciate the journey.

1. Remember What You Do

One of the first things I do when I'm asked to evaluate an organization's process position is to ask the group for its mission statement. Lots of times I get a blank stare. No one really knows what I'm trying to get at. Sometimes I get a suspicious stare. Those people do know what I'm trying to get at, and they know they haven't got it.

What I'm after when I ask for a mission statement is this group's official take on what it is they do, what they are about, what they're here to achieve. That's what you hope to see in a mission statement.* And I always look to see if this statement is prominently displayed around the organization.

---

* I know that mission statements can often become window dressing in an organization. They can even become curtains to hide what's behind the window. But I'm taking the more positive approach in my discussion here. I'm going to assume that an organization's mission statement is at least a close proximity to what the organization really thinks its job is, what its values are, and what goals it is built to address.

I recognize the possibility that these kinds of corporate communiqués may be little more than high-touch management mantras, but even so, even when that's all they really are, I do get one thing out of them: the sense that the members of the organization know who they are (or think they know, or at least want to know). And in cases where the mission statements are genuine, when they have been carefully thought out and committed to, I get a whole lot more.

When I am brought in for a process consulting engagement, I always recommend that we begin with a mission statement. If one already exists, we revisit it, even if only to confirm that it is solid. If one does not exist, I recommend that we put one—even a light one—officially into place. The reason is, I think, clear. Your process program, in order to be effective, in order to be sustained over the course of business life, needs to be intricately tied to what your business is all about. And this link needs to be continuously reinforced across your working groups. And the only way to forge this link is to begin by understanding the mission of the organization, by knowing what its purpose is and what contributions it is equipped to make to the larger business mission. Once this is understood, a process program can be forged that will help sustain this mission.

But for every IT shop that has a firm grasp on who it is, I bet there are 10 that have only the vaguest of ideas. It might be something like, "Serve the IT needs of the organization." Or "Deliver high value to customers." But as missions go, those don't go very far. For sustained process improvement, an organization must know what it does. And I don't think that this is a question of "Do what you do best." It's, "Do what you do the best you can." And that's what I want to see established in an IT shop: the understanding of what is required of the group and a commitment to doing it the best they can.

A good place to begin is to focus on the customer-product relationship.

Focus on the Customer-Product Relationship

Chapter 3 looked at techniques for establishing a process program in the organization. One of the first considerations we looked at was the importance of planning the shape of the program around the company's overall business objectives. That's important, maybe preeminently important, for a single reason. For any company in any business, the only real path leads to one certain outcome: providing customers with a product or service. If your customers find value in what you bring them, you can be successful. If they don't, success will be hard to find.

That's a basic business principle. But what's often forgotten is the process end of it. Or, rather, the process beginning.

Think of the fact that there's no such thing as a disorganized organization. There are poorly organized organizations, and there are well-organized organizations. And there are many in between. But all operate according to some guiding principle, even if it's only the uncertainty principle. And that shows itself in the production process, in the steps a group takes to move from idea to deliverable. And so process, like it or not—know it or not—

ultimately leads to the customer. By experiencing your product, they experience the processes you work by.

Because business will change, customers will change, and products must change, sustained process improvement means evolving process improvement.

The sharpened critical viewpoint, then, appreciates the link between customer satisfaction and process. And so you should periodically reexamine who your customers are. Reach out to them, talk to them. Try to get the feel of what they might be looking for from you.

In the IT world, there is often a wall set up between the shop and the customer. But go through that wall. The keys to how you should evolve your program are ready to be given to you by your customers. There's a real benefit to be gained here: synergy between your shop and your customer base. This is a proactive focus IT managers should be happy to take. It is not complacency that delivers sustained process performance. It's energy.

Knowing your customers, appreciating what they want, and working to ensure they get it may be the best expenditure of energy you can make to keep your process program on track and delivering the kinds of benefits you designed it to deliver.

Shape Your Process Program to the Voice of the Customer

You'll see later on that the term *voice of the customer* is big in Six Sigma. The members of ISO have introduced a similar concept into ISO 9001. This focus on the customer is not really a new thing, but it's refreshing that the idea has moved to center stage in the field of process improvement. All too often it's easy to forget about the customer in the routine of daily business. Many times the people who work in technology environments may even feel that the customer is pretty far removed from them. They might feel that what they do has a preordained customer tie, and they have little influence over what those ties might be. Or they may even feel that what they do won't even touch the customer, that it provides only some other tangential function.

But in reality, everything we do should be somehow traceable to satisfying the customer.

That's why it's so important for an IT shop to know who its customers are and what the customers hold to be valuable. If you can string this philosophy through your processes, you'll strengthen the link between your shop and the customer. Just as important, you'll provide an avenue to help your people appreciate their impact on the client. And when people know this—whether the impact be big or small—you'll find that their job direction becomes clearer. And when they can link what they do to what the customer wants, they can link what they do to business success. And when they have a process that they trust to take them both ways, you'll find that the people use the process more, take advantage of its full attributes, and work to improve it.

By knowing what you do, doing it the best way you can, and shaping it to meet the needs of your customer, you'll be able to shape the kind of process program that will deliver sustained benefits over time, one that can grow with your company as it grows.

2. Weld Business Success to Program Success

Jim Ditmore is Chief Technology Officer for Wachovia Banks, one of the nation's largest financial institutions. His offices in Charlotte, North Carolina, overlook a series of rooftops, all from fellow bank corporations. He has led strategic initiatives at a host of major companies and is one of the most experienced and knowledgeable process professionals I have ever worked with. Jim understands the discipline from the floor of implementation to the walls of strategic design. And one of the fundamentals he stresses when it comes to sustained process improvement is the importance of welding the performance of the business to the use of the program.

He tells one story about implementing a process program for one of the very first online banks. His process manager was having a hard time enforcing the program she had built. She had built a good program. It was not too heavy. It fit the culture well. The issue was simply one of motivation. There was no real active resistance, but the various groups within the bank that should have been adopting the program were slow to do so. Other priorities always seemed to take precedence. The line managers did not seem too concerned about this as long as the regular work was getting done in a reasonable amount of time. And no one was complaining too loudly.

Jim's architect—I'll call her Kate—was frustrated because she was in many ways accountable for the success of the program. But she felt that her powers as a lateral enforcer were not enough to make people notice. She wanted Jim to step in with a bigger stick.

But Jim took a different approach. I have since borrowed it from him, and it seems to work pretty well wherever I am able to employ it. Jim told Kate not to worry. She shouldn't feel frustrated at the slow pace of adoption. He would soon drive the demand to her.

Jim used his position as a C-level executive to reshape the organization's view of process and its role within the business. He met with the various representatives of IT management and instituted a new series of performance reports, reports that were based on measures of general IT performance. The reports would be assembled every week and presented to the CEO. The trends in the reports would be discussed with the CEO and with the board of directors when needed.

What Jim knew (because he had helped position it) was that Kate's process program directly addressed the performance of the organization along the exact lines that were being measured. From that point on, when IT management got together and the reports were distributed, here is what people began to see. Some of the groups were doing well. Their numbers looked good. Some other groups were not doing so well. Their numbers were not impressive. Everyone knew this data was going to the top of the company and that the top was paying attention to it. Jim made sure of that. And so what happened in a relatively short span of time were three things in pretty quick succession.

First, management became motivated to find out what they had to do to get off the Bad list and onto the Good list. Kate was able to assure them that she had some new procedures and practices that were designed to do just that. Management went to their people and told them to work with Kate to get this new stuff in place. To them it wasn't about process improvement at all; it was about the perception of performance. Jim had in fact driven demand to Kate.

Next, when the weaker groups began to appear stronger on the numbers reports, the stronger groups wanted a way to get back out front. And so they began to go to Kate to add some extra capabilities into their toolkits. Within a span of time, adoption was not the issue. A sense of competitive accomplishment had been introduced among the groups, and because of the measures, the group had a way to regularly look at who was taking the lead and who might be falling behind.

The last thing that happened in this stream was that executive management—the CEO and the board—began to appreciate in their own way the process program Jim and Kate were supporting. The simple fact that they were able to see in a single metrics report a picture of performance over time (and in this case it was a very positive performance trend) caused them to want more. They began to not only rely on the program and on the data it helped generate, but they began to query about new ways it could help the organization, new ways it could reveal opportunities for improvement and at the same time work to document success.

Jim's strategy here was very astute. He knew the benefits of linking business success to process success. If you can do that for your management as well as your work force, you'll find that they will back the program once they begin to see the benefits it brings.

3. Participate

You'll see a theme repeated throughout this book. It's valuable to those just starting down the path of process improvement. That is the theme of executive commitment: dedicated and focused executive commitment is essential to the success of any process initiative—in fact, to any business initiative.

When you create a process program, you are not creating an end product. You are setting down the first stone in what will eventually (hopefully) stretch into a well-worn path. But, of course, the stone is not the path, and all the good work of your process team has not laid the brush aside. It has delivered a direction and a map. Now the real test comes.

There's always a strong leadership presence in successful process programs: the champions, the visionaries, the true believers. Maybe those labels are too strong to apply to many process initiatives. But you probably understand the directive behind them: make executive commitment a visible thing. To do that, it is essential to participate in the life of the program. Management must lead the way.

Appear in the Valley

It's no doubt easy sometimes to look down on company operations from high up. The view from there can often appear placid, orderly. And there's an argument to be made that heavy executive management across all layers of an organization might not be a good thing. After all, if you hire competent people, you should probably get out of their way and let them do their jobs. That's my philosophy, too. But it's a general philosophy, good for routines that have stabilized

But for new or emerging process programs, the stability is usually not there, at least not in most companies. In these situations, visible executive commitment and support become especially important.

By the term "appear in the valley," I mean to suggest that management appear as a guide. They are not there to audit, or to check up on people, or to peer over shoulders; they show up to show your people that they are interested, that they want to see results, that the company will be patient, as long as progress is being made. And also that the company will be tolerant when missteps are made, that those kinds of trials will no doubt arise, but that they are OK as long as they are indicators that people are moving into the program.

Be Content with Commitment Equal to Yours

The last thought here on the subject of participation is the level of commitment you should expect from your people as your program becomes a part of the way you do business. The level of commitment you show—openly and visibly in the organization—is the level of commitment you can predict will permeate through your process program.

You probably know this already. Think of your management partners: will they share this commitment with you? This form of on-floor encouragement does not require an inordinate amount of attention. If you've designed the process program so that it fits the organization well, then it shouldn't be a struggle to fit it into daily and routine business activities. But especially at the outset, the program will be new to people, maybe a little strange or a little daunting. If senior management can be seen as imminently interested in how people are adjusting to it and strongly committed to seeing it succeed for the organization, then that attitude will go a long way to ensuring adoption, attenuation, and integration into work group cultures.

4. Training

If I were asked to pinpoint two of the most critical factors in achieving a successful process program, I'd cite executive commitment and training. Not one after another, but both together. I see them as being equally crucial.

Chapter 3 looked at the importance of training when it comes to establishing your process program. There it is essential, because it preps your people to begin using the program effectively. But training should become an ongoing and permanent part of your program, just as improvement is.

Naturally your program is going to evolve over time. So the best way to have a better program is to have better people. Such an ongoing commitment to training works best when it takes on a two-dimensional shape.

The first is focused on growth. This includes the growth of your program, the growth of your people, and the growth of your business. Training addresses all of these. As a manager, in addition to all your other duties, you are the caretaker of your people. Like a football coach, you should want to turn them into the best players they can be. And so it's good practice to seek and support their personal career goals in ways that line up with the mission of the business.

This area can include professional training and often includes training that is not directly relevant to the process program. For example, you may have some network people in your group who would like to obtain Cisco CCNA certification. You might have programmers on staff who want to obtain MCSD certification. These paths are designed to help produce better network analysts and better programmers.

If parts of your business objectives are to improve network efficiency or to program .NET more effectively, then this form of growth training will bring advanced knowledge, skills, and practices into the organization. And this will provide a foundation of fresh knowledge and new perspectives that can be directly applied to improving the process program.

The second facet of this two-dimensional shape is process training. Your organization should establish some form of training program to support the use and evolution of the process program across the organization. There are some sound reasons for this.

First, you'll no doubt be bringing new people into the organization on something of a regular basis. And you should have some sort of mechanism in place for training these people in their jobs. Part of their job will be to follow the processes established to carry out the work. You can facilitate this with formal classroom-style training, with coaching and mentoring, maybe even with computer-based instruction.

At the same time, you'll want to remember that your process program will be evolving over time: changing to become better and changing to keep up with shifting business environments. This will require process refresh training at certain intervals. Depending on the size and reach of your program, you may set up some type of fixed training regimen or curriculum that requires attendance by certain job roles for mini sessions once a quarter, twice a year, or even annually.

The issue of training, once your program is moving under its own steam, can easily lose its focus. But it's wise to keep a steady handle on it. If you appreciate the fact that your program will change—that you actually want it to change—and that your people's ability to use the program effectively is key to its success, then you will have little trouble justifying the importance of training and the contribution it can make to sustained process improvement.

5. Support Compliance

I work pretty regularly with two process consultants, Kricket Ichwantoro and Nicole Whitelaw. I bring Kricket and Nicole in on lots of different kinds of jobs. They're great program developers, they're really strong at pre-assessments, and they know how to accurately gauge the scope of how much process is right for particular groups. But what I like to use them most for is what I call Project Quality Assurance. Depending on the improvement model or the industry it's in, Project Quality Assurance goes by other names: auditor, inspector, assessor, etc.

The Job of Project Quality Assurance

The job of Project Quality Assurance (PQA) is straightforward enough: keep the project team on process. (This role is directly called out both in ISO 9001 and in CMMI.) In the effort to institutionalize a process program, this may be one of the most neglected or least appreciated roles. People might logically assume that since a process program represents a way to do business, people should follow that way without much prodding. Or they may think that the addition of people to oversee the use of the program amounts to unnecessary overhead. Or that maybe it implies distrust.

While I can understand those attitudes (at least a little bit), I've got to maintain that they aren't completely accurate. Not only is the role of Project Quality Assurance essential to sustaining a process program, the job of the PQA analyst may be paramount.

Follow Kricket Ichwantoro and Nicole Whitelaw around on a project, and you'll see what I mean. The first job of the PQA analysts is to know the process program inside and out. Since they are key to making sure everyone on the project team is able to conduct their jobs according to the procedures and activities of the program, they will need a deep, workable understanding of the program.

Next, the PQA analysts actively help plan the project. The project manager probably takes a planning view that focuses heavily on budget, schedule, and resources. The PQA analysts can complement this view. Working with the project manager, they can help provide a compliance plan for the project—one that details what key activities will be monitored over the course of the project, what work products will be required for delivery, what artifacts will be expected to be produced. This plan represents a compliance contract for the project team. It defines what compliance means. And it serves as an aid to the project manager who is also responsible for following established processes.

Then, during the various project phases, the PQA analysts execute the PQA plan. They are involved with the project team. They announce scheduled audits well in advance, perform the audits in accordance with current standards, note issues of noncompliance, and then help the team get back into compliance where needed or document the valid reasons for being out of compliance. Regularly they release summaries of all their audit reports, noting areas of strong performance and areas where performance might be improved.

If every IT project had a Kricket or Nicole working with it, team members would quickly see that process, when well planned and designed, does not interfere with project work. It complements it. It promotes it. It serves as an aid to using consistent solutions for moving in predictable directions, along a clear-cut path.

When an organization supports its process program by instantiating the role of Project Quality Assurance analyst, it sets up a framework of dependability, one that different project teams can use to not only make sure they stay on process but also to help saturate process into their teams, so that over time the program becomes a natural—almost unnoticed—way of doing business.

Provide Coaches, Not Cops

A great way to help sustain your process program is by supporting compliance, but there are different ways of approaching this task, some not as effective as others. One term that the improvement industry has unfortunately picked up over the years is "compliance cop." That's the person you think of as always looking over your shoulder, checking up on you, auditing you on a whim. The spirit most often associated with the compliance cop is that of catch-and-correct: catch someone doing something the wrong way and then push them (usually by consequence) into doing it the right way. I guess in basic training that approach might work—there, it's probably the smart approach—but in the business world, that approach is not going to be very effective. It will probably backfire.

The better approach is to set up your PQA analysts as process coaches. They should be charged with helping your people gradually grow into the program, not in a passive, observational way but in an active way, while engaged in the program, while using it.

When your PQA folks are seen in this supportive way, the issue of compliance changes. It moves from being perceived (perhaps) as an intrusion to a tool, one that might need some getting used to, but a tool nonetheless. And the PQA analysts themselves begin to be seen as a visible sign of executive commitment to the program. These analysts are not, per se, linked to the project teams. They are part of the organization at large, and their willingness to help the teams move through process, engage in process appropriately, and realize the benefits of the program communicates management belief in the program.

The success of your process program will hinge on its long-term adoption by the people in your company. If the program has been designed well, it will probably meet the business needs of the organization. The key then is to get people using it until it becomes habit, until it is the natural *modus operandi* of the culture. A very effective way to help this come about is through the use of PQA analysts. By seeding these process coaches within teams across the organization, projects can stay on process, people can work with and appreciate process program elements, and the benefits of the system can begin to saturate the organization.

6. Active Feedback Mechanisms

You may be the sponsor of your organization's process program; you may even be accountable for it, liable for its success. But your people really live with it. After all is said and done, the final test of the program's effectiveness will come down to how well it fits the way your people do their jobs. If the fit is good, people will use it. If the fit is poor, they won't. And so it's important that you continually monitor the program's fit with your organization.

So far in this chapter, we've looked at a few ways you can do this. But here we discuss a technique that carries with it a singular importance: feedback.

Organizations are dynamic enterprises. They're ever-changing. So is the blend of people in the organization. So are trends in the marketplace. So are business objectives. The world of business is in a busy state of continuous flux. And because of this, you need to make sure that your process program does not remain fixed. It needs to evolve with your organization, to remain in sync with your organization. The best way to do this is to work with those closest to the program, your frontline people. This is where feedback comes into play. Your people—working the program every day—need to know that what they think and need can directly impact the shape of the program.

Through their feedback, you can work effectively to make sure that your program retains its goodness-of-fit for the organization. Here are four ways you might consider to help you establish feedback mechanisms in your organization that can work to sustain your process program.

Let Them Know Who the Ears Are

People are usually willing to provide constructive feedback when given the chance, but organizations often fail to identify who the ears are—that is, who it is they can talk to, who they can come to with ideas and requests.

Some organizations try to compensate for this by setting up web sites people can use to submit feedback. Or suggestion boxes placed around an office to collect ideas. But these are only half measures. Web sites and boxes are usually perceived as black holes: nothing that goes into them ever seems to come out.

Feedback needs human contact to make it valuable. People need to know who they can go to—not what—to offer up thoughts and ideas that can be used to make business processes more effective. It's the organization's responsibility to let them know who those ears are.

Provide a Means of Communicating

Now that your people know who they can go to with process improvement ideas, it's important to set up communication channels to encourage and foster this feedback. There are various ways to do this. You can give out a map to your office. You can hand out your phone number. You can walk around and solicit ideas. You can also conduct more formal activities.

One commonly used activity is to hold formal process program review meetings at regular intervals. You can think of these as user-group meetings, where you bring together the people who use the program (maybe for a day or two each year) and gather ideas for making the program better.

You can take smaller actions, too. You can hold focus group sessions with targeted groups within the organization, looking at specific performance areas of the program. You can use the suggestion boxes and email centers I talked about earlier, but now with a real person waiting at the other end.

Use your creativity and experience here. The goal is to encourage the various work groups to think about how they use elements of the process program, to come up with ideas and suggestions to make it better, and then to know what to do with those ideas and suggestions, how to share them with the right audience.

Provide Evidence of Actions

The positive power of feedback will quickly lose its energy if you only pay lip service to it. Unfortunately that is often what many company managers do. They *say* they want to hear from the workforce; they *want* to think that they are responsive to what their people might express. But when it comes down to hard tack, they prefer the status quo. Or if change is required, it's better if it's their change. Of course, people see through that position pretty quickly.

Realizing the value of feedback requires two assumptions: that the frontline workers probably know how best to get a job done, and that the processes you've put into place to assist job performance could be improved. In my mind, those are pretty safe assumptions. Take your position along those lines, and you'll quickly come to welcome feedback.

Feedback also requires two actions. First, demonstrate that you are collecting and analyzing the feedback you get (and accept that this will take a degree of work and energy on your part). You can do this several ways. You might create a public process improvement log or database that everybody has access to and is able to enter new data into. You might post what you judge to be the top five improvement ideas every month in some conspicuous place within the company.

Next, *implement* the ideas that really add value to your program. In other words, act on the feedback. That's the best way to get your people involved in the program, to get them feeling that the program is really theirs, that they exercise a degree of control over how it's shaped, and that they have a real and tangible stake in its outcome.

Seek the Wisdom of Balance

Hopefully, if you've let your people know who they can come to with ideas, and if you've opened up accessible communication channels, you'll be getting a lot of feedback. Some of it will contain gems: really solid and pertinent ideas that can be used to significantly improve the efficacy of your program.

Another portion will contain some pretty good ideas for minor tweaks and adjustments.

And then a portion of it, while sincere, may prove not really relevant or practical, or contain no real improvement value.

The point I'd like to make here is that sometimes the act of implementing an improvement idea carries with it more value than the idea itself. Now you are not going to want to continually change your process program. It needs to be seen as a stable, well-managed methodology. But you will want to make revisions to it on something of a fixed schedule, and when those times come, it might be important to your people that they see some of their ideas being incorporated into the refinements you have endorsed.

Use these opportunities to look at their suggestions. And don't just look for the Big Ideas. Small changes might not mean much to you (and so might be very easy for you to implement), but they may very well mean a lot to the people who suggested them. They may see the incorporation of these ideas as recognition of their business savvy and acumen. And when your program is supported by people like that, it soon becomes a solid asset within the company.

7. Promote Performance Incentives

In the business world, people are compensated for doing a job. They are often rewarded for doing the job well. These basic performance assumptions can be carried directly into your process program.

Chapter 3 established some general process program guidelines: identify business objectives, design processes to support these business objectives, and create activities within the processes to guide business activities. If you have done that, you have helped create a way for your people to do business in your organization. In fact, it should be the preferred way of doing business. Therefore, if the business is important and if your process program guides business activities, it should be important to your organization that your people become proficient in your process program.

The idea here is that if your people follow the program, they should be able to perform well in their jobs. In fact, process compliance should be seen as part of their job. And when they prove that they are able to work efficiently within your program using processes and procedures to get work done, they may well deserve to be rewarded.

Linking process proficiency with job performance evaluations is a good way to sustain process improvement across the organization. Following are four techniques that you can apply as a way to create performance incentives that encourage people to adopt and use the process program in place for your business units.

Link Performance Objectives to Program Components

Your process program, taken as a whole, may be a big thing, and its full scope may reach outside of most people's day-to-day activities. However, people have specific jobs to do, specific contributions to make, and so they should be familiar with those parts of the program that impact their business views. These areas should be—at some level—represented in the program.

To foster compliance and the ongoing use of the program, then, part of management's job—part of their own business view—should be to link the employee's performance with proficiency in those program elements.

To do this, up front and early on, you can work with your people to establish these relationships and then use the traditional MBO (management by objectives) techniques of defining goals and then defining a path to achieve them. In this case, one objective could be to learn and use the program as part of overall job responsibilities. MBO is a technique that can help set a host of performance goals: increase revenues by three percent, reduce downtime to half a day per quarter, meet installation commitments 98 percent of the time. Those examples all have to do with job action. Other examples, those related to your process program, could be tied to job knowledge and job proficiency: train at least three new employees in our up-time maintenance procedures every month, participate in three process improvement committee sessions each year, attend two process program refresher courses. By setting these kinds of objectives, you begin to link business performance objectives to process program proficiency.

This will serve as a common yardstick you and your people can use to measure not only your increased knowledge and use of the program, but also to monitor overall organizational commitment to sustained process improvement.

Tie Performance Reviews to Program Proficiency

When you manage your teams, in part by setting them with objectives that stress process program integration, you should naturally expect them to work to achieve those objectives. And because you have made these objectives a tangible and measurable part of job performance, you should make sure that their work toward accomplishing these objectives is recognized in performance reviews.

In many organizations, job reviews and performance appraisals are handled as little more than chat sessions. They run as casual conversations that dip in and out of performance assessment topics. In other organizations, reviews and appraisals are structured along much more formalized lines. Whatever path your organization takes, it's important to remember the commitments you share with your people, especially (for the focus of this book) those that deal with process proficiency. Bring these commitments up at reviews and appraisals and discuss them. For those people you feel have met or exceeded their process performance objectives, ensure that you can reward them in an appropriate manner.

Establish formal rewards

Because an organization's process program should reflect the way it conducts business, the program should be officially viewed as a core business essential. From the perspective of human-resource management, process performance should therefore be officially tied to compensation. Salaries, benefits, bonuses, and perks should in some way be a reflection of that person's ability and experience working within the program, as well as that person's ability or potential to refine, improve, or promote the program.

You can move a long way toward sustaining process improvement activities in your organization when your people begin to understand that their levels of compensation are directly linked to the level at which they embrace the program. This should probably be an early consideration in the development of the program. It's a good idea to work with your management to define the importance of process as a strategic initiative and then seek their buy-in to include process allegiance as part of performance reviews and personnel appraisals.

Establish informal rewards

You need not wait for annual or semiannual performance reviews in order to recognize achievement. You can use informal awards spread out over time that let people know you are following their progress and are recognizing the work they are doing. Actually, I have found that informal awards sometimes have more impact the formal ones. I have seen managers give people what I call "visible thank-yous" that really reinforce commitment and promote enthusiasm. Things like a dinner out on the town, tickets to theater or sporting events, special plaques, team lunches, or even success banners all provide a visible show of support to members of the organization. They are valuable reminders that the process program is important, and that the people who help it succeed, even in little ways, are sincerely appreciated.

View from the Top

SUCCESS BUILDS ON SUCCESS

"There's great value in interpreting, selecting, and internalizing those portions of CMMI, ISO, and Six Sigma that line up with your needs. The key is to take these parts and then shape them to fit the organization.

"A common idea is to apply process improvement to those areas in an organization that have the most problems, or substantially lack process. But an approach that's often better is to focus process improvement on areas in the company that have already made progress in process management. These groups will typically make the most of improvement opportunities, and you'll often see a faster ROI on their efforts. Also, they stand a strong chance of standing out as a success story in the organization. Nothing succeeds like success."

—Bruce A. Brown, Senior Vice President and CIO, T-Mobile USA

---

8. Celebrate Success

If you are sincerely committed to nearly any path of action, you'll probably run into success sooner or later. A struggling actor will land an off-Broadway part. A young father will get a "Best Dad in the World" T-shirt. Same for your process program. As a matter of fact, compared to the actor, the chances for big success are probably much better for your process program. But big success will take time. In the meantime, and probably more important, small success will arrive quietly through small doors, at gradual intervals, reminders of measured progress.

Often these small successes are overlooked. In this field, people tend to want to peer out to the horizon, looking for the tip of the mast of the S.S. Major Accomplishment. But I like for people (and companies) to focus on incremental progress. The good thing about that view is, if you roll your program out properly and you and your management team are truly committed to it, there will be plenty of incremental progress to appreciate.

I once worked with Dan Payne, a senior IT Project Manager for Cingular Wireless. We worked to implement a CMMI program that Dan and his team had pretty much built from scratch, and we helped roll it out to various organizational groups. In any engagement like this, the word "smooth" is a relative term, but Dan kept the Big Goal in mind. He coached his people through the rough spots and supported them as they maneuvered through new activities. He was always, and actively, looking for signs of success, even the smallest of signs, and at each sign, he demonstrated his enthusiasm for the program and for the effort his team was making to implement the program.

Of course, this attitude became contagious. His different teams began to enjoy making the program work. The idea of failure had been quietly removed from the equation. They weren't afraid of any "invisible consequences" that might come from trying. Because the light was shed on success, they adopted the attitude of "let's try until we succeed." What a great attitude. It worked very well.

So, as your process program spreads out in your organization, train your eye to spot the small successes. There's a popular acronym that's been floating around for centuries: QED. It's from the Latin phrase *quod erat demonstrandum*. It means, "There's the proof!" My friend, Alan Mann, a quality specialist working in the Washington D.C. area, named a quality program he helped design QED: Quality Execution and Delivery. After it was in broad use, whenever he would notice another of a series of small successes, Alan could feel justified in announcing, "QED!" In other words, "There's the proof, guys, that our process works."

To encourage sustained process improvement, look for success everywhere you can. Do it by walking around and observing. Do it by finding true pleasure in your people working toward goals they've set. Seek out feedback. People will be anxious to tell you what's working well, proud to announce what they have *discovered* to work well.

Celebrate these small successes. Let people know you are aware of the progress, that you appreciate it, that it means something to the company. You might consider small tokens of appreciation. Even silly things like awarding process progress cakes to a group or awarding success plaques to teams can be very positive reinforcements. As long as you yourself take these little gestures seriously, you can be pretty much assured that your teams will accept them gratefully.

9. Public Announcements

As we discussed earlier, it's important to visibly demonstrate support for your process program. If the program is seen as being an integral part of the business and an important part of the overall corporate culture, then the program will probably be embraced. That's why it's important that executive management shows they are behind the program. And that's why it's important to tie incentives to the program.

Along these same lines, it's important to keep the message of process improvement and program commitment alive in the day-to-day culture of the organization. A good way to promote this is through public announcement.

Many companies are required to report how they are doing financially. They issue quarterly and annual reports. Those are forms of public announcements. You should consider doing the same thing, internally or even externally, for your process program.

There are many ways you can do this, but they all aim to hit the same target: communicating your process commitment and your process achievements as forms of business success. From time to time, the company should publicly announce its progress and its goals in terms of improvement. Some ways of making these kinds of public announcements are:

Newsletters

Regular articles in company newsletters that report on process program use and efficiencies in the organization

Press releases

Sent to local and national media sources that announce program success, extensions, and recognition

Posters

Displayed around the facilities that remind people of the company's reliance on process and the part it plays in the organization's overall identity

Inserts

Perhaps in pay envelopes or company communiqués that ask for improvement ideas, nominations for process awards, or new support suggestions

There are a couple of good reasons for supporting your program with these techniques.

It Makes Good Business Sense

Public announcements of your company's commitment to process and its evolving success with process tells a good business story. It's one that Wall Street is learning to pay attention to. More and more, financial analysts and institutions are including process-related questions in their assessments of corporate value and stability. What was your IT spending last year? How critical is the growth of IT in your strategic plans? Do your IT units have a process program? What kind of program is it? How is it being managed? When you begin to communicate inside and outside that process is part of your business tool set, you gain the perception that you take your business seriously, that you are working to strategically position it for continued success.

Shows Commitment at the Highest Level

When the executive suite invests in public announcements of process progress, the rest of the organization will begin to pick up on the vibe. Of course, the communication must reflect a true commitment to process improvement—that's what the line force will really pick up on—but the visible expression goes a long way to expressing that commitment.

You've seen how it's important to expect only the kind of commitment to the program that you're willing to make. This idea of public announcement, of open announcements, is an extension of that. These techniques keep the voice of commitment resonating in the hallways. I have just completed an engagement with a major Medicare claims management company. Naturally, any company dealing with Medicare claims must comply with a host of regulations; it's essential to the integrity of the business. Everywhere you walked around the place—and this was a huge campus—you would see signs that read, "Compliance. It's not a style job. It's a job style." That's the kind of message that after a while really takes hold in the culture of the organization.

10. Measure, Measure

Measuring is important in process improvement. You've probably heard that. Maybe a few times. The problem I have found is that the people who are the ones saying it may seem to believe it, but they don't seem sure why. That often leads to a common misdirection with process improvement programs: thinking you have to support it with a complex measurement program.

When people are led down that path, the result can indeed be a very complex measurement program, maybe even a good one, one that on paper promises to reveal a host of nuances and facets of your process set. But then comes the chore of doing the measuring: finding someone to amass and collect the data, analyzing and figuring out what the results might indicate, reporting and communicating the results, and then deciding what to do with it all.

What happens next—after the paper program is admired—is often nothing. It takes work to collect measures. It takes energy. And resources, and time, and (admit it) interest. When an organization drifts from the chief purpose and use of process program measurements and creates a mathematical and statistical Methuselah, no one wants to be bothered with it. No one wants to look at it. It appears too cumbersome, too tangled, or like too much work. Besides, people might think, why are we collecting all this data anyway?

Measuring *is* important in process improvement. But the reason is simple. Measurements tell you how you are progressing. They help show you the direction you are moving in. A trip odometer is a measurement system. A compass is a measurement system. Kricket Ichwantoro and Nicole Whitelaw, the process quality analysts I try to work with whenever I can, know the measurement conundrum well. They often step in to help IT shops plan for and develop metrics for new or existing process programs. Their common philosophy is pretty straightforward: keep it straightforward.

The measurements you define will work best when they possess three traits:

- The measures tie to hard business objectives.
- The measures give you meaningful information.
- The measures are things your people can identify and collect.

With those traits in place, you don't need a complex measurement approach to help analyze your process program. If the approach you design reflects real business needs, if it contains data that means something to the organization, and if it focuses on data that's readily available, you can go a long way toward setting up the foundation of what can become, with use and improvement, a solid metrics-analysis program.

To begin with, though, two things are handy to consider: measure to monitor and measure to know.

Measure to Monitor

The concept of *measure to monitor* sets the stage for the opening advantage metrics can deliver. Regularly measuring your process program is an effective way to monitor the program's affinity with business objectives and project efficiencies.

As mentioned in Chapter 3, one of the key factors in establishing an effective process program is to tie the activities in your program to overall business objectives. It's important to shape your program to the needs of the business, and it's important to demonstrate that your program is helping your organization achieve those objectives. And so, as you decide what kind of measures you might begin to trace through your organization, think about what you'd like to demonstrate.

Is fidelity to schedules a point of special interest? Is the rate of resource churn of particular concern? Budget? Length of project phases? The number of change requests?

All of these kinds of metrics—quantitative snapshots of evolving activity—can be used to help you monitor how your projects are doing. Not just in retrospect, but in real time as your project unfolds, so that you can better manage the unfolding.

Measuring can also help you monitor the performance potential of your processes. Not just how things are working now, but how things will probably work later on: process performance. Even if your measures begin simply in a qualitative mode, you can begin to discern how well the processes, procedures, and other tools that you've implemented are working for your teams.

With time, this facet can become the greatest growth factor of a process program. The ultimate achievement is to measure the performance of your processes to such a degree that your people, by implementing the processes, can predict quantitatively how they will perform and thus anticipate how the overall project will perform.

That's quite an achievement. And many process-centric companies have attained that achievement. But for now, for what we are after—sustained process improvement—a little less is just as respected. You needn't begin with what you know you know. It can be just as valuable to begin with what you'd like to know.

Measure to Know

Over time, as your measurement repository grows, the information that begins to accrue will point toward opportunities for improvement. The repository will give you a foundation to know what to improve. The following is an example.

If you're monitoring how well your teams comply with published processes, and your auditors are recording noncompliance issues, their measures might indicate that for one particular process, noncompliance is abnormally high. This might indicate a few things. Maybe your training needs to be beefed up for that procedure. Maybe team members haven't been trained to effectively follow the process. Then again, maybe the teams are regularly avoiding the procedure because it doesn't fit the way work flows. Or maybe the way it's built does not allow for the kinds of tailoring that's needed for the particular activity across different projects.

So measurements, carefully designed to reflect your business and your program, can help you know what you might need to improve.

Measurements can also establish avenues to improve elements of your program in specific ways. As you begin to look at ISO 9001, CMMI, and Six Sigma in Part 2 of this book, you'll see how these models place particular emphasis on metrics. And with greater levels of capability and sophistication come increased measurement. The idea these models support is that metrics provide valuable information for making data-driven decisions. In other words, your experience, judgment, and intuition are valuable assets for your process improvement strategies. But a strong complement to these is the solid component that data supplies.

Measuring the right things in the right amounts will help you sustain process improvement activities by providing you with hard data that can complement your experience and judgment when it comes to refining the program for more efficient use in your organization.

11. Periodic Reassessment

To successfully sustain your process program over time, so that it develops in sync with your business operations and in line with the responsibilities of your workforce, you will need to periodically assess the program.

After all, business changes over time. Objectives change. Technologies change. People change. Your process program, being a reflection of your business activities then, should also be expected to change.

As discussed in "6. Active Feedback Mechanisms," earlier in this chapter, you can support this by setting into place a series of feedback mechanisms within your business units. These mechanisms give your people a path for making improvement suggestions over time. At the same time (as discussed earlier in "3. Participate"), you, your process teams, and your executive management have all been actively involved in monitoring the program and in assessing its effectiveness on a daily basis. The result is that your organization should be able to accumulate a good foundation of improvement information that can be used to refine program operations.

The balance to seek in refining your program comes with the frequency of updates. Continuous improvement is the governing theme in almost all process and quality management systems. But that doesn't mean constant change. In fact, one could argue that too much improvement can actually wreak more havoc than no improvement at all. Process programs are intended to help an organization achieve a degree of operational stability. And for this to be true, the program itself must achieve a degree of stability.

This brings us to the concept of strategic reassessment.

The idea here is that the organization should reassess its program at set strategic intervals. In well-designed systems, business success ties closely to process program success. To help keep the two in line, you and your process teams should plan to review the program in depth at certain defined intervals. And the organization as a whole should be aware of these intervals.

The frequency here naturally depends on the particulars of your program. In dynamic organizations in emerging markets, with new processes, the reassessment period could be as short as every six months. For more stable businesses, in mature industries, and using well-refined processes, the period might be every three years or so.

But in each case, the strategy is the same: to refresh the program as needed for its next cycle of productivity.

Chapter 3 looked at the steps you typically undertake to establish a process program within an organization. Some of those steps included establishing your process objectives, performing an analysis of existing business practices, and then creating and refining processes to better tie the practices to the objectives. These happen to be the same kinds of steps you'll take when you conduct a reassessment. It represents its own process improvement project, and so it should be treated as such, coordinated through the organization as both an executive and strategic effort.

In brief, there are 10 steps you usually follow when coordinating a reassessment of your program. Here they are:

1. Establish the reassessment period and scope, and communicate it to the organization.

2. Collect feedback and observations over time, positioning for reassessment.

3. Plan the reassessment activities.

4. Announce the reassessment initiative to impacted business groups.

5. Create improvement data review committees (as appropriate).

6. Create improvement teams as appropriate.

7. Conduct reassessment activities.

8. Analyze, validate, and prioritize assessment results.

9. Create improvement plans.

10. Implement improvement plans.

These steps will help you execute the reassessment in a smooth manner, and in a way that involves as many of your line people as practical. The push of this approach is to first establish the assessment interval. This will help orient people as to how often they can expect the program to change. This will steer them away from making frequent and willy-nilly recommendations, and focus their inputs where they will have the most impact. Next is the action to conscientiously collect and store feedback and observation improvement data over the time between intervals. Don't simply rely on the assessment period to find out what you might need to do. Reference all the data your people have been providing you. Then thoroughly plan the assessment activities. You want to have a solid pan here for two reasons. One, you'll no doubt have limited time to perform the assessment. Two, you'll want to coordinate assessment activities in a way that reaches the broadest groups of people while intruding on normal work duties as little as possible.

After that, you should appoint people inside the organization to participate in the assessment activities. You'll want groups to evaluate existing process improvement recommendations, and you'll want groups who can go out and investigate current activities across the organization.

Once the planned activities have been conducted, you should have the groups analyze, validate, and prioritize improvement opportunities according to their potential impact and their promise of positive influence on business activities. From this, you can begin to create improvement proposals that address specific ways in which the elements of your process program can be adjusted or refined to increase efficiencies.

After a review and a decision as to which improvements might work best for the organization at this point in time, you can move to implement the refinements.

For some, the effort of conducting periodic reassessments of your process program may seem like a major task. And in fact, it should be treated as a serious effort. It is certainly a significant and important task. But similar energies are spent on business infrastructures and regulatory positions all the time. Why shouldn't similar energies be spent on the program that guides what might be a major portion of the business?

The sustainability of any process program is one of the surest guarantors of success that a program can demonstrate. And effective sustainment comes from ensuring that your program retains its business relevance in the organization. This relevance links your program to productivity, to workplace efficiencies, and to acceptance by the work force. At the same time, it serves as one of the key controllable assets that drive achievement of business objectives. Given all this, periodic reassessment might well be considered as basic a practice as changing the oil in your car or replacing the filter in your air conditioner.

12. Appreciate the Journey

Process improvement is not a project in the sense that we think of for IT projects. There are no start and end dates; it is not a single, self-bounded initiative. And it is not a goal, someplace where you arrive and then issue congratulations all around for a job well done.

Process improvement is a Way. It is the way you see your company. It is the way you do business. And so the only time it should draw to a conclusion is when your business draws to a conclusion. It is a way to plan for business, to manage core business activities, and to oversee business progress and success. And it is a way to forge tangible links between the three core elements of any organizational design: people, activities, and technology.

Process improvement, and its larger discipline, process management, are also about standards, consistencies, and common expectations. They can be used to set the bar for performance, for production, for service, for responsiveness. And they can provide much needed benchmarks for creating and delivering the most important business differentiator of them all: quality.

Performance standards, operational efficiencies, quality: these three ingredients—this mix that makes up success—have been recognized as sound operating principles in most business markets for decades. Look at Detroit. Look at the way cars roll off the assembly line. The days of the Gremlin, the Vega, and the Chevette are long gone. What are rolling now are rock-solid, dependable automobiles. It's nothing today to think that your new car will deliver 200,000 miles with few if any headaches.

Look at Coca-Cola. That brand is recognized worldwide and sold in more countries on planet Earth than any other drink product—probably any other food product. That's because the formula for Coke is a success formula. And all the structures and processes that drive that bottle to market drive toward the single goal of supporting and maintaining everything that Coke has come to mean to a global marketplace.

Why the technology markets have been slow to embrace process in a similar way has always puzzled me. Maybe it's because the industry as we know it today is relatively young—barely 40 years old. Maybe it has a right to be immature. Maybe it's because so many of it top managers have risen from the ranks of technical development. Maybe they know more about technos than technique. Then again, maybe it's because the pace of change here is so fast, so prevalent that the temptation to run with the latest and the greatest overcomes any strategic notion toward stability.

Whatever it is, the shortcoming of our IT organizations—the shops that more and more run American business—cost over $50 billion last year. That's $50 billion in lost profits, in misdirected energies, in lost opportunities, in abandoned projects.

When you look at it long enough and think about it deeply enough, process improvement and process management are not esoteric philosophies or abstract theories. They aren't amorphous approaches or wall-mount placards. They are programs of action steps, concrete catalysts. They push you to the action of externalizing the fundamental understandings of any business enterprise: Why are we here? What do we do? Why do we do it? How do we do it so we make a difference?

Visit a large IT shop nearly anywhere. Ask those questions. More often than not, you'll hear confident concordance that all that's clearly understood. But then ask individuals. Chances are you'll get a surprisingly wide variety of differing responses. Have those crucial and elemental defining points been externalized into guiding principles? Have they been shaped into structures and avenues that unite and coordinate? You probably know the IT industry well. What do you think?

Is process the "capital A" answer? Is it the silver bullet? No. But I do know this: the process program you create is the vessel that holds the answer. And it will often come to the aid of the company in ways that look like a silver bullet.

What the program holds is your expertise, the experience of the people in your organization. Designed properly, it should carry the best of what your organization has to offer. And so the program should hold a central position within your organization. But it is not an end-all in and of itself. It is a way that you establish to guide your people along a managed and conscientious business path. That's the aspect of the program that should be most appreciated. It is a journey to quality, an ongoing momentum leading to increased business success.

Summary

Sustaining process improvement requires more than setting a process program in place. It requires attention to the program from multiple directions. To help sustain process improvement in your organization, consider employing some of the following techniques:

- Remember what you do. Understand your products and your customers so that your process program can continually reflect the needs of both.

- Weld business success to program success. Engage upper management in program commitment and use by tying business performance and process performance together.

- Participate. Visibly participate in the program's organizational use. This demonstrates that all levels of the company find value in the program and are committed to its success.

- Train. Remember to provide adequate training to the organization so that various work groups can use the program in an informed and appropriate manner.

- Support compliance. Provide resources to monitor process program compliance and provide guidance and support when teams need to better adhere to process guidelines.

- Seek active feedback. Seek open and regular feedback on ways to improve the program.

- Provide performance incentives. Give your people formal and informal awards to encourage their use of the program across daily business activities.

- Measure, measure. Collect and analyze measures that help you understand, from a data viewpoint, how the program is working for you and the different business teams.

- Implement periodic reassessment. Periodically reassess your program, seeking opportunities for refinement and improvement.

- Appreciate the journey. Understand that process improvement is not a goal; it has no end point, no finish line. It's a cultural atmosphere that seeks to continually make business more efficient and more effective.

PART TWO

Three Major Process Improvement Standards

In Part 2 of the book, I'll look at three of the IT industry's leading quality management and process improvement standards. These are as follows:

ISO 9001:2000
  The generic quality standard from the International Organization for Standardization in Switzerland.

The Capability Maturity Model Integration
  The technology development process improvement framework from the Software Engineering Institute of Carnegie Mellon University in Pittsburgh.

Six Sigma
  The process improvement program based in statistical application and quantitative analysis developed and made popular by companies such as Motorola, Honeywell, and General Electric.

When I am out in the IT community—at trade shows, conventions, or visiting client sites—these are the three programs I am most often approached about. People want to know which one is the best, which one is right for them. The most common misconception is that there's a clean answer to those kinds of questions. Each of the three look at process improvement in a slightly different way, with a different focus on the issues of design, management, and refinement. I think it is a valuable move for everyone in IT to know at least something about these three standards. And so now I'll look at general summaries of each. These summaries are not intended to provide the most complete detail available. There are other books, dedicated to each, that can do that for you. But here you'll get a good feeling about what each one is about, how they might help you, and what you might be able to use from each to better promote your own internal process improvement initiatives.

CHAPTER FIVE

ISO 9001:2000

ISO 9001:2000 IS A PRODUCT OF THE INTERNATIONAL ORGANIZATION FOR STANDARDIZATION, AN organization that works to establish standards for worldwide use across a broad range of disciplines.

Most of us appreciate the value of standardization. Water hoses fit backyard faucets everywhere. Light bulbs fit light sockets no matter who made them. Twin sheets cover twin mattresses pretty much the same way. But the concept of standardization as we know it today is a fairly recent one. International standardization began, interestingly enough, with technology, or at least with the rise of electronics and electrical equipment. This was around 1900, in Europe.

Nations saw the advantage of regulating the production of electrical components so that trade and commerce would be able to cross boundaries with a minimum of adjustments. In 1906, to support this new view toward standardization, the International Electrotechnical Commission (IEC) was established. For the next 20 years, the IEC made successful headway in establishing common and successfully embraced standards. Then a partner organization was established, the International Federation of the National Standardizing Associations (ISA), set up in 1926. The ISA expanded the scope of standardization, focusing heavily on mechanical engineering, another rapidly growing field.

However, Europe in the late 20s and 30s was not the best place for the growth of international cooperation. With the outbreak of the Second World War, nations focused internally on more pressing matters, and both organizations quickly lost their influence. Both vanished with the rise of hostilities.

But the economic advantages of standardization could not be long squelched. Just after the close of the war, in 1946, delegates from 25 countries met in London and decided to create a new international organization, one designed to define and establish common, unified industrial standards for the whole of the European community. Such standards would provide for the simplified design, manufacturing, and maintenance of products across borders and international boundaries. The new organization, *Organisation internationale de normalisation*, officially began operations in February of 1947.

Today, the ISO—headquartered in Geneva, Switzerland—is made of up representatives from 148 member countries and has published nearly 14,000 standards. These standards cover dozens of industries and manufacturing specifications, including screw threads, fasteners, roller bearings, metallic fittings, ship and marine technology, boilers and pressure vessels, and—as its history might lead us to expect—information technology.

To date, its most influential, widely adopted, and recognized standard is its ISO 9000 family of standards, those that deal with a focus on quality, quality management systems, and process improvement.

A Brief History of ISO 9001:2000

For 40 years, the ISO led the way in establishing standards for consistency, interchangeability, and design. But by the late 1970s, the Western world—Europe and the United States—began to look east: to Japan. For three decades, that country had been quietly taking the lead in quality control. Evidence had begun to surface in distinctive ways, really since the 40s. But in the 1970s, the first transcontinental shockwave was felt—in the automobile industry. Japanese car manufacturers like Toyota and Honda began to draw away American buyers by the millions with economical and reliable imports. While American designers embraced the concept of built-in obsolescence, believing that Americans wanted to trade in every four years, the Japanese focused on dependability and value. If you were around at that time, you might remember embarrassments like the Chevy Vega, the AMC Pacer, and the Chrysler Reliant. These cars seemed to roll of the assembly line already rattling. There were no Japanese counterparts to these engineering Frankensteins—nor have there ever been.

What secret had the Japanese uncovered? The ironic note here is that the Japanese were just doing what the Americans and Western Europeans had taught them to do for years.

Think back to the close of World War II. In the late 1940s, Japan was little more than rubble. Literally. Over 60 percent of the country had been flattened. Part of the job of the occupation forces was to rebuild the country's infrastructure. And so the process began. The U.S. helped erect new factories across the land, new factories that featured the latest innovations in manufacturing techniques. Japan was getting the biggest modernization face-lift in the history of the world.

What's more, the people of Japan were taking this fresh start seriously. Their manufacturing leaders, visionaries, and managers began to read and absorb American business school literature: works by people such as Deming, Crosby, and Juran. These quality pioneers introduced such concepts as Total Quality Management, zero defects, Continuous Quality Improvement, and promoted the mantra "quality is free." And they gave new definitions to the concept of customer satisfaction. But by the 1960s, in America, these subjects— once fresh and inviting—had slowly been pulled out of the realm of application, relegated back into the halls of academia. They became interesting concepts, ideas for students to ponder. Meanwhile, American manufacturing (with Europe following lead) concentrated on volume, on turnover.

The Japanese, however, took quality seriously. They were attracted to the ideas of quality and continuous improvement and reliability. They appreciated values of consistency and repeatability. They believed what we preached. And so they began to build their manufacturing techniques around these concepts. They quickly proved adept at getting results.

By the 1980s, Japanese products were known for their superior engineering and solid performance. And not just in the automotive industry. Companies such as Mitsubishi, Sony, Sanyo, Hitachi, and Canon were market leaders. And so the West went East.

We began to send our people over there to find out the secret we had once discovered and then lost. In the mid-1980s, the concept of Total Quality Management attained renewed interest worldwide. The ISO recognized this revitalization, and in the wake of an ongoing technology revolution, it appreciated the need for a new worldwide standard, one that would embrace the ideas of quality and quality controls in manufacturing environments.

ISO 9000

In 1987, the ISO released the first version of its first international quality standard: ISO 9000. ISO 9000 was designed as a generic quality standard. It provided for the implementation of a quality system into just about any manufacturing environment. A coat-hanger factory could implement ISO 9000. A guided-missile plant could implement ISO 9000. A trucking company could do it. Your local pharmacist could, too.

The idea behind ISO 9000 was that in any manufacturing endeavor, there are opportunities in which quality can be controlled. These opportunities—often called quality gates— can be identified and then proactively managed so that the production process, once thought of as an unstoppable assembly line, could now become a specimen for fine-tuning. The standard had two basic objectives: to prevent a defective product from getting out the door, and to remedy the missteps that caused the defect in the first place. This was done by continuously examining and measuring the way you created your product.

While the foundation concepts inside ISO 9000 were *thematically* generic, the ISO realized that different types of manufacturing organizations would probably need different emphases.

Ensuring that coat hangers drop off the assembly line properly twist-tied probably requires a different focus from that of a group that wants to make sure the guidance system of a nuclear warhead operates in subfreezing temperatures. And so ISO 9000 was designed and released as a *family* of standards. It consisted of five individual but related international standards on quality management and quality assurance. The five standards were known as ISO 9000, ISO 9001, ISO 9002, ISO 9003, and ISO 9004.

The first and last in the family—ISO 9000 and 9004—served as bookend documents. ISO 9000 was titled "Quality Management and Quality Assurance Standards—Guidelines for Selection and Use." This document explained the purpose and use of the middle three standards and provided guidelines that adopters could use for selecting the appropriate standard for their organization. ISO 9004 was titled "Quality Management and Quality System Elements—Guidelines." This document featured guidelines for understanding and selecting the elements that would go into the quality management system being established.

The middle three documents contained the three independent quality standards that made up the core of the ISO 9000 family. ISO 9001 was titled "Quality System—Model for Quality Assurance in Design, Development, Production, Installation, and Servicing." ISO 9002 was titled "Quality Systems—Model for Quality Assurance in Production, Installation, and Servicing." And ISO 9003 was titled "Quality Systems—Model for Quality Assurance in Final Inspection and Test."

ISO 9001 was intended for use in organizations that are involved in the full design/production/maintenance life cycle. These companies typically create custom products specific to the needs of their clients (think of Jet Fighters, McDonald's uniforms, or anything having to do with Jennifer Lopez). They create a unique design based on the customer requirements, produce products from this design, and then perform maintenance once that product is installed in the field.

ISO 9002 was intended for organizations that produce full life-cycle products but do not rely on custom designs. They base their products (or service)—like the manufacturers of 10 p nails or 5 mg aspirin tablets—on generic specifications and uniform requirements common to all customers. These agencies are not required to create and verify unique designs.

ISO 9003 featured the narrowest scope of the three standards. It was intended for organizations, or groups within organizations, that are only concerned with the inspection and final testing of products (or services) prior to shipping. Think of the people who employ "Inspector Number 6."

ISO 9001:2000

Within a few short years of its release, the ISO 9000 family had become one of the world's leading quality standards. There are solid reasons why. It incorporated the latest quality management philosophies, it was supported by a recognized international organization, it was flexible in its implementation, and it was shown to produce results. ISO 9000 became the most widely disseminated and adopted standard in ISO history.

The ISO refined the standard in 1994 and then began almost immediately on a major revision. The impetus was consolidation. After nearly a decade of adoption, implementation, and observation, ISO members had expressed the need for a single consolidated standard. Such a standard would apply to any manufacturing entity by providing a series of truly generic quality practices. These practices would be expressed in a way that allowed for even more openness in interpretation and flexibility in implementation.

The ISO acted on these inputs and organized a major revision effort. In December of 2000, the organization released version 1 of ISO 9001:2000.

ISO 9001:2000 is a single quality standard. It replaces ISO 9000, 9001, 9002, 9003, and 9004 by incorporating the best practices of them all.

People familiar with the ISO 9000:1994 family will instantly recognize the push and focus of the 2000 standard. But its approach has been condensed to harmonize the goal of common application.

If you were to distill the essence of ISO 9001:2000, you would finish with five core directives:

1. Understand the requirements.

2. Establish processes to meet those requirements.

3. Provide resources to run the processes

4. Monitor, control, and measure the processes.

5. Improve continuously based on the results.

1. Understand the requirements

Like the best quality programs, the ISO 9001:2000 Standard carries a heavy focus on customer satisfaction. Because the term "quality" can be shaped to mean almost anything at any time, the best way to manage it is to tie it to customer satisfaction, or rather customer expectation. The assumption is, if you build what your customer wants, the customer should be satisfied with your work. Build in too little, and the product won't perform; too much, and it may be full of irrelevance. The best way to achieve agreed-upon quality then is to first know what it is your customer needs.

Understanding what your customer wants comes from understanding the requirements. But reaching that point of understanding takes work. You may begin by accepting a set of requirements from your customer. These may appear to be complete and valid, but it's important to confirm that. So you and your team might need to analyze these requirements. Through analysis, you may come up with questions, or you may derive additional logical requirements. You may then want to work closely with your customers to review and discuss, as necessary, this full set of requirements. Once you are both able to agree that you now have a solid benchmark for commencement, you'll be in a good position to design, build, and deliver a quality end product.

2. Establish processes to meet the requirements

The next core directive in the quality standard is to establish processes to meet the requirements. This is the functional heart of ISO 9001. As with any quality standard, the program is built upon documented, repeatable processes. These processes guide the many different activities your teams may have to undertake in the production regimen.

The use of common processes is important for three reasons. First, it externalizes the knowledge of the organization. Look at shops that work without processes. You'll see that they are commonly pretty ad hoc places. The success of their work is almost exclusively dependent upon the skills of the people performing the work; the organization provides little guidance. So your strongest team members will be able to produce as needed. But your weaker team members may fall behind, or produce inconsistently. Without a balance between these two, the success of a project on the whole may be unpredictable. By creating processes that reflect your most efficient work paths, you externalize the expertise in the organization, transferring it from inside the domain of *individuals* into the realm of the *group*.

Second, processes add visibility to the production activities. Effective managers and team members see value in this visibility. When an organization prefers to blindly throw components over walls—from team to team—it experiences a fragmentation of effort. Activities become micro-focused on bounded sets of actions. The big picture of what the end product should be can easily become lost. A well-balanced process program helps prevent this. With the walls down, all teams can understand how the components move through the system, and what value the system should add at each step. This harmonizes and consolidates the energy of a project team.

Third, processes provide for effective management of budgets, schedules, resources, and functionality. They're a mechanism to plan, predict, monitor, and control.

When the design of the process program is geared to meeting the requirements, you reap all these benefits. The processes are then able to shepherd project activities to create components that effectively meet the customer requirements. Such processes can help you control designs. They can help you assemble appropriately. They can help you test thoroughly. Ergo, quality.

3. Provide resources to run the processes

In point 2, processes are designed to fulfill the requirements: to help focus project activities on meeting the requirements. Here, from this third directive, you make a formal commitment to the process program by providing resources to run the program. In other words, the organization provides the overhead necessary to put the program to work. These resources typically include several elements. To begin with, the program will need people to disseminate, use, and monitor the processes. It may require that you provide office space, desks, and computers for these people. It may require that you publish guides and process flows, and perhaps create training materials for the various teams who will use the processes. Providing adequate resources gives life to the process program.

4. Monitor, control, and measure the processes

What makes quality programs (and the standards they spring from) effective is management's insistence that they not remain still, that they don't stagnate. The idea of continuous quality improvement therefore is woven throughout ISO 9001. No single process program starts out in perfect form. And no process program will probably ever evolve into a perfect methodology. But when a program is implemented in such a way that it is regularly monitored, its efficiencies observed, and its effectiveness measured, management then has the means to refine the program, to make it more effective, to make it more efficient, to make it better able to meet the goals of the organization.

Measurement is the key to this kind of real improvement. Measurement provides data—hard numbers—that can be used to make decisions with quantitative support. Often, organizations make decisions on how business processes are governed or on how process activities are undertaken based on instinct, gut feel, intuition. Such moves may turn out to be effective, but that is not really the best way to chart a course. Data is a much more precise way to understand, shape, and direct. It's the foundation for intelligent, fact-based decision-making.

5. Improve continuously based on the results

The final directive built into the structure of ISO 9001 is to use the measurements and data that come from regular monitoring of the quality program to make improvements in the program. This captures what is essential to the success of any quality program: the commitment to long-term adoption. Implementing a quality program should never be viewed as a quick fix.* Quality programs require time to become institutionalized, to saturate an organization's culture, to become refined, and for their benefits to become recognized.

For this reason, the ISO Standard provides requirements and recommendations that promote continuous measurement, analysis, and actions, all aimed toward improvement.

These five traits make up the core focus of ISO 9001:2000. The requirements, structural elements, and recommendations contained in the Standard are all designed to promote these traits and, in doing so, promote effectiveness and, in the end, tangible results.

ISO 9001 Ownership

In Chapter 6, you'll learn that the Capability Maturity Model, developed by the Software Engineering Institute (Pittsburgh), is a public-domain quality model. Because the SEI is a federally funded research and development center, the products it releases, including CMMI, are all in the public domain. Anyone can take the text of the spec and copy it,

---

* However, I'll be the first to admit that many organizations adopt ISO 9001, CMMI, and Six Sigma hoping that they will provide quick fixes. These organizations are usually in a jam and are looking for a fast way out.

distribute it, and give it away. Laura Allen could set up a booth in downtown Smithtown and hand it out freely to passersby.

In Chapter 7 of this book, you'll see that Six Sigma is even less controlled. It's not governed or maintained by any independent or third-party organization. It's as close to an open source quality program as they come. It is as free as algebra, and only a little more regulated. Six Sigma practices and methodologies are disseminated by a common user community. They are not owned by anyone.

ISO 9001:2000 is a different matter. Look inside the front cover of the official 9001:2000 tome, and you'll see this familiar statement:

> All ISO publications are protected by copyright. Therefore and unless otherwise specified, no part of an ISO publication may be reproduced or utilized in any form or by any means, electronic or mechanical, including photocopying, microfilm, scanning, without permission in writing from the publisher.

The Standard, funded by the member nations of ISO and created by technical teams made up of those members, remains the property of the organization, protected by international copyright. If you wish to implement a fully compliant ISO 9001:2000 program, especially if you have a view toward eventually becoming ISO-registered, you should certainly acquire an official copy of the spec from the ISO. There are many "interpretations" of the Standard available in the marketplace. They do a good job of explaining ways and methods of implementing ISO 9001, but they are prohibited from printing the exact wording found in the Standard. So to make sure you understand exactly what 9001 is asking of you and your organization, it's wise to acquire the official text.

The Structure and Design of ISO 9001:2000

ISO 9001:2000 is designed as a *generic* quality management standard. It can be used by just about any manufacturing organization to control the production of its components in such a way as to ensure control, visibility, and adjustability in meeting preset quality objectives. There are distinct advantages to implementing a 9001 program, but the degree to which you are bound by the design and structure of the program depends upon one factor: whether you wish your organization to become ISO-registered.

ISO registration is the process of having your 9001 Quality System audited and then having compliance rated against the Standard. If you pass the audit, your organization can register this result (active for a period of three years) with the ISO. You are then recognized as operating in a way that satisfies the performance criteria in the Standard. ISO registration is seen as a mark of distinction, as a competitive advantage, and as a required entry into certain market segments. But registration is not a required activity for all those who adopt ISO 9001. 9001 can deliver its benefits to an organization without that organization needing to move through the registration process.

With this objective removed, an organization is free to use any or all parts of 9001, in full or partial implementation, in such a way as to improve the areas it wishes to improve. This approach—implementation without third-party recognition—probably represents the best approach to process improvement. (And as we saw in Part 1, this is probably the best approach no matter which standard you select.) Using this approach, the organization takes on the commitment to get better, not to get applauded. And so a software development group, a washing machine factory, and a landscaping company might all adopt ISO 9001. They would use the same specification, but out of it would be born three distinct programs. However, to implement it in its intended spirit, all three would be bound by the standard's structure. Basically, there are three stipulations the Standard makes of its implementers.

Shall Statements

The first is to recognize the word "shall" as a requirement of the Standard. You'll find many such "shall" statements throughout ISO 9001: "The organization shall maintain control over nonconforming product." "Management shall establish and maintain a quality manual." And so on. There is a lot of flexibility and room for interpretation in the Standard, but if you want to be in compliance, you must (you *shall*) do what each shall statement defines. These are required components of ISO 9001.

Required Records

The next structural component is the collection and maintenance of required records. As you implement ISO 9001, you'll no doubt encounter many opportunities to record activity, events, data, and other artifacts. But there is a core set of records that you are required to keep. All in all, there are about 23 required records defined in the Standard. For example, you are required to keep an updated Quality Manual (that's considered a record). You are required to keep records of what you did with defective products. You are required to keep records of management reviews. And so on. You are free to format and shape these records according to the needs of the organization, but they must appear in some form or another and meet their defined intentions.

Common Structure

All organizations implementing ISO 9001 will create a Quality Management System that is, by and large, composed of four major sections. These sections may be integrated or segmented in any manner best suited to the organization. But they will need to demonstrate some degree of traceability back to the Standard's specifications. This common structure is briefly described here and then expanded in later sections of this chapter.

The Quality Management System is a collection of policies, procedures, and processes used to manage selected work in the organization. The QMS will be realized in some external form, such as a Quality Manual. This manual will include requirements on how the organization will control the use and retention of documents impacting project work activities, and how it will control the use and retention of records concerning project work activities.

The Quality Management System will also contain procedures to define management responsibilities for the system's use and upkeep. This includes establishing a high-level management commitment to the QMS and ensuring that the system is focused on customer satisfaction. This is typically achieved through the use of a Quality Policy. Management responsibility will also include establishing the quality objectives the QMS should address and then planning the QMS so as to meet those objectives. Management is also responsible for assigning appropriate stakeholders to maintain, manage, and use the QMS, and to provide open communication channels among those stakeholders. Finally, management is responsible for periodically reviewing facets of the QMS (inputs and outputs) to ensure the system is operating efficiently and effectively, and in line with the established quality objectives.

The next common element of an ISO 9001 quality program is resource management. Each program will identify how it will provide material and technical resources to support program operation. It will also identify how it will provide qualified human resources to execute program operations.

All ISO 9001 programs will also contain definitions and processes for managing the activities involved in product realization—creating the components or products asked for by its customer. This will include definitions for planning product realization, for determining requirements related to the product, and for establishing customer communications. It will also contain processes and procedures for planning design and development, the inputs and outputs required for each, and the adequate reviews and approvals of production milestones. Product realization will also define how activities around purchasing will be managed, how production and service provisioning will be carried out, and how the measuring and monitoring devices in the production process will be controlled.

Lastly, all ISO 9001 quality programs will contain management procedures for measuring the effectiveness of the quality program, analyzing these measures for meaning, and then improving the program based on these analyses. The program will include mechanisms to measure customer satisfaction, process effectiveness and efficiency, and product quality, and to define how the organization will deal with nonconforming products. This part of the program will also describe methods for acting on this information: ways to remove causes of defects in the production process and ways to prevent defect potentials from entering the production process.

That's a brief look at the design and structure of the ISO 9001:2000 Standard. Now let's begin to move deeper by looking at the first three sections of the specification.

ISO 9000: Sections 1 Through 3

The ISO 9001:2000 Standard is organized (roughly) into two basic parts. Sections 1 through 3 provide introductory and overview material. Sections 4 through 8 provide the requirements for the makeup, management, use, and maintenance of the quality management system. Sections 4 through 8 of the manual are discussed in some detail in this chapter, but before I look at these sections, I'll touch briefly on Sections 1 through 3, as they set the stage for the intention of the Standard and its particular audiences.

Section 1. Scope

Section 1 of ISO 9001 defines the scope of the Standard. Basically, it defines in two subsections the intended audience for the Standard—that is, the types of organizations it is designed for and how it might be used by them.

1.1. General (documents the specification as an official standard)

This section begins by specifying that the document represents an international standard for quality management systems. This is an ISO organizational requirement, a seal of authenticity. All official ISO Standards carry two common marks. The first is the registered ISO logo. This shows that the document has been officially released by the International Organization for Standardization. The second is the statement that the document is an international standard. The ISO releases many documents over the course of a year: reports, analyses, study results. But not all are to be taken as official standards. The "international standard" statement confirms the nature of the document. These two marks — the logo and the statement—appear on all 1,400+ standards that the ISO maintains.

This section then looks to the intended purpose of ISO 9001:2000. It states that ISO 9001 is intended to be used as an aid for organizations that have one (or both) of two objectives in mind. First, the standard is designed for organizations that want to demonstrate in an objective and broadly recognized manner that they have the ability to perform in a way that consistently meets customer and/or applicable regulatory requirements. Second, it's intended to help organizations that want to enhance customer satisfaction through the use of a formalized model, one that is based on consistent and repeatable processes and that has at its foundation the philosophy of continual improvement.

So, in essence, use of ISO 9001 can be applied to organizations operating toward three subobjectives (as shown in Figure 5-1):

- A focus on meeting customer requirements
- A focus on management through process
- A focus on continuous process improvement

1.2. Application (defines the Standard as "generic"; applicable to many industries)

The audience descriptions found in Section 1.1 are extended here in 1.2. This section is titled Application. Application has to do with the applicability of the requirements found in the 9001 Standard. The requirements contained here are defined as being "generic"— that is, they are not industry specific. They can be applied to all types of organizations, regardless of size, structure, or industry focus.

This is an important trait of ISO 9001. It can be used just as well at a shoestring factory as at the Jet Propulsion Laboratory. The requirements are articulated in such a way that they can be applied to just about any manufacturing, production, or service provisioning activity. *How* you apply them will depend on the needs and operational characteristics of your organization.

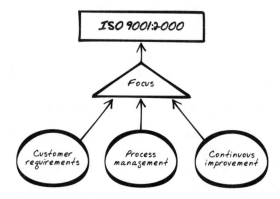

FIGURE 5-1. ISO 9001:2000 is focused on establishing mechanisms to meet customer requirements, to manage this through the definition and use of processes, and to work to always better meet the requirements by continuously improving processes.

With this in mind, this section also allows an exclusion. It states that where a certain requirement proves to be irrelevant or impractical for a certain organization or for a certain product it produces, the requirement may be omitted. However, you should take a certain amount of care with the generosity of this exclusion. Such omissions are limited only to the requirements stipulated in Section 7 of the Standard (Product and Service Provision; see page 169). These requirements impact how your particular production process is managed, monitored, and controlled.

What may not be excluded are the requirements in the other sections of the Standard. These requirements are in place to ensure that the organization establishes a formal focus on meeting customer and regulatory requirements, on establishing a formalized process-based quality program to meet its quality objectives, and on making a commitment to continually improving the program.

These core activities of ISO 9000 are essential to its nature. Without them, the intention and benefits of the Standard become severely compromised, and so, in the spirit of compliance, they should not be omitted.

Section 2. Normative Reference (the Latest Issue of This Standard Can Be Used As a Legal Reference)

This section provides a dose of legalistic *caveat emptor*. Because ISO 9001 is an official international standard, parties can enter into legal agreements based on the requirements and definitions of the Standard, and these requirements and definitions can be expected to be held up as "superlatives" should any disagreement or dispute arise between the parties. That is, in fact, one of the strengths that using an ISO Standard provides. It is globally recognized as a common benchmark.

But Standards and their requirements and definitions can, and do, change over time. This section therefore also reminds us of that. The intention here is to encourage parties adopting, referencing, or using the 9001 Standard to make sure the material they have acquired represents the latest version available and that all parties have settled on this most recent version.

Section 3. Terms and Conditions (Some Modification of Terms from Previous Versions)

This section provides some basic update and addendum data on the use of certain terms and definitions that appear throughout ISO 9001. Basically this section endorses the definitions contained in the glossary of the ISO 9000 family of standards (9001, 9002, 9003). Inclusion of this glossary is out of the scope of this review, but the same glossary is brought forward in the 9001 document, with the exception of three definitions.

The term *customer* has been refined to place more emphasis on the independent nature of the party (whether internal or external). The customer has one or more of the following traits: it's the person or party that pays you to perform the work, it's the person or party to whom you have a contractual relationship, or it's the person or party to whom you are required to deliver the product.

Another change comes with the term *supplier*. This has been updated to *organization*. In the 9000 Standard, *supplier* was used to indicate the entity managing the ISO quality system or seeking ISO registration. But that term was deemed to be somewhat imprecise, not taking into account terms used to identify subcontractors and supplying vendors. *Organization* was selected as being clearer.

And so the term *sub-contractor* was elevated to *supplier*. *Supplier* now indicates a subcontractor, consultant, or vendor from which the organization obtains goods or services.

Section 4. Quality Management System

The heart of the ISO 9001:2000 Standard begins with Section 4. From Section 4 through Section 8, the Quality Management System is described in detail.

In the view of the ISO, what is a quality management system? It's a series of components, logically linked, that when taken together give an organization the controls and measures it needs to manage and improve how it produces product. As you'll see with the descriptions of CMMI and Six Sigma, the Quality Management System (QMS) of ISO is a self-contained process improvement program.

Section 4 is divided into two parts and is used to establish the structural criteria for the QMS.

4.1. General

This section, as its label suggests, provides a series of general requirements that your QMS should possess. You'll see in later sections that this structure holds up throughout. All the sections are based on these criteria. Basically your QMS should support six elements:

1. Your QMS should identify the processes that your program will use. This is an explicit requirement. Often, organizations will rely on implied processes. They may see no

need to define how they conduct daily business; they might think they know it so well that habit is enough, that they need no such reference. But with ISO—and this is true of most all process programs—the way of doing business needs to be documented. It needs to be externalized. If process is only implied, the organization has no choice but to leave it up to the individual to honor it; it's internalized. And if it's internalized, it becomes close to impossible to manage, measure, or improve. So the first recommendation in the standard is to explicitly identify your processes. Write them down, document them, describe them.

2. Your QMS should describe the sequence and interaction of the processes. This is an important characteristic of any process program. In the most concrete of processes— say, the gearing of a grandfather clock—the reason becomes clear. The gears, levers, and springs are arranged in a precise order. When one part is set into motion, the other parts move in harmony. And the clock keeps accurate time. The same is true with a systems or software process program. The elements are interrelated. They have the potential to affect one another. Some should occur before others, others after. So in addition to defining the individual processes, it's helpful to understand—and to document—their logical sequences and interactions.

3. The Standard requires that you ensure adequate resources are available to manage the system. It may seem surprising, but this is an often overlooked factor. Many times people work hard to define and create a quality management system and then forget that it takes people to run it. However well you define your program, you should realize that it will take resources—perhaps full-time, perhaps part-time—to execute it. And these resources will need the appropriate level of support and infrastructure to successfully carry out their duties.

These first three requirements describe how to structure your program. The next three describe what to put into place so that you may gradually grow and improve your program.

4. You must provide mechanisms to monitor and measure the performance of the processes. This is integral to all process improvement efforts. It shows up in CMMI, and it shows up in Six Sigma. In order to get better at what you do, you need to know your starting point. No beginning Quality Management System is going to perfectly solve every issue thrown its way. Processes, like people and organizations, need to mature over time. If you monitor and measure the performance of your processes, then over time, you'll begin to gather enough data to show you how well they are working. More important, they will show you where things are not working so well, and this will help you pinpoint areas for improvement.

This may be the single most neglected aspect of process improvement. It's nice to think that once the design work is done and a process program is in place, you can just leave it alone to do its thing. But like any tool used in the organization, your QMS should be regularly monitored to ensure that it's doing its job even as the organization itself matures and evolves.

5. The Standard requires that your QMS contain criteria used to judge how effective the process interactions are. This is really an extension of point 4. The idea is to monitor and measure not just the individual processes you have designed, but to define criteria that you can use to weigh whether or not the interactions between the processes are working. You may have a series of successful processes in place—a collection of finely minted gears—but if they don't fit together well (if the interfaces have gaps), the program as a whole may not live up to its promise. So you should define the criteria to measure the interactions. The criteria you select are up to you, and naturally depend on the types of processes you implement and the type of work your organization is engaged in.

6. You should examine the results of points 4 and 5—measuring your processes and their interactions—and then improve the Quality Management System based on these analyses. Improvement is one of the chief goals of any QMS. The idea is that you should see better quality as your QMS gets better. But changes to your QMS should be regulated. They should not be willy-nilly. You don't want the system to exist in a constant state of flux; people wouldn't be able to get used to it. You also don't want it frozen in time; it wouldn't be able to move with your organization. A better approach is to make changes to the QMS at regular intervals and based on tangible facts: the results of your measures. Gut instinct and intuition are valuable commodities, but these are best balanced by hard data when tinkering with what is basically the holding tank for your business systems.

These six elements describe the requirements for a sound Quality Management System (illustrated in Figure 5-2). Looking further now, a QMS is naturally composed of many parts. There are policies, procedures, processes, forms, artifacts, and so on. For the system to be effective, manageable, and measurable, it needs to be documented.

The next part of Section 4 describes the documentation requirements for the QMS.

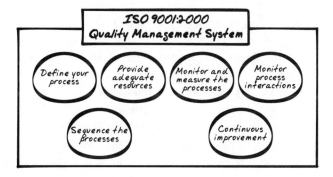

FIGURE 5-2. The Quality Management System should possess six general characteristics: processes are defined, processes are sequenced, adequate resources are appointed to manage the processes, process performance is monitored, process interactions are monitored, and processes are continuously improved.

4.2. Documentation Requirements

ISO 9001 takes documentation seriously. (You'll find that CMMI and Six Sigma take it seriously, too.) Section 4.2 describes the physical manner in which Section 4.1 can be realized. It's organized into four parts: a general description of the kinds of documentation you should have, a requirement for the management of your program's Quality Manual, requirements to control your various quality documents, and requirements for controlling the records that emerge from using the quality system. Let's take a brief look at each section.

4.2.1. General

This section provides general requirements for the kinds of documentation needed to support your program. Basically you'll need to create four categories of documents.

The first is a document that defines your organization's quality objectives.* This is a critical component of your quality program. It may be the single most critical element.†

Your quality objectives will shape the focus and structure of your full program. The objectives should be carefully thought out. Because they are of strategic importance, they are usually developed by senior management. The objectives represent the quality goals you are aiming for. They can be expected to change over time, but to create the initial program, some of the main ones need to be understood and defined in advance. Naturally these will be defined based on the type of technology business you are in, the current structure of your organization, its market imperatives, and the internal characteristics of your production processes. This document need not be extensive; it need not establish a mission to solve every issue you might be facing. But it does need to be focused on key goals, and it needs to spell your objectives out in concrete terms, terms that can be tangibly targeted and implemented.

The second requirement is to document a Quality Policy. This is a logical extension of the documented quality objectives. In fact, the policy is a document that will normally contain the objectives. It is an executive tool that sets the tone for the organization's quality program. It demonstrates executive commitment to the quality program. Again, this document is typically authored by executive management. A policy might, for example, be created to focus energies on on-time delivery, on schedule management, and on customer communications. These are all good objectives around which one can build a quality program. Once it is in final form, ready for approval, the policy should be signed: this is a sign of visible backing by management. And once signed, you should ensure that it is made readily available to all members of the organization. From time to time, as your program grows or your organization evolves, it is a good idea to revisit the policy to keep it current.

---

* I describe each of these documents as if they are standalone units. You can create them in that way if you'd like, but you can also combine these into consolidated documents. Select whatever approach you think is best and easiest to maintain for your organization.

† For more information on the importance of quality objectives, see Chapter 3.

The third requirement is to create your organization's Quality Manual. This is the document everyone usually thinks of as the ISO 9001:2000 program. It contains the full set of processes and procedures and interactions you build to satisfy the ISO requirements described in Section 5, 6, 7, and 8 of the Standard. This may be one manual or it may be a collection. One group may own it, or it may be shared across many groups. However you structure it, it represents the heart of your Quality Management System. Most of the rest of this chapter describes what components should go into this manual.

The fourth requirement is to document the records required by the Standard. In ISO 9001, you are required to keep 21 types of records. These records become the artifacts you'll collect for three purposes: to provide evidence that the program is being implemented, to help move processes and procedures along their integrated paths, and to provide material for measuring the effectiveness of your program. You should probably consider creating these records as blank forms or templates that can be used across the program and across different groups. These records are described in their respective sections later in this chapter.

4.2.2. Quality Manual

The previous section described what types of documents you'll need to support your QMS. Section 4.2.2 is specific to the Quality Manual.

The requirement here is to establish and maintain the Quality Manual.

The phrase *establish and maintain* is important to understand. It is a common process improvement term that implies three things. The first is clear: the system needs to be documented. By being documented, the program it contains can be made available to everyone in the organization who needs it. In addition to this, it needs to be maintained. This requires two other things. The manual needs an owner: someone or some group in the organization charged with maintaining its integrity. And maintaining the integrity means that it needs to be updated as your quality program changes over time. The two need to be kept in sync.

4.2.3. Control of documents

This section is related to Section 4.2.2. Your Quality Manual may include a number of documents, or it may reference other documents. To ensure the ongoing integrity of all the documents that impact your QMS, you should set into place proper versioning and access controls.

As mentioned above, the Quality Manual should be under the care of an owning group in your organization. This ownership carries with it certain access privileges. With any evolving quality program, change is to be expected. However, change needs to be controlled. You will not want just anyone in the organization to have the ability to make modifications to your QMS or to the Quality Manual. And so you will want to govern the ability to make changes to the manual or to any documents related to the manual. In addition to this, the owning group should have some form of version control in place, a system to mark or number releases of documents so people can reference the latest, most current versions. By implementing this requirement, the organization adds a protective layer of quality control over its Quality Management System.

4.2.4. Control of records

Just as you need to protect the integrity of the components of your quality program, you also need to protect the records that emerge from the regular use of the program. These records are important to the organization. They help demonstrate compliance with the Standard. They help move processes through their defined stages. And they provide useful measurement material. For these reasons, it's important to gather and store the records in a place that is secured and safe from accidental loss or corruption. As an example, for paper records, this may mean making copies and storing them in a fire safe or an off-site storage warehouse. For electronic records, this may mean making regular backups, archiving data to a safe media, and then storing this media in a safe place.

Required Records

To ensure that you have met the requirements of Section 4 of ISO 9001, one record is required: the Quality Manual. If you choose at some time to be officially audited, the ISO auditor will look for this manual as confirmation of Section 4 compliance. As noted earlier, this manual may be one large document, or it may be a collection of documents.

The required records for Section 4 include the Quality Manual.

Section 5. Management Responsibility

Section 5 of the ISO 9001:2000 Standard describes management's responsibility in establishing and maintaining the organization's Quality Management System.

The requirements here are not extensive or demanding, but they are of special importance.

ISO 9001 places particular emphasis on the participation of management in the quality program. In some organizations (and we've probably all seen this), management may have the inclination to vouch audibly for process improvement and quality management, but when it's time for the rubber to hit the road, the work is delegated somewhere downstream, out of management's sight. But with ISO 9001, benign acquiescence is not the way.

Management is required to work as a key partner in the program's use, evolution, and ultimate success. In fact, this involvement is a big part of the 9001 audit process. Management must demonstrate its close involvement with the program.

To support this, Section 5 is organized into six requirements: management commitment, customer focus, Quality Policy, planning, accounting for responsibility and communications, and management review.

Next is a brief description of each.

QUALITY MANAGEMENT SYSTEM

Establishing your Quality Management System requires a series of initial steps that will later govern the shape of your quality program. These activities include:

- Identifying the processes the program will encompass

- Defining the sequence and interaction of the processes

- Planning adequate resources to run the program

- Defining how to monitor and measure the performance of the processes

- Establishing criteria used to judge how effective the process interactions are

- Defining strategies to improve the Quality Management System based on performance measures

Once the above are in place, you can document the quality program through the design of the following types of program components:

- Quality objectives

- Organizational Quality Policy

- Quality Manual

- Procedures to establish and maintain the Quality Manual

- Procedures to allow proper versioning and access controls

- Methods to document emerging quality records

- Methods to gather and store the quality records

5.1. Management Commitment

The main requirement in this section is for management to demonstrate its commitment to the Quality Management System.

The term *management* here implies full management, from the executive level down to line management. And the word "commitment" means full and real commitment. Commitment with a capital C.

This breadth of commitment is essential to any quality program. In fact, it's essential to *any* program within a company. Employees tend to be a sharp, observant group of people. If they perceive that management lacks the interest to see an initiative through, they will quickly conclude that it's OK to skirt it themselves. Recognizing this, the 9001 Standard defines five requirements necessary to demonstrate and maintain quality-program commitment across the life of your program.

The first is to establish quality objectives. This was described in Section 4, but here the responsibility is laid at the feet of management. It is up to management to define what the QMS will be designed to accomplish, what its focus will be, how it will be directed. This is an important activity. From this, the full QMS will eventually emerge. This should not be a harried activity, nor rushed. It should be carefully thought out. And it should not be conducted in isolation. It may be management's responsibility to define QMS objectives, but management should do so with plenty of input from as many voices across as many levels of the organization as are practical. This will help ensure that the objectives address the true needs of the company.

The second requirement is to establish the Quality Policy. This policy, being a tangible document, represents the visible flag of management commitment. There are a few points to note about the Quality Policy. At its heart, the policy should reflect the quality objectives that management has established for the organization. These should be clearly but concisely described in the document. In fact, "concise" is a good word to apply to any policy. Policies are not programs or processes, which may require a great deal of description. Policies direct people to programs and processes. The best policies are precise. They are short and to the point. Your 9001 Quality Policy might be a couple of pages long. The best policies I have seen, and those that I have helped shape, have been a single page. Above all, the policy should be signed—with confidence—by management, the higher the positions the better. This is the cap on the visible flag of commitment.

The third requirement is for management to communicate the importance of the QMS to the organization. This is typically done through broad dissemination of the Quality Policy. The policy might be emailed to all employees. It might be tacked on bulletin boards around the company. It might be formally discussed at staff meetings. This communication can also take other forms: team meetings, newsletter communiqués, annual report statements, and so on. The central idea here is to let the whole organization know that the QMS is a core ingredient to the way business is conducted by the company, that this system is viewed as critical to corporate success, and that management wants this way to be commonly understood across the organization.

The fourth requirement is to ensure that adequate resources have been assigned to implement and run the QMS. Quality programs don't run themselves. It takes people to make a program work, and one of the chief reasons quality programs fall short is because the right people are not in place to take care of them. With the 9001 Standard, management is required to fortify the program by adequately staffing for its use.

The fifth requirement is to conduct management reviews of the program on a periodic basis. A guiding philosophy behind ISO 9001:2000 is that adoption of the program represents a strategic move on the part of senior management, a move that shifts the culture of the organization to one with a distinct process focus. That being the case, management should not leave the success of the program solely in the hands of those down-line of the executive chain. Management must monitor and review the effectiveness of the QMS on a regular basis. This can be done several ways: through group discussions, through project reports, through off-site meetings. The regularity of such evaluations is up to management. It might be quarterly, it might be at the close of each major project, it might be linked to other management evaluations. However conducted, the point is the same: management takes an active and ongoing role in evaluating the effectiveness of the QMS and guiding its evolution.

Figure 5-3 illustrates the five domains of management responsibility.

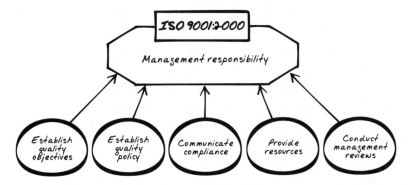

FIGURE 5-3. Management responsibility under ISO 9001 falls into five domains. The first is to establish quality objectives for the organization. Second is to establish the organizational Quality Policy. Third is to communicate the importance of the policy and the program. Fourth is to provide adequate resources. And fifth is to conduct periodic management reviews of the program.

5.2. Customer Focus

You'll see later in the discussion of Six Sigma that one of its major directives is to find and listen to the "voice of the customer." With the 9001:2000 revision of the ISO Standard, the place of the customer has taken on a similar and heightened prominence. Section 5.2 requires that the QMS be shaped specifically to help meet customer requirements, thus better ensuring customer satisfaction.*

This is a relatively new emphasis in the realm of process improvement. Many organizations shape their process programs from a strictly internal view. How can we streamline X to reduce waste? How can we improve Y to speed up delivery? How can we manage Z to add more features?

All of those may be good ideas, but they may have little to do with customer satisfaction. Your customers may not care about waste reduction, faster delivery, or added features.

---

* The "customer" here can be anyone: an internal organization, an external client. The basic definition of a customer is the party paying you and your people (in whatever currency) to perform work or produce a product.

The point of Section 5.2 is that you should shape your program, first of all, to help fulfill the requirements of your customer.

If the requirements are fulfilled, your customer should be content, and that contentment should translate (in their minds at least) to quality. That should then contribute to business success for your enterprise.

5.3. Quality Policy

A key component of management's commitment to its QMS is to produce the Quality Policy. I discussed some of the characteristics of a Quality Policy in Section 5.1. In Section 5.3, the Standard sets forth four requirements that the ISO expects to see in a sound policy.

The first requirement is that the policy reflect the mission of the organization. This mission statement is important. It helps ensure that management is able to articulate its mission precisely. Surprisingly, many management teams find this difficult to do. They may have a feeling about it. They may think it's obvious enough. But when it comes to putting the mission into words, they struggle. This requirement also links the quality program to the mission and encourages management to articulate that in real terms.

The second requirement is for the policy to reflect the organization's defined quality objectives. Defining these objectives is a crucial management activity. The objectives shape the form and tenor of the quality program. They point it in the direction it will set sail. The Quality Policy is a natural home for these objectives, as evidenced by the next requirement.

The third requirement is to communicate the policy to the organization. Since the policy holds the quality vision of the organization, this document needs to be shared throughout the organization. This communication helps saturate the vision. It will also aid in its consistent implementation throughout the organization. You'll find that the idea of communication is one broadly implemented throughout the 9001 Standard. Effective communication—sharing, evaluating, and using information—is a key to effective teamwork. Since the Quality Policy gives the team its charter, this first-tier document should be shared with everyone.

The fourth requirement is that the Quality Policy be maintained and reviewed for relevance. You'll find that your quality program will grow and evolve over time. Your business will undoubtedly grow and evolve over time. For these reasons, your Quality Policy must be kept up-to-date with the mission of the company. From time to time, your management team should review the policy, make sure it reflects current quality objectives, and (if needed) revise the policy and then redisseminate it within the organization.

5.4. Planning

Planning under ISO 9001 is another key management responsibility. In fact, in all quality programs or process management systems, planning is always an important consideration. In Section 5, management is required to assume planning responsibility in two areas: planning (defining) the organization's quality objectives and planning the overall Quality Management System. Let's take a quick look at each of these requirements.

5.4.1. Quality objectives

You've seen earlier that one of the first steps in creating a Quality Management System is to define the objectives of the system—that is, what the system is designed to accomplish.

This requirement promotes management to establish relevant quality objectives.

The term *quality objectives* may seem a little broad. And it's admittedly easy to move down two obscure paths with this requirement. The first is for management to adopt broad-stroke objectives. Here are a couple of examples: "Become the nation's leading provider of Sales and Tax Management software" or "Produce products that are renowned for their quality performance." Those may be good objectives in and of themselves, but they are at such a high level that they beg for clarification. The second path is at the other end of the spectrum. The objectives are far too detailed or numerous, vivisected to the point where you can't see how they tie into a cohesive picture.

The word "relevant" helps with this requirement. Management is responsible for defining relevant quality objectives. These should be goals that the organization can use to devise plans of action, to establish routes that can move teams to their quality targets. As with all plans and policies, management should review the quality objectives from time to time to ensure they remain in sync with the organization's evolution.

5.4.2. Plan the QMS

You've seen earlier, in Section 4, that ISO 9001 requires the development of a Quality Management System. Here, the Standard makes the creation, planning, and maintenance of the QMS a specific management responsibility. This requirement emphasizes the importance of the QMS. By assigning it to management, the implication is made that the QMS is an integral component of the organization's overall business strategy. It is not a side project, nor a low-level initiative.

This does not mean that the Quality Management System should be planned or executed without the input of your working teams. Just the opposite is true. As much as practical, the whole organization should become involved in the molding and shaping of the program. This will help ensure a secure cultural fit. But management should handle the production reins. It should not delegate QMS development ownership out of its domain. Management remains the party responsible for making sure the system is created, published, disseminated, used, and maintained within the organization.

5.5. Responsibility, Authority, and Communication

This section of the standard establishes accountability for the QMS. In other words, management is required to create the right infrastructure to support the implementation of the system.

Many organizations have created quality programs without accounting for this infrastructure. As a result, many fine programs are today sitting on shelves somewhere collecting dust. The concept of responsibility, authority, and communication is crucial to the successful rollout and implementation of any quality program. To support this, the ISO Standard specifies three requirements:

1. Stakeholders are identified.

2. Management representatives are designated.

3. Communication channels are established.

Let's briefly look at these three.

5.5.1. Identify stakeholders

All Quality Management Systems have stakeholders.

A stakeholder is usually defined as a person who will take an active role in the execution of the quality system or who is significantly impacted by its use. This may be a person who owns a process, whose activities influence a process, or who must interact with a process or collection of processes.

Identifying these stakeholders is important for two reasons. First, it lets the relevant people know their roles in using and managing the QMS. Second, it helps establish the basis for defining the resources needed to adequately run the system.

5.5.2. Appoint management representatives

The stakeholders identified in the previous section will typically use the QMS on a day-to-day basis. But the stakeholders need the presence of management to maximize the productive use of the system. Should issues arise, or questions concerning system use surface, the stakeholders need to know who they can turn to for resolutions. And so management needs to appoint representatives who are—perhaps as part of their other duties—responsible for the operation of the system within the organization.

The management representatives and identified stakeholders should work as a team to propagate the QMS throughout the organization in a coordinated manner.

5.5.3. Establish communication channels

In the two previous sections, the ISO Standard defines the two parties that will manage the Quality Management System: stakeholders and management representatives. Here in Section 5.5.3, the Standard requires that management establish channels of communication between these parties.

These communication channels are defined to allow stakeholders to bring to management's attention ideas and issues related to the use of the QMS. They are also defined to describe how management can communicate changes, revisions, or addenda concerning the QMS to the stakeholders. As with any effective communications plan, rigidity is best avoided. The more effective path is to set into place a two-way street, with open access and encouraged participation.

5.6. Management Review

The core idea behind Section 5 of ISO 9001 is that management take ultimate responsibility for the system's use, maintenance, and effectiveness.

Section 5.6 describes requirements for ensuring that management's relation to the system remains active. This is done by management periodically reviewing the effectiveness of the QMS within the organization.

Three requirements are set into place for this:

1. Management conducts the periodic reviews.
2. Management reviews data on how the system is working and how it might be improved.
3. Management reviews any outputs from actions taken based on the reviews.

These are described next.

5.6.1. General

The first requirement is for management to review the QMS at regular intervals.

The spacing of those intervals depends on a few things. The size of your QMS, its reach within the organization, and its current level of maturity can all dictate how often management meets to review it. Perhaps with new and unfolding programs, management might meet quarterly. With large, well-established programs, it might be necessary to meet only annually. You will find that you are the best judge of this when it comes to your own program.

5.6.2. Review input

Management's responsibility to meet and review the effectiveness of the Quality Management System is defined in Sections 5.6.2 and 5.6.3. In 5.6.2, the Standard requires that management's review of the QMS be based on actual data, not merely on an internal agenda from the group. This data is termed input, and as ISO 9001 is used over time, plenty of input should accumulate. There are many sources of this input.

One source could be the results of audits conducted for the program. As a project moves through the quality management process, there are preset milestones at which audits are conducted to make sure compliance is being honored.

Another source could be customer feedback. I mentioned earlier that ISO 9001 places particular emphasis on customer satisfaction. In line with this, the Standard promotes seeking feedback from the customer as often as possible. This feedback can be a valuable source for improving the QMS.

Another source might be process performance measures. ISO 9001 specifies in Section 8 of the Standard that the organization regularly monitor and measure the performance of its processes. The results of these measures can provide insight into improving the QMS. The status of corrective actions is another good source of review data, as are follow-up actions on any current issues.

Reviews of all these sources of data—all this input—can provide objective and tangible information that can be used to improve the QMS.

5.6.3. Review output

By reviewing the input described in the previous section, management should be able to take concrete action to better shape the QMS to the needs of the organization. These actions should be set into place, and the results of these actions—the output—should also be reviewed by management as part of its ownership of the system.

In this regard, management should look at two areas. The first is to look at improvement measures that have been taken. If the program is in any way reshaped or the processes re-engineered, it's a good practice to review how well the changes are working for the organization. Another view is just as useful: to look at the improvement of your products. That's the ultimate objective of any quality program: produce an improved product. By looking at the quality trends of your products (or their components), you can acquire a good gauge of the effectiveness of your quality system.

Required Records

Section 5 of ISO 9000 requires that the organization retain records of its management reviews. These records can be evidenced in many ways. One common form is to keep them as meeting minutes of review meetings. (Another record that usually comes from the requirements of Section 5 is the Quality Policy, but that is usually accounted for in the Quality Manual, which is the record requirement of Section 4.)

Examples:

- Notes from reviews of the QMS
- Reports from results of QMS audits
- Customer feedback
- Process performance measures
- Status of corrective actions
- Records of improvement measures
- Analyses of product improvements

MANAGEMENT RESPONSIBILITY

Section 5 of the Standard defines requirements that involve management's responsibility for the Quality Management System:

Management commitment
Management demonstrates its long–term commitment to the Quality Management System by establishing the Quality Manual, the Quality Policy, and communicating the importance of each to the organization.

Customer focus
Management designs its quality objectives and the working of its QMS to specifically address the needs of customers as expressed by customer requirements.

Quality policy
Management defines the Quality Policy to reflect the mission of the organization and to align it with established quality objectives. Management then communicates this policy to the organization at large and maintains it for ongoing relevance and currency.

Planning
Management defines the business and quality objectives the QMS should address and then actively coordinates development of the processes and procedures that make up the QMS and typically make up the Quality Manual.

Responsibility, authority, and communication
Management identifies the stakeholders of the QMS, appoints management representatives to oversee its use, and establishes communication channels to support the QMS throughout the organization.

Management review
At regular intervals, management reviews the QMS and analyzes inputs and outputs that indicate how well the system is performing for the organization.

Section 6. Resource Management

Under ISO, management is assigned the responsibility of providing adequate resources to manage and operate the Quality Management System. Section 6 defines a set of requirements dealing with resource management.

To most people, the idea of resource management involves only people—for example, identifying the stakeholders and the management representatives. But in ISO 9001 (as well as in CMMI and Six Sigma), resource management means more. It means providing people, yes, but it also means providing them with the right tools and environments they need for their jobs.

The resource requirements are described next.

6.1. Provide Resources

The first step in resource management is stated simply enough: provide resources. There are two objectives to this requirement. The first is to provide the right resources to manage the quality system—that is, adequate people, tools, and environments.

The second objective is related to the first and appears, maybe at first glance, to be a bit vague. The requirement is to provide adequate resources to help meet requirements and "make customers happy." This enhances ISO's focus on customer satisfaction.

As noted in Section 5.2, one responsibility management has is to shape the Quality Management System as a tool that increases the organization's ability to meet customer requirements. This focus is further developed here.

Customer requirements serve as the benchmark for customer satisfaction. So, the organization should structure resources so that it can understand, construct, and deliver on customer requirements. This should arise as a natural offshoot of providing resources for the QMS.

6.2. Human Resources

Assigning human resources is key to the success of any process improvement program. This is an often-neglected component. Of course, it's an accomplishment to design and build a Quality Management System. And sometimes you'll see that that effort tires out an organization. After that effort, the QMS might sit unused unless the organization backs up its plan with action.

The action is to assign people to carry the system into the organization. But the action should not be blind: it requires two motivations. These are described next.

6.2.1. General

This requirement is labeled "general," but it is actually quite specific: assign competent people.

That may seem obvious, but an organization can often be tempted to throw bodies at the QMS initiative (indeed, at *any* project). ISO 9001 promotes assigning people who are capable, backed by experience and background, and who have the ability to control, manage, and monitor the system.

6.2.2. Competence, awareness, and training

This second requirement supports Section 6.2.1. The organization should naturally assign qualified people to the QMS, but it also needs to support these people. It needs to ensure that the team responsible for the effectiveness of the QMS is competent, aware of the requirements of the system, and trained in its use. This is done three ways.

The first is to assess the skills of your team members. The skills assessment is designed to provide a basis for team strengthening, for improvement. Out of the assessment comes the second way: to fill any skills gaps by providing training. This may be training in the QMS, general process training, technical training, or a combination of these. The third way to maintain the competence of your team is to periodically evaluate the performance of the members.

The human resources requirement is illustrated in Figure 5-4.

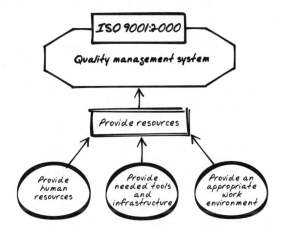

FIGURE 5-4. Under ISO 9001, resources are required to operate and manage the Quality Management System. This includes human resources, people qualified to perform their duties; the right tools and the infrastructure to carry the duties out; and a properly configured work environment.

6.3. Infrastructure

Assigning a competent team to work and maintain the Quality Management System is crucial to the program's success. To support this, the team needs the right tools to perform the tasks associated with the QMS.

This infrastructure may consist of several components. It may include the Quality Manual itself. It may include any forms, templates, or guidelines you have in place to support the QMS. It may include the computers and software your team members use. It can even include the office space you have allocated to the team.

This infrastructure requires an investment on the part of the organization. But it is necessary to ensure the QMS is backed up with the framework it needs to support its mission.

6.4. Work Environment

This section of the Standard focuses on providing the right resources to manage the quality system.

Resource requirements include hiring competent people, regularly assessing their skills, providing training as needed, and providing the team with the tools and infrastructure they need to maintain the system.

The idea here is to make sure that the work environment supports the quality objectives, that the environment does not serve as a benign or overt disruption to the QMS. This is a requirement that is reflected in management's responsibility, as described in Section 5.5. Management can keep the work environment and the QMS in harmony with one other through a variety of mechanisms, by:

- Identifying stakeholders, management assigns daily ownership of the QMS, a responsibility that should carry over should there be any environmental changes.

- Appointing management representatives to oversee the QMS, an avenue is provided for high-level support of ongoing system compliance.

- Establishing communication channels between the stakeholders and management representatives, support is further enhanced.

Of course, all organizational environments change. It's a natural part of business. Employees come and go. Policies may shift. Market trends change. Business objectives are adjusted. But these crests and troughs of business life should not be allowed to negate or overshadow the Quality Management System. It is management's responsibility to keep the two in line, each working to complement the other through an effective two-way environment.

Required Records

Section 6 of ISO 9001 requires the organization to maintain records that evidence skills of its stakeholders and management representatives, records of education (whether academic or professional) that demonstrate its people have the base knowledge to carry out their responsibilities, and records of training to evidence that its people have been appropriately trained in the scope, maintenance, and use of the Quality Management System.

Required records for Section 6:

- Records of skills
- Records of education
- Records of training

Examples:

- Résumés
- Assignments to project works
- Performance evaluations
- Employee assessments
- Continuing education records
- Professional association records

PROVIDE RESOURCES

Section 6 of the Standard requires management to assign adequate resources to manage organizational use of the Quality Management System and to ensure that customer requirements are appropriately accounted for. This is done through three categories of resources:

Human resources
Assign competent people to manage both the use and evolution of the QMS and the customer requirements, and also to periodically assess skills and job performance.

Infrastructure
Provide the team with the tools it needs to perform its various tasks.

Work environment
Manage the work environment in a way that will support the quality objectives of the organization.

Section 7. Product Realization

Section 7 of ISO 9001 can be considered the technical heart of the Standard. You can think of the three previous sections—4, 5, and 6—as preparatory.

Section 4 describes the requirements of the Quality Management System and the need for a documented Quality Manual. That's the foundation of your quality program.

Section 5 describes the responsibility of management in providing for the proper oversight, reviews, resources, and communication channels required for the program's successful deployment.

And Section 6 describes the requirements for providing the right human resources to manage the program, the right tools for the team, and the right environment for the team to work in.

With those elements in place, the organization has an infrastructure that can support the rollout and ongoing evolution of the Quality Management System.

Section 7, Product Realization, defines the core requirements regarding what the QMS (as reflected in the Quality Manual) should contain. It is your process program.

Product Realization is all about steps for creating a quality product, steps that move from planning to requirements, all the way through to production and delivery. To describe it in adequate detail, Section 7 is divided into six subsections. These subsections are:

- Product planning
- Customer-related focus
- Design and development
- Purchasing
- Product and service provisioning
- Control of monitoring and measuring devices

Let's take a brief look at each.

7.1. Planning of Product Realization

Planning is an integral part of the QMS management process. It should also be a cornerstone activity for any quality or process improvement program. Planning is a control and measurement tool. It helps you chart an intelligent course, navigate that course, and judge how well you are staying on course. When you begin a project under the requirements of ISO 9001, the first activity you undertake is to plan the project. This project plan should contain at a minimum the following elements.

Product requirements

This is an essential set of data. Before you can really begin a project, before you can even adequately plan a project, you need to know what the requirements are. You need to know what it is you are going to build. When projects begin without documented requirements (and that is not uncommon in this business), they invariably run into trouble. In the technology business, it's commonly understood that bad, soft, or missing requirements account for about half of a project's problems. But the temptation to begin the work of product realization—that is, building the product—often overpowers common sense. Speed-to-market concerns can push a team to set sail without a compass. This is a surefire way to compromise product quality. The ISO Standard emphasizes the importance of gathering and documenting accurate project requirements first. The requirements are not only a valuable planning reference, they should become a permanent part of the plan's foundation.

Required QMS processes

Any plan is a series of activities or steps you take to reach a goal. The plan then becomes the methodology for achieving the goal. And so the plan here should identify the processes and procedures in the Quality Manual that will be used on the project. Some projects may use all of the contents of the manual, particularly if they are full-life-cycle projects. Other projects—often of limited or smaller scope—may require that you use only a subset of the manual. Whichever path is indicated, the plan should clearly define just what processes and procedures will be employed.

Verification, validation, monitoring, and test activities

As you'll see in the next section (7.2), ISO 9001 places a strong emphasis on understanding, documenting, and meeting customer requirements.

To achieve this, you will need to continually assess your progress to make sure that the customer requirements are being realized in your work efforts and in the ensuing work products. The project plan should reflect this. In the plan, you should identify when verification, validation, monitoring, and testing activities will take place, and who will conduct these activities.

Verification is making sure the requirements are being built into the product properly. Validation means confirming that the end product will work well in the intended environment. Monitoring is the mechanism to make sure proper oversight is being applied to project activities. And testing is the way to confirm that development activities have resulted in appropriately built products and components.

Identify control records

Throughout its scope, ISO 9001 identifies records that are required to be created, maintained, and kept up by the product team.

Some of these records are for the purpose of managing the project. Some are for measuring and improvement purposes. But the critical ones—the ones you should identify here—are used to demonstrate that the finished product meets customer requirements.

You can think of these as traceability records. These are the records that trace how the customer requirements have been verified at key phases of the project.

Figure 5-5 illustrates the four categories required for product realization planning.

7.2. Customer-Related Focus

We've all heard the movie phrase, "If you build it, they will come." There's an assumption there: they will come because you built what they wanted built.

That's true to the spirit of ISO 9001, even though it's a little backward. (ISO wants you to first find out what they want, and then build it.)

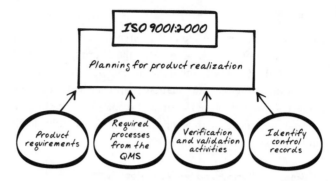

FIGURE 5-5. Planning for product realization requires that four categories of activities and components be accounted for: the customer and product requirements; the QMS processes to be applied on the project; defined verification, validation, and test activities; and the identification of control records to be used across the project.

The ISO Standard requires you to demonstrate a sharp customer-related focus. The reason behind that requirement is a sound one: quality can mean different things to different people. And so it's the job of the business to find out what its customers want, what is important to them, what they will get value from. If we are content to build just what we want (what *we* think of as quality), we may end up being the only ones who want it.

The 9001 Standard supports its focus on the customer with three requirements:

- Working with the customer to determine the right requirements
- Reviewing the requirements to make sure they are complete, consistent, and appropriate
- Maintaining regular communication with the customer to ensure expectations remain in sync over the life of the project

Let's take a look at each.

7.2.1. Determination of requirements related to the product

As a technology professional, you've probably run into this issue before: the clients think they know what they want, but they have a difficult time articulating it. The Standard addresses this by requiring you to work with your clients to document their requirements.

The first step is to document what they know they want. This should include not only what should be in what you deliver but what you may have to do after delivery to ensure the product works as planned.

Next, you should work to document the requirements not stated but known to be needed. This is where your experience comes into play. You probably know more about technology than the clients, and so you should provide insight into what supporting requirements might be needed in order to bring about the desired end result.

You should also work with the clients to document any statutory and regulatory requirements that may exist around the product. These kinds of requirements are becoming more and more common, and many specialized industries have no choice but to comply. Health care, finance, and insurance are just three industries in which technology products and services must meet strict statutory and regulatory rules.

Finally, you should work with your clients to uncover and document any additional requirements you think should be met. These additions may come from brainstorming sessions or review sessions. They may or may not materialize, but the idea is to work through the requirements to make sure that the baseline you end up with is complete enough to meet the intended goal of the project, to produce a product suitable to its anticipated use.

7.2.2. Review the requirements related to the product

The requirements definition process is one of the more amorphous activities in technology development. It rides the fence between concept and conception, and so it's common to feel somewhat ambiguous as to when you're done or not.

On top of that, a project may end up with thousands of requirements. Different people may have been responsible for collecting different requirement sets. All this can make the final product—the requirements specification—a daunting document.

For these reasons, it's important to review the completed requirements with your client prior to committing to irrevocable technical solutions. The review process should be designed to ensure that the requirements are well defined. That means several things. It means that you confirm that the requirements are complete, that no major gaps exist and no critical functionality is missing. It also means that the requirements are understood; that they are clear, concise, and testable; that they do not conflict with one another; and that they are viable.

This review will accomplish two things. First, it creates a commonality among teams. This is a common understanding between the client and the members of your technical and management teams as to the scope, purpose, and use of the requirements. The "daunting" element alluded to earlier will then have been somewhat reduced. Second, it should uncover any problems with the requirements set and give you the focus you need to resolve requirements issues.

Out of this review activity, the requirements should emerge in strong shape. The organization should then be able to confirm that the defined requirements have the ability to meet the client's needs.

7.2.3. Customer communication

Focus on the customer does not end once you understand what the customer wants. It should continue throughout the life of the project.

Staying in touch with your customer is important, because when you boil it down, all projects are partnerships. The customer has partnered with you to create something. And so it is important to maintain communication with the customer over the life of this partnership. The Standard recognizes this through three requirements.

The first is that the organization shall plan communication with the customer. For example, the project plan might contain a section on communications management, or you might even devise a separate communications plan to map out how you'll remain in touch with your customer. However you approach it, the avenue for communication should be clearly defined.

The second is that the organization shall regularly share information with the customer concerning project progress and activity. This sharing typically includes exchanges concerning budget and schedule updates, functionality and product information, contract issues as they arise (should they arise), and changes or adjustments that need to be made from time to time to the project scope or deliverables.

The third requirement is that the organization shall seek regular customer feedback. This implies an open channel of communication between the organization and the customer. This channel should support ongoing discussions, feedback as to how the organization is performing on the project. The organization, in the spirit of process and quality improvement, should also not shy away from any complaints that might come its way through this channel. All information can be used to beneficial purposes.

7.3. Design and Development

The ultimate purpose of any project is to create something. The purpose of a Quality Management System is to help you create that something in an ordered manner. There are two recognized steps in this process: defining the solution and then realizing that solution— design and development.

The ISO 9001 Standard composes the requirements for design and development in greater detail than the information in any other section. Requirements are presented for planning the design and development activities, establishing proper design inputs (such as functional requirements and regulatory requirements), generating appropriate outputs so that products can be adequately verified, reviewing designs and work products, verifying that designs and work products comply with the requirements, validating that the design and work products will function as intended, and ensuring that any changes introduced during design and development activities are properly controlled, tracked, and managed.

These subsections are described in brief.

7.3.1. Design and development planning

Design and development can (and almost always do) involve a variety of activities. To coordinate these activities effectively, they should be carefully planned. Usually this is reflected in a Project Plan, although it may exist as its own Design and Development Plan. The plan then becomes a management tool used to control design and development activities, to monitor their progress, and to provide mileposts for course confirmation and correction as needed.

Proper planning should allow for management along several lines. For example, the plan should break down design and development into a series of manageable stages. This degree of decomposition depends upon several factors, including the scope of the project, the size of the project team, and the management view wished by the customer. The key is to understand what work products will be required for both design and development and then form the stages to accommodate them.

Also, the stages you define for design and development activities can be used as quality gates during the project life cycle. They can serve as milestone points at which work products can be inspected prior to their moving along in the process. The Standard supports this approach by requiring that you plan for the review, verification, and validation of ensuing work products at defined stages.

Effective planning should also require that the organization not only describe what activities will occur and when they will occur, but also who will be responsible for making sure they occur. The plan should reflect this. In it, you should assign responsibility and authority for the design and development activities and ensure that those team members assigned are explicitly made aware of (and prepped for) their duties.

7.3.2. Design and development inputs

This subsection requires that you define and identify in the plan the specific inputs that are going to be related to the design. These are the documents or references that will be needed to produce a design that is complete and viable. These typically include things like the functional and performance requirements you have created through your work with the customer. Also included are the statutory or regulatory requirements that may be mandated by your customer's industry or by government agencies.

In addition to the requirements, you might also point to other reference materials. For example, if you have worked on successful projects in the past using similar designs, you might (with the customer's acquiescence) reference the reuse of certain of those components. You might also do the same with existing code modules for developmental work activities or for any other work products that can be applied on the project.

The goal here is to thoroughly think through the design and development activities and document what existing materials are relevant to these activities. Then you can plan for their acquisition over the life of the project. This ensures a solid degree of readiness for the team and positions the project to move forward in a focused and managed direction.

7.3.3. Design and development outputs

Just as you need to identify the inputs that are going to be used to create the design and guide development, you also need to identify what work products are going to emerge from the design and development activities.

The outputs are typically some form of work product. These products add real value because they allow the team to properly verify and approve the work prior to moving it further along the production line.

> **NOTE**
>
> As your program develops, you'll find that many of the outputs you create in the design stage may become appropriate inputs for later design or development stages.

The Standard requires that the design and development outputs share certain characteristics. The first is that the outputs can be (and are) traced back to the requirements. This is an essential trait of good design and development, and a hallmark of sound quality control. Traceability is the process of tracking each requirement as it migrates across the production life cycle. When traceability is ignored or poorly implemented, requirements can become lost, convoluted, or their operations compromised. This is true especially in large systems with many requirements, or with systems that experience ongoing change. Traceability is a method to help guard the ultimate goal of the project: that what you build ends up containing everything the customer asked for.

Next, the outputs should provide appropriate information for purchasing, production, and service provisioning. This means the outputs should be created with the understanding that they may influence what components, tools, or support materials have to be purchased to support their further development, deployment, or implementation. This information may be embedded as part of the output, or it may be attached to the output as an addendum or reference documentation.

The outputs should also provide criteria for quality acceptance. This means that the work products or components produced during design and development should be established against certain standards. These standards serve as acceptance criteria for moving the product further along the life cycle or releasing the product to the customer. These criteria will vary from one work product to another, depending on the product type, the customer requirements, and the scope of the output. The key here is to ensure that these criteria are defined for each type of output. (These criteria will come into play in Section 7.3.4.)

Finally, the outputs should specify the characteristics of the product that are essential for its safe and proper use. This requirement reflects ISO's manufacturing origins. Certain products' components can carry with them safety issues. You've no doubt read the caution labels on consumer products, such as "Don't spray next to open flame." Lawnmowers carry caution labels; shaving lotion cans carry caution labels. In assembling components for a guided missile, the same type of safety information would naturally apply. The idea here is that, if you are creating outputs (products or components) that need to be integrated or used in a particular way, you should describe what this particular way is and make it available to the handlers of the product or component so that potential misuse can be avoided.

7.3.4. Design and development review

The inputs for design and development help ensure that the technical team knows how to build the right components and products for the customer.

The outputs that emerge from design and development help confirm that the appropriate components and products are being produced. Section 7.3.4 deals with this confirmation process. The idea behind design and development review is to inspect the outputs at specified points in the production process. The inspection should be conducted by a team qualified to evaluate the output against two requirements.

The first is that the team will evaluate the ability of work in progress to meet requirements. This includes assessing the work to make sure it meets (or contains) the requirements it was designed to fulfill. It's also important here to confirm that product functionality can be traced back to specific customer requirements.

The next is corrective. If the team identifies any problems with the work product, it will evaluate, document, and recommend solutions to correct the problem. This process is often called a peer review and is a valuable quality-control tool. It is preventative in nature. Peer reviews are set into place to spot trouble areas as early on in production as possible, where they can be much more effectively corrected than if they show up in the finished product.

7.3.5. Design and development verification

Verification is an extension of the peer-review process.

One can think of the peer review as a team check for quality, a check conducted against a set of criteria. Verification is usually a much more organized effort. It often precedes a peer review or it is employed at certain milestone points: when critical components are integrated for the first time or a product is about to be released.

In the field of technology development, verification is most often associated with testing. Testing can come in many forms: unit testing, system testing, integration testing, acceptance testing. Or it can be shaped as a very formal peer review. However you approach it, all verification efforts in ISO 9001 need to share two traits. The outputs of design and development activities should be verified to ensure that they can be traced back to the requirements and that they meet the intention of the requirements in full. This is most often accomplished through some form of testing procedure or some manner of in-depth inspection and sign-off.

To support the verification process, the team should maintain records of verification results. These records—objective measurements—can be used to assess whether or not the component or product has been adequately realized. If it has been, the production process can continue. If not, corrective action may need to be taken.

Keeping verification results is also a good tool for measuring the quality of team work. As these results collect over time, the organization should be able to see how its quality trends are shaping up.

7.3.6. Design and development validation

Peer reviews and verification activities are all about assessing whether or not the work meets the customer requirements. Validation adds another dimension. Its purpose is to ensure that the product will operate well in its intended environment. This duality can be a stumbling block for technology projects.

For example, you might build a product that meets all of the customer requirements. When you test it on your in-house systems, it performs flawlessly. You therefore deem it ready for deployment. But once it's installed, something happens. Back at your office, you tested it with a team of 13 people banging away at it. But your customer sets 300 people on it and, as they do, performance slows to an unacceptable crawl.

Another case: think of a computerized toaster. You're the software end of that business. Your staff tests a stream of software that sends an electronic pulse to a spring lever when a sensor detects the release of carbon monoxide (the toast is done). The code runs flawlessly on your development boxes. But when the software is embedded in a chip in the toaster, the up-down heat variation causes the silicon to expand and the software to loose its bearings. Proper component and product validation is set into place to anticipate these kinds of issues.

Experienced technology shops will seek out these production requirements early on in the project. They are often defined as performance requirements, environmental requirements, or availability requirements. But whatever types of requirements you get, you should work with the customer to configure and create a validation environment that is as close to a real production environment as is practical. With this environment set up, you should then conduct a series of validation tests or analyses. And, as with verification, you should maintain records of the validation results.

7.3.7. Control of design and development changes

Anyone experienced with development projects knows well that change is the norm. Requirements change, environments are upgraded, systems migrate. A shift anywhere here could cause your work products to fall out of sync, operate poorly, malfunction, or become obsolete. Unless you actively manage such change, you risk losing control over the quality of what you produce. This is where the concept of change control becomes essential to project success.

The ISO 9001 Standard requires that change management be implemented across all design and development activities. Your change-management program should have the following characteristics.

As a part of ongoing quality management, changes should be regularly controlled. That means you should have mechanisms in place to monitor change requests on a set schedule. This may mean establishing a change-control board or change-review committee—or some similar team—and then chartering that group to meet at set points during the project.

The chief purpose of this change-control group is to review change requests and assess the impact and effort required to introduce them into project work activities. In order for this to be conducted in a smooth manner, you'll find that a manageable change control program should contain some or all of the following components:

- Some manner of change-request form with a submission process
- Some form of change-request entry and tracking system
- A change-control authority
- A way to communicate committee decisions

In addition to the above four components, the project team should ensure that change records are maintained across the life of the project.

Figure 5-6 illustrates design and development control.

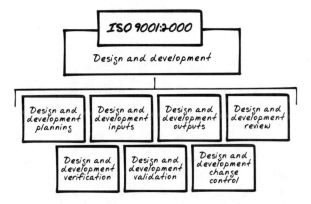

FIGURE 5-6. Under activities for design and development, the program is required to support seven areas of control: planning for design and development, identifying design inputs, identifying design outputs, providing for design reviews, providing for proper verification, providing for proper validation, and managing change in a controlled manner.

7.4. Purchasing

In technology projects, teams often explore what are called make/buy/reuse decisions. That is, they analyze choices when they have to produce something. Do they build it fresh, buy it new, or reuse existing components?

If the team elects to make the component from scratch, they will typically have more control over its ultimate functionality and quality, but heavy costs and efforts may be required. If the team elects to reuse, it can work with something already built, perhaps customizing it to the needs of the project. But the degree of flexibility in such customization may be limited. If the team elects to buy new, it may be able to acquire the component quite cost-effectively, but it may risk introducing a preshaped element into the project, an element over which you may have little control.

The decision to purchase a component and integrate it into the overall product scheme can be an effective strategy if it is managed well. In recognizing this, the Standard supports a considered method for purchasing components for a project. It does this by setting forth requirements for establishing a purchasing process, for defining the criteria the purchased element must meet, and for verifying that these criteria are met when the product is delivered.

7.4.1. Purchasing process

The Standard requires that your Quality Management System contain a documented (and maintained) purchasing process. This process should define how to evaluate suppliers and vendors based on their ability to deliver quality goods. It should also define how the organization establishes the purchasing criteria to be used when third-party products are going to be examined.

The goal of the purchasing process is to give your organization a consistent method for managing "buy" activities. The first part of the process is intended to help you deal with vendors who have the ability to meet your expectations and have proven this in the marketplace. This is important when purchasing. You are, in a very real way, giving up control of some commitments to your customer, placing them in someone else's hands. And so you want to take this step only with qualified vendors.

Next, you want to establish the functional or performance criteria the purchased component must meet. This objectifies the purchasing process. Purchase decisions can often be made based on relationships, or on a perceived "wow factor" in a product. This leads to emotional choices that may not be best for the project in the long term. A better approach is for the organization or the project team to define what the component must do up front in order to meet specific customer requirements and then define some form of comparative checklist that can be applied to product options. This gives the team a sound base for evaluating purchasing choices.

7.4.2. Purchasing information

The evaluation criteria described in the previous section is fully developed here in purchasing information.

The Standard requires that the project team, in working through the purchasing process, describe the product to be purchased in line with customer requirements. This description usually includes the criteria to be used for confirming the product's goodness-of-fit and approving its acquisition. It should also include such considerations as required vendor experience, qualifications, and market stability. To avoid undue outside influence, this information should be prepared by the team in advance of establishing vendor contacts.

This step in the purchasing process is key to the success of the process. This is the action that makes the method a "considered" one. By thinking out and documenting what it is exactly you need to purchase, you increase the likelihood that what you end up buying will be something that fits the needs of the project. It helps to remove (or at least lessen) the potential for impulse buying or for making a purchasing decision based on a relationship, not on the needs of your customer.

7.4.3. Verification of purchased product

The purchasing process also requires you to exercise due diligence for all purchases. The purpose here is to ensure that you are going to purchase components that will add value to the resulting product, that will take you closer to meeting customer requirements and performance expectations. And so the process includes steps for defining just what it is you need to purchase, what vendors are qualified to provide you with the goods, and what criteria you will use to make a purchasing decision. With all of this in place, you can proceed with the acquisition.

But before the deal is done, you need to take one final step: you need to verify that the purchased product does in fact meet those purchasing criteria.

So before you incorporate the component—before you integrate it with other components— you need to take a look at your criteria and inspect the product (what was actually delivered to you) against that. This verification process (you'll typically see this performed as an inspection or a series of acceptance tests) should be incorporated into the purchasing information (see Section 7.4.2). That way, the vendor will know what functional/performance features need to be met, as well as what acceptance process will be undertaken to bring the deal to a successful close.

Once this final step is completed, you can integrate the acquired component with your other elements.

7.5. Production and Service Provision

Section 7.3 sets forth requirements for design and development activities. Section 7.5 rounds this out with requirements for production and service provisioning.

Section 7.5 complements Section 7.3. It adds to 7.3. Design and development contains a series of discrete activities: inputs, outputs, verification steps, and so on. Product and service provision provides a framework under which you can conduct the design and development activities.

This section is organized into five subsections:

Control of provision
> Establishes requirements for ensuring that provisioning activities are carried out in a planned, monitored, and controlled manner.

Validation

Establishes requirements for ensuring that your verification activities are appropriate for the kinds of work products being created.

Identification and traceability

Defines requirements for ensuring that work products moving through the production process are uniquely tagged or otherwise identified so that they may be traced effectively.

Customer property

Establishes requirements for protecting any customer property you might have in your possession.

Preservation of product

Describes how to protect the integrity of your work products during every phase of the life cycle.

Let's take a brief look at each of these.

7.5.1. Control of product and service provision

The processes you use to manage product (and service) production need to provide for an adequate degree of managerial control.

To facilitate this, plans should be set into place for the major development stages: production, installation, and service delivery. These plans should include considerations such as:

- Specifications of the product or service
- Written instructions on how to carry out the work
- Availability of suitable equipment
- Adequate tools for monitoring and measuring product or process characteristics
- Definitions of specific activities for monitoring and measuring product or process characteristics
- Criteria for release, delivery, and post-delivery activities

By accounting for these planning parameters, the organization sets into place control mechanisms that will ensure work products are generated in an orderly manner, one that is visible for inspection and quality confirmation.

As with all quality-control methods, the idea here is to plan, follow the plan, and then evaluate progress for effectiveness. It is through this path that the organization's product and service provision methodology can become refined and improved over time.

7.5.2. Validation of processes for production and service provision

As you've seen, ISO 9001 contains description of two general inspection activities: verification and validation.

Verification is usually linked with activities like testing and product inspections. The goal of these activities is to confirm that the work products you've built satisfy the requirements that were specified by the customer. Verification is all about meeting requirements, and should really be chiefly focused on that.

Validation is a little different. In one way, it's an extension of verification. The goal of validation is to ensure that the work products you produce operate in their intended environments. This is usually accomplished through some form of performance, load, or production mock-up testing. Validation helps ensure that the system interfaces work as planned, that the system will be able to stand up in the production environment, and that it will perform as expected during peak production activity.

To support this, your Quality Manage System should contain processes for ensuring proper and appropriate validation checks of the product.

Because validation is a key to product quality, the organization needs to plan its validation activities carefully. Processes here typically describe several activities, such as:

- How the product will be validated
- How each validation activity will be reviewed and approved
- What validation equipment or environments will be needed for the process
- What records will be kept of validation results
- How the validation process will be assessed over time for effectiveness

Finally, the process should contain criteria for product acceptance—that is, what validation results should be reached for the product to be deemed production-worthy.

7.5.3. Identification and traceability

Take a look at a bottle of Tylenol or a can of Thrifty Maid green peas. Somewhere on each container is the stamp of a batch number. That is about the cleanest example of identification and traceability I know of.

If the peas I buy turn out to be moldy, that might indicate more than a bad can of peas. It could point to a larger production problem, one that might require the recall of lots of cans of peas. With that batch number, the manufacturer will know just which cans went through a shared process, when they were produced, and where they were shipped. Because that batch of peas has been identified and is traceable, the manufacturer can move effectively recall the cans, wherever they've ended up.

This process of identification and traceability is valuable in the ISO world from two perspectives. First, it strengthens the capability of internal product management. You can keep a tight track on where your components are during each step of production. Second, you can know comfortably later on where your products are in the field, should you need to find or monitor them there.

In the field of technology, identification and traceability are tied closely to configuration management (reflected in Section 5.5.5, "Preservation of product"). Good configuration management maintains an audit trail of your work components as they move through the various phases of the production process. And it keeps unique identifiers attached to these components so they can be easily identified, detached, rolled back, or discretely managed. Identification and traceability are also important from the perspective of customer satisfaction.

You can see how this requirement is useful for forward management. But it is also useful for backward management, as a tool to trace the functionality in each component back to the requirements that the customer specified. By ensuring that you can trace requirements in such a manner, you add a level of confidence that your end product does indeed meet initial customer specifications.

7.5.4. Customer property

Often during project work, you'll find that your team is required to work with customer property. This may come about from working at the customer site, using specific customer equipment, or using intellectual property unique to your client. The Standard recognizes this and sets forth the requirement that you shall take good care of customer property.

In other words, when placed in your care, you are responsible for making sure that the property is guarded against harm. This includes protecting it from damage, ensuring its safe and proper storage, and granting access to it only from authorized parties.

If anything should happen to the property, you are required to record data about the incident and promptly report it to the customer.

7.5.5. Preservation of product

As a technology organization, you may be producing software, circuit boards, system designs, or laptop computers. But whatever it is, you have to handle it at some point. ISO 9001 requires that your QMS contain a method for the proper handling of your products and their individual components.

The Standard states that the organization shall take care to preserve the product and components during handling, packing, storage, transport, and delivery.

With an otherwise sound QMS, you can create reliable deliverables. But if you drop them on the floor, bang them into a wall, overwrite them with a previous version, or erase them outright, your work can come to naught. That why it's important to "preserve" the products from the time materials come through your door on through each production phase, until they are finally delivered and installed.

In the field of technology, this is typically part of your configuration management activities.

Configuration management guards the state of your components. It preserves their integrity. Configuration management ensures that your team members have access to the components they need, and that they don't have access to things they don't need. It ensures that your team members are working on the latest version of a component (with the latest specs) as it matures over time. It makes sure that products are migrated from one staging area to another in an orderly and consistent manner. And it enforces guidelines and rules for promoting a product into production or packaging it for release.

Good configuration management is an integral part of the ISO 9001 quality program. With it, you can be confident that your materials are handled properly and transported safely.

7.6. Control of Monitoring and Measuring Devices

The final section under Product Realization is Control of Monitoring and Measuring Devices. (This subject is extended with additional detail in Section 8 of the Standard.)

In ISO 9001, the use of monitoring and measuring devices is essential to effective product realization. The monitoring and measuring devices you employ are the tools that enable you to confirm that what you have realized is satisfactory for release. Because these devices are so important to overall project success, it's important that they are properly controlled at all times on any given project. Therefore the Standard requires that you define what monitoring and measurement devices will be needed across the realization cycle. This can include—for technology projects—what inspections and tests you'll conduct to ensure that the work meets customer requirements and operates in the intended environment. Additionally, you will want to establish processes to make sure that the monitoring and measurement activities are carried out in a coordinated manner.

At heart, the Standard wants you to measure and monitor three things:

- Customer satisfaction
- Process effectiveness
- Work product quality

To do this effectively, your Quality Management System will need to contain definitions of how to measure these. You will need to define, for example, how to measure customer satisfaction. This might be done through a customer survey, through tracking technical support calls, by tracking the number of complaints, or any combination of these.

Process effectiveness might be measured in throughput times, in defect occurrences, or by comments made in process review sessions. Work product quality might be measured in terms of reliability, requirements traceability, or cleanliness from defects.

Once you have defined how you will measure these attributes, you will then need to build the processes (procedures and formulas) for monitoring, collecting, and analyzing the measurement data. These processes should then be incorporated into the project plan, with time and resources allocated for the activities around them. This will ensure proper control of the monitoring and measurement activities.

Required Records

Section 7 of the Standard requires the collection of the most records: 13 in all. These records serve as artifacts that help you manage and control the product realization processes and they also serve as artifacts to show that you are complying with the requirements of this part of the Standard.

Required records for Section 7:

- Inputs related to product requirements

  Examples:

  — Customer business requirements

  — Performance requirements

  — Regulatory requirements

  — Technical requirements

  — Alternative solution analyses

  — Similar past performance records

- Customer and product requirements

  Examples:

  — Customer business scenarios

  — Workflows

  — Customer business objectives

  — Industry standards and statutes

- Design and development requirements:

  — Records that demonstrate the product meets the defined requirements

  — Records of product reviews across the production process

  — Records of design and development reviews

  — Records of verification activity across the production phases

  — Records of validation activity across the production phases

  — Records of any design or development changes, and actions related to each

  Examples:

  — Requirements-review meeting minutes

  — Peer-review records

  — Status reports

  — Analyses of technical designs

  — Test environment configurations

- — Production-simulation environment configurations
- — Change requests
- — Change-control-board meeting minutes
- — Configuration management systems
- — Configuration management records
- — Test plans
- — Test cases
- — Test results
- — User-acceptance test plans
- — User-acceptance test cases
- Purchasing requirements:
  - — Records of supplier evaluations and any resulting actions

  Examples:
  - — Preferred supplier database
  - — Product evaluation criteria
  - — Supplier rankings and categorizations
  - — Supplier agreements
  - — Product-acceptance criteria
  - — Product-transition criteria
- Product and service provision requirements:
  - — Records of validations on product and service provisioning
  - — Traceability records of product components across production
  - — Records of any loss of customer property
  - — Records of product verification

  Examples:
  - — Traceability matrices
  - — Defect-tracking mechanisms
  - — Defect reports
  - — Verification configuration environments
  - — Validation configuration environments
  - — Verification plans
  - — Validation plans

PRODUCT REALIZATION

Section 7 of the ISO 9001 Standard deals with the technical heart of the Quality Management System: how the products (or services) you create are planned, provisioned, and assembled. This section focuses on six broad areas:

Planning of product realization

> Here you are required to thoroughly plan all the activities that will impact the production process. This includes gathering and understanding the customer and product requirements; identifying which processes of the QMS will be used to manage the project; what verification, validation, and testing activities will be employed; and what records will be created and kept to help control project activities and demonstrate general process-program compliance.

Customer-related focus

> Product-assembly activities should always retain a focus on realizing what it is the customer has asked for. This customer-related focus is central to the mission of the Quality Management System. And so for planning, you should highlight those customer requirements that are critical to customer satisfaction and establish a customer communication plan that will foster two-way communication across the project life cycle.

Design and development

> The design and development activities represent a major portion of this part of the Standard. They involve ensuring that the right inputs are considered for the design, that the proper outputs are produced and used to further the production process, and that verification and validation procedures are undertaken to ensure that the components meet customer requirements and operate in the intended environments.

Purchasing

> Part of product realization is the management of any purchasing activities that you undertake during the production process. This area includes establishing criteria for selecting and evaluating potential vendors, creating a process for delineating purchasing information, and defining criteria for verifying that acquired products and components meet the needs of the organization.

Production and service provision

> This section deals with the control of product and service provision through proper configuration management and change control procedures. It also deals with issues of identification and traceability, and the manner in which products can be tracked in the field. Finally, it defines requirements for the proper handling of customer property.

Section 8. Measurement, Analysis, and Improvement

At the base (but not the basement) of most process improvement programs, you'll usually find a set of recommendations or requirements that focus on measurement, analysis, and improvement. CMMI and Six Sigma have them as well.

These activities are important because they provide you with the empirical data and objective insight to assess your program and make it better. The measurements show you how you are doing. The analyses help clarify how you might do things better. And the improvements are your actions in response to the data.

Here is the natural cycle of process improvement:

1. Implement a process.

2. Observe it in action for a while.

3. Measure its performance.

4. Analyze the measurements to see what is working well, what has potential for refinement.

5. Make refinements.

6. Begin the cycle again.

Section 8 of ISO 9001 deals with the cycle of measurement, analysis, and improvement. This section sets forth requirements for collecting measurement data on customer satisfaction, process performance, and work product quality. It also establishes requirements for controlling products that do not conform to quality standards, for analyzing measurement data, and for ensuring that QMS refinements are implemented through a culture of continual improvement using corrective and preventive actions.

Section 8 addresses these topics in five subsections:

1. General

2. Monitoring and measurement

3. Control of nonconforming product

4. Analysis of data

5. Improvement

These are described next.

8.1. General

The general requirement for Measurement, Analysis, and Improvement is that the organization shall *plan* and implement the measuring, analysis, and improvement processes needed to demonstrate that the products being produced conform to the established requirements, that they were created using the mechanisms provided in the QMS, and that improvement data was collected for future work. In other words, the organization needs to plan to collect measurements that will demonstrate compliance.

In short order, this subsection summarizes the whole intention of the ISO 9001 Standard. The previous statements represent the Standard's three overriding philosophies:

- Build a product according to what your customer wants, not what you think the customer wants.

- Use a Quality Management System as a managerial guide for the development of the product.

- Work to continually make the QMS better by collecting improvement data at regular intervals.

8.2. Monitoring and Measurement

In order to meet the three goals, your organization will need to monitor a series of activities and collect measurements from these observations to improve your QMS.

The subsections under 8.2 detail four kinds of measures that should be taken. Before I look at this, I'll briefly touch on measurement regularity. This is one area where organizations can easily swing wrong in one of two directions: either they don't measure the effectiveness of their program often enough, or they attempt to measure the thing too much. Each route can introduce obstacles to productivity.

If you don't measure enough, you'll be hard-pressed to collect enough data to show where your program might be improved. If you try to collect too much in very short cycles, you might get bogged down in number crunching at the sacrifice of program execution. So this falls to the judgment of the individual organization.

Ultimately, you and your people will know your QMS best. You'll know how products and projects cycle through it, and you'll gather a sense of what measurement and analysis schedules work best. The general rules here are twofold: select a set of measures designed specifically to help you improve your program, and then conduct measurement activities based on a schedule suitable to the general throughput of your organization.

8.2.1. Customer satisfaction

The first measures that the Standard stipulates are measures of customer satisfaction.

The requirement is that the organization determine and document how it will collect customer satisfaction data. As mentioned earlier, ISO 9001 is structured with a keen focus on customer satisfaction. The concept of "quality" can be defined any number of ways, but a safe way to get a handle on it is to link it with customer satisfaction. If the customers are content with the products you've produced, chances are you've meet their quality needs. You haven't underestimated or overestimated what they wanted. They'll probably return.

The trick can be finding ways to measure this satisfaction. (Some companies find the very idea intimidating.) But there are lots of established paths.

You can conduct focus groups. You can send out surveys. You can count support calls. You can track external change requests. You can subscribe to competitive analyses. You can send your people out on the road to go and *ask* customers if they're happy with you.

The idea is to position your organization to work in line with what the customer wants. That's the surest way to ensure both quality and success. By defining and then collecting measures of customer satisfaction, you can direct your organization appropriately.

8.2.2. Internal audit

The next set of measures has to do with your Quality Management System. The requirement here is that the organization shall conduct internal audits to ensure that the QMS conforms to ISO standards and that it is effectively implemented and maintained.

I alluded to this earlier in the discussion of Section 4. The Quality Management System is not a static entity. It is not a fixed program; it is a dynamic one. It evolves over time. It should change to meet the changing needs of your organization, its business, and market demands. Because of this dynamic trait, you should periodically measure your QMS to keep it on course, to make sure it has not inadvertently drifted off mission. To ensure this, you should measure your QMS along three lines.

First, you should measure it against the requirements of ISO 9001:2000. This is a type of gap analysis in which you map the requirements of your QMS to the requirements of the Standard.

Next, you should take measures of how effectively the QMS has been implemented within the organization. These measures usually have to do with overall compliance with the QMS from project to project.

Finally, you should collect measures on how well maintained the QMS is. This has to do with confirming the proper configuration management and version control of the Quality Manual, and the records that indicate these activities have been formally conducted.

8.2.3. Monitoring and measurement of processes

The measures specified previously help you assess how well the QMS fits into your organization: how well it's been integrated into your work teams, how well it's been adopted, and how efficiently it's being maintained.

Here in Section 8.2.3, you begin to measure how well the QMS is performing and how effective it is within the organization. The requirement is that the organization shall monitor the processes of the QMS and measure selected ones to make sure the QMS as a whole is meeting the quality objectives of the organization.

I mentioned this earlier. The QMS needs to be founded on a series of quality objectives, objectives that tie in with the overall mission of your organization. And so the processes and procedures (and all else) contained in the QMS should be verified from time to time to show that they really are helping you meet your quality goals.

This does not mean that *everything* in the QMS has to be measured. A more efficient approach is to periodically select a subset of processes and measure just those. The measures can be anything that you find meaningful. This might include a count of noncompliance issues around a process, the estimated time a process helped save for a certain project activity (or the time it cost), the number of change requests a process helped you analyze, and so on.

The goal here is to go beyond simple process execution. The better path is to execute with an eye toward evaluation, understanding, and improvement.

8.2.4. Monitoring and measurement of product

The flip side of measuring process effectiveness is to measure product quality. The two should actually tie together pretty closely.

A common mantra in the field of process improvement is that the quality of a product is heavily influenced by the quality of the processes used to produce it. So here the requirement is that the organization shall regularly monitor the characteristics of the product to verify that the requirements are being met.

Again, this turns back to customer satisfaction. If the goal is to build what the customer has asked for, it becomes important to regularly measure how fully the product components or the full product meet those specific requests.

In addition, the organization should collect and maintain evidence of this conformity at various stages in product development. If problems with meeting the specified requirements are uncovered, further promotion of the product might need to be postponed until the issues, whatever they may be, have been properly addressed and authorization to continue has been given.

Monitoring and measurement of the product is probably the most immediate of ISO 9001's measures. It is an online activity. It is active, not reflexive. That is, it influences the throughput of product realization. If the measures indicate a conformance problem, production should be addressed. Someone should hit the red button on the assembly line. If this is not in place, the organization runs the risk of introducing problems into the final production product, which could amount to a high-risk situation for the company further down the line.

Figure 5-7 illustrates monitoring and measuring requirements.

8.3. Control of Nonconforming Product

"Control of nonconforming product" is a technical way to spell out how to deal with products (or product components) that don't turn out right: those that come out defective.

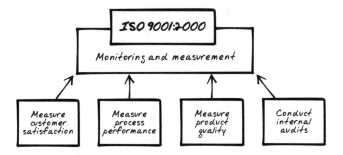

FIGURE 5-7. An ISO 9001 Quality Management System is required to provide for monitoring and measurements along four lines: to periodically measure customer satisfaction, measure process performance, measure product performance or product quality, and periodically conduct internal audits to help gather and analyze these measures.

In Section 8.2.4, the Standard describes the requirement for monitoring and measuring product quality. This is an ongoing activity, carried out as a product is created and assembled across the many stages of its life cycle. These measurement and monitoring activities help detect any defective outputs.

Here, in this section, the idea is to introduce ways to control the nonconforming products when you do find them.

Naturally, if at all possible, customers should be spared an encounter with a failed product. One DOA package out of 1,000 can make the whole lot suspect.

And so the Standard requires the organization to be proactive with nonconformance: it (the organization) shall ensure that product components falling out of conformance are identified and controlled to prevent unintended delivery. In other words, keep an eye on construction at critical steps. Inspect what you produce. Keep an eye out for the worms.

But it's not enough just to keep the bad parts from slipping by; the organization shall deal with nonconforming product by taking one of three actions. First, it should take action to eliminate the nonconformity. This is a two-dimensional requirement, implying steps. The organization should inspect the defective product with a view toward fixing it. If it can remedy the defect, the product can be shipped; if not, it should be discarded (or labeled as unsuitable for use). Any product that goes through a remediation step should also be subjected to reverification. Taking this further, the organization should investigate the source of the defect—investigate what condition introduced the error in the first place—and work to remove that source from the production process.

As an option to that, the organization can discuss the nature and severity of the defect with the customer. If the customer deems that the defect is of an inconsequential nature, then the organization is free to release the product to the customer. However, if either the organization or the customer has reservations about the suitability of the unit, it should, again, be either marked as unsuitable or discarded.

Finally—and of significant impact—if for some reason products that do not conform to the requirements are released into the field, the organization shall take remedial action to mitigate the risk of poor or irregular performance. Actions here might be to initiate field corrections, to send out errata data, or to issue a product recall.

Controlling nonconformance is essential to controlling the ultimate quality of products in production and the quality of the production process itself. In line with this, a final requirement of the Standard is that the organization shall establish and maintain records of nonconformance instances as they occur.

8.4. Analysis of Data

As described earlier in the three previous subsections, ISO 9001 requires that an organization collect measurements across its activities to gauge performance in four areas:

- The institutionalized use of the Quality Management System by the organization
- The overall effectiveness of the Quality Management System
- Supplier efficiency
- Customer satisfaction

Section 8.4 makes use of this collected data by requiring that the organization analyze and interpret measurement data to determine how well the organization is meeting its quality objectives.

This is a cornerstone activity within the ISO Standard. Here you tie actual performance to your previously defined performance goals. In Section 5, I discussed management's responsibility for establishing quality objectives for the organization and the QMS. This was a basic first step in creating the Quality Management System. The general design of the QMS should come from these objectives. Once it has been in use for a while, management should analyze its performance to see how well the system is meeting these objectives.

Analysis of data can take many forms. For this reason, it's important to understand up front how you plan to measure the success of your QMS. "Soft" quality objectives such as "achieve industry-leading customer satisfaction," or "meet or exceed customer expectations" may be founded on noble intentions, but they are difficult to measure. They are not very precise. The goals you establish for the QMS work better if they are more quantitative and less qualitative.

Here are examples of three solid goals for a Quality Management System (and the program that will come out of it):

- Reduce the occurrence of product defects by 5 percent in year 1.
- Increase the throughput of shippable components by an average of 12 percent per month.
- Reduce the need for component rework by 2 percent each quarter in year 2.

These goals provide two benefits for a quality program: they are easily measurable and verifiable, and they provide the focus needed to design the QMS. Once data has been collected from the activities that impact those goals, an analysis will readily reveal how well the QMS is working to meet those goals.

If it proves to be working well, you know you're on the right track. If it's having minimal impact, you know you might need to revise (sharpen) the QMS.

8.5. Improvement

An inescapable theme in all quality programs—CMMI and Six Sigma included—is the focus on improvement. A characteristic of quality programs that is often under-stressed is that they are not about being perfect. The nirvana of zero defects has pretty much been discarded in the commercial realm. Rather, quality programs are about becoming better, about continually improving over time. This idea is brought out here.

ISO 9001 focuses on continuous improvement in two ways. The first way is to take action to correct or refine the quality management system when weaknesses are found or opportunities for improvement are discovered. The second is to build safeguards into the program (efficient processes and procedures) that prevent defects or errors from being introduced into the production life cycle.

Let's take a brief look at each next.

8.5.1. Continual improvement

The first requirement under Improvement is that the organization shall continually improve the effectiveness of its QMS.

The term *continually* implies two actions in practice. The first is the *regular* assessment of the system. *Regular* means at scheduled intervals. The actual schedule selected will naturally depend upon the needs of your organization and the maturity of your QMS. A small organization using a relatively new QMS may find it beneficial to assess the program's effectiveness on a quarterly or semiannual basis. A larger organization using a well-established QMS may find that it needs to assess the system only every other year. These types of assessments can be considered major. But for both organizations, management should assess components of the QMS on a more frequent basis. This leads to the second implication: "continually" implies conscientiousness.

Continuous improvement is not haphazard improvement. Nor is it change for the sake of change. Continuous improvement should be a conscientious activity in which the organization engages in carefully planned analyses of the effectiveness of the QMS, studies the results of these analyses, and then derives ways to make the system more effective. This may be the single strongest indicator of the success of any Quality Management System: the degree to which the organization is committed to its improvement.

8.5.2. Corrective action

One of the fundamentals behind process improvement is to fix things in your system that are weak or show opportunity for improvement. This can be called corrective action.

The ISO requirement for corrective action is as follows: the organization, when encountering nonconformity, shall take corrective action to remove the root cause of the problem.

In other words, you shouldn't be content with just fixing the faulty component or element. ("Get that worm out of here!") You should make an effort to determine where, how, and why the problem occurred, and then take steps to remove that potential from the system.

To support this, the organization should maintain a documented procedure used to govern how nonconformities are reviewed, how root causes are determined, how potential solutions are evaluated, and how corrective actions needed to remedy the situation are implemented to prevent the same kinds of errors from bring introduced in the future.

As a potential part of measurement activities and to provide a history of process improvement activity, the organization should also work to record the results of improvement actions taken and review the effectiveness of these actions on a regular basis.

8.5.3. Preventive action

In addition to taking corrective action to remove the root cause of problems in the Quality Management System, the Standard also requires that the organization take a proactive stance when it comes to defect prevention.

The requirement here is that the organization shall take action to eliminate the potential for nonconformities creeping into the system. This means that the organization should work to anticipate the possibility of trouble before it occurs. To support this, the organization should establish a documented procedure that governs how it will define potential nonconformities and their causes, how it will evaluate the need for action to prevent the potential, and how it should implement the actions needed to ensure the continuing integrity of the system.

As a potential part of measurement activities and to provide a history of process improvement activity, the organization should record the results of the preventive actions taken and review the effectiveness of these actions on a regular basis.

Figure 5-8 illustrates the improvement requirements of the Standard.

Required Records

Section 8 of the Standard requires the collection of measurement records that quantify program performance and provide a basis for making future decisions about potential process improvements:

- Records of internal audits

- Records of assigning and authorizing personnel

- Records of nonconformity

- Records of actions to correct nonconformity

- Records of preventive actions

    Examples:

    — Audit criteria

    — Audit reports

    — Audit plans and policies

    — Staff assignment forms

    — Staffing notifications

    — Noncompliance records

    — Defect-tracking systems

    — Defect-tracking and management reports

    — Process improvement plans

    — Process performance measures

    — Process improvement results

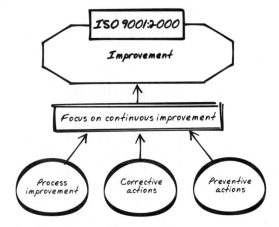

FIGURE 5-8. The focus on improvement runs throughout ISO 9001:2000. The Standard requires three areas of concentration. First is a focus on continuous process improvement. Second is a focus on taking corrective actions to mitigate any poorly performing elements of the system. Third is to take preventive actions so that defects do not enter into the system or into production lines.

MEASUREMENT, ANALYSIS, AND IMPROVEMENT

This final section in the Standard sets forth requirements for improving the QMS through the implementation of measurements and the analysis of the measurement data. This is described in three subsections:

Conduct measurement activity

> The section calls for establishing ways to measure customer satisfaction, ways to monitor and measure the performance of your processes, and ways to measure the quality performance of your products.

Control nonconforming product

> The Standard sets forth requirements for controlling products and product components that fall out of specification. These include guidelines for correcting faulty components and for isolating defective components that cannot be corrected.

Analysis of data

> This subsection defines requirements for taking corrective action to repair or remedy defective products, and for taking preventive action to remove the root cause of problems so that they do not recur.

For a Deeper Look

The following books and references can provide you with a deeper look at the ISO 9001: 2000 Standard:

ISO 9001: 2000 for Small Businesses by Ray Tricker (Butterworth-Heinemann)

> This book focuses on the implementation and use of 9001 in small businesses. The focus is on using ISO 9001 in a way that reflects the objectives and directives of your organization without moving into the realm of developing heavy or cumbersome policies and processes. The book also helps you if your organization is migrating from the 1994 Standard. It describes many of the additions, changes, and differences you should consider when making the move up.

ISO 9001, The Standard Interpretation by Leland R. Beaumont (ISO Easy)

> Beaumont's book focuses mainly on the differences between the 2000 Standard and the 1994 Standard. But it also contains a pretty complete explanation of what you should understand and appreciate about ISO 9001, especially if you're new to this specification. The book is written in a casual, friendly style, with good side-by-side explanations of all sections of the Standard. It may not be the most exhaustive work on ISO, but it makes for a good introductory or exploratory look.

ISO 9001:2000 for Software and Systems Providers: An Engineering Approach by Robert Bamford (CRC)

Because ISO 9001 is known as a generic standard, it can realistically be applied to just about any manufacturing environment: toothbrushes to missiles. This book focuses on application in technology environments, and in doing that, you can garner a good comparative picture of what ISO offers compared to programs like CMMI and Six Sigma. The book's approach is comprehensive and thorough. Because it focuses on considerations of engineering shops, it can at times get a little technical. But it's the kind of detail technical people will appreciate. And the general recommendations are appropriate enough for the typical process improvement audience.

Systematic Process Improvement Using ISO 9001:2000 and CMMI by Boris Mutafelija and Harvey Stromberg (Artech House Publishers)

A lot of the value of this book comes from two angles. First is its very thorough approach to discussing the role of ISO 9001 in the realm of rigorous process improvement. Second is its inclusion of CMMI as a potential partner for ISO-based solutions. The authors do a good job of explaining how a CMMI program can comfortably fit under the larger umbrella of ISO. They also present good explanations of the reach and scope such a program might include. This is a solid resource for technology shops that want to understand not only the values of process improvement, but how these two standards might be harnessed to pull together effectively.

ISO 9001:2000 Explained by Charles A. Cianfrani et al. (ASQ Quality Press)

This is a good book to turn to if you'd like a dedicated and complete presentation of the scope, purpose, and structure of the 9001 Standard. Cianfrani describes the sections and requirements of the Standard and combines this with explanations of how typical implementations are accounted for. The focus of this book is not on any one industry sector. And so it maintains a generic approach that supports the generic purpose of the Standard. A good general reference.

Summary

ISO 9001:2000 is a generic quality standard developed and sponsored by the International Organization for Standardization in Geneva, Switzerland. The ISO is made up of over 140 member countries and is the largest developer of recognized standards in the world.

ISO 9001:2000 is a quality standard that can apply to any manufacturing environment, including information technology. The focus of ISO 9001:2000 is to:

- Understand the requirements of a product to be built for a specific customer.
- Establish processes to meet those requirements.
- Provide resources to run and manage the processes.
- Monitor, control, and measure the performance and effectiveness of the processes.
- Improve the system continually, based on the measures of process and product performance.

CHAPTER SIX

The Capability Maturity Model Integration (for Development)

SINCE ITS INTRODUCTION JUST OVER 15 YEARS AGO, THE CAPABILITY MATURITY MODEL HAS QUICKLY become a major player in the IT world of process improvement and quality management. Today, it runs second only to its more established relative, the ISO 9001 program, in acceptance and use around the world. And in terms of momentum, CMM is probably leading. It is being adopted as the preferred IT quality standard by more and more businesses, organizations, and government agencies. With ISO and Six Sigma, it has taken its place as one of a trio of quality management options the executive world is looking to. Its rising popularity can be attributed to many factors. It is relatively compact. It is specifically shaped to the needs of technology development. And it is a public-domain specification, free to anyone who wants to use it.

Perhaps more important, the CMM framework has been proven to work. Its benefits have been demonstrated both quantitatively and qualitatively. The corporations that have adopted its recommendations and consciously applied them within their technology development projects have seen measurable performance improvements. Planning estimates and projections have become more accurate. Work paths have become more established. Efficiencies have increased. Defect rates and rework have dropped.

And so, CMM's potential for impact makes it a worthwhile model that should be at least tangentially understood by IT management across corporate America. For that reason, I'll now take a look at what the Capability Maturity Model is all about.

I'll do that in this section by presenting an overview of the most current version of the Capability Maturity Model, the CMMI-DEV. The "I" in the model's name stands for "integration." As we'll see, CMMI is an extension of the CMM. It both expands and refines the CMM by incorporating generic approaches for software engineering, systems engineering, and integrated process and product development together into a single framework. And it does this while allowing for greater flexibility in reaching the model's goals. The "Dev" stands for Development. The CMMI-Dev (version 1.2) is the model useful for technology organizations that have to develop products, processes, or both for their customers. (There is also a CMMI-ACQ model for Acquisitions, but discussion of this model is not in the scope of this book.)

But before we look at the components that make up the Capability Maturity Model Integration, let's take a brief look at the history of the model and its parent organization, the Software Engineering Institute.

A Brief History of CMMI

The Capability Maturity Model, and its evolution into CMMI, began in the wake of the PC revolution in the early 1980s. During that time, data-processing departments across America underwent an abrupt and radical change. The once predictable landscape of centralized processing, batch loads, and dumb terminals gave way to a kaleidoscope world of personal computing. This change split the discipline of data processing two ways. First, it discarded the concept of "stability through limitation." Computer departments were now faced with a myriad of options, a constantly changing (to this day) sea of choices. New architectures, programming languages, database systems, spreadsheets, and communications avenues all promised to deliver a host of rich and robust capabilities that were faster and cheaper than ever before.

Second, and perhaps more important, the control of technology moved from the back room to the front desk. Personal computing became people computing. Users gained an unprecedented degree of control over what popped up on their screens. And they quickly became a savvy bunch to deal with.

In the span of a decade, factors such as choice and accessibility, falling costs, and rising performance flipped data processing from being load-driven to being demand-driven, so much so that today we no longer "process data," we "manage information." DP is now IT. And software, once an adjunct to any business, has now become fully absorbed by business. The two have become inseparable. This integration became apparent quickly. Even in the mid-80s, the dominance of this trend was making headlines in technology circles. And its impact was being seriously assessed. The effective management of software and technology directly translated into business success. This rationale extended a step further: for America to compete in a rising global economy, it needed resources for effective technology management.

That conclusion did not go unnoticed by technology theorists, politicians, and corporate strategists. These new technology dimensions were recognized as part of a permanent shift in the dynamics of information management. And the theorists, politicians, and strategists knew the weight of this shift. These disparate parties organized their voice into one and appealed to the U.S. Congress to establish a national resource for advancing knowledge of software engineering and technology, and to address what was seen as a growing need for effective technology-management models.

Congress responded by establishing the Software Engineering Institute at Carnegie Mellon University in Pittsburgh, Pennsylvania. The SEI was chartered to operate in the public interest as a federally funded research and development center. Placed under the sponsorship of the U.S. Department of Defense, the SEI began its mission with work on a framework for quality management in the arena of software development. That framework became the Capability Maturity Model.

At the time, quality management models for the manufacturing industry were in full bloom. The ISO 9000 series was enjoying broad interest. Japanese innovations like Just-in-Time delivery, Assembly-Line-Control, and LEAN were attracting worldwide press. Six Sigma was emerging at places like Motorola and General Electric. The SEI was taking a close look at all of these. And it was also dissecting the work of noted American experts on quality. The work and philosophies of quality pioneers such as Philip Crosby, Malcolm Baldridge, George Box, and Edwards Deming were explored and analyzed for application. This effort culminated in 1987 with the publication of Watts Humphrey's book *Managing the Software Process* (Addison-Wesley Professional). The book synthesized the critical thinking in quality management and applied it to a series of practical steps, organized by maturity levels, that an organization could undertake to manage its development projects. Later that year, the SEI used Humphrey's approach as the basis for version 1.0 of the Capability Maturity Model. The name reflects the attitude of the quality approach: the more mature an organization becomes in its use and management of process, the greater its capabilities grow.

The CMM was founded on two well-known quality principles. The first is the idea that "process works." In other words, in the manufacturing realm, where you execute a series of distinct steps to create a final product (whether that's coat hangers or surgical lasers), a proven, tested process will ensure better quality than a haphazard, ad hoc one. The second principle is "a performing organization is a learning organization." The idea here is that successful cultures succeed through continuous innovation and improvement, and for those traits to exist, the organization must operate in *learning mode*, in a mode where it regularly assesses its performance and looks for ways to do its work better. The organization welcomes self-consciousness.

Those two principles were new to the newly transformed technology industry. But the Department of Defense, the SEI's official sponsor, saw the value and was first to broadly adopt the model. Soon it was able to demonstrate CMM's effectiveness. That led to the CMM's wide dissemination. Within five years, over 5,000 IT organizations had adopted the CMM as a working quality model. The SEI meanwhile was taking the base concepts of process improvement and applying them to a wider range of IT disciplines. The original

CMM was termed SW-CMM, since its primary focus was on process improvement for the tasks of software engineering. The SEI then designed a similar model for the discipline of systems engineering, SE-CMM. Later it shaped a model for integrated product and process development, IPPD, and Supplier Sourcing.

Each model found its niche in IT departments around the world. But soon, users discovered they were employing several models within the same organization to meet different but similar needs. They expressed the desire for a single integrated model that could be followed for systems engineering, software engineering, or integrated product development. The SEI saw this as an opportunity not only to consolidate several models into one, but also to simplify and, to an extent, "genericize" the requirements of CMM, no matter what its flavor.

The resulting integrated model was released in 1999 as CMMI. Then in August of 2006, the SEI released updates to CMMI (with some streamlines and consolidations, and the introduction of "constellations" of models) known as version 1.2. From this came CMMI-Development for product and process development, and CMMI-ACQ for acqusitions. In this book we discuss the CMMI-Dev model. For the sake of convenience, we'll refer to it simply as CMMI.

CMMI, then, can be seen as a gift from America to America, as a toolkit to help make American IT enterprise remain innovative, competitive, and productive. But it has actually become more than that. Today, we can see it—as many people in other countries doubtlessly do—as a gift from America to the world. In the following section, I'll look at the question of ownership regarding CMMI.

CMMI Ownership

When it comes to CMMI, the issue of ownership is easy: all citizens of the U.S. own it. If you're an American, you own CMMI because you paid for it. As mentioned in the previous section, CMMI is a product of the Software Engineering Institute (SEI), and the SEI is a federally funded research and development center sponsored by the Department of Defense. So CMMI belongs to the American people. If you're an American, you get full use of it, free and clear. But you don't just own CMMI. Just as important, you—and everyone else—have access to just about all the programs developed by the SEI. These include programs to help you implement CMMI, programs to help you assess your implementation, tips and techniques for your staff, and methods for technology management in areas other than the systems and software development fields. You can take a look at everything the SEI makes available to you at its web site, *www.sei.cmu.edu*. There, you can browse through an extensive library of programs, papers, analyses, reviews, and studies, all geared to helping you make your IT program stronger.

Because most of the work of the SEI is released into the public domain, you get unlimited distribution rights to the material as well. That means you can download any of the specs from the SEI and make copies for everyone in your organization at no charge. You can share them, teach them, even write books about them. You can hand them out on street corners if you want. The only requirement is that you respect the copyrights. You can't, for example, republish CMMI as "Joe's Maturity Model." Other than that, the field is yours.

This ownership status brings with it one advantage that the ISO 9001:2000 Standard and Six Sigma can't offer. CMMI is a fully supported program that is free to implement. ISO 9001 isn't. Sure, it is indeed a fully supported program; the ISO is a highly organized enterprise. And it has been able to develop and refine its Quality Management System standards in a smooth and successful manner. But you have to pay a fee to get the standard. It is not free. It is copyrighted, and that copyright is tightly enforced. If I wanted to publish a book on how to implement ISO 9001:2000, I would be allowed to present only my *interpretation* of the spec, not the spec itself. If I retyped the official ISO spec, I'd have attorneys from Geneva knocking at my door as fast as an SST could cross the Atlantic.

With Six Sigma, the view is a little different. Six Sigma is free, free in the same way that mathematics is free. If you know how to do it, you can do it any place and any time you want. What Six Sigma currently lacks is a recognized, centralized governing body. There are solid organizations out there that can mentor people into the Six Sigma fold (places like Six Sigma Academy and the American Society for Quality), but Six Sigma has not yet emerged as a coordinated, programmatic standard.

CMMI has the advantage of being both free and centrally maintained. This brings us to a paradox inherent in CMMI's "free" status. Created for the U.S. by the U.S., it has become immensely popular worldwide, in large part because it is free and it is so well supported. Companies around the globe are taking advantage of this; some think India probably has more Maturity Level 5 organizations per square mile than any other place on the planet. The government of Poland has made CMMI certification a required part of its national IT project bid process. The government of Tasmania is exploring initiatives to support CMMI adoption. The University of Ulster has been chartered by the UK Ministry of Defense to provide CMMI solutions in the Northern Ireland IT business sector. The Japanese government is contemplating establishing a CMMI Research Center to support CMMI in its territories. I have personally worked with representatives from Sweden, Portugal, Spain, and the Ukraine, all actively pursuing CMMI programs.*

So what started out as a strategy to hone American competitiveness has transformed into a worldwide quality standard. That's probably a good trend. The broad acceptance of CMMI and other SEI programs will no doubt have a consolidating effect on the standards world. Even now, the SEI and ISO are working together to design what may become a single method for program appraisals, applicable to both CMMI and 9001:2000 models.

What you own then is a CMMI that is robust, effective, and positioned for future growth. What lies at the heart of this successful model? That's what I'll look at in the next section. I'll explore the design, structure, and components that make up CMMI.

Technology Disciplines Covered Under CMMI

As noted earlier, the Capability Maturity Model began as a process improvement framework for the field of technology engineering. The structure of the original CMM reflects

---

* See *http://www.sei.cmu.edu*, "Breaking Barriers."

that focus. But as the CMM's popularity grew, the SEI (and the CMM user community) began to see potential for applying the model to a broader group of IT activities. And so the SEI developed extensible forms of CMM, with the base version becoming know as the SW-CMM. A version was tailored for the processes and activities of systems engineering, known as the SE-CMM; a version was tailored to address the unique needs of strategic product and service acquisition (Supplier Sourcing); and a version was developed for the broad applicability of Integrated Product and Process Development, the IPPD-CMM.

Each of these models enjoyed acceptance and success in the various disciplines it addressed. Yet they all still retained many common elements. After a few years, many organizations that used all four disciplines began to ask for a model that capitalized on the common elements and at the same time allowed for a degree of flexible configurability. CMMI was the initiative to regroup these various tailored versions into a single, configurable model for all four disciplines. The Capability Maturity Model *Integration* represents the end result.

Today, CMMI-Dev v1.2 includes practices and program components for the following IT disciplines:

- Systems engineering

- Software engineering

- Integrated product and process development

In CMMI, these disciplines are keyed to a series of Process Areas that contain the recommended practices that make the model work.

For IPPD, the full model applies—all Process Areas are relevant. IPPD is typically employed on only the largest of projects, or the most disparate, in which multiple organizations or reporting groups from different disciplines must be allied with a common vision to execute multiple project components in a highly coordinated manner.

For systems and software engineering, all Process Areas apply, with the exception of the IPPD principles and practices.

Practices for supplier sourcing are addressed under "Supplier Agreement Management," later in this chapter.

CMMI-Dev Structure and Design

CMMI-Dev is specifically structured for the IT industry. As discussed earlier in Chapter 5, ISO 9001 can be employed for almost any manufacturing environment. Six Sigma can be used anywhere (or best) where transactions are recurrent. CMMI can (and has been) used in non-IT environments, but its *raison d'être* is to help IT organizations develop highly reliable management, engineering, and quality-support systems.

CMMI is focused on the concept of process improvement. It assumes that process works, that following a tried and true path gets you where you want to go most times you travel it. It also operates under the postulate that successful organizations (and by this they mean organizations that have shown themselves to be successful over time) tend to be process-mature. They design processes, implement them, study them, and then refine them over time.

In the parlance of Deming and Baldridge, the honored approach is to Plan, Do, Check, Act.

A Goal-Oriented Design

CMMI is structured as a series of Process Areas (PAs). You can think of each Process Area as a collection of best practices that help a technology organization manage its activity and control its quality. The full model contains 22 Process Areas. As an example, one of the Process Areas is called Project Planning. Naturally, it provides guidance for effectively planning projects. Another PA is called Requirements Development. This PA provides guidance on eliciting, describing, and documenting customer and product requirements.

Each Process Area within CMMI establishes one or more goals that should be achieved in order for an organization to be able to claim that it is truly following the program. There are two kinds of goals in the model: specific goals and generic goals. The *generic goals* represent the "common elements" of CMMI. The *specific goals* shape the direction of each Process Area.

Additionally, each goal is supported by recommended practices. You'll find that the goals are typically expressed in high-level terms, while the practices are expressed in more concrete, "actionable" terms. The assumption with the goal-practice structure is that if you implement the practices described for each goal, you'll meet the intention of the goal itself.

There are specific practices for the model's specific goals, and there are generic practices for the model's generic goals.

By way of strict interpretation, the practices are optional. Were an organization to be officially appraised, the job of the lead appraiser would simply be to collect ample evidence that the goals are being met. Yet, most organizations (and certainly most appraisers) find that the best route to compliance—and to realizing the benefits of CMMI—is to largely use the practices to get to the goals.

I summarize the specific goals and practices of CMMI in the section "The Process Areas of CMMI," later in this chapter. But this is probably a good time to take a look at the generic goals and how they contribute to the model's use.

Generic Goals of CMMI

There are five generic goals in CMMI. They are labeled Generic Goal 1 (GG1), Generic Goal 2 (GG2), Generic Goal 3 (GG3), and so on. The naming here is a little awkward. You can implement CMMI one of two ways: the Staged Representation or the Continuous Representation (more on this in the section "Implementing CMMI," at the end of this chapter). If you elect to implement the Continuous Representation, all five generic goals may be applied. That's what will get you to a specific capability level.

For example, if you wish to be known as a CMMI Capability Level 4 Project Monitoring and Control shop, you would need to meet all of the specific goals for the PM&C PA, as well as generic goals GG1 through GG4.

In the Staged Representation, the designation is really about maturity level. With the Staged Representation, you reach a maturity level by implementing a set series of PAs. For Staged, there are only two generic goals that need to be applied, GG2 and GG3. Generic Goal 2 is applied when an organization is building a Level 2 program; GG3 comes in when the organization moves up to Level 3, and then sustains the program through Levels 4 and 5. There are no other generic goals required for any higher maturity levels; GG2 and GG3 are it.

The generic goals play an important role in implementing CMMI. They define and support the framework each Process Area needs to operate consistently, predictably, and manageably. In the language of the SEI, the generic goals provide the commitment, ability, directed implementation, and verification needed for each PA. They help you *institutionalize* a Process Area.

This being said, let's look at CMMI's generic goals.

Generic Goal 1: Achieve Specific Goals

Generic Goal 1 simply states, "Achieve specific goals." It is supported by one Generic Practice, 1.1, that states "Perform base practices."

The intention here is naturally basic. The goal simply directs the organization to achieve the specific goals defined for each Process Area it elects to implement, and then to achieve the lowest level of recommended practices for each goal under each of those PAs.

Generic Goal 1 applies to Continuous Representation.

Generic Goal 2: Institutionalize a Managed Process

Generic Goal 2 directs the organization to "institutionalize a managed process." What that means is, in order to implement a maturing process program (even if it's for only one project), you need to create and manage (that is, use and control) the process just as you create and manage project work. At Level 2, the organization is free to experiment with an evolving set of processes across its projects, learning along the way, keeping the good and discarding the bad. That's the idea behind "managed." To help you meet this goal in a way that provides strength to the project or organization, CMMI supports Generic Goal 2 with a set of 10 generic practices. Very briefly, these are:

Generic Practice 2.1, Establish a Policy
> Create an executive-level policy that demonstrates the organization's commitment to the use, monitoring, and maturing of its process.

GP 2.2, Plan the Process
> In other words, when you embark on a project, make sure the process and its associated activities and responsibilities are recognized by project management and integrated into a project plan (or at least referenced in the plan).

GP 2.3, Provide Resources

It's not enough to simply create a process and then plan for its use. The organization should ensure that the proper resources are in place to successfully carry out the process. This could include anything from the right people to computers, process forms and guides, work space, etc.

GP 2.4, Assign Responsibility

This practice is related to 2.3. Processes don't work very well on their own. Someone needs to execute them, to be responsible for carrying out the defined activities. And this assignment should be explicitly made as an official appointment.

GP 2.5, Provide Training

This practice, plain as it is, can be interpreted. If the resources that are responsible for managing the process are not familiar with the process, you should ensure that they receive the proper training they need to get up to speed—before the process work begins. If they are obviously experienced enough to work their duties (documentation helps here), a training waiver (or some other indicator) could suffice.

GP 2.6, Manage Configurations

When you plan a process for a project, you'll probably end up with process artifacts: schedules, staff assignments, forms, and so on. To keep these items current with project progress and evolution—to keep expectations at a set level of commonality—the process work products should be, at the least, version-controlled. You may elect to formally configuration-manage items deemed critical to project success.

GP 2.7, Involve Relevant Stakeholders

This generic practice can be a little fuzzy. What is a stakeholder? Actually it's anybody with an interest in the outcome of the process or the project. But that's not very helpful. Remember earlier, in GP 2.4, where you assigned specific responsibility for carrying out the process? Link that here. This practice recommends that you (perhaps the project manager or executive management) make sure that the people assigned to project or process work are kept in the loop—that your team is unified through the informed involvement of those people charged with making it a success.

GP 2.8, Monitor and Control the Process

The processes that you have embedded into your project exist to promote the success of the project. And so they should be treated by project management in the same way that major milestones and client deliverables are. Process activities should be regularly tracked against the plan to ensure that their executions are going as planned.

GP 2.9, Objectively Evaluate Compliance

In order for your processes to be effective, they must be complied with. They've got to be honored. Even if they have weaknesses, they will never improve if they are not worked. This generic practice recommends that an "objective" party periodically evaluate the degree to which the process is being complied with on the project. The concept of "objective" is important here. It avoids potential conflicts of interest or pressures from varied agendas and is typically realized through a set of independent evaluation criteria.

GP 2.10, Review Status with Higher-Level Management

As you'll see later, project management involves, to a large degree, process management, managing the parts that make a project a whole, that make the project move as it should. This can't be maximized without the involvement of upper management. To help ensure that the processes being applied to a project are contributing to the success of the project, process discussions should be held with higher-level management from time to time. What is "higher-level management"? Usually a level above project management. This will naturally vary from organization to organization. But the practice is intended to keep the voice of the process (or the process owner) within earshot of higher management.

Ten generic practices for Generic Goal 2 admittedly are a handful. But this bulk occurs only with GG 2, and if you think about each recommended practice, you'll see how each one is important to supporting a process improvement program. CMMI is often described as a process improvement framework, and it is the generic goals—especially Generic Goal 2—that hold up the framework.

Generic Goal 2 applies to Continuous Representation and Staged Representation.

Generic Goal 3: Institutionalize a Defined Process

Generic Goal 1 is set into place to point an organization toward the specific practices of CMMI's Process Areas. It's there to forge a beginning. Generic Goal 2—the heavyweight of the GGs—is designed to provide for the considered care and management of each PA.

Generic Goal 3 assumes a higher level of maturity, one in which the organization has learned enough—over time—to define for itself a set of standardized processes, a set that can be tailored for each new project the organization engages in. There are two generic practices defined for GG3:

GP 3.1, Establish a Defined Process

When an organization is ready to implement Generic Goal 3, it will have established a "defined" set of processes for the organization's Process Areas. This is different from the "managed" form of Generic Goal 2. A *defined process* (or process set) is a method of planning and management that the organization has adopted across its relevant operating groups. It has become the standard. And though the processes can be tailored to the specific needs of each project, considered guidelines for how to shape processes that have been set into place.

GP 3.2, Collect Improvement Information

We mentioned earlier that, with Generic Goal 2, the organization becomes self-conscious. It's aware of its activities and so plans and manages them with oversight. With Generic Goal 3, the organization takes a step further. It begins to analyze how its processes are working and starts to gather empirical data on their performance. Empirical here is intended to mean objective, observed, comparative. The next logical step—quantitative data collection—comes with the next generic goal.

Generic Goal 3 applies to Continuous Representation and Staged Representation.

Generic Goal 4: Institutionalize a Quantitatively Managed Process

IT organizations that have reached a point at which they are ready to implement Generic Goal 4 have reached a high level of maturity, one in which process drives the organization, and now one in which quantitative numbers drive the processes that drive the organization. It is here that the organization adopts tools similar to Six Sigma (see Chapter 7). To adopt the quantitative environment suggested by Generic Goal 4, the organization is encouraged to realize two generic practices:

GP 4.1, Establish Quantitative Objectives for the Process
> To measurably demonstrate improvement or effectiveness, we are wise to rely on numbers. Qualitative measures may "suggest," but they don't "prove." And so with Generic Practice 4.1, the organization sets quantitative performance standards for its processes. For example, the organization may decide that a project of a certain scope and technical approach should take 120 hours to plan. That is a quantitative objective. When such a project appears, the planning process is observed and timed, and the results are analyzed. This becomes the de facto approach for every process in the organization's defined process set.

GP 4.2, Stabilize Subprocess Performance
> This practice is related to the one above. Stabilize means to meet the quantitative objectives by analyzing a process and its subcomponents and fine-tuning them for performance. Again, this involves using numbers: observing, measuring, collecting, modeling, analyzing. To say we have entered the scientific realm here is not an understatement. At Generic Goal 4, the organization adds a new layer of management: quantitative performance management. It is certainly effective, but it requires a new layer of commitment as well, a commitment to continuous and rigorous data collection.

Generic Goal 4 applies to Continuous Representation.

Generic Goal 5: Institutionalize an Optimizing Process

Process improvement is a continuous way of doing business—whether you are General Motors moving engine blocks along an assembly line or Jack 'n' Jill's Web Shop designing eChocolate.com. Its goal is to help the organization mature. But can there be an end to the maturation process? Tools change. Market demands change. Cultures change. The business world is not a stable one. And so when one adopts Generic Goal 5, one is really adopting all the recommendations of Generic Goals 1 through 4. It is a commitment to an ongoing process improvement program, an institutionalization of the culture of process improvement. In other words, to always be optimizing.

I recommend two generic practices here:

GP 5.1, Ensure Continuous Process Improvement
> Here the organization sets into place a culture of continuous process improvement. There's enough for a book in that statement alone, and this being a survey of three popular process improvement choices, I can't get into the powerful detail here. But the

idea is solid, and it holds. The organization ensures—by fiat, by culture, by command—that its process improvement program will continue to shape how it produces its products and, ultimately, how it measures its quality.

GP 5.2, Correct Root Causes of Problems

This generic practice, in my opinion, can be closely associated with Generic Goal 4; at any rate, it's a crucial ingredient to process maturity. The recommendation is to "correct the root causes of problems." This is kin to the quantitative analytical nature of Generic Goal 4. The concept here though deserves a brief look. Correcting the cause of root problems means boiling it down, not sliding backward. The data you collect at Generic Goal 4 should support your actions in correcting the root causes of problems. I mentioned earlier the usefulness of symptoms. They are barometers of things hidden or things to come. Here, the organization by habit, by charter, looks for the causes of the symptoms of quality issues. And then it works consciously to remove those causes.

Generic Goal 5 applies to Continuous Representation

The Link Between Generic Goals and Process Areas

In the realm of CMMI, a project is an organized collection of people, product activities, and process activities. For any business, the chief job of any of these components is to produce effectively. This usually means two things: make a profit and make the customer happy. When the two go hand in hand, you have a successful business.

Though it's often unappreciated, that is the ultimate aim of process improvement. The driving philosophy behind CMMI is that, if you use effective processes, you'll produce effectively—and if you produce effectively, you'll be able to better manage both costs and quality.

To support this, CMMI supports a series of 22 best-practice Process Areas (PAs). Each Process Area promotes a set of activities that augment the production process. In the next section, we'll look at these Process Areas, but first it's important to understand the link between the Process Areas (with their own goals and practices) and the generic goals and practices just discussed.

Think of it this way. The generic goals can be applied to each Process Area, and they are in place to ensure that the right support exists for that Process Area. The generic goals exist to guide how you manage each PA. And so they are an integral part of the overall model.

The Process Areas of CMMI

The full CMMI model contains 22 Process Areas, each containing a series of practices designed to accomplish one or more goals. As a general rule, each Process Area can be implemented on its own, independent of the others. Yet as you become familiar with the model, you'll find that many of the Process Areas in CMMI are related to each other, add strength to each other, and build upon each other.

You might find it helpful or handy to interrelate Process Areas by grouping them into functional categories. Using or even recognizing this grouping (which the SEI has used in the past but doesn't really push now) is not mandatory for model success, but you might find it's a useful way of organizing things in your head. The grouping is sorted like this: in the model, six Process Areas (PAs) deal with project management, six deal with engineering, five others deal with the support functions of project execution, and five deal with process management within the organization.

Here's how the PAs are organized by functional category.

Project Management:

- Project Planning
- Project Monitoring and Control
- Integrated Project Management
- Quantitative Project Management
- Risk Management
- Supplier Agreement Management

Engineering:

- Requirements Management
- Requirements Development
- Verification
- Validation
- Technical Solution
- Product Integration

Support:

- Process and Product Quality Assurance
- Configuration Management
- Measurement and Analysis
- Decision Analysis and Resolution
- Causal Analysis and Resolution

Process Management:

- Organizational Process Focus
- Organizational Process Definition
- Organizational Training
- Organizational Process Performance
- Organizational Innovation and Deployment

In the following sections, I'll take a look at the Process Areas in CMMI and briefly describe the purpose and scope of each. The descriptions begin with an overview of the main objectives of the Process Area, followed by a summary of the specific goals defined for each PA, a concise core action statement, a category indicator, and a final list of the IT disciplines to which the PA applies.

Project Management Process Areas

The following sections detail the Process Areas specific to project management.

Project Planning

In my opinion, the Project Planning Process Area is the single most important PA in the entire CMMI model. Others might dispute that point (and validly), but what's generally accepted is that a reliable quality result can only come from up-front planning: the more, the better. That's why CMMI places such a strong emphasis on planning (just as ISO 9001 and Six Sigma do).

The structure of the Project Planning PA helps an organization resist the temptation to hurry up and go. Today we have ample data on what happens when pressure to begin pushes a project into premature action. Issues with resource allocation, budgeting, scheduling, scope, and functionality crop up early and plague a project across its life cycle.

Planning is a way to reduce these kinds of problems (and the risks they bring). A well-designed planning program provides two key benefits to any project effort: it provides a road map for thinking a project through prior to making commitments, and it delivers a medium for agreement between parties as to how the project will be managed.

Three specific goals

There are three goals in the Project Planning PA, each designed to strengthen your position in meeting a project's objectives:

1. Establish estimates of what it will take to see a project through from start to finish. These estimates include such things as the size and scope of the end product, the number of resources required, special skill sets needed, types of computing resources required, and so on. These estimates can be derived from formal models, from similar projects from the past, or from consensus of experienced opinion. However you approach it, the idea is to estimate intelligently using as much data as is available to you.

2. Create (and document) a plan based on the estimates. Since a complete project plan will typically contain a good bit of data to support the estimates, it's a good idea to document the plan using a standardized template. The use of a template helps different project managers in the same organization plan in a consistent manner from project to project. It also helps ensure that a core set of planning data will be addressed in each plan. The plan will contain all the detail necessary to carry forth the estimated scope and activities. And, just as important, it will serve as the chief control mechanism for managing the project across its life cycle.

3. Obtain commitment to the plan. This step is essential to smooth execution. Here you circulate the plan among team members and relevant stakeholders to elicit feedback and approval. Once agreed upon, the plan can serve as a contract of agreement between you and the team (and the customer) as to the scope of the project and how it will be managed.

Core Project Planning actions

Document a project plan using the best estimates and information at your disposal. Then involve team members and stakeholders in reviewing and approving the plan in order to establish a contract of agreement among parties as to how the project will be managed.

Applies to Project Management:

- Systems Engineering
- Software Engineering
- Integrated Product and Process Development

Figure 6-1 illustrates the Project Planning PA.

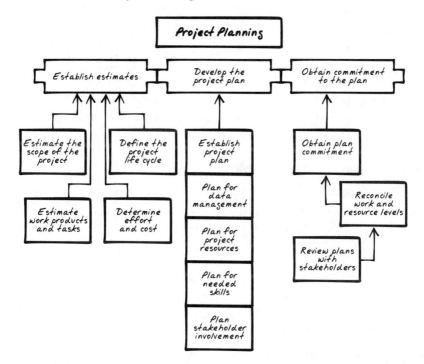

FIGURE 6-1. The activities that make up Project Planning center on establishing a viable and practical plan for the project. This includes first establishing estimates of the scope and size of the project; defining management activities for resources, schedules, budgets, stakeholders, and data; and then working with the organization to review the plan and ultimately obtain commitment to it.

Project Monitoring and Control

The Project Monitoring and Control Process Area is a logical extension of Project Planning. In planning, you document the resources, activities, and constraints anticipated for a project. You then use the plan as the chief reference tool for monitoring the project's progress. Effective monitoring includes the use of regular status meetings, stakeholder communications, product inspections, and audits. Control is the proactive counterpoint to monitoring. When the *actuals* on a project—the details of what is actually transpiring—begin to vary significantly from what was planned, you should take corrective action to bring the plan back into sync with the project, either by reversioning the plan or adjusting the scope of the project.

Two specific goals

CMMI assigns two goals to Project Monitoring and Control:

1. The project manager should monitor the project against the plan. This includes monitoring the planning parameters (resources, costs, schedule), tracking project commitments and risks, and ensuring stakeholder involvement. These moves can be accomplished through regular formal status meetings, through informal status check-ups, and through other available communication channels.

2. The project manager should track risks and emerging variances across all phases of the project life cycle, following the issues to closure. When variances begin to become significant, the project manager should initiate some form of corrective action to bring the plan and the project back into alignment. To do this effectively, the project manager will typically identify variances as they begin to rise, monitor their rate of escalation, and then move to mitigate their influence at preset "take action" points.

Core Project Monitoring and Control actions

Project management tracks the actual progress of the project against documented projections in the plan. When significant variance occurs between what was planned for and what is actually happening, the PM takes corrective action to realign the plan with project activity.

Applies to Project Management:

- Systems Engineering
- Software Engineering
- Integrated Product and Process Development

Figure 6-2 illustrates the Project Monitoring and Oversight PA.

Integrated Project Management

Integrated Project Management supports the coordination of disparate work groups and elements within a project. It combines the facets of Project Planning and Project Monitoring and Control with activities to focus these elements for enhanced project control. This Process Area includes practices that help project management identify and select the right

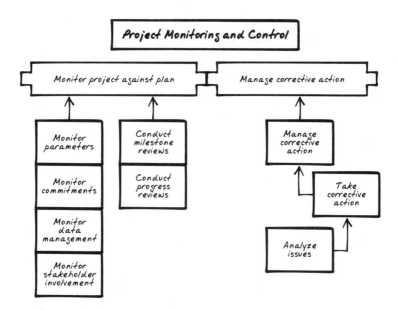

FIGURE 6-2. Project Monitoring and Control is the natural extension of Project Planning. Here, actual project activities are monitored against what was anticipated in the plan. Monitored items include the budget, schedule, risks, stakeholder involvement, and milestones and deliverables. When corrective action needs to be taken, the actions are tracked to closure.

processes for a particular project from the organization's process repository (see "Organizational Process Definition," later in this chapter). Also included are activities to tailor the processes to the needs of the project, managing the project objectives with the active involvement of designated stakeholders, creating and communicating a shared project vision with the stakeholders, and creating integrated teams based on the specific technical and production needs of the project.

Three specific goals

CMMI defines three goals for Integrated Project Management:

1. Project planning and execution should be based on the use of the organization's defined processes. This goal sets in place recommendations for selecting process sets from the organization's process repository and tailoring those to the needs of the project as part of integrated planning activity.

2. Project activities should be coordinated with relevant stakeholders, allowing for ample collaboration and exchange. This involves forging a broad team partnership by identifying relevant stakeholders and then ensuring that project communications and activities are continually coordinated with these parties over the life of the project.

The third goal is for use when you are using CMMI for Integrated Product and Process Development:

3. Apply IPPD principles to the project activities and structures. This goal—exclusively for IPPD efforts but useful wherever you might see fit—puts forth practices to help

align multiple project teams, often with disparate charges. Practices deal with establishing shared vision statements and creating integrated teams.

Core Integrated Project Management actions

Project management coordinates the use of organizational process sets, integrates plans and teams, and ensures stakeholder involvement across the life of the project.

Applies to Project Management:

- Systems Engineering
- Software Engineering
- Integrated Product and Process Development

Figure 6-3 illustrates the Integrated Project Management PA.

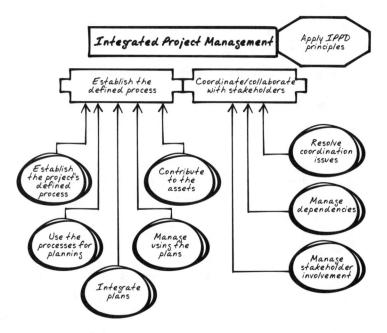

FIGURE 6-3. *Integrated Project Management is the natural extension of Project Monitoring and Control. Here, institutionalized processes are defined for the project, stakeholder involvement and coordination is promoted, and IPPD principles, where applicable, are applied.*

Quantitative Project Management

Quantitative Project Management is an advanced technique used by mature organizations to plan for and gauge project success. This Process Area extends the reach of Project Monitoring and Control and Integrated Project Management. The basic modus operandi of PM&C is to track actual values against planned values. The values here are usually snapshots of substantial project components, such as the schedule, the budget, the number of resources, the risks, and so on. When one or more of these values begins to vary significantly from what was planned, the project manager takes corrective action. The concept of "significant variance," however, is not really tangibly defined with PM&C; that call is left to the experience and intuition of the project manager. The corrective action is likewise a discretionary move.

Quantitative Project Management adds a layer of engineering granularity to this process. To begin with, under QPM, progress is mapped numerically. For example, a measure that shows the design phase as being three days ahead of schedule might be calculated as being 109 percent on target. That percentage is more meaningful (for analysis and reporting) than, say, "+3 days." With such measures, project management also monitors the efficiencies of subprocesses within the project. Quantitative measures are taken to assess the performance of these processes against anticipated or expected goals. As another example, a requirements review process that was executed with 4 missed steps out of 20 might receive a performance score of 80. That hard score can then be compared against other projects or a preset scorecard to determine the success of the process for that project.

Effective Quantitative Project Management relies on a backlog of accumulated project performance data, thoughtful and analytical project planning, and firm control over the execution of a project.

Two specific goals

CMMI defines two goals for this Process Area:

1. The project is managed, in part, by using quantitative measures of quality and process performance objectives. Meeting this goal requires that the organization capture enough history from prior projects so that it can effectively quantify benchmarks that indicate quality and progress baselines and targets. Quantitative measures can be defined in the absence of history, but these benchmarks add maximum value when they are derived from the organization's typical production flow. The use of predictive tools (such as Earned Value Management) is also appropriate in support of quantitative project management.

2. The performance of selected project subprocesses is statistically measured against preset goals for efficiency and effectiveness. This goal provides a method for measuring the engine that drives the project, which comprises the various processes and their subcomponents as employed. Here, processes are tracked by their constituent steps. The organization's experience with its process set should be such that it can estimate the duration of each within a project. By tracking the duration and success of each process substep, project management can accrue measures on the efficiency of the processes. This leads to greater and more accurate project control and provides data for future process improvement considerations.

Core Quantitative Project Management actions

In addition to the basic monitoring of schedule, funding, and resource attributes, project management performs oversight on the project by regularly comparing quantitative measures of quality, performance, and process efficiencies to preset goals around process performance.

Applies to Project Management:

- Systems Engineering
- Software Engineering
- Integrated Product and Process Development

Figure 6-4 illustrates the Quantitative Project Management PA.

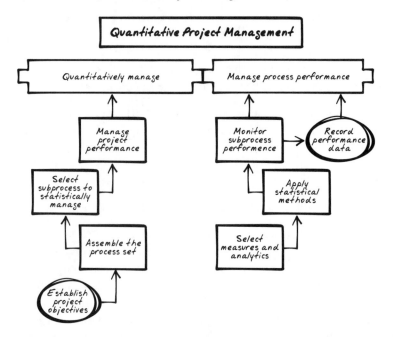

FIGURE 6-4. Quantitative Project Management is a high-maturity, high-capability Process Area. Here the team uses quantitative measures and statistical techniques to monitor the performance of selected project processes to ensure that their performance will meet targeted expectations. Of special interest are subprocesses. These are continually measured across the project to anticipate current performance and predict future performance.

Risk Management

The Risk Management Process Area extends the capabilities of Project Planning and Project Monitoring and Control. Basic project planning calls for the identification of potential risks. And basic project monitoring calls for tracking risks that could threaten a project. Risk Management introduces an organized and planned approach for continuously dealing with risks, one that uses a proactive organizational methodology. This methodology takes what could be thought of as free-range risks and corrals them into categories. The organization then develops strategies to address the inherent traits of the different risk categories. These strategies are then applied at the project level, where potential risks are explicitly identified and their impacts assessed as early as possible. The mitigation steps that emerge from this activity are then encompassed in a Risk Management Plan that becomes part of the overall project plan.

The Risk Management Process Area represents a step to quantify (to a degree) something that we typically regard as a hazy intangible or, at best, as a distinct but removed potential. It helps an organization forge a set of tools useful in circumventing the pitfalls that come from avoiding the issue of risks or from dealing with them in a reactive, half-considered manner.

Three specific goals

CMMI defines three goals for Risk Management:

1. The organization should prepare a risk-management program. This includes defining typical sources and categories of risk, determining risk parameters, and establishing a general strategy for managing risk that can be applied to all organizational projects.

2. For each project, the project manager (with assistance from selected members of the project team) should identify and analyze risks. This includes defining potential risks as part of the planning process, assessing the potential impact of each risk, and then prioritizing risks according to impact, likelihood, and complexity.

3. The project manager should document a series of mitigation steps that can be employed to deal with the risks, should they materialize.

The risk plan—risks identified and prioritized, with mitigation actions—can then become a component of the overall project plan.

Core Risk Management actions

The organization defines the types of risks its projects typically encounter, identifies specific risks for each project, and develops a management plan for each project, which details how risks will be mitigated should they materialize.

Applies to Project Management:

- Systems Engineering
- Software Engineering
- Integrated Product and Process Development

Figure 6-5 illustrates the Risk Management PA.

Supplier Agreement Management

The Supplier Agreement Management Process Area addresses the need to acquire outside products or services that are required to fulfill the expectations or scope of a development project. As an example, a project intended to create an online e-store might seek to acquire a piece of finished code that processes Visa and MasterCard transactions. To ensure that this acquisition process is structured with adequate quality controls, the organization should establish a program that manages interplay and agreements between

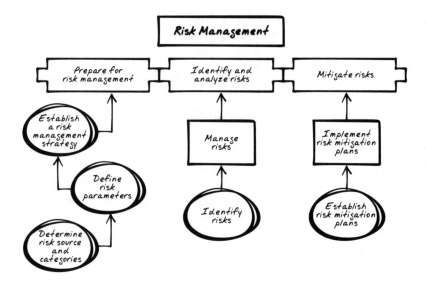

FIGURE 6-5. Risk Management is designed to help project teams plan for risk and then effectively mitigate the effects of risks on project plans and objectives. This involves a preparatory step: defining currently known risk categories and acceptable plans to address them. As a project unfolds and risks emerge, risk plans are developed, implemented, and tracked for effectiveness.

suppliers and the organization. The Supplier Agreement Management Process Area provides the framework for such a program.

This Process Area helps organizations establish standards for determining the type of acquisition required, criteria for selecting qualified suppliers, considerations for executing and managing supplier agreements, protocols for product inspection, and guidelines for transitioning acquired products into the organization.

Two specific goals

CMMI defines two goals for Supplier Agreement:

1. Establish formal agreements with your suppliers. This goal helps objectify the process of selecting and managing vendors whose products you wish to acquire. Here the organization should begin by categorizing, in some manner, the type of acquisitions it makes and then apply those criteria when amassing a potential supplier base. The organization should also develop some type of supplier selection criteria, a checklist to provide consistency when evaluating potential vendors and their products. Then, in anticipation of a purchasing choice, formal agreements should be drawn up (governing interactions, legal rights, product distribution, etc.) that can be used to establish an understanding between the organization and the supplier.

2. Satisfy the executed agreements. To meet this goal, the organization should work to meet the tenets of the executed supplier agreement. These tenets typically include stipulations to monitor select supplier processes and product development activities,

examine the product (or product suite) for suitability, establish terms for acquisition, provide for the transfer of the product into the organization (with appropriate documentation, support, and other necessary materials), and then describe the steps needed to integrate the product into the organization or project team.

Core Supplier Agreement actions

The organization defines the methods for acceptable selection and use of third-party products and services, detailing supplier selection criteria, product suitability requirements, and boilerplate supplier agreements. Also promoted is the monitoring of selected supplier processes and iterative work products.

Applies to Project Management:

• Supplier Sourcing across all disciplines

Figure 6-6 illustrates the Supplier Agreement Management PA.

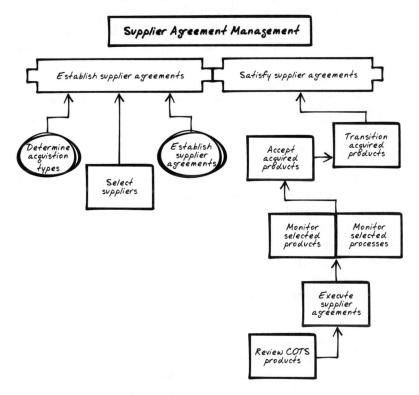

FIGURE 6-6. Supplier Agreement Management is designed to help organizations deal with external suppliers effectively, ensuring the integrity of acquired deliverables. This includes understanding types of acquisitions made, providing for a means of pre-inspection of available products, selecting qualified suppliers, and formalizing criteria for deliverable acceptance and transition.

PROJECT MANAGEMENT PROCESS AREAS

The six Process Areas (PAs) in the Project Management category of CMMI are set in place to help you plan, manage, and report on project progress. Here's a brief take on each.

For Maturity Level 2:

Project Planning (PP)

Three goals are established for Project Planning: create formal estimates for the scope, size, duration, and resources needed for the project; develop a comprehensive project plan based on the estimates and management expectations; review the plan and obtain commitment to it from team members, management, and stakeholders.

Project Monitoring and Control (PMC)

Two goals are defined for Project Monitoring and Control: monitor actual performance and progress of the project against what you documented in the project plan, and take corrective actions when the project's performance or results deviate significantly from the plan, managing these actions to closure.

Supplier Agreement Management (SAM)

SAM has two goals: agreements with suppliers are established and maintained, and agreements with the suppliers are satisfied by both the project and the supplier.

For Maturity Level 3:

Integrated Project Management (IPM)

For Project Management, three goals govern IPM: conduct the project using a set of defined processes that are tailored from the organization's set of standard processes, coordinate and collaborate with relevant stakeholders across the full life cycle of the project, and apply IPPD principles on projects as needed.

Risk Management (RSKM)

Three goals are defined for Risk Management: prepare for risk management during planning activities; as part of project management, identify and analyze risks as they appear in order to determine their relative importance; and mitigate risks to reduce their impact on project progress.

For Maturity Level 4 PAs:

Quantitative Project Management (QPM)

For this Process Area, there are two "high maturity" goals: quantitatively manage the project using statistical techniques built around quality and process-performance objectives, and statistically manage the performance of selected subprocesses within the project's defined process.

Engineering Process Areas

The following sections detail the Process Areas specific to engineering.

Requirements Management

If the IT industry as a whole were asked to isolate one activity that led to more problems than any other, it would probably be requirements management. Poor requirements—incomplete, inconsistent, ill-expressed—have been known to derail a project faster than almost anything else. Without sound requirements, a project operates in an amorphous world where nothing can be fixed, where no quality mark can be set. Therefore, sound requirements—at least a baseline of sound requirements—should be in place before you embark on any development effort.* It's a critical path item for project success. It's not hard to see why. If your project team has no methods or tools for managing requirements, no degree of effective oversight or engineering talent will keep a project on its rails. The tracks have been greased for slipperiness from start to finish. Requirements Management then is an essential characteristic of any quality model.

At its core, Requirements Management is a control technique that should be adopted as early as possible in a project's life cycle. Because it recognizes that people change their minds, that business rules fluctuate, that no one thinks of everything at once, requirements management serves as a facility to handle change in a manner that promotes the clean intake of requirements, their smooth integration into project plans, and their eventual evolution across project phases.

One specific goal

CMMI defines one basic goal for Requirements Management: that requirements are managed. By this, the spec implies five common practices, each one leading from and building on the other:

1. The engineering team should have the opportunity to review the requirements prior to adopting them. In other words, the team should get the chance to understand the requirements before committing to their implementation.

2. The project team, including relevant stakeholders, should formally approve the agreed-upon requirements as a group, establishing a common base of understanding.

3. Once approved, the requirements should be tracked and monitored to maintain their consistency with project plans and work products across the life of the project.

---

* The term *requirements* can refer to any form of scope definition. Here we most often think of the functional requirements that stipulate how a system should operate. But before that, there had to be some form of requirements to generate those requirements—perhaps module descriptions. And before that, there needed to be requirements for what modules an application of a certain kind should possess—perhaps a business vision. The point is, a reliable starting mark—something that describes what the end should look like—is always needed to reach that end.

4. Traceability should be established in order to verify that the proper requirements have been incorporated into the proper functioning components and work products of the system.

5. If inconsistencies are discovered between the requirements and their work products, corrective action should be taken to realign the two.

Core Requirements Management actions

The team agrees to a core set of requirements and then actively tracks and monitors their evolution across every phase of the project.

Applies to Engineering:

- Systems Engineering

- Software Engineering

- Integrated Product and Process Development

Figure 6-7 illustrates the Requirements Management PA.

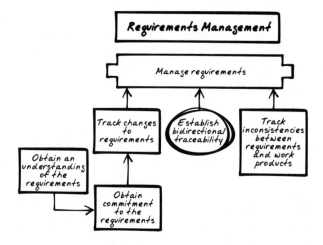

FIGURE 6-7. Requirements Management is focused on how requirements are reviewed, approved, and baselined for project work. This includes obtaining an understanding of the requirements, obtaining commitment to the requirements prior to work, tracking changes to requirements, and keeping requirements and work products consistent with each other.

Requirements Development

Requirements Development is the logical "pre-extension" of Requirements Management. It deepens Requirements Management, a technology-engineering task, by linking it with a primary systems-engineering task, the development of the requirements. In the CMMI model, Requirements Development is concerned with producing requirements through interactions with customers and then analyzing those requirements to validate their completeness.

Developing requirements is a big job any way you look at it. And CMMI doesn't describe in detail just how the job should be done. It outlines at a high level the tasks of stakeholder coordination, elicitation, documentation, verification, and communication. Its main concern is that requirements development is conducted through a set process, a process composed of defined steps. The use of process is especially important here: requirements development is a notoriously intuitive regimen. By its nature, it's in the business of translation, and translation is always open to misinterpretation and missing detail. A process won't make the regimen perfect, but it will give your people an arena to operate in that promotes consistency and thoroughness, and it will foster mechanisms for feedback and review. With those kinds of elements in place, your Requirements Development effort should become cleaner and cleaner over time.

Three specific goals

CMMI identifies three goals within the Requirements Development Process Area:

1. **Develop customer requirements.** Customer requirements are those requirements that define the customers' (and relevant stakeholders') expectations of the system. These requirements usually deal with fulfilling specific business and performance needs. The job of your analysts—and usually this is an iterative job—is to elicit these needs and then document the customer requirements based on them.

2. **Develop product requirements.** Product requirements are usually a finer, more detailed set of requirements that work to realize the customer requirements through more technical descriptions. This step includes defining the product makeup and its constituent components and then allocating requirements to these components and their linking interfaces.

3. **Analyze and validate the requirements.** This step calls for your analysts to organize the documented requirements into operational concepts and scenarios, extract and map the resulting functionality, prioritize the functionality, and then validate that this functionality meets the business and performance expectations of the customer.

Core Requirements Development actions

Your business analysts work with customers and other selected stakeholders to elicit and document customer requirements and product requirements. These requirements are then analyzed for completeness, suitability, and viability.

Applies to Engineering:

- Systems Engineering
- Software Engineering
- Integrated Product and Process Development

Figure 6-8 illustrates the Requirements Development PA.

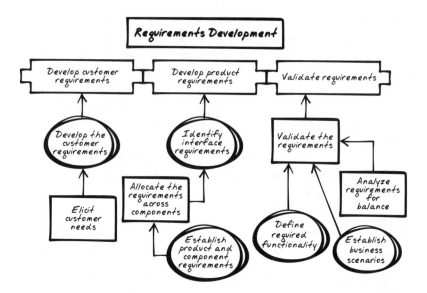

FIGURE 6-8. *Requirements Development deals with the elicitation, composition, and analysis of requirements. The activities provide structure for tasks to develop customer requirements, develop product component requirements and any interfaces needed to link the components, and develop methods for prioritizing and balancing requirements across the project life cycle.*

Technical Solution

Technical Solution is designed to provide the organization with guidelines for determining the technical direction of a project, then organizing and implementing an appropriate design. This Process Area is in many ways an extension of the two Requirements Process Areas: Requirements Management and Requirements Development. Those Process Areas provide means for eliciting, documenting, and managing the requirements that form the basis of a development project. They can be thought of (if you prefer to think of these Engineering PAs in a traditional SDLC order) as the first two Process Areas of CMMI. The Technical Solution PA moves you from requirements to design.

Here the model makes recommendations for evaluating, organizing, and implementing an appropriate design for the project. The focus is on finding the right technical solution, one that makes sense based on the needs of the project as a whole and on the different sub-components of the project.

Three specific goals

This Process Area comes with three specific goals:

1. Select the right product-component solution (or solutions). This first goal provides guidelines for investigating the best architectural path to apply to the project. This involves developing alternate solutions against criteria of the performance and technical capabilities of the organization, and then examining the requirements to determine which available solution fits best. Many IT organizations are tempted to

simply apply a solution that fits their current strengths, such as "We're a .NET shop" or "We do Java better than anyone" or "MQ Series can handle anything." The practice specified here encourages a more considered approach. It gives you and your development team a mechanism to formally hunt for the best technical solution for the project.

2. Develop the designs for the solution. This goal sets guidelines for creating the overall design (and any necessary subcomponent designs) based on the architectural solution established through Goal 1. This includes establishing the technical tools and resources needed, defining the product components in detail, and defining and detailing any interfaces that will be needed to link the components together.

3. Implement the designs across the project. This third goal carries out the defined activity in Goal 2. You create the design according to the specifications you defined for it and implement it in an appropriate way (i.e., coding the solution). In addition, the team develops the supporting documentation (here called a technical data package) required to support the implementation of the design.

Core Technical Solution actions

The project team uses the requirements as a base for determining and implementing an appropriate product design, one that accounts for all product components and interfaces. This is based on evaluations of viable alternatives, as well as on the technical capabilities of the organization. The designs are then implemented.

Applies to Engineering:

- Systems Engineering
- Software Engineering
- Integrated Product and Process Development

Figure 6-9 illustrates the Technical Solution PA.

Product Integration

Product Integration is concerned with the gradual, prescribed assembly and delivery of the developed product along with its accompanying materials. This Process Area is related to Configuration Management (discussed later under "Support Process Areas") in that it deals with how configured components are linked, compiled, and assembled for delivery. It is also related to Validation (discussed later in this section), in that what are being validated are the final integrated components. The purpose of Product Integration is to ensure that a method is in place that provides for the orderly assembly of what can often be many product subcomponents, often at different life-cycle phases. Additionally, Product Integration exists to provide a mechanism to determine whether the assembled subcomponents function properly before they are released as an integrated whole. In general, the process of Product Integration is one of planning, confirming, assembling, and—finally—delivering.

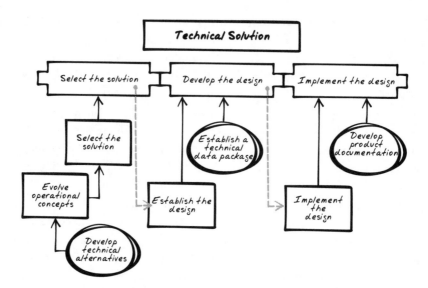

FIGURE 6-9. Technical Solution contains practices for deriving the right technical solution for a project, and then implementing an appropriate design based on the solution. This Process Area also includes implementing the design (through coding, construction, etc.) and establishing a technical data package to support the design.

Three specific goals

CMMI provides three goals for Product Integration:

1. **Prepare for Product Integration.** This is a planning and documentation process, one that deals with how you'll plan and define the process that maps out how the product components fit together. Here the engineering staff defines the product's components, the sequence in which they should be integrated, the configuration of the integration environment (what's needed to fit the pieces together), and the criteria to use to determine if the assembly (the integration) has been successful.

2. **Ensure interface compatibility.** This goal is designed to account for the various interfaces that link project components into an integrated whole. This part of the integration process should include a definition of the interfaces and how they fit together. This is important because interfaces have a tendency to be overlooked from time to time, the focus being on the major product parts. But interfaces—because they too can change and evolve over time as the product develops—need to be given the same attention and focus on integration.

3. **Assemble the defined components and deliver the product.** This step includes confirming that the components are ready to be integrated—that they have reached that final phase of development—then assembling the components using the criteria and procedures you have developed, verifying that the resulting product is operational, and then delivering the assembled product with relevant supporting material to the customer.

Core Product Integration actions

The engineering team devises a coordinated method for linking all components and interfaces of a product into an integrated whole, one suitable for delivery to the customer. The team then assembles the product following this method and delivers the product to the customer.

Applies to Engineering:

- Systems Engineering
- Software Engineering
- Integrated Product and Process Development

Figure 6-10 illustrates the Product Integration PA.

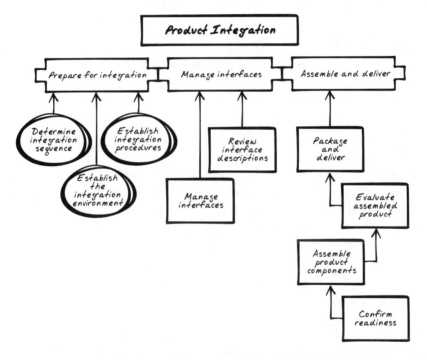

FIGURE 6-10. Product Integration is often seen as the next step following Technical Solution. The practices contained in this Process Area focus on defining how the product components should be assembled, what the integration environment should be, and what the assembly procedures should address. Interface management is another aspect of Product Integration. Interfaces should be regularly managed to be kept current with the components being assembled.

Verification

The purpose of this Process Area is to ensure that selected work products produced across the project life cycle have been developed according to appropriate requirements, standards, and formats. Verification can be thought of as an extension of the Process and Product

Quality Assurance Process Area (discussed later under "Support Process Areas"). But (as you'll see) while PPQA is an independent, "external" quality-compliance component, Verification is internal to the project team. Verification is typically implemented in phases across the project, usually at selected milestones and in the form of quality gates. This Process Area serves its most effective use as a means for accomplishing the smooth transition of work products from one team to another, on through product delivery. We typically think of Verification in terms of peer reviews and functional tests. Here, peer groups are organized to conduct product inspections, comment on their quality and completeness, and approve their downstream transition. And like teams are formed to put product components through tests to verify compliance with requirements.

Three specific goals

The Verification Process Area has three goals under CMMI:

1. Prepare for Verification. This is the planning phase for this Process Area. It usually occurs (and probably *should* occur) prior to project execution. Here you define—for the full length of the project—what work products will be subject to the verification process. Then you define what inspection criteria you'll use to verify these key work products and product components. For example, you might define the format, structure, and contents of what you'd expect to see in an acceptable design document. This will then serve as the basis for evaluating that document later in the project.

2. Perform peer reviews. This is an oversight facet of the verification process. Peer reviews are an exercise in which members of the project teams inspect and evaluate each other's work to ensure that it is ready to move on in the production process. For this goal, material is organized for each peer review, peer teams are identified, inspections are conducted, and resulting recommendations are analyzed for any further actions deemed appropriate.

3. Verify the selected work products. This is the closing step of Verification. Here, selected follow-up recommendations that arose out of the peer review may be acted on. Additionally, major work products and product components are subjected to the robust verification evaluations planned for in Goal 1. (The classic form of this is system and regression testing.) The result should be products that pass verification criteria and are ready to move on into further project activity, or perhaps on to Product Integration actions.

Core Verification actions

The project team inspects selected work products based on preset criteria (i.e., appropriate requirements, content, format, and standards). Products that fall outside of these criteria are reworked before moving along the project life cycle.

Applies to Engineering:

- Systems Engineering
- Software Engineering
- Integrated Product and Process Development

Figure 6-11 illustrates the Verification PA.

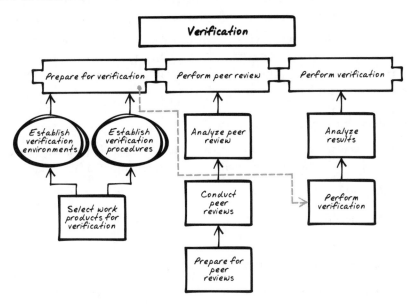

FIGURE 6-11. Verification is often thought of as "test," but it includes more than that. It contains activities that help ensure that the product components truly reflect the requirements given to the project team. This involves establishing verification environments and procedures, performing peer reviews, and then executing verification activities as planned.

Validation

The Validation Process Area presents a method for ensuring that a developed product operates in its intended environment according to performance expectations. This Process Area is related to Verification and might be seen as the end point in the Verification line. Validation is concerned with the delivery and deployment of the product, but it should take place well before deployment. The process of validation works best when conducted using, as close as possible, the operational environment intended for the product in the field. The overall intention of validation is to confirm that the product will work in the field as the customer first envisioned.

Two specific goals

Two goals exist for Validation. The structure is very similar to that of Verification.

1. Prepare for Validation. This is the planning phase for this Process Area. Here the team selects the products that will be put through validation exercises. Then the team identifies the proper configuration that will be needed to replicate the field environment and, based on that, defines what tests and exercises will be required to confirm that the product operates in the intended environment in the intended way.

2. Validate the product and its product components. Here the validation plan is executed, and the results are analyzed. Based on this analysis, the product may be deemed suitable for production, or it (or some of its components) may be returned to the engineering process for refinement.

Core Validation actions

Selected products (or components) are exercised and evaluated in production-like environments to ensure that they meet operational and performance field expectations.

Applies to Engineering:

*   Systems Engineering
*   Software Engineering
*   Integrated Product and Process Development

Figure 6-12 illustrates the Validation PA.

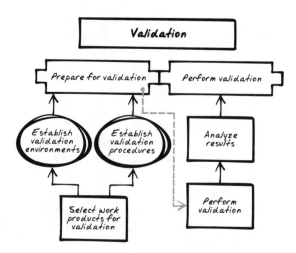

FIGURE 6-12. Validation sets into place activities to help ensure that the product built by the project team will operate properly in its intended environment. The activities defined here include defining the validation environment, establishing validation procedures and criteria, performing validation tasks as defined, and analyzing the results of the validation activities.

ENGINEERING PROCESS AREAS

The Process Areas (PAs) that deal with engineering under CMMI are focused on establishing workable requirements, developing appropriate solutions, assembling components into an integrated whole, verifying product features, and validating product performance. Here's a brief recount of the six Process Areas:

For Maturity Level 2:

Requirements Management (REQM)

This Process Area has one goal: manage requirements in a way that ensures consistency and control, and then allows for tracking and tracing over the life of the project.

For Maturity Level 3:

Requirements Development (RD)

Three goals are defined here: elicit customer requirements, develop appropriate product requirements based on the customer requirements, and analyze and validate the requirements to establish order, relationships, and priorities.

Technical Solution (TS)

Three goals are defined for this PA: evaluate alternatives to select the best technical solution for the project, develop a design that accounts for the proper product components and interfaces, and implement the solution based on the technical approach and the design.

Product Integration (PI)

Product Integration has three goals: prepare for Product Integration by defining how the product components and interfaces will need to be assembled, ensure that interface specifications and versions remain compatible as product components evolve, and assemble and deliver the product according to the criteria and instructions you've developed.

Verification (VER)

Three goals define this PA: prepare for Verification by defining inspection criteria for the different work products you will need to verify, perform peer reviews on selected work products as they move through the production process, and perform verification on key work products prior to integrating them into deliverable components.

Validation (VAL)

Validation has two goals: prepare for Validation by establishing validation procedures and defining the proper validation environment; and perform validation based on the procedures and the predefined environment configuration.

Support Process Areas

The following sections detail the Process Areas specific to support.

Configuration Management

The role of Configuration Management in CMMI covers two areas: technical configuration management and change control. Configuration Management is a discipline designed to ensure the integrity of the work products that impact project success. In the realm of systems and software development, this most often includes configuration management of source code, code compilers, and key technical documentation. But in mature organizations, this usually expands to include other items as well. Often you'll find that it's beneficial to configuration-manage such products as the requirements specification, system designs, test plans, and even such management items as the Project Plan. The scope of Configuration Management naturally depends upon the scope of your project. But whether you elect basic or comprehensive configuration management, the practices remain the same.

The other focus is change control. As change is a natural component of any project, it is important that the organization set into place some form of change management. A basic change-control program typically includes such elements as a change-control process (for introducing and assessing change requests), some manner of change-management system, and a change-management body such as a change-control board.

Both these facets—version control of configured items and change management—serve as support arms for project management. They provide for the incorporation and coordination of change over a project's progression across time.

Three specific goals

CMMI presents three goals for Configuration Management:

1. Establish baselines of selected work products. Here, the configuration manager ensures that some form of Configuration Management system exists for the project and then works with project management to identify which work products produced by the project team will be placed under Configuration Management control. From this planning activity, the configuration manager can then create and release baselines of these products for use by the team.

2. Track and control proposed and adopted changes to the work products. Here, the configuration manager (and perhaps a change-control board) employs some manner of change-control system to track change requests as they come into a project and to monitor change actions that are approved for incorporation. The configuration manager is also responsible for managing how those approved change items are integrated into product baselines.

3. Establish and report on the integrity of the work products. This goal is in place to ensure that items under configuration control are regularly monitored for integrity.

This usually includes conducting configuration library audits and issuing regular audit reports to the team.

Core Configuration Management actions

The configuration manager monitors and controls a defined set of project work products through a Configuration Management system by creating baselines, tracking changes, and periodically reporting on the integrity of designated work products.

Applies to Support:

- Systems Engineering
- Software Engineering
- Integrated Product and Process Development

Figure 6-13 illustrates the Configuration Management PA.

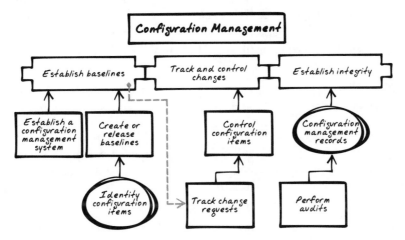

FIGURE 6-13. *The purpose of Configuration Management is to control the integrity of a work product across the life of the project. This includes practices in three areas. First, the team establishes a Configuration Management system it can use to control and release baselines. Second, the team sets change-control mechanisms in place to track and analyze change requests. Third, the team periodically audits the contents of the Configuration Management system to ensure work product integrity.*

Process and Product Quality Assurance

The PPQA Process Area in CMMI is the model's core compliance component. Process and Product Quality Assurance is in many ways kin to Configuration Management. Its function is to ensure the integrity of a project's work products and processes from a standards viewpoint. A PPQA analyst* assigned to a project monitors two operational areas. First, the

---

* I call this role an *analyst*. That's just my term. This can be a full-time role, a part-time role, or a role shared by multiple members of your teams.

analyst is responsible for work *product* compliance. Key here is confirming that selected work products produced during the various phases of a project are created in accordance with established formats, content guides, and scope projections. Second, the analyst is responsible for *process* compliance. This involves the work activities on a project. The goal here is to confirm that the major work activities for a project are conducted in compliance with published process standards.

The chief tool of PPQA is the audit. Through the use of a PPQA Plan, the PPQA analyst identifies certain milestone points in the project where product and process audits should take place. The audits are then conducted against a checklist of compliance items, and the results of the audit are distributed to project managers, identified team members, and executive management.

As noted earlier, this PA is also related to Verification. But it differs in one key way. Verification contains a peer-review process conducted by team members reporting to project management. PPQA is an activity typically managed by a function that reports to executive management in addition to project management. The main job of the PPQA analyst is to provide *objective* evidence that project teams within the organization at large are conducting project activities according to established processes.

Two specific goals

Two goals are defined for Process and Product Quality Assurance:

1. Objectively evaluate processes and work products. This goal is in place to ensure that each project team is provided with objective criteria that can be applied to evaluate process compliance and work product suitability. The key is to remove as much subjectivity as possible so that performance expectations and suitability standards are clear to everyone and can be consistently evaluated.

2. Provide objective insight into the efficiency and effectiveness of project processes. This goal provides the documentation and measurement component for this Process Area. Here, the PPQA analyst communicates and tracks noncompliance items to make sure they are remedied in an acceptable manner, and also records measures of these events and audits in general to provide a basis for future process improvement.

Core Process and Product Quality Assurance actions

A Process and Product Quality Assurance analyst, using objective criteria, works with the project team to audit activities and work products to make sure that they are being conducted in a manner compliant with published processes, procedures, and standards.

Applies to Support:

- Systems Engineering
- Software Engineering
- Integrated Product and Process Development

Figure 6-14 illustrates the Process and Product Quality Assurance PA.

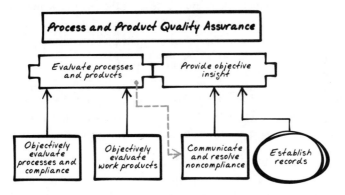

FIGURE 6-14. *Process and Product Quality Assurance is often seen as the process-oversight arm of a project effort. The focus is on ensuring that the project team is following defined processes and is producing appropriate work products in line with standards. Regular audits are planned and conducted, results are communicated, and noncompliance issues are managed to closure.*

Measurement and Analysis

The Measurement and Analysis Process Area presents the foundation for quantitative analysis (and process growth) within project management and across the organization as a whole. As it is introduced here, this Process Area need not be thought of as a full-blown metrics program. Measurement and Analysis may begin small and then lead to a fuller metrics approach to process improvement and program management. Here, each project (coordinated mainly through Project Management, Configuration Management, and Process and Product Quality Assurance) defines a set of measurements that will be collected at various points during the life of a project. These measurements are then incorporated into an M&A plan that specifies how the data will be collected, who will collect it, where the data will be stored, and how it will be used.

The main objective of this Process Area is to create a metrics repository—a central database for measurement storage. In the short term, this data can be analyzed as a way to measure variance, as an early indicator of project trends, and as a numeric mechanism to compare projects. In the long term, the repository will serve as a base for establishing quantitative project management measurements and for studying causal analysis with a view toward defect resolution and prevention.

Two specific goals

CMMI defines two goals for Measurement and Analysis:

1. Align defined measures and analyses with project activities. In other words, make sure that what you want to measure is in harmony with the activity occurring on the project. This involves defining the measures to collect over the course of a project and specifying how the measures are to be calculated and collected, how they are to be stored, and how they are to be analyzed.

2. Provide measurement results. This goal defines how the collected measures are to be compiled and reported both to the project team and executive management. This can include such facets as reporting regularity and responsibility, report formatting, communication avenues, and data retention policies.

Core Measurement and Analysis actions

Measurements are identified, defined, and collected for key activities and project phases. Once collected, they are used by project management and executive management to interpret project progress and as a mechanism to quantify project and process improvement as a whole.

Applies to Support:

- Systems Engineering
- Software Engineering
- Integrated Product and Process Development

Figure 6-15 illustrates the Measurement and Analysis PA.

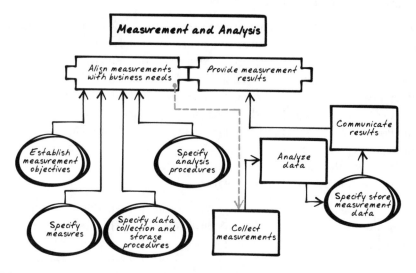

FIGURE 6-15. Measurement and Analysis deals with collecting process and project-performance measures that can eventually be used to help make improvement decisions. The practices here are designed to target meaningful measures, measures that reflect appropriate business objectives. Once defined, the organization specifies how the measures will be collected, how they will be analyzed, where they will be stored, and how measurement results will be communicated.

Decision Analysis and Resolution

The purpose of Decision Analysis and Resolution is to give teams a path to follow when making major decisions with the potential to impact the course of a project over its life cycle. Such decision making is common to all projects. At issue here is the manner in which decisions are arrived at. In organizations that lack sufficient or mature processes, projects are usually managed by intuition, by the "gut feeling" of the project manager. In this case, the better the project manager, the better the decisions being made. But this approach does not add much stability to an organization's operational capability.

A better approach is to provide a team with decision-making guidelines that promote analysis and the evaluation of alternatives. This approach is not designed to eliminate intuition or experience in project management. Its aim is to augment those qualities within a more regulated framework, one that sets methods for establishing alternatives, weighing the viability of alternatives, and selecting alternatives appropriate to the decision at hand.

One specific goal

CMMI has one goal defined for Decision Analysis and Resolution:

1. Evaluate alternatives before making a decision. This goal is based on a series of activities undertaken to guide the decision-making process. First, the organization establishes guidelines for decision analysis. This typically includes categorizing the major types of decisions addressed over the course of a project (decisions like budget changes, schedule adjustments, resource allocations, etc.). Next, these decision types are defined through a set of evaluation criteria, criteria that help establish the scope and impact of the decision on the project. Based on this, the team can explore alternatives that address these criteria, with each alternative being ranked by the suitability. Through this effort, a specific decision can be made that is best suited to the situation at hand.

Core Decision Analysis and Resolution actions

The organization provides project teams with a method for evaluating and weighing alternatives as part of the decision-making process.

Applies to Support:

- Systems Engineering
- Software Engineering
- Integrated Product and Process Development

Figure 6-16 illustrates the Decision Analysis and Resolution PA.

Causal Analysis and Resolution

Causal Analysis and Resolution addresses the issue of defect analysis and prevention. The purpose here is to investigate the potential causes for the occurrence of defects (in processes and products) and then design solutions to remove these causes from current and future project work. This Process Area requires several things of the organization. First, the organization must be adept at defect tracking. This typically involves some formalized process for product inspection (see the Verification Process Area, under "Engineering Process Areas"), as well as procedures for thorough process analysis and in-depth product testing. These procedures should provide the organization with a repository of defect data,

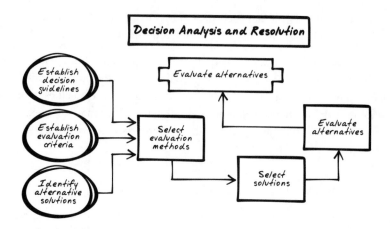

FIGURE 6-16. Decision Analysis and Resolution is designed to provide project teams with a mechanism to guide critical decision-making. The goal is to identify those kinds of decisions that should move through the DAR process and then provide activities that will encourage the evaluation of alternatives and the selection of appropriate solutions based on objective criteria.

sources, and frequencies. Next, the organization should have a method in place (with appropriate resources) to select and investigate a set of priority defects. These defects are analyzed to determine possible causes, and from these possible causes, corrective-action options are defined. Further production investigation is undertaken to verify defect causes, and then appropriate actions are selected to remove the causes.

Causal Analysis and Resolution is an ongoing process in an organization. It can be applied to all manner of work products and activities. And it represents a core focus of any advanced process improvement program.

NOTE

This Process Area bears a direct relationship with the DMAIC process in Six Sigma. For more information on this, see Chapter 7.

Two specific goals

Two goals are defined in CMMI for Causal Analysis and Resolution:

1. Determine the causes of defects. This goal establishes practices to pinpoint focal points for defect prevention: in code, in work products, in processes. This includes examining defect data sets to decide which analyses will prove most beneficial to the organization. Using these defect sets, an appointed team then investigates potential causes further, identifying the highest-profile or most likely causes.

2. Address the identified causes of the defects. This activity takes action from the first goal. Here, the team decides how to remove the causes from the production process. This usually involves a choice among possible actions. The team should evaluate

which choice holds the most promise for the situation at hand. Once this is decided, the team implements the corrective actions and monitors the result of this adaptation. If the change has proved effective, the team can focus on other defect areas; if not, further action may be called for.

Throughout this process, the team records its findings in a repository for future process improvement information.

Core Causal Analysis and Resolution actions

The organization examines sets of defect data to determine likely causes, modifies processes to test potential solutions, and then records the validity and effectiveness of these solutions.

Applies to Support:

- Systems Engineering
- Software Engineering
- Integrated Product and Process Development

Figure 6-17 illustrates the Causal Analysis and Resolution PA.

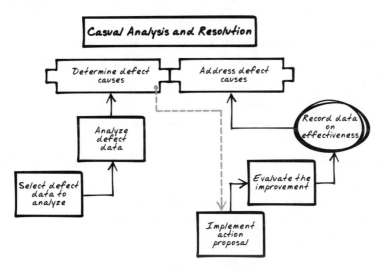

FIGURE 6-17. Causal Analysis and Resolution is a high-maturity Process Area that uses quantitative analysis and statistical analytics to determine the sources of defects in process performance, and then provides guidelines for addressing the removal of those sources.

SUPPORT PROCESS AREAS

The Support Process Areas (PAs) are designed to provide the kind of infrastructure that management and engineering need to execute project activities in a well-ordered and controlled environment. In brief, these PAs are as follows.

For Maturity Level 2:

Configuration Management (CM)

> Three goals are associated with Configuration Management: with the aid of some form of Configuration Management system, create and release product baselines when useful for project management; track changes and change requests as they are introduced into a project; and establish and maintain integrity by periodically auditing the CM system.

Measurement and Analysis (MA)

> This PA has two goals: define appropriate measures that will be collected and make sure they are aligned with business objectives, and provide results once the measures are collected and analyzed.

Process and Product Quality Assurance (PPQA)

> The PPQA PA has two goals: evaluate processes and work products using objective criteria, and provide objective insight to the project team and executive management concerning process and product compliance.

For Maturity Level 3:

Decision Analysis and Resolution (DAR)

> DAR has one goal: evaluate alternatives when making key business decisions, using objective criteria and weighting factors.

For Maturity Level 5:

Causal Analysis and Resolution (CAR)

> Two goals exist for CAR: based on accumulated defect data, study the data to determine likely causes of the defects, and address the causes of the defects by implementing solutions to prevent them from reoccurring.

Process Management Process Areas

The following sections detail the Process Areas specific to process management.

Organizational Process Focus

Organizational Process Focus is an activity the organization implements once it has reached a certain level of maturity. It's reached that level when the organization is ready to institutionalize a set of common processes and practices across all its groups. With this step comes an organizational focus on process improvement. Previously (and here I'm talking specifically about maturity levels, but the basic idea holds true for implementing processes in general), process sets were managed at the project level, each project team working with a set of procedures, activities, and artifacts that met its needs. Here the focus shifts higher up to the executive level. With Organizational Process Focus, process-centric strategies and targets are put into place to support the analysis, planning, development, and execution of all process program components. Then these components are collected and managed by a chartered group within the organization.

From this point on, the organization makes strategic decisions as to how its process program should be shaped as the needs of the organization evolve over time.

Two specific goals

CMMI defines two goals for Organizational Process Focus:

1. Determine process improvement opportunities. This goal involves the whole organization, but it is typically coordinated through senior management or a centralized Process Management Committee. Through the use of measurements, feedback, and outside knowledge, the organization defines its process needs. It establishes where its current program stands and in what direction it should evolve. The organization then appraises these needs and identifies process improvement initiatives that will most likely lead the organization to these defined improvement goals.

2. Plan and implement the process improvement activities. This second goal follows from the first. Once process improvement initiatives have been identified and prioritized—a strategic plan set into place, so to speak—the organization works to plan for, design, and implement the improvements across the organization.

Core Organizational Process Focus actions

The organization establishes strategic goals and objectives for its process program and coordinates the deployment of process improvement initiatives over time throughout the organization.

Applies to Process Management:

- Systems Engineering

- Software Engineering

- Integrated Product and Process Development

Figure 6-18 illustrates the Organizational Process Focus PA.

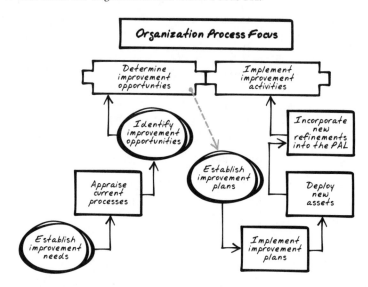

FIGURE 6-18. Organizational Process Focus provides a strategic approach for planning and managing process improvement activities. Here, the organization develops targets and objectives for process improvement activities, and then develops tactical plans for implementing the improvement activities across the organization.

Organizational Process Definition

This Process Area works in partnership with the Organizational Process Focus PA described previously. While OPF introduces centralized and coordinated management of the organization's process improvement activities, OPD centers on the management and deployment of the organization's process asset library, including those assets dealing with IPPD (when needed). The process library is a repository of standardized items available for use by the project teams as guidelines to work activity, product creation, and project management. This repository typically includes descriptions of processes and process elements, descriptions of life-cycle models, process tailoring guidelines, process-related documentation, measurement repositories, and other management tools and guidelines.

The purpose of Organizational Process Definition is to provide a program that promotes a consistent and predictable mode of operations for management and development efforts across the organization. Further, this Process Area provides a resource for best practices, lessons learned, and metrics consolidated from groups across the organization.

Two specific goals

Two goals are defined for Organizational Process Definition:

1. Establish a repository of organizational process assets. This goal involves institutionalizing a set of standardized processes that can be applied to (or tailored for) all organizational development projects. Included here are process descriptions, life-cycle models, tailoring criteria and guidelines, metrics databases, training and tutorial materials, and other relevant resources.

2. Enable IPPD principles. This goal deals with establishing the right environment for integration, including team unification, coordination, and collaboration.

All of this is typically organized into a library, version controlled, and made available to members of the organization.

Core Organizational Process Focus actions

The organization establishes a central repository of process assets and IPPD assets (as needed) and makes this repository available for organization-wide use.

Applies to Process Management:

- Systems Engineering
- Software Engineering
- Integrated Product and Process Development

Figure 6-19 illustrates the Organizational Process Definition PA.

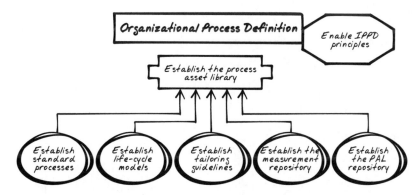

FIGURE 6-19. Organizational Process Definition is centered on establishing a commonly used set of process assets. Housed in a Process Asset Library are such typical components as process descriptions, life-cycle methodologies, tailoring guidelines, and the measurement repository. Another activity is to enable IPPD principles when needed in the organization.

Organizational Process Performance

Organizational Process Performance is a Process Area related to Quantitative Project Management. As noted earlier in this chapter, under "Project Management Process Areas," the goal of QPM is to provide a set of guidelines and activities that project management can use to quantitatively measure project activity and performance over time and against a set of predefined benchmarks. That same concept applies here, but with a slightly different focus. Organizational Process Performance is managed and used (by designated team members) to regularly track the efficiency and effectiveness of the processes used within projects. Processes are observed and then measured to produce a base set of metrics used to predict how the processes will influence project performance. Process performance baselines, models, and trends can then be charted. When implemented on future projects, management can use these metrics as part of the planning process, and as an aid to predicting schedules, budgets, and resource needs. Further observations can also be used as a source for process improvement data.

One specific goal

CMMI defines one goal for Organizational Process Performance:

1. Establish performance baselines and models for elements of the process set. This goal includes selecting a set of processes to focus performance measures on, quantitatively measuring them, establishing their performance benchmarks, and creating performance models that can be applied to the planning and estimating and tracking efforts of the organization. Naturally this is a Process Area that requires a high level of maturity, one in which performance data and other metrics have been plentifully amassed over time.

Core Organizational Process Performance actions

The organization quantitatively measures a selected set of process elements and then uses these measures as predictors of performance and efficiencies for future projects.

Applies to Process Management:

- Systems Engineering
- Software Engineering
- Integrated Product and Process Development

Figure 6-20 illustrates the Organizational Process Performance PA.

Organizational Training

This Process Area is designed to support the institutionalization of a comprehensive process program throughout the organization. The success of any such program is contingent upon the knowledge your people have of it and their ability to use it. In light of this, training is a key way to ensure that your people are familiar with your program and know how

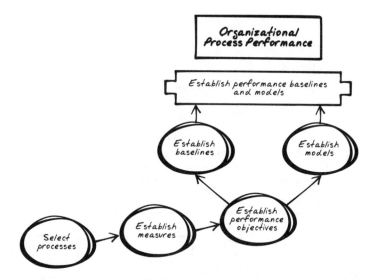

FIGURE 6-20. *Organizational Process Performance is another high-maturity Process Area. Here, the organization establishes baselines and models of process performance based on detailed measures of past process performance. The baselines and models can then be used to predict future project performance.*

to use it. The Organizational Training Process Area promotes a series of practices. These include defining what courses are needed to support your program, designing and publishing course material, accounting for the availability of training facilities, and arranging for competent instructors to conduct the classes. This PA also provides a framework for establishing training recommendations for the members of the organization, identifying the training needs of employees, arranging for class participation, and establishing methods for keeping and tracking training records.

Two specific goals

There are two goals established for Organizational Training:

1. Establish an organizational training capability. Through this goal, the organization builds its training program. It does this by defining its strategic training needs, determining what training it can contract outside of the organization and what training it must own, and then establishing training facilities, curriculum, and course materials.

2. Provide the necessary training to people within the organization. This goal involves targeting the right people in the organization for the right courses, conducting those training sessions, maintaining training records, and periodically assessing the effectiveness of the training program as a whole.

Core Organizational Training actions

The organization establishes a training program to educate its people on the use of its process set, and then implements appropriate activities to deliver the training.

Applies to Process Management:

- Systems Engineering
- Software Engineering
- Integrated Product and Process Development

Figure 6-21 illustrates the Organizational Training PA.

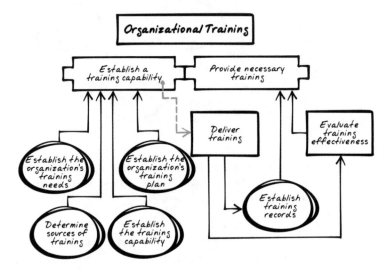

FIGURE 6-21. Organizational Training deals with helping the organization establish a training capability to address ongoing training needs. This includes developing training objectives, devising training responsibilities, and creating a tactical training plan. Also included are activities for delivering training, for maintaining training records, and for assessing overall training effectiveness.

Organizational Innovation and Deployment

The purpose of Organizational Innovation and Deployment is to select and deploy incremental and innovative process program improvements that measurably improve the organization's management processes and technologies. The improvements support the organization's quality and process-performance objectives as derived from the organization's business objectives. This Process Area represents the culmination of process management in CMMI.

Two specific goals

Two goals are defined for this Process Area:

1. Select process improvement activities for the organization. This goal involves strategically deciding which process improvement activities to undertake within the organization. In order to do this effectively, the organization should assess all opportunities for improvement, weigh the benefits and investment required for each, choose those opportunities that provide the best benefit/investment mix, and pilot

them within the organization. Those pilots that show benefit to the overall process program should then be prepared for deployment.

2. Deploy the improvements across the organization. This goal realizes the activities of Goal 1. Here, a plan is created for the coordinated deployment of the improvements into the overall process program. This deployment is then managed according to plan, and measures are taken of the overall improvement in the program due to the enhancement.

Core Organizational Innovation and Deployment actions

The organization strategically develops enhancements to its process program and then deploys these enhancements in a coordinated manner.

Applies to Process Management:

- Systems Engineering
- Software Engineering
- Integrated Product and Process Development

Figure 6-22 illustrates the Organizational Innovation and Deployment PA.

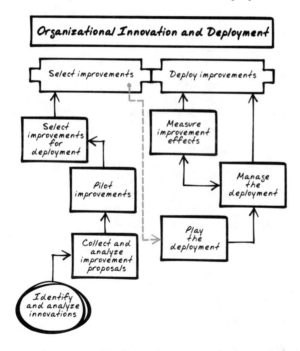

FIGURE 6-22. Organizational Innovation and Deployment provides for practices that help an organization roll out process improvements in a planned and coordinated manner. Activities in this area include selecting improvements to implement, piloting improvements to ascertain effectiveness, rolling improvement out across the organization, and measuring the effectiveness of the new and enhanced processes.

PROCESS MANAGEMENT PROCESS AREAS

The five PAs that address Process Management under CMMI deal with how the organization manages, maintains, and institutionalizes its process program and the assets it contains. The focus is on strategic management, improvement, and deployment. The Process Areas include the following.

For Maturity Level 3:

Organizational Process Focus (OPF)

Two PAs are defined for OPF: determine strategic process improvement opportunities within the organization, and develop plans and actions to implement these process improvement activities.

Organizational Process Definition (OPD)

Two goals are established for OPD: establish a centralized, managed repository within the organization that holds the process asset library, life-cycle model descriptions, process tailoring guidelines, and measurements databases. And, when needed, enable IPPD principles within the organization.

Organizational Training (OT)

Two goals exist for OT: establish an organizational training capability that accounts for the process and technical training needs of your resources, and provide the various forms of training you've identified for the organization.

For Maturity Level 4:

Organizational Process Performance (OPP)

This high-maturity PA has one select goal: establish performance baselines—that is, use quantitative performance data to create models that can be used to predict future performance.

For Maturity Level 5:

Organization Innovation and Deployment (OID)

This is another high-maturity level PA, with two goals: based on your empirical analysis improvement opportunities, select those opportunities with significant paybacks, and develop a plan to deploy those improvements across the organization in an orderly fashion.

Implementing CMMI

As we have seen so far, CMMI is a collection of Process Areas (PAs)—all in all, 22 of them—and under each is a series of recommended practices. Each PA is supported by one or more specific goals, which can be reached using the recommended specific practices. To support the implementation of each PA, CMMI also uses generic goals. The generic goals help institutionalize the activities of a Process Area into a project. There are five generic goals, each with its own generic practices.

That's a lot of best-practice data. And if you were to look at the CMMI components as a single model, the way that ISO 9001 and Six Sigma are, you might reach the conclusion that there's more than enough there, maybe too much. But CMMI was designed with scalability in mind. In fact, you can implement CMMI within your organization one of three ways. In each way, you select only certain portions of the model to use: portions that best suit your own process improvement needs, portions that address your chief management concerns, portions that get you to your process goals.

One way is called the Continuous Representation. Another is called the Staged Representation. The third way—and this is my term—is called the "any way you want" way. Let's take a look at each.

The Continuous Representation

The Continuous Representation is designed to address specific areas of need within an organization. Here, you select those Process Areas that you want to focus on, maybe those that need shoring up, and you implement them. It's a way to direct process improvement along very specific lines. For example, if you manage a technology shop that produces code very effectively but has a hard time managing budgets and schedules, you might elect to implement two PAs: Project Planning and Project Monitoring and Control. A different shop might have a different problem: project components might be slipping from team to team with noticeable defects or functional mismatches. This shop might elect to implement three PAs: Configuration Management, Verification, and Validation; those give you practices to deal with those kinds of issues. With Continuous Representation, the choice is yours.

As a process improvement tool, the Continuous Representation measures your progress along a six-tier capability scale. It is specific to each Process Area you work with. The assumption is that the higher up the scale you move, the more capable you have become with each Process Area.

The capability scale is as follows:

0. Incomplete
1. Performed
2. Managed
3. Defined
4. Quantitatively Managed
5. Optimizing

Incomplete

At Capability Level 0, the Process Area, although it may be partially in line with CMMI, is not yet in compliance with model recommendations.

Performed

At Capability Level 1, the organization has implemented Generic Goal 1 (which says follow the specific goals) and has also implemented, for the Process Areas it has elected, the specific goals and the recommended Level 1 specific practices. When implementing the Continuous Representation for any PA, you'll find that the vast majority of the recommended specific practices come into play at Level 1.

THE CODING SCHEME EXPLAINED

This is a good point to explain the coding scheme behind the model. It's helpful to understand. As noted, the model is composed of specific goals and specific practices, and generic goals and generic practices.

Specific goals are coded as SGs, specific practices are coded as SPs, generic goals are coded as GGs, and generic practices as GPs. As an example, under the Process Area Technical Solution, there are three specific goals. They are coded as SG 1, SG 2, and SG 3.

SG 2 states, "Develop the Design." Under this goal, there are four specific practices: SP 2.1, SP 2.2, SP 2.3, and SP 2.4. So, SP 2.3 can be read as, "This is a specific practice for Specific Goal 2, and it is practice number 3."

After this, you'll see a hyphen and then a final number—for example, SP 2.3-1. The 1 indicates the capability level at which the practice should be implemented. SP 2.3-1 then can be read as, "This is a specific practice for Specific Goal 2, it is practice number 3, and it should be implemented at Capability Level 1, Performed."

Managed

At Capability Level 2, you've kept your Level 1 program in place but have augmented it by implementing Generic Goal 2, a step that broadens the depth at which the processes are deployed on your projects. Along with Generic Goal 2, the organization also implements those Level 2-specific practices recommended in the model.

Defined

At Capability Level 3, the use of your Process Areas has matured to the point where the organization can adopt them for organization-wide use. Here, the organization adds to its

Level 2 program by implementing Generic Goal 3 and the Level 3-specific practices recommended in the specific goals.

Quantitatively Managed

At Capability Level 4, your Process Areas are reaching a high degree of capability. Here, you add to you Level 3 program by adopting Generic Goal 4. No new specific practices are introduced at Level 4. At Level 4, the organization takes a growing quantitative approach to process management. Precise measures of expected process performance are established, tracked, and used for process improvement.

Optimizing

The Continuous Representation reaches its apex at Level 5, the optimizing level. Here, the organization adopts Generic Goal 5 for its Process Areas and realizes a culture of continuous process improvement and defect prevention for each of those Process Areas it has adopted.

That's a quick look at the Continuous Representation. Let's summarize a few of the more important points. The Continuous Representation is centered on those Process Areas you elect to implement. Logically, it's better to select Process Areas that can deliver distinct benefits to your organization, that can help you improve management, production, and quality. You may elect one or many PAs to implement. And since the sophistication of a Process Area is rated along a six-tier capability scale, the measurement 0 to 5 indicating how capable each PA is, you can raise the capability level of each Process Area at its own rate, independent of other Process Areas.

If you implement the Continuous Representation and then choose to be formally appraised, the appraiser will evaluate each Process Area independently of the others and then award a capability rating to each Process Area. With all PAs combined, you'll then have a capability profile.

There are many professionals who feel that the Continuous Representation is the best choice when implementing CMMI. Since process improvement is all about getting better at what you do, at minimizing weaknesses, the Continuous Representation shares that end. It lets you select where to target your efforts, where to focus your energy.

The Staged Representation

The official SEI alternative to the Continuous Representation is the Staged Representation. The Staged Representation takes a different perspective on process improvement using CMMI. With the Continuous Representation, the focus is on the *capability* of Process Areas. And you choose the Process Areas. With the Staged Representation, the focus is on organizational *maturity*. Here you implement predefined sets of PAs.

With the Staged Representation, projects—or the organization as a whole—work a process improvement program that moves through a series of five maturity levels. At each maturity level, the project or organization adopts more and more Process Areas. The five maturity levels of the Staged Representation are as follows:

1. Initial
2. Managed
3. Defined
4. Quantitatively Managed
5. Optimizing

This five-tier scale has some commonality with the six-tier scale of the Continuous Representation. You'll notice that Levels 2 through 5 share common names. And in fact their intended outcomes are pretty well aligned. But there is one big difference, and that has to do with the generic goals.

Generic goals in the Staged Representation

As we have seen with the Continuous Representation, CMMI has five generic goals. Under each goal is a set of recommended generic practices. As a Process Area increases in capability, it implements a successive number of generic goals. For example, for the Project Planning Process Area to be profiled at Capability Level 4, its team needs to implement the specific goals and specific practices defined for that Process Area, as well as the Generic Goals 1, 2, 3, and 4.

But with the Staged Representation, only Generic Goals 2 and 3 apply. You implement the practices of Generic Goal 2 when you are forming your Maturity Level 2 program. You implement the practices of Generic Goal 3 when you are forming your Level 3 program. Maturity Levels 4 and 5 require the addition of no new generic goals.

Following is a brief description of each maturity level in the Staged Representation.

Initial

When an organization or project is at the initial stage, it has no consistent process program in place. Shops that are run this way typically manage projects in an ad hoc fashion. The goal is simply to get the work done, and any way that gets it done in even a close-to-acceptable condition is OK.

Here's what you'll commonly find: organizations in the initial phase are *personality-driven*. Project success depends largely on the talents and the temperaments of the people working the project. The term "hero-dependent" is often employed here. It takes the tireless efforts of heroes in the organization to bring projects off. There are obvious drawbacks to working this way. First is the waste of effort. Without process or a program of improvement in place, the team learns little about how to do things better. The wheel is constantly being reinvented in these shops. Second, visibility is low. Management has little view as to what is going on inside project activity. And so management has little control over cost, accountability, or quality. This "just do it" environment might work well for an exercise program, but it'll do little for product development. Finally, shops in the initial stage operate with very low predictability. And with low predictability comes high risk: risk of schedule overruns, risk of cost overruns, risk of missing functionality.

All in all, it's a risky way to run a business. But it's easy. And more times than many IT professionals might like to admit, easy wins out.

Managed

Maturity Level 2 is the Managed level. Here, the project or organization makes a conscientious move into the culture of process improvement. The following seven Process Areas are implemented: Requirements Management, Project Planning, Project Monitoring and Control, Configuration Management, Measurement and Analysis, Process and Product Quality Assurance, and Supplier Agreement Management.* The recommended generic practices of Generic Goal 2 are also implemented.

Notice this: the focus at the Managed level is on two key factors. The first is project management: effectively planning, managing, and controlling project components. The second is process management: implementing a program to ensure that the established processes are being honored in a company.

Defined

At the Defined level, the organization has learned enough and tested its processes thoroughly enough that it can now standardize on a full suite of process assets. This is—in my opinion—the biggest leap in the Staged Representation of CMMI. Here the organization augments its Level 2 program with a host of new Process Areas, including Requirements Development, Technical Solution, Product Integration, Risk Management, Decision Analysis and Resolution, Verification, Validation, Integrated Project Management (with extensions for IPPD), Organizational Process Focus, Organizational Process Definition (with IPPD extensions), and Organizational Training. The organization also implements Generic Goal 3. The move here is substantial. At Maturity Level 3, the organization has a broad and robust process management and improvement program in place that reaches into the areas of project management, engineering, process management, and support.

Quantitatively Managed

At Maturity Level 4, the organization begins to shape its process and management programs through the use of empirical measurements. Just as moving to Maturity Level 3 signifies a major step forward in the commitment to process improvement, the move to Level 4 marks another major advancement. Data takes on a new importance here. Decisions are

---

* They can be implemented for a single project, or they can be implemented for the entire organization. The usual recommended path, when viable, is to let projects develop their own processes. That way the organization can try out many different approaches, keeping the best of what's developed over time.

now in large part data-driven (similar to Six Sigma). Here the organization implements two new Process Areas: Organizational Process Performance and Quantitative Project Management. No new generic goals are required at Level 4.

Optimizing

The final maturity level is Level 5, Optimizing. Notice the verb form used. Optimizing is an ongoing process. Here, the organization adopts two final Process Areas: Organizational Innovation and Deployment, and Causal Analysis and Resolution. (Again, no new generic goals are required at Level 5.) At this point, the organization has entered a level of maturity in which the full enterprise is focused on continuous process and product improvement.

> **NOTE**
>
> As with the Continuous Representation, the Staged Representation consists of specific goals and specific practices, and generic goals and generic practices. But with the Continuous Representation, the coding scheme is important in that it shows you what practices to implement at what levels. For the sake of continuity, the Staged Representation retains the same coding scheme, but here it loses its significance. When a Process Area appears at a certain maturity level, all the recommended specific practices under the specific goals apply.

That's a quick look at the Staged Representation. Let's summarize a few important points about it.

The Staged Representation is centered on a series of five maturity levels, the levels moving from 1, the initial stage, to 5, the optimizing stage. At Maturity Level 1, the organization has not fully implemented its process program or any set of CMMI's Process Areas. At Level 2, the Managed Level, a series of Process Areas is implemented to guide project planning and management, process management, and related support functions. Level 2, even though it is constrained in scope, is usually the toughest leap for an organization. Making the move from Initial to Managed requires a cultural shift that many organizations find difficult to maneuver.

Level 3, the Defined level, is arguably the biggest leap in the Staged Representation. Here, the organization adopts a host of new Process Areas that address project management, engineering, supplier management, and support functions. All in all, 18 Process Areas can come into play at Level 3.

At the high maturity Levels 4 and 5, the organization moves to a more quantitative approach to decision making, to proactive defect prevention, and to a coordinated method for innovation and deployment.

If you implement the Staged Representation and then choose to be formally appraised, the appraiser will evaluate your project or your organization (using a sample of typical projects) against implementation of the Process Areas for a predefined maturity Level (and the Levels under that).

Just as the Continuous Representation has its advocates, there are many professionals who feel that Staged is the best choice when implementing CMMI. Staged is an ordered way to integrate a suite of process improvement practices within an organization. And it provides a path the whole organization can follow on its way to increased maturity.

The "Any Way You Want" Way

The third way is the "any way you want" way. This is just what it sounds like: you implement the best practices described in any Process Area any way you want to, according to the needs of your organization. In fact, this is the probably the best way to use CMMI. (It's probably the best way to use any formalized process improvement program.) The whole idea behind process improvement is to establish a road map you can follow to steadily move toward the goals of increased predictability, reduced risk, and stronger quality controls. The need is an *internal* need. In the purest sense, organizations should implement process improvement not to receive an award, like a formal maturity rating. Rather, the evolution of getting better—of delivering heightened quality—is the real reward.

Organizations that make the commitment to process improvement might find that the Continuous Representation or the Staged Representation include recommendations that don't fit the group's current quality position. In cases like these, it's probably better to take a simple three-step implementation approach in line with the any-way-you-want way.

First, assess your organization. Understand what it does well; know what its strengths are. At the same time, take a critical look at areas where performance is not all it could be. Pinpoint opportunities for improvement. This is the beginning of any improvement strategy.

Second, study the CMMI framework. Acquire a solid understanding of the scope of CMMI, the goals and practices it promotes, and the estimated level of effort you think will be required to realize the recommendations that seem to address your needs.

Third, target select practices based on these needs and then implement them in the way you deem to be the most effective, the way that will have long-lasting impact and benefits for the organization.

In terms of a solutions approach, the any-way-you-want way probably provides the best goodness-of-fit for an organization. It allows for maximum customization and the sharpest degree of focus. Of course, this approach limits the external recognition of your program. The SEI actually enthusiastically endorses the any-way-you-want way. But, when it comes to official appraisal recognition, it can only recognize the Continuous or Staged Representations. The same holds true for authorized Lead Appraisers. They can only perform a SCAMPI* appraisal using the Continuous or Staged approach. And it's true that many organizations that adopt CMMI do so because they want the rewards of process improvement along with official external recognition. They need it for competitive advantage, or for marketplace requirements, or because headquarters says so.

If you're free of those requirements, you may be able to focus solely on getting better, on the tangible benefits of CMMI's proven practices. In that case, the any-way-you-want way may be the best way to go.

For a Deeper Look

The following books and references can provide you with a deeper look at Capability Maturity Model Integration:

CMMI, Guidelines for Process Integration and Product Improvement by Mary Beth Chrissis et al. (Addison-Wesley Professional)

> This is the official CMMI specification, published by the Software Engineering Institute through Addison-Wesley. The book is organized into three main parts. Part 1 describes the model's approach to process improvement and presents the methods by which CMMI can be implemented in an organization. Part 2 contains full descriptions of each of the 22 Process Areas in CMMI. Part 3 contains an extended glossary and other reference material.

CMMI Distilled by Dennis M. Ahern et al. (Addison-Wesley Professional)

> This book offers tips and techniques for implementing CMMI, whether the organization is starting with a "fresh" process program or is migrating from an established one into CMMI. There is a lot of advice here on how the CMMI team might be structured and what responsibilities it should undertake. And the authors offer their own lessons on how to make implementations the most effective. The book also provides descriptions and guidance concerning SCAMPI, the CMMI appraisal process.

Real Process Improvement Using the CMMI by Michael West (Auerbach)

> This book presents what might be called a critical look at implementing CMMI. The author focuses on the practical application of this framework and leaves theory for other works. I sat with the author's wife, Jitka, at an SEI training session, and she

---

* SCAMPI is the SEI's name for its authorized appraisal process. The acronym stands for Standard CMMI Appraisal Method for Process Improvement. It's a clunky name, but an effective methodology. If you wish your organization to receive official recognition for being CMMI-compliant, you will need to undergo an authorized SCAMPI A appraisal. This is conducted by an SEI authorized Lead Appraiser who is bound to follow the guidelines set for SCAMPI. These guidelines ensure consistency across the discovery and evaluation activities and reduce the degree of subjectivity that might creep into an appraisal.

Aside from the Class A SCAMPI appraisal, there are also Class B and C appraisals. These are lighter forms of the full-blown Class A appraisal. Typically, companies conduct internal Class B and C appraisals for one of two purposes: 1) to gain a picture of their current quality position when they are first developing a CMMI program, and 2) to make sure the organization is ready for a forthcoming Class A appraisal.

stressed the value of this "practical" approach. The book works to establish real-world expectations of how CMMI can benefit an organization and provides practical tips on realizing the full value from an implementation.

Software Process Improvement with CMM by Joseph Raynus (Digital)

This work is addressed to project managers and management looking to get a practical understanding of process improvement using the CMM. The CMM is an earlier version (now sunset) of CMMI, but the book's focus on implementing CMMI processes across the phases of a project life cycle is very well done and thorough, and the advice still remains true for CMMI. So it's still worth a look.

Interpreting the CMMI: A Process Improvement Approach by Margaret Kulpa and Kent A. Johnson (Auerbach)

This significant book lays out recommendations and advice for using CMMI as a foundation for organizational process improvement. The book presents the details of what the specification recommends in terms of goals and practices. But its real focus is on techniques for interpreting the model so that it best fits with the culture of the organization and also addresses the core process improvement needs within the organization.

Practical Insight into CMMI by Tim Kasse (Artech House Computing Library)

This work presents a general picture of the kinds of activities in software and systems engineering shops that can benefit from the implementation of CMMI Process Areas and practices. The book describes the roles and responsibilities that are required to advance the use of CMMI and offers advice to project managers, technical managers, and senior management. Available as a digital download.

Summary

Capability Maturity Model Integration is a process improvement framework established by the Software Engineering Institute of Carnegie Mellon University in Pittsburgh, Pennsylvania. CMMI represents a collection of 22 Process Areas consisting of a series of industry-recognized best practices for IT development. Adopters use the Process Areas as a foundation upon which they develop processes and process program components.

Unofficially, the Process Areas can be organized as falling into four general categories:

- Project management: process areas to help you develop estimates, plan projects, monitor and control project status, manage suppliers and vendors, address and mitigate risks, and quantitatively project progress and process performance

- Project support: process areas to help you ensure the integrity of work products, address change control and change management, guide critical decision making, plan for and deploy root-cause analyses, measure process performance and product quality, and audit process and standards compliance

- Engineering: process areas to help you elicit, define, and manage requirements; develop and deploy appropriate technical solutions; coordinate product integration and assembly; verify and validate product performance; and conduct peer reviews

- Process management: process areas to help you institutionalize process assets across the organization, provide training on process program elements, and establish an environment for overall process improvement

CHAPTER SEVEN

Six Sigma

BRIAN NEELY IS **CTO** OF A MAJOR SYSTEMS INTEGRATOR BASED OUT OF THE **W**ASHINGTON **D.C.** AREA. I was speaking to Brian recently about his own focus on process improvement and how he sees process contributing to the success of large companies. "At one level, it's about expanded potential," he said, referring to the use of process programs within various company subsidiaries, "but at the executive level, it is about performance, especially performance measures."

Brian's focus is on empirical process improvement, the ability for operating units to demonstrate efficiencies through data and to establish performance trends over time through the analysis of data. That's a somewhat typical viewpoint for CFOs. Companies use financial standings, projected revenues, and burn rates as reliable predictors of success. The story is in those numbers. But that's a relatively advanced viewpoint for CIOs and CTOs. However, it's becoming more and more common. And more and more popular. As the IT industry begins to increase its appreciation that process lies at the heart of any technology development effort, the interest in process performance should increase proportionately.

That brings us to the subject of Six Sigma.

In the previous two chapters, you got an overview of ISO 9001 and CMMI. You saw that these programs were geared toward helping an organization implement process programs, perhaps to refine a current process position or to create a program from the ground up. In essence, those programs—those approaches—are all about instituting best practices. They help an organization set into place the structure for process improvement and, by default, quality management.

Six Sigma is different. Six Sigma has recently stepped into the field of IT as a Hot Topic. It has generated a lot of buzz, even more so than ISO or CMMI. People seem to be talking about it, discussing it, trying to figure out what place it might have in their organizations. Six Sigma is different from ISO 9001 and CMMI in that its focus is on measuring existing processes with a view to making them more efficient and effective.

Six Sigma assumes you have processes in place. Maybe they are formal, maybe they are informal, but you are definitely doing something to produce something. At its core, Six Sigma is a way to measure processes and then modify them to reduce the number of defects found in what you produce. With this program, you study the sources of defects and then analyze ways to make the processes more resilient, so that defects are not introduced or have fewer opportunities to creep in.

Many people think that the idea behind Six Sigma is to have a system that produces zero defects. That's not really true. But, statistically, the rote measure of "six sigma" means that your system will turn out only 3.4 defects per million opportunities for defects. (I'll look at this in more depth later.) But even that is not a really accurate representation of the intention of Six Sigma.

The real idea behind Six Sigma is to manage process improvement quantitatively. It seeks to put measures and controls in place so that you can readily and regularly monitor the performance of your processes and, using performance data, adjust them to maximize their ability to produce predictable, quality results.

You can think of Six Sigma as the evaluation side to a process improvement program. That's why many organizations pair Six Sigma with programs like ISO 9001, CMMI, or LEAN. Six Sigma gives you the tools you can use to rate how well these programs are performing for you. And this rating is not qualitative. It is not instinctive or intuitive. It is a rating based on hard data, on fact.

As this chapter looks at the high-level focus of Six Sigma, you'll see that it is a cycle of seven general steps:

1. Look at the product. Put a critical eye on what you produce. Continually examine what it is you make and how you make it so that you can always seek ways to make it better. There are few sacred cows in Six Sigma.

2. Identify defects. Examine your product and identify defects. Count them. Measure them. Know what you mean by the term "defect." You can think of a defect as anything that holds your product back from being the best it can be in the minds of your customers.

3. Look to the process. If the product is not all it can be, then chances are your processes could be improved. Examine your processes. What's happening with your current processes that might be letting defects in? What opportunities might you see to keep defects out?

4. Determine sources of defects. Analyze how the process works. Study its flows and structure to determine where in its operations defects are seeping in.

5. Improve the process. Based on your analysis of process performance and your understanding of the process structure, you now adjust the process with the intention of improving its performance. The goal is to lock defects out.

6. Use the new process. Now that you have improved the process, put it to work. Set it into the production environment and let the improvements make their mark.

7. Look at the product. Take a fresh look at the product. Did your improvement make a difference? Is the product better? If it is, look for new improvement opportunities. (And the cycle continues…)

Before we take a look at the push and structure of Six Sigma, let's go through a brief recap of the history of Six Sigma.

A Brief History of Six Sigma

The foundation of Six Sigma was created at Motorola around 1979. Two engineers, Art Sundry and Bill Smith, were the pioneers. They were involved in the company's pager business at the time. And the business was having quality problems. The demand for pagers was skyrocketing, and Motorola was cranking up production to take advantage of the demand. But the pace proved to be somewhat hectic, and problems began to pop up.

Out on the factory floor, when a pager rolled off the assembly line, before it was packaged, it went to Test. If it passed there, OK. If it failed, it was rerouted to Repair. Once Repair fixed what was wrong, it went on to packaging and then shipping. When more and more pagers started finding their way to Repair, Sundry and Smith, both intrigued by this growing quality problem, began to track the lives of the troublesome pagers once they got out into the field, and they noticed an interesting fact. The pagers that failed initially in Test failed more often in the field even though these were the ones that had gotten that extra shot of quality control by going through Repair. The pagers that passed Test originally tended to operate defect-free in the field.

Sundry and Smith knew that Motorola was committed to customer satisfaction and looked around to see how the company was dealing with this. The model they saw was from the Classical School. Motorola was committed to a large in-house repair facility to fix anything it could find before it got into the field. And it also invested in many repair shops in the field, so customers wouldn't have to deal with dead pagers for long. This was the American business trend of the early 80s: Motorola was keeping its customers happy by reacting to (correcting) problems in the field. But Sundry and Smith had the following revelation. They saw (just like Philip Crosby knew) that quality through reaction is expensive. It takes a lot to support a reaction strategy. More people, more materials, more steps, more time, especially more money.

That's when they realized that the defect-free pagers were not only superior and imminently more reliable, they actually cost the company less money. The lesson was clear: improving quality reduces costs. It reduces costs by reducing activities and materials. The American business climate at the time thought pretty much the opposite: it costs too much money to build quality in; it's cheaper in the long run to deal with it in the field.

Sundry and Smith—both experienced engineers—began to develop statistical measures so that they could empirically analyze Motorola's production process to find out why these defects were creeping in. This analytical, numerical approach was essential because the pager-making process was large. It was complex. It had lots of interrelations. It was clear in this case that "gut feeling" was not the way to make improvements. What was needed was hard data. Lots of it.

Over a period of three years, Sundry and Smith implemented measures and techniques, casually labeled Six Sigma, across Motorola, measuring, measuring, analyzing, and improving. This new approach—the new program they had worked out—worked. It worked out very well. From 1985 on until today, Motorola has documented over $16 billion in savings from their Six Sigma efforts.

In 1995, Jack Welch adopted Six Sigma for General Electric. Jack Welch made Six Sigma a part of GE culture. He is largely credited with widely promoting the success of Six Sigma at GE and its potential for successful use throughout corporate America. His famous quote is that Six Sigma "changed the DNA of GE."

Jack Welch and his team are the people who shaped Six Sigma into the program we know today. GE popularized and formalized Six Sigma through such concepts as Critical to Quality, the Voice of the Customer, and the DMAIC methodology. Jack Welch has credited Six Sigma with saving GE hundreds of millions of dollars in 10 years of use. Six Sigma is so important at GE that today you can't be promoted at the company without being Six Sigma-trained and -certified.

In the last 10 years, Six Sigma has risen to the top as one of the most talked about process improvement and quality management programs available. It rivals ISO 9001 and CMMI in interest and adoption. But of the three, it is often the least understood. There are a couple of reasons for this. The first is that compared to ISO and CMMI, Six Sigma has the potential to be imminently more complex. If you move seriously into its statistical and quantitative aspects, it can be both powerful (to the informed) and powerfully daunting (to the uninformed). And then there is the question of what Six Sigma actually is. Is it GE's property? Did Motorola get a patent on it? Who is the owner of Six Sigma?

Six Sigma Ownership

The International Organization for Standardization publishes, revises, and governs ISO 9001:2000. The Software Engineering Institute publishes, revises, and governs CMMI. Six

Sigma is different. Folks at Motorola created it. Honeywell added to it. GE refined it. Ford put its spin on it. But no one owns it. It is like an open source standard, shareware in the world of process improvement. In a way, that's understandable. No one owns algebra or differential calculus or regression analysis. On the other hand, Six Sigma is supported by a well-published methodology: DMAIC.

The folks at Motorola and GE (notably former GE CEO Jack Welch) publicly promoted Six Sigma and encouraged its adoption without putting any ownership or copyright constraints on it. There's no doubt those were beneficent gestures. Those two companies invested millions in developing the methods, protocols, and structures associated with Six Sigma. When they set Six Sigma and all its parts free, they gave a gift to the worlds of manufacturing, IT, and process control. But when they relinquished control, they also left Six Sigma to itself. Or rather to us, to do with it what we saw best.

That leads to what might be called Six Sigma's chief weak point. There is no central governing body for the program. Many organizations have picked up the mantel, but there is no consensus as to what the agenda is for promoting or growing the body of knowledge. Respectable institutions like Villanova University, the American Society for Quality, and an organization called iSix Sigma have each established training and guidance programs. GE has a well-maintained Six Sigma web site. But all these groups are working in their own directions—not necessarily in conflict. There is just no unifying center for Six Sigma coordination, standardization, and development.

For some people, that is not a constraint. It's a good thing. For others, the lack of centralization could be an issue. But for Six Sigma, right now at least, that's the way it is.

Six Sigma Structure and Design

To understand the structure and design of Six Sigma, it's helpful to first understand the philosophy of Six Sigma. The philosophy behind Six Sigma could be summarized as "Deliver Quality." That capital Q in Quality is important. It implies a certain kind of quality, and that is what Six Sigma drives at, a very special definition of quality. Quality is not whatever happens to be the biggest, the strongest, the prettiest, the best, or the coolest. It is not what your organization says it is. It is not what your competition thinks it is. In the world of Six Sigma, quality is what your customer wants. That is all it is. The meaning of the word *quality* comes from that source and that source only. Nothing else matters. Everything else is irrelevant. GE calls this the Voice of the Customer (VOC).

The Voice of the Customer

You'll see VOC mentioned a lot in Six Sigma descriptions. Six Sigma springs from this idea. Jack Welch made this a popular mantra at GE. The Voice of the Customer means that you listen to the customers and give them what they want, what they need. Do they want light bulbs shaped like question marks? Not if we're listening. They want light bulbs you only have to change every seven years.

The concept of the Voice of the Customer makes perfect business sense. It's a perfectly logical basis for defining quality. Most consumers (customers, clients, call them what you will) want a product or a service that fills a need. But they don't want an ongoing relationship with a company. Paradoxically, free them from needing you and they will regularly return. "Brand loyalty" springs from a product (or service) that matches what a customer expects from it. I am spending time on this because many companies prefer to think that they know what their customers need. They think they have a bead on the business they are in. They know best. Maybe they've been in the business for 10 years. Maybe they have a "vision." Maybe they are driven to be the best. And so they think their customers will buy whatever they sell. But that's not the Six Sigma approach.

Six Sigma is all about making a commitment to delivering what the customers want. And if maybe the customers don't know, your job is to find out what they want. And once you know this, you then align your production processes to create what it is they want. When you produce that, you've built a quality product. That's what quality is in the realm of Six Sigma.

That's the starting point: build what your customer wants. The next steps into Six Sigma move us into the realm of quantitative analysis. Let's begin with a simple formula:

$X=f(Y)$

X is a function of Y.

That's a way to look at Six Sigma problems. Cause and effect. X is always a function of Y. Business is down (X) because our umbrellas ship late (Y), the polka-dot design is unattractive (Y), and they tend to leak in the rain (Y).

It's helpful to realize that we can't really control X. Business is down. That's X, and that's the result of a culmination of factors. We can't change the result by focusing on the result. It's a good thing to know, sure, but it's a summary at best. What we can control is the Y. We can pin down the folks in shipping. We can influence the designers. Six Sigma focuses in on the Y. With Six Sigma, once you've heard the Voice of the Customer, you can move forward by defining your own $X=f(Y)$ equation.

Define X as your business goal. X may be "a light bulb you only have to change every seven years." It might be "sales of $100,000." It might be "98 percent on-time shipping." Then look at that goal and deconstruct it into its functional elements. Identify each element of your operations that may impact the goal. Then look at those elements. Study them. Turn a critical eye to them. Lock them down. Measure them. Evaluate them. And then, for those elements that are not getting you to the goal they way they should, change them. Improve them.

You change them by collecting and analyzing performance data.

Let's take this example: a bulb that lights for seven years. One of the Ys that can impact that X is the carbon coating of the filament. Our scientists tell us that a coating 5 microns thick will deliver the desired longevity, give or take .25 microns. But that's a lab number, that's ideal conditions. On the factory floor—with varying environmental conditions—our carbon-coating machines fluctuate more than a few microns. A few microns here, a few there, and our bulbs lose hours on hours of performance. So the idea is to find out two things.

First, discover the "real" performance of those machines under typical floor conditions. How close to 5 microns can they consistently hit? And so we measure the machines. We collect the data. We look at the data. If the data tells us that the variance is within our limits of performance, then that Y is OK. Let's focus our efforts on other Ys.

But if the performance varies too much—if the machines coat too many filaments with too-thick or too-thin carbon coatings—we better take a closer look. We should find out the second thing: the thing that is causing that variance. Until we get control of that, our goal of a light bulb that burns for seven years will only be a goal. Just a goal. We'll have no practical way of getting there.

Why Is It Six? Why Is It Sigma?

Six Sigma is all about the spread of variation in a set of data. In a normal distribution, data tends to spread out in a very predictable pattern. Most of the values fall around the middle. Some fall more or less to either side. If you plot the result, the figure will look like a bell. Let's move away from light bulbs. Think of another common example: people's height. If you measure the height of 100 18-year-old males, you'll end up with a range of heights. Some will measure 6'2". Some will measure 5'5". Some, 5'11½". Some 6' even. And so on and so on. But most of the 18 year olds will measure 5'9½". In theory, 18-year-old males can be any height. But in nature, the average height is 5'9½", and the natural distribution tapers off evenly on both sides of that number. It looks something like Figure 7-1.

A chart such as that illustrated in Figure 7-1 is called a *normal distribution*. It has the general shape of a bell, and we know from statistics that's a normal way that data like that should fall.

That brings us to Six Sigma. Six Sigma predicts that when you run a process, the way the performance varies over time will dance up and down around the center line, the average line—just like the range of heights in nature. (There are two caveats here, but don't worry about them right now. I'll look at them later.) But here is the key with Six Sigma: it wants you to put techniques in place to control what numbers (what data points) are going to most influence the average.

The common understanding of achieving Six Sigma performance is that for every 1,000,000 data points, only 3.4 will deviate from either side of the average. In a grossly exaggerated example, that might look more like Figure 7-2.

In Figure 7-2, we see hardly any variation. Everything is grouped right at the middle. In general, that's not a bad understanding. But the technical explanation is better, and it

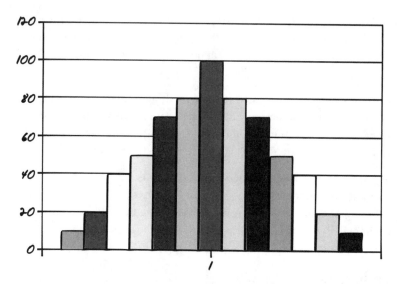

FIGURE 7-1. The traditional bell curve shows a normal distribution of data. The "average" values fall in the middle and the less common values fall to either side of the center.

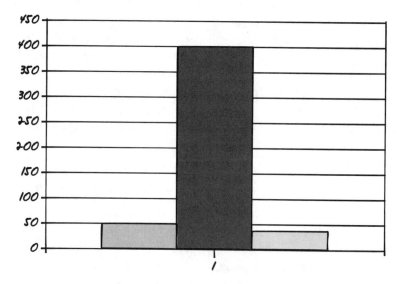

FIGURE 7-2. Here we see a very controlled sample set. We have been able to get most of the values to fall into the center, with very few falling to either side.

sheds more light on the purpose and design of Six Sigma. Let's get at this by looking at the name Six Sigma.

Sigma means the same thing as standard deviation. *Standard deviation* (SD) is a well-founded measure of the range of variation from the average for a group of measurements. In any set of data, 68 percent of all the measurements will fall within one standard deviation of the average. 95 percent of all the measurements will fall within two standard deviations of the average. By the time you're out to six standard deviations—six sigma—

you've accounted for 99.9997 percent of the data. Practically nothing is out of those bounds.

At first blush, that might seem like the opposite of what Six Sigma promotes, conformance to the center. But now here's the push: Six Sigma is about good numbers and bad numbers. Good numbers are measures of performance you deem to be acceptable: the numbers you want to hit, the number range in which you want your process to perform. If you're an inventor out to clone The Average Male, you might decide that "good" heights for the clones would fall only between 5'9¼" and 5'9¾". Any other height would be deemed a failure. And so if you were to develop a cloning process performing at six sigma, you would find that 99.9997 percent of the 18-year-old males you turned out would stand between 5'9¼" and 5'9¾" tall. That's a very predictable process. That's a process under control. For every 1,000,000 transactions, that process would turn out only 3.2 defects, taller or shorter males.

So Six Sigma is about process control. The more you are able to control a process, the better you will be able to make it hit the performance numbers you want.

Forget Six. Forget Sigma.

Six Sigma is a program that works best when it uses hard data as the foundation for process improvement. That's why one of the general interpretations of this program is that it is heavy on statistics. So far, we've looked at a few common Six Sigma concepts: Voice of the Customer and $X = f(Y)$. Here's another one: DPMO.

DPMO is Defects Per Million Opportunities for defects. When you are building a product, you want your production processes to be predictable. You want to know how many microns of carbon coating they are going to lay onto a filament. No process is perfect. No process operates without variance. One of the things you need to establish with Six Sigma is the number of process variations.

Think of a simple example: catching a baseball. The outcome is either/or. You catch the ball, that's success. You don't—you drop or miss the ball—that's a defect. If you want to measure how good a catcher is, you have to measure only two things: the number of throws and the number of catches. You could generate a pretty good sigma rating by throwing the ball to the catcher a million times and then analyzing the outcome.

To get a valid statistical indicator of the reliability of this process (the talent of the catcher), you have to repeat the transaction over and over. Measure and measure. When you have a process that achieves statistical six sigma, you can pretty much guarantee that you'll have only 3.4 defects for every million transactions. That's 3.4 misses for every million throws. Whatever you are doing, it is so controlled, so streamlined, so proven that the outcome is a safe bet.

Sigma (statistical standard deviation) is used as a measure of process capability. In the realm of Six Sigma, you can measure your processes and then, through analysis, generate a performance sigma for each one. But most companies—even machine-driven companies—have not achieved six sigma in their processes. And they probably don't need to. Even if they have stringent quality goals, they can probably get there without getting to the 3.2 DPMO goal.

Six Sigma, then, is not about achieving six sigma. And so the "six" in Six Sigma is not a mandate. And generating process sigmas is not an absolute requirement. This is often misunderstood. Six Sigma is about putting in place the tools you need to control your processes to the point that they meet customer expectations. That's all. In your business, you might find four sigma is fine. With three sigma, you're hitting the mark 93 percent of the time. If you're in the pizza delivery business, that may be OK if you used to be able to make on-time delivery only 80 percent of the time. So an essential part of any successful Six Sigma program is defining what process sigma you should strive for in order to be successful. Decide—in the interest of quality, in the interest of the customer, in the interest of your business goals—what level of certitude is practical for you and your business teams.

Six Sigma Methodologies

Six Sigma employs two basic methodologies to problem solving. The first is termed DMAIC. DMAIC is used to improve existing processes in an organization. The other methodology is DFSS. It is used when you want to design a new process and introduce it into an organization in a way that supports Six Sigma management techniques.

DMAIC is the one that gets the most press. There are five basic steps in the methodology: define, measure, analyze, improve, control. DMAIC is used to improve and increase the efficiency and reliability of processes that exist in an organization. It is a process improvement methodology that employs incremental process improvement using Six Sigma techniques.

DFSS stands for Design for Six Sigma. It is also sometimes referred to as DMADV. This methodology also has five steps: define, measure, analyze, design, verify.

DFSS is used when an organization wants to design and produce new products in a timely, cost-effective manner to meet exact customer needs. It is a business development methodology. The core steps, DMADV, are used to create reliable processes in an organization that does not have processes, or when an organization must discard a deeply faulted process. DFSS is a process design approach.

Between DMAIC and DFSS, DMAIC is probably the one used by most people most often when implementing a Six Sigma project. The two are strongly similar, so I will focus on DMAIC for this chapter.

Define

The D in DMAIC is for define. For any process improvement initiative, you must first decide what you are going to do, why you are doing it, how you'll get it done, and what results you'll hope to achieve. Six Sigma places special emphasis on these definition activities. This is because Six Sigma doesn't want you to engage in process improvement just for the sake of process improvement. The understanding behind the program is that tinkering with process is serious business, and so you should not take it lightly. Businesses run on processes. Products and services are released through processes. Company success is based on processes. So what you do to your processes is going to make a difference, one way or another.

If there is a central idea behind this first step, it is to pick wisely. Choose an issue that will make a demonstrable difference in the company's ability to achieve its goals. Look for opportunities to tangibly affect efficiencies, to drive out costs, or to eliminate waste. Look for change that will alter what you produce in ways your customers will notice. A good place to begin is to define what it is that probably should change.

Figure 7-3 illustrates the define phase of DMAIC.

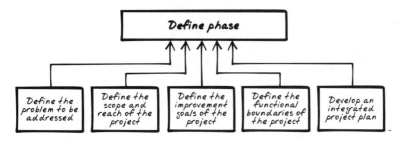

FIGURE 7-3. In the define phase of DMAIC, the objective is to shape the Six Sigma program so that it can be executed in an orderly fashion, with an empirical focus based on data control. This involves defining the problem to be addressed, shaping the scope of the project, defining the goal to be accomplished, setting functional boundaries in place, and then developing a detailed project plan that will be used to govern the project.

Define the Problem

Lyndon Johnson once said that the tough thing about being a leader isn't doing the right thing. It's knowing what the right thing is. The same could be said of this step in Six Sigma. For your process improvement efforts to be successful, they need to be focused on a targeted problem. In terms of the definition stage, this may be the most important element you'll identify. What do you want to improve?

How you approach this tactical alignment will naturally depend upon the size, shape, and culture of your IT organization. But there are three broad categories of "improvement management" that may be used to help you pinpoint what you'd like your teams to work on:

"It's broke. Fix it." category

This is the easy one. If you have a process or activity that is essential to your business and it's falling apart all over the place, then that will probably stand out readily in everyone's minds as a necessary improvement target. The word *improvement* here naturally indicates major work, given the degree of failure that so strongly stands out. In most circumstances where Six Sigma is applied, you'll probably find that the obvious targets—those that scream at you for action—are (thankfully) few and far between. Six

Sigma works best, and is most appropriate, when you want to continue making incremental improvements to existing processes performing to a known level of efficiency.

"Opportunity target" category

We've seen earlier that Six Sigma's approach to process improvement is based on data-driven decision making. That is, the organization collects information and measurements over time, analyzes this data, and then uses the results to point to practical and viable improvement opportunities. In these kinds of organizations, you'll typically find that Process Action Teams maintain a queue of improvement opportunities already somewhat defined. In ongoing continuous improvement environments, the teams will methodically manage the queue, adding new items as they emerge in the organization, sorting and prioritizing existing items, and selecting items in the queue to begin work on. Here opportunities already exist. By managing them in an active queue, you and your teams can select the targets you deem ripe for improvement actions.

"Listen up" category

This may be the easiest way to define the problem you want to address. It's easy because you basically have no choice. Management steps in one day and says "Listen up—here is what we are going to work on." No analysis required on your part. No sorting, no prioritization. Bingo, there it is. The "listen up" category of problem or target identification usually springs from executive initiatives or strategic directives that address high-level organizational objectives. In some cases, the assignment will make perfect sense to the process teams. In others, the rationale or logic may seem a little vague; the teams may not be cued in to what criteria drove the choice. But, whatever form it takes, it's an avenue that often introduces improvement opportunities into your domain.

When you are able to define the problem, you are in a position to begin defining how you will address the problem and how you will manage work surrounding a solutions approach.

Define the Project

Once you've defined the problem or the issue or the target you want to address, you are, for all practical purposes, ready to begin a project. I put this step in early on in the cycle of definition activities, but it can occur in many places. Some organizations like to do a lot more analysis and refinement of the idea before developing a plan (see the following two sections). Others prefer to begin with a simple, executive-level plan, get that approved, and then move into more in-depth planning. Whatever approach your organization takes, the basic activity of developing a sound project plan still stands.

When you read about ISO 9001:2000, you saw how that Standard strongly emphasizes the need for planning. You saw the same attribute with CMMI. Planning is essential to the success of any process program. It's essential to the success of any process environment. When you begin a new Six Sigma effort, you should give the concept of project planning the same degree of focus. The following sections address some items you might consider including in such a plan.

Define the mission statement

The plan you develop will be used for three purposes: it will serve as the chief tracking device for managing project resources and team activities, it will serve as a communication and status mechanism to inform management of project progress, and it will serve a similar function in keeping customers and stakeholders up-to-date on how the project is going. And so—to aid all three of these purposes—it's useful to develop the mission statement for the project. The mission statement will usually describe the problem or opportunity to be addressed, the goals that the organization hopes to achieve from the effort, and the business benefits that can be realized when these goals are met.

The mission of the project should quickly become common knowledge in the organization and among the various working teams. But having it ever-present in the plan serves as a good reminder as to the scope of the work. And it can help reinforce resource and team energies in the event of change requests and shifting business dynamics.

Establish executive sponsorship

All business activities require the sponsorship of management. Often this sponsorship is implied. A better path is to make it explicit. So in your Six Sigma project plan, it's useful to identify the branch of the company that will serve as the official sponsor. In the realm of Six Sigma, this sponsor is often referred to as the "champion." That's a good term for the role, but it's not a necessary one. Call the role whatever you and the sponsor would like.

By identifying who the sponsor is in your plan, you help establish organizational support for the project. You can do this by including an organization chart that ties your project to a branch of the organization. You can provide a simple narrative description of the reporting chain for the project. You can include a table of relevant stakeholders, indicating the chain of command there. Once that sponsorship is in the plan, the plan can be seen as representing an official activity, not just for you and your teams but for the whole company as well.

Develop the project charter

A project charter is a useful management tool in the same way that an org chart is a useful tool or a departmental charter is a useful tool. An organization is usually made up of a collection of permanent departments. The departmental charters describe the job of each department within the overall company: what roles will be filled and how the department interacts and supports others. The org chart shows the relationships among all departments in an organization. The charters and the org charts are a way to define a new company or to link an existing company together.

It's the same way with projects. Projects are pretty much like company departments. Only they usually aren't as permanent. Like departments, they exist for a particular purpose. They require specific job roles. And they interact with other organizational units in specific ways. That's why it's helpful to set up a charter for your Six Sigma project. The charter, in a subtle way, can make the project "real" in an organization.

The charter will usually describe the objectives of the project, define the roles required for the team and the responsibilities of each role, detail how the chain of command will be structured, and describe what the project's operational scope and reach will be.

Define the team and resources

Defining the project and the charter are good steps to solidifying what it is you are going to accomplish with this Six Sigma initiative. But you won't get far without a team and the right resources to get the work done. This may seem like an obvious point, but I have always been surprised to see it handled very poorly (or casually) in some organizations. What happens in these kinds of initiatives is that everyone agrees that there is a problem to be solved, that attention needs to be focused on it. But when it comes time for the rubber to hit the road, people are reticent to commit resources in a specific way. They may give lip service to the idea. They may even casually indicate that so-and-so could help out (usually during "down time"). When resource assignment is handled this way, you can just about bet that the project will hit major snags. People will get pulled away from the work when other "more pressing" needs appear. Tools and facilities won't be available when needed. Things won't happen.

That's why early on you should explicitly define who the team is, what members of the organization are going to fill the roles described in the charter, and what level of allocation will be required of each. This should be followed up with specific communications to these team members so they are informed firsthand of their involvement. Likewise with resources: the tools, facilities, and availabilities you'll need all need to be clearly spelled out.

Any process improvement project, whether its Six Sigma, CMMI, ISO or any other type, is ultimately the work of a team. And a team is a collection of people. Identify the right people, get them committed to the project, ensure that they'll have the right resources, and you'll go a long way to making your project a success.

Define the Goal

Defining the problem and defining the project will help us establish the scope of the Six Sigma initiative. We understand what it is we'll look at and how we will approach what it is we might want to modify. Another important attribute we should define is the goal. What is it we want to achieve?

This activity has a special meaning in the domain of Six Sigma. We have seen earlier that all activities should be planed to fall in line with the Voice of the Customer: what we know the customer wants, what we believe the customer needs. It is the Voice of the Customer that drives everything about Six Sigma. The goal we want to achieve, then, should have a direct and tangible link to the customer. If it doesn't, what we are seeking to do might end up being irrelevant to the company. If what we modify, tweak, or adjust doesn't make the product more appealing to the customer, then there was probably little real impetus to do it. We should care about what we know the customer cares about. When we define the goal, we should think in terms of reaching an objective that will help make a difference to the customer.

Identify the (real) customer

The goal we are after should always be a goal our customers would want us to achieve. That's why it's important when we are setting goals for a Six Sigma project that we take time to identify who the customer really is. This can be tricky in large organizations. The people in marketing might think the customer is one person, while the people in engineering might be thinking of someone else. Management might have yet another view. I routinely encounter this issue in technology shops. IT managers think the customers are the business managers who fund their services; those are the people they want to make happy. The business analysts think the customers are the people who will ultimately use the applications they help design; they think the focus should be on the users. The technical architects think the real customers are the people in the data centers; since they have to operate and maintain the systems, architects think those are the folks who should receive the majority of consideration.

If you define the real customer as the person having the closest relationship to your product, then you could make a case for any of the groups mentioned previously. I don't have an easy solution to this business dilemma. And, though it will likely add a degree of complexity, you may be smart to think of all of them as the real customer, each with their own set of expectations, requirements, and influences.

I work with an associate, John Porzio, whose wife Kelli is managing a DMAIC project at the hospital where she works. Her mission is to improve Operating Room utilization. For this project, an unbooked OR equals waste, a booked OR that cancelled inappropriately is a defect, and so on. And in this case, her customers are clearly defined too: they are the hospital administrators charged with keeping the place fiscally efficient. It is their view of quality that Kelli will structure her project around.

Define Critical-to-Quality issues

The Six Sigma acronym CTQ stands for Critical to Quality. CTQs are issues, elements, traits, features, benefits, or other product attributes that your customer perceives as being essential to quality. For a pizza shop, one CTQ might be on-time delivery. Another might be order accuracy. A third might be delivery temperature. So far in this activity, we have defined the problem to be addressed, we have defined the project we'll use to address it, and we've defined the goal we want to achieve. As we begin to identify the Critical-to-Quality issues, we want to remember to stick with those that are relevant to the problem at hand. If the problem we want to address is on-time delivery, then we want to focus on issues critical to the quality of on-time delivery. This might include things like store location mapping, phone call routing, and delivery time estimation. But it wouldn't necessarily deal with things like oven temperatures or box insulation. Those issues can indeed be CTQs, but they probably belong in the domain of delivery temperature. They are out of the scope of our current focus.

CTQs are not issues you should dream up on your own. You can, of course. But then they become your Critical-to-Quality issues, not your customers'. CTQs should be collected over time, through interaction with your customer base. They should provide an open channel of communication that allows for the free exchange of information. A good organization will seek out this communication. By learning what it is your customer would like to see made better in your current product or designed into your next generation of products, you can identify what your improvement goals should be. And you can do so in ways that are tangible, actionable, and greatly assured to increase customer satisfaction.

Establish a definition of quality

At this point, you are ready to establish a definition of that elusive term *quality*. This is one of the features of Six Sigma that I like best. In ISO 9001:2000, we see that the focus is on building a QMS, a Quality Management System. And in ISO, there is certainly a strong focus on customer needs and quality. But that Standard doesn't go a long way toward giving you a way to define quality. In CMMI, we see only tangential references to quality. That model operates from the perspective that, if you implement recognized best practices for technology projects (and the customer is indeed included in many of these best practices), then you'll emerge with a quality product. But Six Sigma takes a direct bead on establishing what quality is, and what it is specific to the effort you are working on.

When you establish a definition of quality for your Six Sigma project, you are also defining success criteria. Your definition is born out of the two preceding activities. You identified who your real, or essential, customers are, and from them, you elicited their Critical-to-Quality issues. From this data, you can now pull a subset of those CTQs and build your quality definition around them.

For example, you work in a Fortune 500 IT shop. IT management has been getting burned at executive meetings due to IT's weakness in reasonably estimating project completion times. You formulate a Six Sigma initiative aimed at addressing this problem. You move out into the organization and, through meetings and discussions, you identify the managers of Marketing and Field Operations as being the core customers in this domain. After all, 80 percent of IT's work is delivered to these two groups. They are the ones with the staunchest complaints. With this focus in place, you then identify their CTQs and discover three essential issues:

1. Marketing and Field Ops can live with a two-week variance in promised delivery dates.

2. They appreciate IT's concern over their situation and will acknowledge progress if they can see IT moving steadily to hit that window.

3. If IT will open a broader channel of communication between itself, Marketing, and Field Ops, the customer will assist in ways it can to help ensure delivery dates.

You can now establish a pretty concrete definition of quality from these inputs. Here's one version: for the coming fiscal year, ACME IT will meet its delivery commitments within a two-week window for 75 percent of all system projects, to be managed by a supporting Partner Communication program.

The definition of quality is very serviceable for two reasons of its own:

1. It directly reflects the needs and concerns of the customers.
2. It provides an empirical foundation for improvement and refinement.

With this quality definition in place, we can now define the project's strategic objective.

Define the strategic objective

Everything we've looked at in this section has been centered on establishing the goal of the Six Sigma project. In the realm of corporate directives, that goal should be properly expressed as a strategic objective. This strategic objective should be featured prominently in your project plan. It describes the goal as a strategic target with distinct business benefits. The strategic objective is the culmination of all the investigation and defining you have done up to this point.

For this IT example, you might express the mission as a two-point strategic objective:

- Enhance ACME IT's current delivery capability from meeting 52 percent of its commitments within a four-week time frame to meeting 75 percent of its commitments within a two-week time frame.

- Establish a Partner Communication process that will enable ACME IT and its customer representatives to monitor and control delivery commitments across operating groups.

This form of expression gives your project a target to shoot for, and it does so in language that is meaningful and relevant to management.

Define Boundary Conditions

The physicist Stephen Hawking says that understanding the boundary conditions of the universe may be the single most important thing to know about it. If it is positively curved, the universe will ultimately fall back in on itself and end in a Big Crunch. If it is negatively curved, it will expand forever, the cosmos forever spreading apart in an ever-thinning soup until it winks out in cold darkness. Boundary conditions are important to Six Sigma projects, too.

Defining boundary conditions is a way to constrain and manage the scope of the project. It helps you avoid having to look at everything in your quest for improvement. And it is also a mechanism handy for continually focusing your efforts along lines that remain in harmony with the strategic objective. Let's take a brief look at ways to define boundary conditions for your project.

Target relevant processes

Six Sigma is fundamentally a process improvement tool. We use it to make our processes better; ideally, they will become measurably better. Once we have established a focus for our project and we know what we want to improve and how, in general, we want to improve it, we can begin to plan how we will move into the organization and make the improvements happen. One of the first steps in this direction is to target the processes in use in the organization that are relevant to the mission at hand. It won't do any good if you spend your time adjusting activities that ultimately have little to do with the problem at hand. So it is important to define just what the relevant processes are. To do this effectively, you will need a solid understanding of the process program at work in the organization. If you and your team lack such a full understanding, you will need access to the people who possess it.

So study the processes. Know what parts of the product they touch or influence. Trace your goals and objectives through the program. Map it out. Code a thread. Whatever path you take, identify the processes that are impacting the result or results you wish to modify. Identify these and then verify with the experts that these are indeed the right ones to target.

Define what a defect is

This is an essential part of any Six Sigma program. I see it as crucial. The idea is to bind the definition of a defect so that you'll know it when you see it. Think back to the pizza shop. The issue is still on-time delivery. Factors that influence this include such things as effective call routing, counter wait time, and drive time. Call routing concerns the central switchboard's ability to route a delivery call to the store closest to the caller location. Counter wait time deals with how long the pizza waits on the counter before a driver picks it up for a delivery trip. And drive time deals with the window of time between when the pizza is boxed for delivery and when the driver arrives at the customer's destination.

What is a defect with regard to call routing? It could be any number of things. It could be a call that is transferred to a location over a mile away from the caller's destination. It could be a call that is transferred to a store during that store's usual rush hour.

The same is true of counter wait time. A defect here might be counted as a pizza sitting on the counter four minutes or more after it has been removed from the oven. The same with delivery time. Maybe a defect here is a driver receiving a boxed pizza less than 10 minutes prior to the committed delivery time.

Defects can come in many shapes and sizes. Your team will need to look at your processes and define what a defect means in those domains. But however you end up slicing it, remember that your definition of a defect must continue to jibe with two traits. First, it must be a misstep that threatens Critical-to-Quality issues. And second, it must be something you can measure. You are going to structure your Six Sigma project around an analysis of opportunities for defects and the occurrence of actual defects. So defects must always be events you can measure in a practical and quantitative way.

Establish the Data Collection Plan

In any system, there are opportunities for defects. You'll often see this acronym pop up in Six Sigma discussions: DPMO. That stands for Defects Per Million Opportunities. If you were to operate a single-thread process rated as performing at six sigma, the process would produce only 3.2 defects for every million transactions (or opportunities) that were run through it. All systems have opportunities for the introduction of defects. Whenever you have inputs and outputs, manipulations or transformations, the risk is there. What you will be looking at in your Six Sigma project is a running process. You should analyze the process to understand how it works and where it has points for defect opportunities. You can map those points and put together a Data Collection Plan.

The Data Collection Plan describes what you'll be looking at, what kinds of defects you'll recognize, and what kinds of collection tools you'll use to capture process performance, measure process variance, and count defect occurrences. The importance of the Data Collection Plan should not be underestimated. Take time to get the detail here right. After all, this plan will cover a lot of the up-front project work. Lots of your initial time will be given to studying the system and making measurements. How you collect this will have a lot to do with the quality of data you end up with and the types of analyses you will be able to apply against the data.

Establish the Data Analysis Plan

Here's another acronym you'll encounter in the Six Sigma world: DOE. That stands for Design of Experiments. If you employ Six Sigma to its full extent, then any project can be thought of as a scientific experiment. You come up with a theory: "Something can be improved if we look at this." You put that "something" in a controlled environment and observe it—i.e., data collection. Then you analyze the data and draw conclusions as to how you might change that something. Basic science. Design of Experiments is a discipline that helps you set up the right kinds of measures and identify the appropriate type of analyses that will let you make statistically accurate assumptions about what it is you looked at. For example, here's an experiment. You collect a lot of measures on people's height and weight. Then you analyze this data by dividing the average weight in pounds by the average height in inches. You conclude with the assumption that one inch of growth will typically equate to the addition of X number of pounds. That seems logical, but is that a sound methodology? Is that a well-designed experiment? Of course not. It's silly. It's pointless.

The point is, you can spend just as much time on a useless experiment as you can on a productive experiment, so you should make sure up front that you have a well-supported Data Analysis Plan to control the design of your Six Sigma experiment. Design of Experiments is a big topic, and I don't have the space in this short-form review of Six Sigma to go into it as much as it warrants. But keep in mind the importance of your Data Analysis Plan.

The Data Analysis Plan is just as important as the Data Collection Plan. Here you should identify what statistical techniques you will use to analyze the data, why those techniques are appropriate to the kinds of data being collected, and what the results will tell you within a statistically dependable degree of confidence. There are many simple forms of data analysis that can be applied. Averages, modes, and medians deal with normal distribution. T-tests, chi-squares, regression analysis, and ANOVA are more sophisticated techniques. Six Sigma routines employ formulas for predicting percent noncompliance and for generating process sigmas. The data analyses you elect will naturally depend on the problem you're trying to understand, the kinds of business environments you're in, and your team's own statistical and quantitative abilities.

Document the Project Plan

With the problem defined, and with the mission, sponsorship, team, and resources established, you are now able to begin putting together a plan to carry out and manage the project. You may elect to include the previous items as a formal part of the plan, or you may elect to keep them separate. (In the next two sections, I'll describe some additional sections of information that you might find useful to feature in your plan.) But as you build your plan, make sure that at least the fundamentals are in place. There is a set of generally accepted items that are typically considered fundamental. One is the project schedule. This is typically expressed as a work breakdown structure, a running series of activities that, taken as a whole, describe the project effort. Another is the budget, which details the costs of personnel, facilities, tools, and other resources. There are benchmarks and milestones, representing significant points of anticipated project progress or work product delivery. There might be a communication plan detailing how the project team will communicate status and progress to management, the customer, and other relevant stakeholders. And you may consider adding a section on assumptions, constraints and risks: issues you may have to deal with as the project moves forward and begins to evolve over time.

The depth of your plan and the type of plan you produce will depend on your own culture. If you build a realistic plan, one that reflects that culture, it should work well for your project.

Initiate the Project

Planning tells the tale of the project. If you've planned well, your project should run well. Here we have established the following things: we defined the problem with the issues we want to address, we defined the scope and mission of the project, we defined the strategic goals we want to achieve, we defined the boundary conditions that will guide the project efforts along focused lines, and then we used all of that to create a project plan.

The following sections cover the rest of the DMAIC methodology. But in a very real way, you've looked at it already. The methodology should be reflected in your plan. Specifically, the steps to measure and analyze have been detailed in the plan. How you improve and control will come from the results of the project.

But at this stage, you are ready to implement the project. And the first step there is to go out into the organization and begin to measure the performance of those processes you targeted.

Tools for the Define Phase

Some common managerial and statistical tools that can be used in the define phase include:

- Process analyses
- Flow charting

- Value stream mapping
- Check sheets
- Pareto analyses
- Cause-and-effect diagrams
- Failure mode effect analysis

Quick Take

DEFINE

The first phase in DMAIC is Define. The intention of the activities here is to establish the purpose, scope, and structure of the Six Sigma project. This typically includes:

Defining the problem

Define what it is that the project should target. This may be an existing problem, a newly surfaced problem, or a strategic mandate.

Defining the project

Establish the scope of the project in relation to the problem. Begin to assemble the appropriate team, seek executive sponsorship, and begin initial planning activities.

Defining the goal

The definition of the goal provides the project with a focused path to guide activity. The goal establishes the success criteria for the project.

Defining the boundary conditions

The boundary conditions help constrain the scope of the Six Sigma project. These conditions establish limits as to what will be measured, what will be analyzed, and what is subject to improvement.

Developing the project plan

With the above areas addressed, the team is now ready to develop a detailed project plan. The plan contains all of the information needed by the team, management, and organizational line workers concerning the purpose, scope, duration, and reach of the project.

Initiating the plan

With the plan developed, it should be reviewed and approved by all impacted parties. Once this is done, the plan is used as the central tool to execute and manage the project.

Measure

The M in DMAIC is for measure. Measure, measure, and measure. In organizations based on Six Sigma principles, measurements are an ongoing activity. The organization is always measuring, always collecting data. Data is the key to knowing how things are going, how things are really going. Considered measurement is the best way to amass the right data in the right manner.

As you saw in the previous sections, for a Six Sigma project, you create a series of plans, including a Data Collection Plan. This is where you map out what process elements and components you'll be measuring. The objective with this activity is to capture an empirical picture of current performance. These are three general steps involved here:

1. Prepare to measure.
2. Measure.
3. Protect the integrity of the data you've collected.

Figure 7-4 illustrates the measure phase.

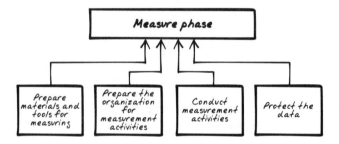

FIGURE 7-4. In the measure phase of DMAIC, the objective is to begin executing the project according to plan. The first field activity is typically to collect the data. This involves preparing the organization for data collection activities, performing the measurement activities and assembling the raw data, and then ensuring that the integrity of the data is continually protected.

Prepare to Measure

Measuring can be an invisible activity, or it can be an intrusive activity. If you're measuring air pressure, temperature, and humidity, a barometer sitting silently on a wall will do the job. If you're measuring worker efficiency or workflow variation or other such subtle activities, you may need a stronger presence. When your measurements call for you and your team to enter the work environment in a way that might impact what it is you'll measure, you will need to prepare the environment for your visits. And so when it comes to measuring, you want to accomplish three things:

1. Measure properly.
2. Measure cleanly.
3. Measure efficiently.

Preparing to measure is an activity that should be thought out in part in the planning stages. The first steps you take here are going to prepare you to measure properly. You want to measure the right things, the things that will help you make significant process improvements.

Create (or reference) detailed process maps

Process maps are depictions of your processes that show the detailed ins, outs, and flows of the system. A good process map will show you all the "joints" of your system, and this will help you determine good points to plan for and collect measures. Well-documented systems should have process maps available for your review and planning purposes. If the documentation is not available, you may find that it is advisable to create it. This will, of course, require extra work on your part. Maybe a good bit of extra work. But the one caveat that Six Sigma springs from is the concept that you already have processes in place. Six Sigma is not at heart a process-creation program. It is a process improvement program. And to improve a process, you've got to know what it's supposed to do and what it is doing. This requires documentation.

Use the process maps in your planning activities to decide where you can measure activity efficiently and cleanly. And then plan your measurement activities appropriately.

Validate the process maps

As you review the process maps, keep the idea of currency in mind. This is an administrative reminder. You want to validate that the documentation is still current, that it really does reflect the way the system works. This is a common problem. Documentation tends to collect dust after a while, especially with systems that change over time. And so before you begin designing the kinds of measurements you'll take of the system and before you use the process maps to determine what points you'll focus on to collect the metrics, confirm that what's in the process maps is really what's happening on the floor.

Validate the measurement system

A counterpoint to validating the process documentation is to validate that the measurement system you plan to use is also valid. Some kinds of measures are appropriate for certain kinds of situations. Others work for different situations. If you want to determine the performance of a process in which pressure molds plastic, it may be accurate to measure the temperature of the injection mold, but it may be more valid to measure foot-pounds of pressure instead. People can identify ways to measure many things. And they can collect all kinds of measures of those things. The key is to validate that the measures you plan to take are in line with the current state of the system.

Coordinate moving about the floor

This is a tactical step. It's probably also a courtesy. Before you begin collecting the measurements, it's a good idea to coordinate the collection activities with the process owners and with the people who may have to help you with the activity. This should be done with appropriate advance notice. Let the relevant parties know what is about to transpire. Seek their acquiescence if that's appropriate. Explain the purpose of the activity and what goal you are seeking to achieve. And then let them know the schedule of when the measuring will begin and how they can help in the effort.

Measure

Now go get the data. If you've examined the processes and planned for the kinds of metrics that will help you analyze performance, and if you've cleared the way with relevant parties to move into the field to get the data, then the actual measurement collection should be a relatively straightforward affair.

A couple of tips here. Collect data from many similar sources. Measure over time and hold on to the time sequence. This is essential to protecting data integrity. The data as it emerges over time tells a time-sequence story that you can use when making improvement decisions.

Just as important, use new measures. Fresh data is important. You may have access to existing or archived data, but this may not accurately portray the current situation. Use your judgment when it comes to existing measures if they are available, but at the very least, augment this with an adequate amount of current measures.

Protect the Data

This is an important concept, and yet it's one that is often not emphasized enough for Six Sigma projects—or for that matter, for many technology projects. When an organization elects to use data as the basis for making decisions and when it plans to subject that data to detailed analysis, it's critical to know that the data it's got is good. And so when you collect data, you should do so with two things in mind. The first is to guarantee the integrity of the data. In systems development, teams typically employ configuration management and version control as mechanisms to protect data. The same concept applies here. Your measurement teams should work to ensure that the data they collect is protected in a way that ensures it stays viable for the analyses to come.

And there is the consideration of data confidentiality. This is also not stressed often enough. We might get permission to collect reams of data, and it's possible that this data will pile up quickly over a short period of time. We may have so much of it and such easy access to it that we begin to take it for granted. But it's important to remember that data tells a story. It tells a performance story. It tells an efficiency story. It tells a success story. And so we should consider that any data is sensitive data and should be treated confidentially.

Analyze

The goal of this chapter is to present you with a general feeling for what Six Sigma is about: its focus, structure, and emphasis on data. Like ISO 9001:2000 and CMMI, Six Sigma is an in-depth process improvement program. The intention of this book is to give you a summary of each of these three leading standards so that you can begin to assess which one might be right for you, or—better yet—what parts of each might help you reach your quality goals. And that brings us to the A in DMAIC.

The A in DMAIC is for analysis, analysis of the data you have collected. This is a big subject, and it is not one that this chapter can explore to the depth that might be warranted.

MEASURE

In organizations that rely on Six Sigma for process improvement, measuring is an ongoing and continual activity. For specific projects, measuring has three dimensions:

Prepare to measure

Here you prep the organization for the measurement activities. Sometimes measuring can be a passive, invisible activity. Often it requires some degree of intrusion into the environment. For the activity to be as smooth as possible the organization needs to be properly prepared for it.

Measure

The act of collecting measurements is central to the success of a Six Sigma project. What is to be measured and how the measures are to be collected should be carefully thought out in the define phase. The quality and relevance of the data you collect will have great impact on the quality of the improvements you are able to derive later in project activity.

Protect the data

The integrity of the data you collect needs to be protected to avoid corruption. The data also needs to be protected from a confidentiality standpoint, especially if it contains sensitive or proprietary information.

But the central idea here—and the central activity—is to analyze the data you've collected in order to determine the root causes of defects or poor performance, and then to establish an empirical basis for improving the process.

The key is to identify root causes of process variation, or instability, not just the symptoms. The symptoms are almost always pretty easy to spot, and they often appear to be easy to fix. A jammed printer is a good example. The paper is all crumpled up around the roller. So we take out the sheet, and we're ready to go again. We fixed the symptom, but chances are, the problem is still there: a dirty roller, a misaligned sheet feeder.

With Six Sigma, the story is always in the data. That's the story of how your systems are really performing. And with Six Sigma, the solution is always in the data, too.

Data analysis can be simple or it can be complex. In traditional Six Sigma projects, quite a few complex statistical and quantitative analyses can be used. We take a very brief look at some of these in the next section. But the techniques don't always have to be complex.

For example, you might run a process and then collect data on process performance values. Say you have a process to create a Configuration Management Plan for software projects. You gather the time it takes your configuration analysts to create plans for 12 projects over the period of four months. You look at the data. The value set might look like this: (3 hrs, 4 hrs, 2 hrs, 7 hrs, 3.5 hrs, 2.9 hrs, 3 hrs, 2.5 hrs, 4.5 hrs, 5 hrs, 4 hrs, 4.5 hrs). You total those values up and get 45.9. You then divide that by 12 and get 3.8 hrs.

That's the average amount of time it takes your configuration analysts to create a Configuration Management Plan for one of your software projects.

If that number seems high to you, you might look a little deeper. You might look at your plan template and see if maybe it's calling for too much information or if maybe the template is somehow confusing. You might check to see if the analysts have been properly trained in how to fill out the template. This data can point you to multiple improvement potentials.

The point is that you did a simple average analysis to get this insight.

The kinds of analyses used on project data will naturally vary from organization to organization. This is influenced by factors such as the type of problems being investigated, the kinds of data collected, the capabilities of your team, and the kinds of solutions you are looking for.

Six Sigma typically employs formulations for such indicators as:

- Measures of central tendency
- Histograms and data shapes
- Process capability indexes
- Percent noncompliant calculations
- Upper and lower control chart limits
- Data segmentation and stratification
- Correlation and regression (linear, multiple)
- Process performance (Cp, CpK, Pp, PpK, CpM)
- Short-term versus long-term capability
- Non-normal data distribution transformations
- Central Limit Theorem
- Goodness-of-fit testing
- Hypothesis testing
- Analysis of variance (ANOVA), two sample t-tests, chi-square tests
- Design of Experiments (DOE): full, fractional factorials

These are great tools and techniques, but even though Six Sigma has a deep foundation in these capabilities, you don't have to feel that you are honor-bound to adopt these for your Six Sigma projects. Use the analytical techniques—sophisticated or simple—that best help you understand your data in meaningful ways.

Figure 7-5 illustrates the analyze phase of DMAIC.

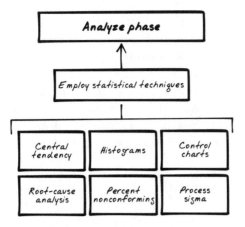

FIGURE 7-5. In the analyze phase of DMAIC, the objective is to draw the performance out of the data. This is where most of the well-known Six Sigma techniques come into play. The use of histograms, measures of central tendency, control chart derivation, process capability indexes, and process sigmas can all be used in this phase.

The Statistical Route

I'll repeat my basic premise about our look at Six Sigma here: this book is not intended to be a complete tome on the statistical and analytic techniques applicable to Six Sigma projects. The intention is to give you a pretty good feel for the structure and focus of Six Sigma. If it seems that this program may be helpful to your organization, then you can move forward to deeper investigation. However, in this section, we'll take a very topical look at a typical statistical path a team might follow when analyzing data on a Six Sigma project.

> ### NOTE
> The statistical descriptions provided in the following sections are presented to give you a feel for the kinds of analyses that can take place under a Six Sigma program. If this is of interest to you, good. If not, don't worry. The statistics described here, while valid and typical, are not essential to your appreciating what Six Sigma might be able to help you with. So you need not pay special attention to the statistics in this section if they hold no real interest for you.

Collect the data

Based on the details described in the project plan, the team collects the field data they acquired from examining process performance. There are a couple of considerations the team should keep in mind. First, collect enough data. The word "enough" is going to depend on the focus, size, and scope of the project. But for basic statistical legitimacy, the minimum number of data points should be no less than 100. Second, keep the data points in time sequence. This is important because the time sequence helps establish the performance patterns in the data.

Plot the data as a histogram

All data sets have a shape. Valid data—data that can be used as a basis for statistical analyses—shows a valid shape. So an essential first step in performing statistical analyses is to determine the shape of your data. If you plot the data and the expected shape begins to take form, you know your data can be analyzed, and so you are free to move forward. But if your data's shape does not take expected form, there's no purpose in going further. You may need to begin again. Maybe you didn't collect enough data. Maybe you collected disparate kinds of data. Whatever the reason, if the data is not amenable to analysis, there's no point in analyzing it.

A histogram is a picture of your data. It's a bar chart, and from this you examine the shape for validity.

Examine the shape of the data

Once you have plotted your data points as a histogram you can examine the shape of the data. Figures 7-6, 7-7, and 7-8 are three sample histograms with valid shapes.

The histogram in Figure 7-6 shows math, reading, and writing scores for school children at varying school grades. Notice that as a child advances in school, scores go up. This is to be expected, and so the shape of this data is said to be valid.

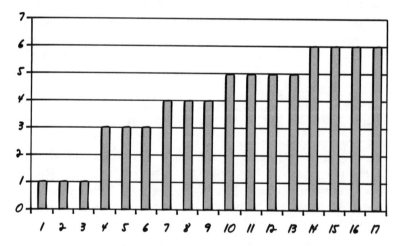

FIGURE 7-6. This data sample, while not a bell curve, shows a normal shape—a trend we would expect: abilities improve with each advanced grade level.

Figure 7-7 shows what appears to be an opposite example.

The histogram in Figure 7-7 has the opposite shape, and so we might think that it is invalid. But this is a histogram of fatigue factors. It shows three people's abilities to lift weights across five exercise sets. The graph shows that the people lift less weight as the number of attempts increase. This is also to be expected, and so the shape of this data is said to be valid.

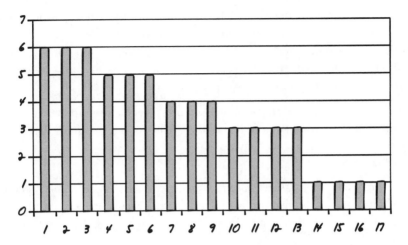

FIGURE 7-7. Here is another example of "normal" data. Lifting weights includes a "fatigue factor." People lift less after lifting for a while.

The shape in Figure 7-8 is also a valid shape. It is the shape of random data. It is the traditional bell curve, with a central tendency and values falling away about equally on either side.

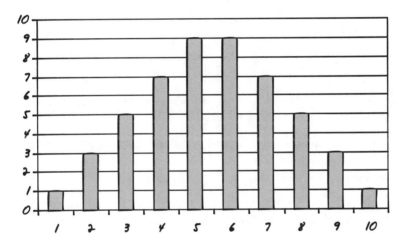

FIGURE 7-8. The traditional bell curve once again shows the tendency for data to cluster around the middle with extreme values falling off to either side.

Valid data shapes are defined as statistical realities. They are not based on simple "expected shapes." But it is safe to say that all data has a valid shape and that it is important to ascertain the shape of your data before you move into further analyses.

Prepare to create control charts

Once you have determined that the shape of your data is valid, you can move forward with the next step. The next step is preparing to produce control charts. Control charts are plotted charts that help you determine whether your process is under control. This is an important concept. A process that is under control is statistically predictable. And because it is predictable, it should be stable. (Even if it is working poorly, it can still be stable.) And in terms of process improvement, you can improve only a stable process, a process that is under control, a process you can control.

Another point to remember is that even stable processes exhibit variation. The core idea behind all process improvement is to reduce the amount of this variation.

Generate the mean

There are three common measures of central tendency: mean, mode, and median. In a sample of data, the *mode* is the most frequently occurring value, the *median* is the value right in the middle on the range, and the *mean* is the average of all the values.

You calculate the mean by adding up all the values in the sample and then dividing that total by the size of the sample.

In the sample (5, 2, 3, 5, 1, 4, 5), the mode is 5 (most frequently occurring), the median is 4 (the middle value), and the mean is 3.57 (the average).

The mean is represented as $\overline{X}$ and will be used in further calculations.

Generate the grand mean

When you collect multiple samples of the same size (a good practice for comparative statistics), you can generate a value known as the *grand average* or the *grand mean*.

In a data set of seven samples, each with a size n=10, the averages may appear as (4, 7, 5, 6, 4, 5, 7). The grand mean for this set would be 5.4.

The grand mean is represented as $\overline{\overline{X}}$ and can also be used in further calculations.

Generate the range

The range defines the degree of variability in a sample. The range is determined by subtracting the lowest value in the set from the highest value.

In the set (4, 9, 3, 3, 2, 5, 6), the range is 7 (9 – 2).

The range is represented as R and can be used when you are creating control charts.

Generate the average range

The average range can be calculated when you have multiple sample sets. You determine the average range by summing the value of the ranges for the individual samples and then dividing by the number of samples.

If you have five samples, and the range values for each are (7, 4, 2, 4, 6, 5), the average range is 4.6.

The average range is represented as $\bar{R}$, and is used when you are creating control charts.

Establish upper and lower control limits for the mean

The upper and lower control limits for the mean are used to develop an X-bar control chart, a form of a control chart. The formula to derive the upper control limit for the mean (UCL$\bar{X}$) is:

$$UCL\bar{X} = \bar{\bar{X}} + A_2 * \bar{R}$$

You calculate this by first knowing your sample size. If you collected 2,000 measures across 5 sampling efforts, your size is 5. If you collected 10,000 measures using only 1 sampling effort, your size is 1.

Knowing the sample size (n), you can now consult a table of Shewhart constants. This is a table of numerical constants used to develop control charts. There is a column on the chart labeled A_2. You align that column with the nth sample-size row. In a sample size of 5, A_2 equals .58.

Next you gather the grand mean from the data as well as the average range (covered earlier). Then you can calculate the upper control limit for the mean. If the average mean is 7 and the average range is 12, the calculation is as follows:

$$UCL\bar{X} = 7 + .58 * 12$$

$$UCL\bar{X} = 91$$

Next you calculate the lower control limit for $\bar{X}$. That formula is:

$$LCL\bar{X} = \bar{\bar{X}} - A_2 * \bar{R}$$

You now follow the same steps as you did earlier, only now the calculation is:

$$LCL\bar{X} = 7 - .58 * 12$$

$$LCL\bar{X} = 77$$

You can now plot the control chart using the upper and lower limits and the values from your data samples.

Establish upper and lower control limits for the range

The upper and lower control limits for the range are used to develop an R chart, another form of a control chart. The formula to derive the upper control limit for the range (UCLR) is:

$$UCLR = D_4 * \bar{R}$$

Just as with the control limits for the mean, you calculate this by first knowing your sample size. If you collected 2,000 measures across 5 sampling efforts, your size is 5. If you collected 10,000 measures using only 1 sampling effort, your size is 1.

Knowing the sample size (n), you can now consult a table of Shewhart Constants. This is a table of numerical constants used to develop control charts. There is a column on the chart labeled D_4. You align that column with the nth sample-size row. In a sample size of 5, D_4 equals 2.11.

Next, you gather the average range from the data (as shown previously). Then you can calculate the upper control limit for the range. If the average range is 12, the calculation is as follows:

UCLR = 2.11 * 12

UCLR = 25.32

Next you calculate the lower control limit for R. That formula is:

LCLR = $D_3 * \overline{R}$

You now follow the same steps as you did earlier, only now you use the D3 column from the Shewhart table.

For this example, the D3 value is 0, so the calculation is:

LCLR = 0 * 12

LCLR = 0

You can now plot the control chart using the upper and lower limits and the values from your data samples.

Plot the X-bar control chart and range control chart

With the upper and lower control limits for the mean and the range in place, you can now plot the X-bar control chart and the range control chart. The two limits are used to frame where normal variation starts and stops with each chart. Now you pull out your data sets and plot each value on the charts.

Figure 7-9 is an example of how the range control chart might look.

Look for special-cause variation

Like histograms, control charts give you a good picture of your data. The charts tell you two things. The first trait they indicate is the stability of your process. As noted earlier, if the process is not stable, you cannot reliably improve it because you can't be sure that what you modify will really have an impact on performance in a consistent way. So if you find from the control charts that your process is not under control, you should probably go back and redesign a new experiment.

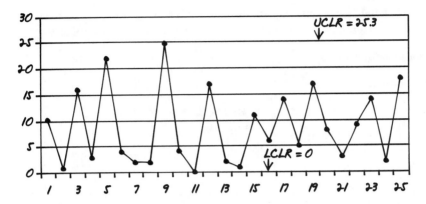

FIGURE 7-9. This is an example of how a control chart might look. The upper limit is set, the lower limit is set, and the values from the sample are plotted in relation to these limits.

How does the control chart show control? Easy. Just look at the upper and lower control limits. If any of the data you have plotted falls outside of that range, you have special-cause variation at work. *Special-cause variations* are factors that affect process performance that are not derived from the process itself. In other words, something outside of the process is impacting process performance. If the data points all fall within the range, then you have a process under control—even if there is a great degree of variability. The way the in-limits points vary from one to another is called *common-cause variation*.

If you find that all the points fall within the limits and your process is under control, then you know you can now begin to move to tighten up the process, bring it more under control, shrink the common-cause variation.

Embrace upper and lower customer specs

The upper control limits and the lower control limits are statistical boundaries imposed on your data. There is another concept in Six Sigma: customer specs. There are two values here, the *upper customer spec* and the *lower customer spec*. These are the process performance limits imposed by the customers. Take pizza delivery, for example. A customer might accept a delivery that is up to 10 minutes early, but no earlier, or up to 10 minutes late, but no later. An automobile company might accept a ball bearing that is 5 mm in diameter, plus or minus .25 mm. These limits are important because they overlay with the upper and lower control limits to give your process measures a focal point in the reality of quality. Here is where you begin to see how closely what your process is doing matches to what your customer wants. The upper customer spec provided is typically called the Uspec. The lower customer spec provided is typically called the Lspec.

Calculate percent nonconforming

Once you have determined all the figures and calculations discussed previously, you may well end up with determining data that will allow you not only to understand how your processes have been performing to date, but predict how they will perform in the future.

In fact—helpfully—you can predict how many defects the process will produce, to close approximation, each time you run it. This is called *percent noncompliance*, or %NC.

The formula for %NC is:

%NC = Zu + ZL * 100

To get to %NC, you will need to generate two Z values: Z_U and Z_L.

The formula for the first is:

$$Z_u = \frac{|Uspec - \overline{\overline{X}}|}{s}$$

To get this figure, you take the upper customer spec and subtract the grand mean from it; then you take the absolute value of that sum and divide it by sigma.

Here is the formula for sigma:

$$s = \frac{\overline{R}}{D_2}$$

Here you go back to the Shewhart constants. You take the average range value and divide it by the D_2 column on the table, lined up with the sample size (n).

You calculate the lower Z value the same way as the upper Z value:

$$Z_L = \frac{|Lspec - \overline{\overline{X}}|}{s}$$

Then to generate %NC, add Z_U to Z_L, and multiply by 100.

Determine process sigma

Now you might want to determine the process sigma. This is done by determining the process yield. Run your process and count the defects (or generate %NC as described earlier). The process yield is calculated by subtracting the total number of defects from the total number of opportunities, dividing by the total number of opportunities, and finally multiplying the result by 100.

Here's an example.

You run a process that produces 18 defects.

You know from the process analysis that there were 12,500 opportunities for defects— chances where defects could have crept in. So you subtract 18 from 12,500 and get 12,482.

You then divide 12,482 by 12,500 to get .99856. You multiply .99856 by 100 to get 99.856. That is your process yield.

The final step is to use the process yield and look up the value on a *sigma conversion table*, such as the following:

Yield %	Sigma	Defects Per Million Opportunities
99.9997	6.00	3.4
99.9995	5.92	5
99.9992	5.81	8
99.9990	5.76	10
99.9980	5.61	20
99.9970	5.51	30
99.9960	5.44	40
99.9930	5.31	70
99.9900	5.22	100
99.9850	5.12	150
99.9770	5.00	230
99.9670	4.91	330
99.9520	4.80	480
99.9320	4.70	680
99.9040	4.60	960
99.8650	4.50	1350
99.8140	4.40	1860
99.7450	4.30	2550
99.6540	4.20	3460
99.5340	4.10	4660
99.3790	4.00	6210
99.1810	3.90	8190
98.9300	3.80	10700
98.6100	3.70	13900
98.2200	3.60	17800
97.7300	3.50	22700
97.1300	3.40	28700
96.4100	3.30	35900
95.5400	3.20	44600
94.5200	3.10	54800
93.3200	3.00	66800
91.9200	2.90	80800
90.3200	2.80	96800
88.5000	2.70	115000
86.5000	2.60	135000
84.2000	2.50	158000
81.6000	2.40	184000
78.8000	2.30	212000
75.8000	2.20	242000
72.6000	2.10	274000
69.2000	2.00	308000
65.6000	1.90	344000

Yield %	Sigma	Defects Per Million Opportunities
61.8000	1.80	382000
58.0000	1.70	420000
54.0000	1.60	460000
50.0000	1.50	500000
46.0000	1.40	540000
43.0000	1.32	570000
39.0000	1.22	610000
35.0000	1.11	650000
31.0000	1.00	690000
28.0000	0.92	720000
25.0000	0.83	750000
22.0000	0.73	780000
19.0000	0.62	810000
16.0000	0.51	840000
14.0000	0.42	860000
12.0000	0.33	880000
10.0000	0.22	900000
8.0000	0.09	920000

Based on the table, your process is operating at 4.5 sigma. Congratulations.

Tools for the Analysis Phase

The analysis phase can employ a good number of statistical tools and analytical techniques. Some of the common ones include:

- Histograms
- Pareto charts
- Time series/run charts
- Scatter plots
- Regression analyses
- Cause-and-effect/fishbone diagrams
- Five whys
- Process map review and analysis
- Value stream mapping
- Descriptive statistics
- Inferential statistics
- Probability analyses and trending
- Cause-and-effect diagrams
- Failure mode effect analyses

Improve

The I in DMAIC is for improvement. Through the collection and analysis of data, the Six Sigma team will reach a point where it has amassed enough information to determine how to make the process better. And so, it then works to improve the process, making changes so the process is more effective, more efficient, or both. All of this comes from the insights provided by the data. With Six Sigma, the solution is always in the data.

Through data collection and analysis, you will come to understand how the process performs, what its strong points are, what its weak points are, what kinds of defects are entering into the system, and where specifically they are coming in.

You can think of the analysis phase of Six Sigma as the point at which you identify the root causes of defects. You can think of the improvement phase as the point at which you remove the root causes.

The improvement phase generally consists of a series of six steps:

1. Assess
2. Develop
3. Select
4. Modify
5. Pilot
6. Verify

Let's take a brief look at each.

Assess

Through the analysis of the data, you and your team will have at hand a collection of improvement indicators. These indicators will point to where the process has significant variation, where it tends to become more unpredictable than at other points, and where it begins to drop its level of control. This is where you and your team should begin to assess your options. You focus on the root causes of defect introduction. The data should give you multiple ideas as to how to modify the work stream. Some of the options will hold more promise than others. Some may appear to hold promise but prove for other reasons to be impractical. Some may appear quick and easy to implement but may not show strong potential for change. Six Sigma is founded in data, but here you should bring your professional judgment into play, and that of your team, too. Assess the options before you. Review them against the backdrop of the organizational culture, the budget for process improvement, the schedule you are working on, and the goals you have established in your project plan.

Once you have critiqued the options, you can begin to develop some of the promising ones.

Develop

There are a few paths you can take when you begin to develop potential process improvement solutions. The analyses might indicate that one path might be to make corrections to existing process components. This may be the most expeditious route. If you can fine-tune process elements that already exist, you may be able to enhance performance without having to perform a lot of re-engineering. In mature process systems or in highly developed systems, this is usually the kind of action taken.

Another path may be to create new work flow extensions to account for missing process components. This comes about through data that shows root causes are due to unaccounted-for activities, the absence of which allows for significant performance variance. These kinds of situations are usually seen in relatively new process systems or in systems that work in dynamic environments where evolutionary change is continually in effect.

A third path may be to define new processes or new components to reroute work flows toward greater efficiencies. This path naturally requires the greatest amount of work. But it does deliver the advantage of allowing for the greatest degree of impact and the greatest degree of control.

The idea is to develop some of these ideas to the extent that their benefits become apparent to you and your team. Then you can make a decision to take the one with the greatest strategic potential and develop it for deployment.

Select

Here's what you've done so far. You have analyzed the data. You have assessed it for solution potentials. You have focused on certain possibilities and have begun to develop them to ascertain their promise for positive impact. Now you and your team can begin to focus on the hard solution. Study the options you have developed and make a prudent judgment to focus on the best one for the project. Select the solution to develop.

Keep the concept of practicality in mind. The solution with the most potential for change may not be the most practical at this point in time. Think through the needs of the organization, the proportions of your project, and the capabilities of your team. Then choose the solution that you know you can successfully implement while obtaining as much of your goal as you can.

Modify

Now you improve the process by eliminating the root causes of defects. You improve the targeted process by designing creative solutions to fix and prevent problems. You can also explore innovations and improvements using relevant technologies and improvement disciplines. The modifications should reflect the trends and constraints reflected in the data. In fact this modification step should be one of the simpler ones in this six-step activity. The only temptation here may be to veer creatively from what the data tells you. Try to resist that. Stay close to the strategic direction you have established so far, and the improvements should work well.

Pilot and Verify

Once you have the revisions down or the new elements in place, you should try to run the process through a real-life-like situation—a pilot. Piloting the solution is helpful for a number of reasons. You want to test the pilot out in an environment as close to production as possible. Test the working of the process and then evaluate the results of the pilot.

Once the pilot is completed and you and your team are fairly certain that the results recommend deployment, you should verify this conclusion with the rest of the organization. Up to this point, the Six Sigma effort has been largely confined to your team. Now, it's important to bring the organization in more fully on your efforts. Even though you may have full authority to deploy any improvements you deem appropriate, you should present your case to the organization in a formal manner.

The first step here is to thoroughly document the proposed improvement. This includes describing the existing process and its performance metrics, describing the proposed enhancements and the performance metrics gained from the pilot, defining the benefits to be realized from deployment of the proposed change, and outlining the kinds of deployment activities that may be required to install the improvements in the existing system.

Once the documentation is complete, you can present it to the organization. This is typically done as a peer-review session. You work with the organization to identify and select those knowledgeable people in the system who will be impacted by the change. They should have a chance to review the documentation, ask questions, and comment on it. The objective is to get the approval of this group, to gain their consensus that the deployment should proceed.

Figure 7-10 illustrates the improve phase of DMAIC.

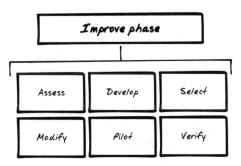

FIGURE 7-10. In the improve phase of DMAIC, the objective is to use the data analyses to formulate a path for improvements, and then take actions to make the improvements. Here you will use the data results to develop potential solutions, evaluate which are the most promising, and then refine the process to reflect the new approach, making it ready for deployment into the organization.

"I" Is also for Implement

The "I" in DMAIC is for "improve," but you can also think of it as standing in part for "implement." We'll see in the next section—in "C"—that the deployment of the improved process can be handled through a Control Plan. But sometimes the Control Plan has more to do with maintaining the performance of the process in the production environment. Where the idea is placed is not as important is that the concepts are carried out. The focus of implementing is to carry the improvement out into the organization, to deploy the solution in a coordinated and organized manner.

Some of the basic tasks here include developing a deployment/implementation plan, socializing this plan with the organization to gain support and cooperation, and then deploying the improvements according to the plan.

Tools for the Improve Phase

Some common statistical tools used in the improvement phase include:

- Design of experiments
- Analysis of variance
- Multivariate regression testing
- Process simulations
- Failure mode effect analysis

Control

The "C" in DMAIC is for control, and this step, like the others, can be thought of in a heavy way or in a light way, depending on the industry you're in and the focus of your project. The basic intention of control is to make sure the organization commits to institutionalizing the revised process and ensuring its enhanced performance. From this viewpoint, every process program needs a "C" step.

As discussed in Part 1 of this book, corporate habits, routines, and cultures can be hard things to change. When you introduce a new process or adjust an existing one, the company may have a tendency to want to revert back to their old ways. That's understandable. The old ways are usually very familiar, so they are easy to use. They seem natural because "that's the way things have always been done." And, good or bad, they were at least predictable. They were known quantities. But honoring such entropy-driven momentum is not a formula for improvement. And it's certainly not a formula for success.

The action behind control is to support the new way with the kinds of resources needed to make the new way the accepted way. To do this, you want to prevent the organization from reverting back to the old way. You want to set controls into the environment to keep the process on a true course.

IMPROVE

The improve phase includes the activities that result in process improvements. Here, based on the analysis of the data you've collected, you focus on potential improvement points to increase efficiencies and remove root causes of defects.

Assess
Examine the analytic results from the data and assess potential opportunities to make improvements.

Develop
Based on the opportunities, develop alternative solutions, documenting the rationale as to how each might result in improved performance.

Select
Evaluate each potential solution and then select the one that appears to promise the greatest return for the organization.

Modify
Modify the existing process in line with the structure of the solution. You'll emerge with a new refined process.

Pilot
Where practical, pilot the new process in a production-like environment; evaluate the changed performance.

Verify
Measure the performance of the process in pilot and verify that it operates as planned. If it does not, you may take it back to redesign. If it does, you can plan to roll it out to the organization at large.

A common disappointment in the field of process improvement is lack of control. We have heard stories of organizations that spend money and time to develop a program, and what they produce may end up being very good. But the program fails to take hold. The organization at large doesn't embrace it. It dissipates over time. Evaporates. The reason usually boils down to the issue of Control. The organization failed to set the right structures in place to control the use of the new program. This, of course, takes planning, and resources, and investment from management.

This is the light view of control. The heavy view is much more rigid and formal. It typically applies to manufacturing environments, where processes are embedded in substantial machinery and robotics. Control here is more than a concept of preparedness. It's the monitoring and maintenance of precise specifications, it's the accurate control of parts inventories, it's rigid adherence to maintenance schedules. But for the purposes of this book, we won't go into the deep end of control. Since we are focused mainly on the use of Six Sigma in technology development environments, we'll keep control constrained to its management meanings. This involves such tasks as the developing a Control Plan, allocating resources, and formally transitioning the processes into the production environment.

Figure 7-11 illustrates the control phase of DMAIC.

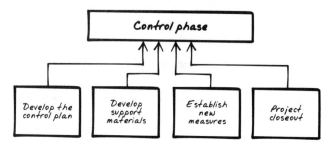

FIGURE 7-11. *In the control phase of DMAIC, the objective is to deploy improved processes into the organization. This involves documenting what the improvements are, how they affect the system as a whole, what training will be provided to process owners, and what support materials are available to operate and maintain the refined processes.*

The Control Plan

You can think of the Control Plan in the same way you think of a deployment plan or an implementation plan in the realm of systems or software development. The Control Plan is a plan you create to coordinate the smooth deployment of the new or refined processes out into the organization. Basically the Control Plan describes what is being introduced, how it is to be used, and what materials exist to support it. Following is an abbreviated list of some of the sections you might want to include in a Control Plan:

Description of the process additions or revisions
    This section describes what is being introduced into the organization. If it is a new process element, the description will include the purpose of the element, the steps involved or embedded in the process, the primary and secondary actors involved, inputs and entry criteria, and outputs and exit criteria. If the element is a revision of an existing process or procedure, then the descriptions are revisions of the existing documentation.

Mapping of the new functionality into existing process streams and flows
    Six Sigma is all about process improvement. But process improvement is not an isolated event. Most of the time, a process is part of a family of processes that represents a system. Systems are interrelated and interdependent entities. One process usually affects another. And so if you alter one process, you should have an understanding of how that change might impact upstream or downstream activities. A good way to do this is with a process map, or with revisions to existing process maps. These may be visual depictions or narrative descriptions. These maps will orient users to the new flows that are being incorporated into the system.

Identification of process owners

Process owners usually include three categories of people:

- The primary actors who are responsible for ensuring that the process is executed properly

- The secondary actors who are needed to provide input into the process or will use the output resulting from the process

- Management that relies on the process to account for standard or regulatory activity

It's a good idea to specifically identify these owners in the Control Plan. This helps establish the required readership for the Control Plan.

Description of production changes

When a process is modified or a new process is introduced, chances are the change will have a material impact on production. The product will change in some way. The change may be in the inputs that are fed into the process. It may be in the form that the outputs from the process take. The change may be in cycle time. A description of this change is useful in the Control Plan. If your people are going to be seeing something new appear in the production process, then they need to be prepped for what that new thing is. Since unexpected newness is typically called a deviation and counted as a defect, your plan should describe what the new processes will be producing.

Location and access of support materials

The new processes you have put into place should be accompanied by some form of supporting materials. These might be flowcharts, procedure manuals, reference sheets, forms, and other similar kinds of process tools. In the Control Plan you should identify what these assets are and where the users can find them. (See the following "Control Tools section.) The location of the materials should describe any access requirements, any check-out procedures, and the rules and standards regarding material versioning. The idea here is to guide the audience to the right materials: the latest and most complete versions. This way, they are ensured to use the most accurate release editions of the materials.

Training schedule

The concept of training should always go hand in hand with introducing new process components into any system. Many times this is a forgotten or neglected consideration. But the issue of training is essential to the successful use of any single process or process program. The deployment of the program is best preceded by some regimen of training. This might be coaching-based instruction, classroom training, computer learning, or video training. But whatever form it takes, the delivery of the training should be coordinated with those who will be required to use and manage the process. And so here it is helpful to define the training schedule and the audience that will be required to attend the training. To facilitate this, the organization should expend some energy designing, developing, and packaging the training materials and their manner of presentation.

Deployment schedule

The training schedule mentioned above establishes the timeline and focus of training efforts related to the process improvements. The deployment schedule serves a similar purpose. Naturally, an organization will not sneak in a process improvement in the dark, fly it in under radar. It should be a visible activity, a lights-on activity. After all, a single process improvement has the potential to touch and influence many parts of a working system. And so the deployment of the improvements should be part of what's communicated in the Control Plan. The deployment schedule usually identifies when the changeover will occur (and this may necessitate some downtime), who will be involved in the changeover, what systems or segments will be impacted (and what the impact will be), and how long the migration is expected to take.

Process performance measures

A final consideration for inclusion in the Control Plan is the performance measures that have been identified for this process. If the measures have not changed, it might be a good idea to still identify them and then reiterate their current applicability. If the process is new or significantly changed, then you may have identified new measures. Here you should consider describing what these measures are, how they are to be collected, what analyses are put against them, and how the analyses are interpreted and reported.

The Control Plan can be used to its best potential as a tool to institutionalize the improvements through the formal modification of systems and structures as articulated in the plan. It is a plan that establishes a path of carrying well-designed improvement into production in a permanent and productive way.

Control Tools

In one section of the preceding Control Plan, I described the process support materials available for the deployment and regular use of the improvements. These materials can be seen as a series of control tools. These are the process assets, such as development documentation and implementation support material, for ongoing use and management of the process.

Policies

Policies are typically used to shape executive-level expectations for process use and to demonstrate executive commitment to process adoption. For the new improvements, consider creating appropriate policies—endorsed by management—that set forth what the organization requires around process use. Policies of this kind are typically short documents (maybe a page or two), and they approach process use from a high level. But they carry the weight of executive mandate, and so they are valuable tools in emphasizing the importance of honoring the organizational way.

Standards and procedures

This is what is usually considered as the "real" process documentation. These tools are the documented procedure manuals, process steps, and activity standards that guide people in very direct ways in the use of the improvements. The common form of these—collected together—is the Instruction Manual. A new automobile—a complex system of interrelated processes—comes with its Owner's Guide. A new medication—a catalyst of complex organic processes—comes with its own Indications and Contraindications Insert. A new human being comes with the 64th edition of Dr. Spock's Baby Guide. These standards and procedures are indispensable components in rolling out new processes or new improvements successfully.

Templates and forms

The standards and procedures just described are often best supported by what are commonly called *reference implementations*. That's a fancy expression for "examples." To augment your standards and procedures, the organization might consider developing such process aids as templates, forms, checklists, and best-case examples. These are tools that the practitioners can use to immediately begin using and managing the process. The better designed ones will actually guide the user to effectively use the process.

Monitoring and control system protocols

Six Sigma retains a deep focus on control throughout its range of activities. This does not let up on deployment. In fact, it takes on a fresh perspective. An organization can use statistical and quantitative techniques to investigate opportunities for process improvement. IT can use the same to determine the most efficient way to improve existing process elements. Likewise, it can—and should—establish ongoing monitoring and control techniques that will help the organization continually collect performance data that can be amassed as a aid to making improvement decisions in the future.

Performance validations

This part of the Control Plan describes process improvement characteristics very particular to Six Sigma. These are the performance attributes that can be used to validate the improvements over time, proving that they were worth deploying after all. This is usually a section that describes new or extended forms of effectivity measurements. These may include such metrics as cost benefits, cost savings, throughput increases, defect reduction, profit growth, risk avoidance, fee avoidance. The kinds of metrics you elect to define here will naturally depend on the processes and the improvements you've set into place.

Project Closeout

The final activity conducted under control is project closeout. Here you are ready to wrap up the project, perform some last cleanup tasks, and then release the resources to new work. You can structure your closeout activities in the way that best suits your organizational needs. But there are five general activities you might consider. These are typically found as part of the closeout tasks on a typical Six Sigma project:

1. Finalize the documentation. Throughout the project, you and your team have been amassing documentation to drive your decisions and creating documentation to support deployment of your improvements. At this point, you should take a careful

inventory of all this material and ensure that it is either ready to be archived for future reference or that it is in a form ready to be published to the relevant groups within the organization.

2. Conduct lessons learned. This is a communal "what did we do right, what did we do wrong" session. This a review session in which the Six Sigma team convenes to identify and discuss the strengths of the current project, and (perhaps more important) to identify and discuss what they did not do so well, and what they might do better the next time around.

3. Communicate the change to the business at large. This communiqué shares the success story with the whole organization. It endorses the concept of continuous improvement and at the same time serves as further evidence that management and the company are committed to the ongoing activity of always making themselves better.

4. Celebrate. Step back and take a look at what you've accomplished. Chances are, what you've accomplished is going to move the company forward, forward in tangible ways. Ways that demonstrably position it closer to its goals. Ways that translates into discrete and measurable factors of business success.

The Six Sigma Team

Even from the light view of Six Sigma taken in this chapter, I hope it is clear that Six Sigma is not a casual, let's-try-it-out approach to process improvement. It's not a simple form of inputs, outputs, actors, and steps. It is a highly structured approach to decision making based on the methodological application of statistical design and quantitative analyses. That's why organizations that religiously employ Six Sigma do so with specialized teams trained in the methods and techniques of the program. You don't just throw a Six Sigma team together. You form a group with a specific set of dispersed skills. Here are some talents the people on your Six Sigma team could do well by possessing:

Knowledge of process systems

Knowledge of process systems is essential for any process improvement team. This is true for ISO 9001 and CMMI, and it is especially true for Six Sigma. The actions you take under Six Sigma are going to quantitatively alter how your processes operate. And improvements designed under Six Sigma are designed to stick. They are designed to be fixed in place. So you teams will be well served to have an appreciation of process systems and the concepts of process improvement. Otherwise they could be setting Six Sigma depth charges off all over the place.

I was recently called into the compliance office of a major telecommunications company to help them overhaul a process program that guided the way their business units engaged with IT. Frankly, the program was a mess: a hodgepodge of patches and fixes that had evolved over time into a convoluted mishmash. My first bits of advice had to do with remapping the program to its original high-level intentions, then flowcharting at descending levels what the program ought to be doing for the company. I got a very

CONTROL

The control phase is used to roll out process improvements into the organization at large. Since the effect here is to change the existing systems, the rollout needs to be conducted in a coordinated manner. This involves establishing a Control Plan and setting into place control tools:

Control Plan

The Control Plan is, in essence, a deployment and implementation plan. It describes what is being changed, who will be impacted, when the change will happen, and what materials are in place to support the new elements. This can include:

- Definitions of new features
- Identification of process owners
- Descriptions of production changes

Control tools

In order to control the proper operation of the new processes, it's important to provide the organization with adequate control tools. These are the assets that the process owners can use to integrate the new functionality into existing systems. This material typically includes elements like:

- Policies
- Procedures
- New measures

Project closeout

The final formal step in control is project closeout. Even though control is an ongoing process, this step signals the official end of the Six Sigma project.

---

bad reaction to that. The people in the compliance office apparently wanted me to take the program deeper. They thought it was failing because it was filled with holes. They never considered that maybe it was failing because it had gone to depths that would pop the rivets off any process program. It then dawned on me that these people, well intentioned as they were, had no real knowledge of process systems, of how to structure an effective process program, or the basic tenets of process improvement.

Knowledge of statistical data management and quantitative analysis

One of the points I've tried to make in this chapter is that you can take advantage of the Six Sigma methodology and the Six Sigma approach without having to necessarily check yourself into the realm of quantitative analysis. However, if you find that you and your team can tackle this aspect of the program, you'll be solidly armed to make both subtle and sophisticated process improvements across a wide range of environments.

One of the mantras of Six Sigma is "data-driven decision making." In other words, you don't decide to alter or adjust a process on whim. You don't do it because you've got a great idea or have developed an intuitive hunch. With Six Sigma, you can't say that things are better until you can show that they are better. And you show it with numbers. Data and the recognized interpretation of data have the power to tell a process improvement story in a totally convincing way. But to get to this point, you need people on your team who are familiar with designing the types of experiments relevant to Six Sigma analysis. You need people who are familiar with statistical techniques and who understand how to apply quantitative analyses.

Industry knowledge

If someone hires you to change the process that etches a microline into a layer of silicon 120 angstroms thick, you probably ought to know something about chip production. Like maybe what an angstrom is. If you're going to create a process used by project managers to estimate the time required to design a payroll system, it would help to know something about accounting. And if you're going to figure out how to time things so that the pizza comes out of the oven precisely 20 minutes before it's scheduled to arrive at someone's front door, it'd help to know how to bake a pizza. Industry knowledge is a great thing to have on your team. All industries are unique. They operate on individual tracks. The best way to begin to improve how the tracks run is to know how they were laid down in the first place and what they are aiming for. In fact, you could probably make a pretty good argument that if you had a choice of hiring really good process people who knew nothing about the industry in which they had to work, or hiring people who knew very little about the mechanics of process improvement but were renowned experts in the field in question, it would probably be the smart move to hire the industry ones. The key is, those guys are probably already process experts; they just haven't realized it. Your job could be to simply refine their way of thinking about process management and process improvement, guiding them as they begin to look into the innards of what they always saw in the past as a seamless whole.

Organizational expertise

Industry knowledge gives your team a degree of expertise on how the industry as a whole operates: the rules, the regulations, the generally accepted practices. That's good, but a great complement to that is knowledge about how the organization works. How your organization works. Every organization has a culture, and culture is little more than unwritten, unspoken, invisible processes woven into the fabric of the daily work routine. A process that might prove efficient and effective for one group might work terribly for another group. Same industry, same practice, maybe even the same job. But if the cultural fit is all askew, it will serve little constructive purpose. That's why with Six Sigma teams you should possess a degree of organizational familiarity. Your people should have a good feeling for how processes work in the culture, what kinds of improvements might be welcomed, what sacred cows should not be touched, and how change could best be introduced.

If you pepper your Six Sigma teams with this kind of qualification knowledge, then the players should be positioned to operate well on your Six Sigma projects.

That brings us to the question of certification. In the domain of Six Sigma, there are recognized roles. These are people who have been recognized through training and experienced to possess the kinds of technical Six Sigma skills that allow them to make specific contributions on Six Sigma projects. Let's take a brief look at what these designations are.

CAVEAT EMPTOR

At this point, I'd like to remind the reader that the following descriptions of what are commonly called Six Sigma Professional Designations are pretty much meaningless. Lots of people take exception to my position on this. But I don't mean that negatively. I mean it sincerely. The problem as I see it is that Six Sigma is not a program or a methodology that is controlled by a central governing body. ISO 9001 has the International Organization for Standardization. CMMI has the Software Engineering Institute. Those bodies train people, audit and register companies, and generally monitor the market's use of their standards.

But that doesn't exist with Six Sigma. And so any organization can claim that it is a Six Sigma training facility or a Six Sigma consulting firm. In metro Atlanta, I can receive a Six Sigma Green Belt Certificate by spending $1,800 for a five-day course offered by Southern Polytechnic, or I can get a Six Sigma Green Belt Certificate by spending $400 for a three-day course offered by "Hexagon Consulting."

Here's the kicker: the $400 course might be exponentially better than the $1,800 one. There's just no way to be sure. And so when somebody presents themselves to you as a Green Belt or a Master Black Belt, I recommend that you appreciate it for what it is, but look closer. As with almost any kind of certification, the proof of competence and professionalism comes not with a degree of accomplishment but through the application of experiential knowledge.

Six Sigma Champion

The Six Sigma Champion is usually an executive or high-level manager in the organization with the ability to promote and sponsor the use of Six Sigma. Champions may manage a series of Six Sigma teams, or they may simply fund and support Six Sigma projects. Champions should have a pretty good working knowledge of Six Sigma, but more than that, they should share an enthusiasm for the promise and approach of Six Sigma, believing in the Six Sigma vision of improvement through data management and quantitative analysis. Well-positioned Champions will possess authority to:

- Control resources
- Allocate budgets
- Assign responsibility
- Set strategic direction

Champions are the executive sponsors of the Six Sigma world, and they usually direct and develop the organization's Six Sigma programs.

Master Black Belt

Master Black Belt is the highest level of Six Sigma certification. This is an individual who has not only had extensive training in the methodology and techniques of Six Sigma, but who has also had extensive experience designing and implementing Six Sigma projects in a variety of organizations. Master Black Belts possess a deep understanding of DMAIC, as well as Design for Six Sigma and the Design Measure Analyze Validate Deploy methodologies. They are considered experts at applying statistical measurements to diverse and heterogeneous data sets, and they have a solid grasp of the use and application of quantitative techniques to understand process performance and derive empirical process improvements.

Master Black Belts have the ability to manage Six Sigma programs as well as program teams. The tradition with Master Black Belts is that they can empirically demonstrate that their projects—designed and managed by them—have saved companies hundreds of thousands of dollars. The term "hundreds of thousands" is not used here for dramatic purposes. It's to be taken literally. In the true Six Sigma culture, no one will call herself a Master Black Belt if she is not able to put that data in front of a client.

Black Belt

Black Belts typically lead Six Sigma projects. They may design the project with the help of a Master Black Belt, or they may design it on their own. They are usually highly trained in Six Sigma methods, with solid experience in DMAIC, DFSS, and DMAVD. Like Masters, they should have sound knowledge in applying statistical measurements to diverse and heterogeneous data sets. And they should have broad experience applying Six Sigma methods to a number of process improvement projects. They should be able to demonstrate very strong statistical and quantitative analysis skills, effective project management skills, strong interpersonal and communication skills, and strong writing and organizational skills. Like Masters, Black Belts should also be able to show empirical cost savings or ROIs as a result of their Six Sigma project work. Most reputable Six Sigma Black Belt courses require that the candidate design, plan, and execute a real-world project with the potential to save an organization at least $100,000.

Green Belt

Six Sigma teams are usually mostly composed of Green Belts. These are people with at least one pretty in-depth course in Six Sigma applications and the interest (and opportunity) to work on a Six Sigma project. They have a beginning ability to produce statistical control charts, calculate percent noncompliance, plot histograms and Pareto charts, identify common-cause and special-cause variation, and calculate process sigmas. They have a good working knowledge of DMAIC, DSFF, and DMAVD and are positioned to participate in Six Sigma projects of varying complexity, size, and duration. They are the field soldiers in the world of Six Sigma.

Yellow Belt

Green Belt, Black Belt, and Master Black Belt are well-accepted Six Sigma designations. Yellow Belt is less so. Many people think there should be no such things as a Yellow Belt. I tend to agree. Because when you think about it, under a Green Belt, a Yellow Belt can only be a Six Sigma team contributor. And if someone is on a Six Sigma team but is not really trained in any of the methodologies, design considerations, or statistical techniques, they can't really be expected to contribute a lot. I guess he could perform measurements and collect data; those are valuable activities, but they probably don't warrant a belt of distinction on their own. What does it take to be recognized as a Yellow Belt? If you read this chapter, twice, slowly, you might be able to qualify.

For a Deeper Look

There are many, many good references available to give you a deeper look into Six Sigma. Here are few that I have found to be useful:

The Six Sigma Handbook, Revised and Expanded by Thomas Pyzdek (McGraw-Hill)
> This is a very complete and comprehensive look at Six Sigma. It covers a good many of the statistical tools you can use in a Six Sigma program, providing a pretty solid picture of Design of Experiments. It also covers the types of management systems that can complement a Six Sigma program.

The Six Sigma Way by Peter S. Pande et al. (McGraw-Hill)
> Here is another thorough look at Six Sigma. *The Six Sigma Way* describes how you can adapt and implement Six Sigma across a variety of conditions and environments. The emphasis here is on designing the program to align with specific business goals and objectives. A large part of the book is devoted to implementing Six Sigma in this way, and the authors don't shy away from the complexities you'll probably face when using Six Sigma to shape corporate strategies and directions.

Six Sigma for Everyone by George Eckes (Wiley)
> This work provides more of a general overview to the theory and practice of Six Sigma. While this book is short and keeps to a general tone, it does provide a good look at the technical and design aspects of the program, featuring lots of statistical charts, graphs, and tables often used in Six Sigma analyses.

Statistics for Six Sigma Made Easy by Warren Brussee (McGraw-Hill)
> The realm of statistics that can be applied to Six Sigma design and analysis is wide and deep, and this book addresses many, many statistical tools and techniques. I don't know if you can call the understanding an easy one—unless statistics is your forte—but this book explains things in a clear and concise way and does a good job of explaining how certain approaches are more appropriate than others for specific types of Six Sigma projects.

What Is Lean Six Sigma? by Michael L. George et al. (McGraw-Hill)

This is a little book—just over 90 pages—but anyone brand-new to Six Sigma will find that it provides a handy overview. It's cleanly written and illustrated and takes the reader through the main topics that surround Six Sigma.

Six Sigma for Green Belts and Champions: Foundations, DMAIC, Tools, Cases, and Certification by Howard S. Gitlow and David M. Levine (Prentice-Hall)

From the title, one would think that this is a general-overview type book. But at over 700 pages, it's really a very comprehensive and detailed look at Six Sigma. Its focus is on information useful to Champions and Green Belts, and from that angle, the authors take a solid look at what it takes to sponsor a Six Sigma program, what it takes to run one, and what kinds of activities and considerations are needed to provide ongoing support for the program.

Summary

Six Sigma is a process improvement tool based on statistical analysis and data-based decision making. The activities in Six Sigma seek to create and refine processes that reflect the Voice of the Customer, those products and service attributes that deal with what the customer wants and needs.

- Six Sigma defines *quality* as any production element that supports the customer's vision of the product (or service).

- Six Sigma defines *defects* as those elements that interfere with the customer's vision.

- Six Sigma follows a general five-phase methodology that works to define and implement process improvements:

Define

Define the problem to be solved, the goal of the project, and the scope of the investigation.

Measure

Collect appropriate measures to determine current process performance levels.

Analyze

Apply statistical and quantitative techniques in order to empirically define performance potentials and identify improvement opportunities and goals.

Improve

Modify the existing processes to reflect improvement opportunities.

Control

Deploy the improvements into the organization with the support material needed to ensure proper operation and maintenance.

- Six Sigma professionals are known as Champions, Master Black Belts, Black Belts, and Green Belts.

CHAPTER EIGHT

Considerations for Adoption

NOW THAT YOU HAVE TAKEN BRIEF LOOKS AT **ISO 9001:2000**, THE **CAPABILITY MATURITY MODEL** Integration, and Six Sigma, you may want to compare these three against some common considerations for adoption.

First, however, it's important to note that these three leading standards are not really choices that are mutually exclusive; they can coexist quite well together. A large company might operate under the umbrella of ISO 9001 and have its IT shops working at CMMI Level 2 under this umbrella. And it might measure the performance of this CMMI program using Six Sigma.

On the other hand, smaller organizations (or those new to process) will probably want to make something of choice, focusing on the standard that, at least initially, appears best suited to its needs.

In this chapter, I'll make a rough comparison between ISO, CMMI, and Six Sigma. I say rough because the three standards do not really share a common structure. And each has a focus that is, in application, somewhat different from the others. But they do have some major traits in common. Each of the three represents an approach to process improvement. Each presents a framework that can be used to structure process improvement efforts. Each has been shown to be effective for the IT industry. And each has a large base of users that constitute a substantial support community.

I'll make the comparison two ways. First, by looking at a series of program traits you might consider when thinking about your organization. And second, by examining a set of traits typically found in quality management and process programs and looking at how each of the three tends to deal with them.

Let's begin with the first. Here there are 12 common adoption considerations. I'll take a look at how each of the three programs compare with respect to:

- Application to IT
- Required knowledge and skills
- Adoption depth
- Cultural shift
- Resource commitments
- Program recognition
- Legislated support
- Support community
- The short-term view
- The long-term view
- Proven effectiveness
- Documented ROIs

Application to IT

ISO 9001:2000

ISO 9001 is a "generic" quality standard. ISO 9001 can be applied to any production environment, including environments that produce technology products. ISO 9001 is expressed at a level high enough that it can fit IT shops. At the same time, it is not built to directly address the industry-specific needs of IT. So while it is not what we might call an IT standard, it is suitable for use in IT development organizations.

CMMI

CMMI is a process improvement framework built specifically for technology development. It contains recognized best practices for systems engineering, software engineering, supplier sourcing, and integrated product and process development. This model was specifically designed for use in technology shops, so much so that it is not readily applicable outside of the realm of IT.

Six Sigma

Six Sigma is typically applied in manufacturing environments or in business environments that are transaction-heavy. Six Sigma can and has been applied in technology development shops, but its full range of application may not be suitable for projects like mid-level software and systems development. Six Sigma may offer greater value to IT operations and system maintenance organizations in which performance has stabilized and can now be measured and improved.

Required Knowledge and Skills

ISO 9001:2000

Required knowledge and skills include those special assets you and your teams will need to implement an improvement program effectively. Aside from basic knowledge of process improvement and a good sense of proportion about what's right for your culture, ISO 9001 does not require a large degree of specialized knowledge and skills. The Standard is expressed in generic language that can be interpreted in ways that will fit within your groups. The most important tip here could be to work with people who know the business you're in and appreciate how process can potentially help it flourish.

CMMI

CMMI naturally requires knowledge of the model and what is recommended under the model. The specific technology slant embedded in CMMI supports the requirement that its implementers be knowledgeable about technology development life-cycle phases and considerations. Additionally, because CMMI emphasizes the application of recognized best practices, its teams should have solid experience with the execution and management of technology projects.

Six Sigma

Six Sigma, when used to its full scope, can be considered the most specialized of the three programs. Like ISO 9001 and CMMI, it uses a set methodology, and its impetus is founded in the principles of process improvement. But Six Sigma carries with it the additional dimension of statistical and quantitative analysis. Concepts like Design of Experiments, control charting, and standard deviation run throughout the program and require a degree of formal analytical and design experience.

Adoption Depth

ISO 9001:2000

Of the three leading standards, ISO 9001 probably has the greatest adoption depth. What makes this Standard different in part from CMMI or Six Sigma is that it is a collection of requirements. To be in compliance with the Standard, you must implement its requirements. And these requirements cover five sections of instruction: Sections 4 (Quality Manual), 5 (Management Responsibility), 6 (Resources), 7 (Product and Service Provision), and 8 (Measurement and Improvement). All of these make up ISO 9001:2000, and so you are required to implement them all.

CMMI

CMMI is a collection of 22 Process Areas. If an organization elects to implement CMMI using the Continuous Representation, then it can choose to work on whatever Process Areas best meet the needs of the company's quality goals. That can be 1, 6, or 20. If the organization uses the Staged Representation, it must follow the SEI's fixed adoption path.

Six Sigma

Six Sigma can be implemented to whatever degree you want to implement it. You can turn teams loose on the whole organization. You can start with one small team looking at one specific issue. Unlike ISO 9001 and CMMI, the methodologies of Six Sigma impact how the Six Sigma team works, usually not how the organization works. And so, Six Sigma can be said to have a shallow adoption depth.

Cultural Shift

ISO 9001:2000

The idea of cultural shift relates to change management. With a process program like ISO 9001, CMMI, or Six Sigma, you are introducing change, something new, something different. That requires an organizational shift. ISO 9001 is structured in a way that allows you to control the amount of shift. It is a series of management requirements, but the requirements are defined in such a way as to promote customization. You can implement ISO 9001 in a "heavy" way, one that pushes for significant cultural shift, or you can implement it in a "light" way, one that calls for less directed shift.

CMMI

Of the three standards, CMMI may—on average—require the strongest cultural shift for an IT shop. This is because CMMI is focused on technology. Its practices are all technology and technology management practices. And so when an IT shop implements CMMI, it is going to impact the way the shop operates. IT activities will change based on the Process Areas being adopted, but they will change. For the changes to be effective and to have their intended impacts, cultural behavior will have to change, too.

Six Sigma

Because Six Sigma employs such a focused methodology, and because it targets very specific issues, it does not tend to have broad immediate cultural impact. But when adopted in the right spirit, the spirit of Six Sigma tends to have a significant influence on the cultural position. With Six Sigma, there are no organizational sacred cows. Everything is up for improvement. And so the organization should adopt the philosophy that business as usual is never good enough. This may be a natural progression for some organizations. For others, it might be torture.

Resource Commitments

ISO 9001:2000

The number and diversity of resources you are required to commit to your ISO 9001 program is going to depend on the scope of your Quality Management System. But at the very least, you will need people to create and document the program, people to run the program, and people to monitor the use of the program. This is very similar to CMMI. The difference from Six Sigma is that ISO 9001 and CMMI reach in to impact all those who operate in the Process Areas that you are defining. With ISO 9001, this touches on management, requirements, design, execution, test, and all the other facets of production.

CMMI

The Process Areas and best practices in CMMI will impact your organization three ways: they have to be created, they have to be followed, and they have to be monitored. That's very similar to ISO 9001. But CMMI reaches down a little deeper, and so it probably involves a greater percentage of the organization. For the program you build from it to be successful, you will need the cooperation of those whose activities are being defined. These people will then have to exercise these definitions in practice, and others in the organization will have to monitor and report on the use of these practices.

Six Sigma

You can implement a robust Six Sigma program without having to commit a lot of resources to it. The commitment you will have to make is to bring in people who are skilled in Six Sigma methodologies, who are skilled in statistical and analytical techniques, and who have some foundation in process improvement and organizational change. But from a sizing perspective, a competent Six Sigma team can be represented by a handful of people.

Program Recognition

ISO 9001:2000

The International Organization for Standardization in Geneva is the most recognized standards body in the world. And ISO 9001:2000 is the world's most recognized quality standard. Because we have no evidence yet of life on other planets, we might say it is the most recognized quality standard in the cosmos. Over its life, the ISO 9001 Standard has become recognized by more countries, industries, and companies than any other comparable offering. It is indisputably the most widely accepted quality standard we have.

CMMI

CMMI is widely recognized, not just in the U.S., its sponsor, but around the world. When it comes to process programs designed specifically for technology development, it's generally seen as the leading contender. Like ISO 9001 and Six Sigma, CMMI has been receiving a lot of press lately, as the value of process and process management becomes more ingrained in IT cultures. There are other options in the marketplace—surprisingly many—but CMMI, ISO 9001, and Six Sigma continue to hold place as entities recognized for their own values.

Six Sigma

Six Sigma is a widely known process improvement program. It has lately received more press perhaps than either CMMI or ISO 9001. There is a lot of interest within the IT community for what Six Sigma might be able to offer IT shops. But the depth of knowledge that gives these shops a critical capability to judge Six Sigma still seems to be maturing.

Legislated Support

ISO 9001:2000

The ISO is made up of over 140 member countries from around the world. These countries fund the activities of the ISO, including standards maintenance and revisions. That makes ISO 9001:2000 one of the best-funded and best-backed quality standards on the planet. There is no doubt that the ISO will continue to develop and maintain 9001:2000 now and in the future. And the organization will no doubt augment the Standard with add-ons and support tools.

CMMI

CMMI's continued development and support is funded in large part by the U.S. Congress by way of the Department of Defense and Carnegie Mellon University in Pittsburgh, Pennsylvania. This level of official support is a great benefit for a process program. It ensures that the standard will continue to be maintained, extended and developed, and monitored through a centrally coordinated governing body and a well-supported user community.

Six Sigma

Six Sigma has no legislated support. It is not an official program of any governing organization. It is a form of shareware. It is a type of open source process improvement program. How organizations develop it, extend it, or augment it is strictly up to individual groups.

Support Community

ISO 9001:2000

Because the ISO is made up of member countries from around the globe, it has a huge support community. There are ISO-sponsored conferences, user-group meetings, and symposiums. There are consultants and auditors through the U.S. who can help you establish a program and then evaluate it for registration with the ISO. There are books, white papers, tip sheets and a host of supporting material from the community to back up the Standard with information and assistance.

CMMI

CMMI has a very large support community, both nationally and internationally. There are annual and quarterly conferences for SEPGs, the Software Engineering Process Groups that are common in organizations implementing CMMI, and these are held around the globe. There are also groups and clubs for CMMI Appraisers and Instructors. And the SEI itself hosts a variety of CMMI symposiums, meetings, and user sessions.

Six Sigma

Six Sigma has a very broad and diverse support community. The plus side to this is that there are multiple and plentiful resources where you can find Six Sigma support, training, and services. The other side to this carries a bit of caution with it. Because Six Sigma is an unregulated standard, there is nobody to govern how the support community uses or shapes the program. In fact, there is no standard shape for this standard. So it's advisable to screen your Six Sigma resources for competency, experience, and credentials.

The Short-Term View

ISO 9001:2000

ISO 9001:2000 provides a basis for establishing a Quality Management System and institutionalizing it inside an organization. Its purpose is to give you a foundation upon which you can build a quality management program. And so we probably shouldn't think of ISO 9001 as relevant to any short-term view of process improvement. It represents an integrated approach to the strategic management of the organization's production activities. Such integration, and its effectiveness, takes time to evolve.

CMMI

Like ISO 9001, there really is no short term for CMMI. The goal of CMMI is to help an organization set processes into place that improve the way it creates technology products. But this proof takes time to realize, just as the results of any change take time to realize. Some organizations move to adopt CMMI because they will be able to win restricted contracts or because their management said they had to, and so they approach the task with the short-term view in mind. But with CMMI, the short term tends to reflect the costs and the investment required. The real benefit does not become apparent until the organization has committed to its use and monitoring over time.

Six Sigma

Of the three standards, Six Sigma probably provides the most potential for short-term success. Because it is used to address specific and pre-identified performance issues, it is by nature a short-term solution. The aim of Six Sigma is not to implement global or strategic improvements. Too many variables exist in those domains. Its aim is to pinpoint and target opportunities to refine current processes. And so you can implement Six Sigma with a view to taking quick action (a relative term) to modify how the organization operates.

The Long-Term View

ISO 9001:2000

ISO 9001:2000, like CMMI, is a strategic solution for organizational quality. It is also a program that touches most groups within an organization that are involved in any aspect of production or production support. Because of its scope and its depth, this is a Standard that performs best when the long-term view is taken. ISO 9001 programs set processes in place to guide, monitor, and measure production work flows. To get the most out of these processes, the organization needs to make a long-term commitment to setting them into place, using them, and working to continually make them better.

CMMI

CMMI has a "great" long-term view. I put "great" in quotes because it's a correlative great. CMMI takes time to show its rewards, and the stretch of time allows in variables. But here is what I can report: organizations that adapt well-designed CMMI programs and stick to them over time tend to demonstrate significant improvement in their abilities to meet schedules, budgets, and quality expectations. They are able to perform in a predictable manner. They are able to control the unforeseen better than in the past.

And so they are able to deliver in much more reliable function. Were other variables involved in this stretch of time? Maybe. But the data reported to the SEI and anecdotal confirmations seem to reliably link one to the other. (See "Documented ROIs," later in this chapter.)

Six Sigma

Just like ISO 9001 and CMMI, Six Sigma can deliver on its promise of long-term results only through the commitment of the organization to its methods and methodology. Relatively speaking, Six Sigma does not provide long-term solutions. It provides for continuous short-term refinements. Over time, these refinements can add up to a significant improvement from where you started and where you are now.

Proven Effectiveness

ISO 9001:2000

In many industries in Europe, you can't even bid on a contract if you do not carry ISO registration. That requirement alone says something about the effectiveness of ISO 9001. Over the years, its effectiveness and value have been well documented. With standards like ISO 9001 and CMMI, there will always be something of a soft fix on issues like effectiveness and ROI. But the fact that ISO 9001 has a track record that is, at the very least, highly correlated with success indicates strongly that the program can and does make a difference when conscientiously applied.

CMMI

Many U.S. and international organizations now insist on CMMI "certification" (not the most accurate term, but it will work here) when contracting out IT work. For example, the U.S. Department of Defense and Housing and Urban Development rely on certification as a way to select qualified vendors. CMMI has the same soft-fix issue when it comes to effectiveness that ISO 9001 has. Organizations don't tend to measure the effectiveness of the program. They tend to measure success factors that tend to come from the program, and so we can only correlate CMMI with proven effectiveness. Nevertheless, there is plenty of evidence that shows this correlation to be strong.

Six Sigma

Six Sigma has a solid track record of proven performance. It lacks the broadcloth application of ISO 9001 or CMMI, but its targeted focus may be seen as a plus for measuring effectiveness. You implement Six Sigma on a targeted issue: to address a specific problem. Because it is applied with such a fine focus, and because it is based on data and data analysis, you can directly tie Six Sigma activities to improvements in environmental performance, efficiencies, and effectiveness.

Documented ROIs

ISO 9001:2000

Studies of ISO adoption show ROIs in the range of 2:1 to 24:1. As you'll see next with CMMI, that's a pretty big range. Measuring process ROIs has always been tricky. It's easy to measure the delta in a product or the improvement in efficiencies, but because systems are usually large or complex things, ROIs can only be generalized because there is a tendency for so many variables to be at play. And then there is the fact that ROIs come in different sizes and shapes, depending on how the program was implemented.

CMMI

Studies of CMMI adoption—admittedly limited in scope and with only medium-sized samples—show ROIs in the range of 1.85:1 to 45:1. That's a pretty big range, and it's one of the problems with ROI data on practice-based process improvement programs. ROIs come in different sizes and shapes, depending on how the program was implemented.

Six Sigma

Six Sigma leads the pack here with documented returns-on-investments in the billions of dollars. Billions. Motorola and General Electric alone have credited Six Sigma with these kinds of savings. Six Sigma lends itself to ROI analysis because of its own empirical data. With Six Sigma, you measure both *before* and *after* performance. So it's relatively easy to see what your process improvements have done for you in terms of investment and return.

In the next section, I'll discuss 23 traits that are usually addressed, in some form or fashion, by quality management program or process improvement methodologies.

The 23 are as follows:

- Third-party recognition
- Customer satisfaction
- Focus on quality
- Documentation requirements
- Required actions
- Management responsibility
- Organizational oversight
- Continuous improvement
- Resource requirements
- Training
- Planning
- Requirements management
- Configuration management
- Design
- Verification
- Validation
- Defect management
- Root-cause analysis
- Measurement activity

- Statistical process controls

- Supplier management

- Reporting

- Auditing

Third-Party Recognition

ISO 9001:2000

ISO provides official recognition of compliance with the 9001:2000 Standard through the use of registration. Select independent companies can act as registration bodies for the ISO. Certified auditors conduct assessments of the organization to ensure adequate compliance with the requirements contained in the Standard. A successful audit results in the organization being registered at the ISO.

- Registration audit

- Conducted by a certified ISO auditor

CMMI

Organizations that adopt CMMI can receive third-party recognition through a SCAMPI A appraisal. This is an event similar to an ISO audit. A Lead Appraiser authorized by the SEI appraises the organization's compliance with selected parts of the model and, based on the findings, awards the organization a maturity-level or capability-level rating.

- SCAMPI Class A (and also B and C) appraisals

- Conducted by an SEI Authorized Lead Appraiser

Six Sigma

Unlike ISO or CMMI, Six Sigma lacks a central governing body. So the program has no form of third-party registration or certification. Organizations that wish to publicize their progress using Six Sigma often publish the sigma levels of their processes, or point to the number of trained Master Black Belts, Black Belts, etc., on their staff.

- No official third-party recognition

- Process sigmas often cited as a level of accomplishment

Focus on Customer Satisfaction

ISO 9001:2000

The 9001:2000 Standard adopted a stronger position on customer satisfaction, perhaps borrowing from Six Sigma. The Standard focuses on the customer by first directly linking the definition of quality to meeting the customer requirements, making this a management responsibility. It then obligates technical and production activities to be responsive to customer involvement. Finally, the organization is required to periodically measure customer satisfaction.

- Section 5.2, Customer Focus

- Section 7.2, Customer Related Focus

- Section 8.2.1, Measure Customer Satisfaction

CMMI

CMMI does not address the topic of customer satisfaction as directly as ISO 9001 and Six Sigma do. The model focuses chiefly on what the organization should do to ensure that it is prepared to manage its projects in a responsible manner and that, by extension, it meets customer requirements. But there are no goals or practices that promote activities centered on customer satisfaction.

- No practices directly addressing customer satisfaction

- Support for eliciting customer needs and verifying customer requirements

Six Sigma

Six Sigma has a strong foundation in customer satisfaction. The program defines quality in large part as an organization's ability to deliver to customers those features and services that are important to them. Using this "Voice of the Customer" approach, the organization designs its efforts around product/service traits deemed to be CTQ, Critical to Quality.

- Strong focus on the Voice of the Customer

- Critical-to-Quality issues directly reflect customer needs

Focus on Quality

ISO 9001:2000

The underlying aim in all three of these programs is better quality management. ISO 9001 has at its base the Quality Management System. The Standard is designed to help an organization thoroughly think through its quality values. First it is required to define its quality objectives. Then it is required to design its Quality Management System around those objectives.

- Section 4.2, Document a Quality Policy and a Quality Management System

CMMI

Two process areas in CMMI address the management of quality in project work. The Process and Product Quality Assurance Process Area is designed as the auditing element of the model. PPQA provides, in part, objective insight into the organization's ability to produce product according to its quality standards. Peer reviews (described under the Verification Process Area) provide a complementary, albeit more technical, level of inspection into the quality of project products.

- Process Area: Process and Product Quality Assurance

- Process Area: Peer-review practices described under Verification

Six Sigma

In Six Sigma, the idea of quality is born solely out of the needs of the customer. The obligation of the organization is to produce products (or services) specifically tailored to what the customer wants. Missing features result in a deficient product. Too many features result in a superfluous one. Both states are considered wanting in terms of quality. The entire focus of Six Sigma is to produce processes and products that meet customer requirements.

- Quality equates to the feature set defined (or required) by the customer

Program Documentation

ISO 9001:2000

The Standard requires the organization to define and document the major elements of its Quality Management System. This includes documenting the quality objectives, the organizational Quality Policy, all the components of the Quality Management System, and the required QMS records.

- Section 4.2, Documentation Requirements

CMMI

CMMI requires that you document your program as it grows in maturity and capability. Generic Goals 1 through 5 direct the organization to "establish and maintain" appropriate sets of processes. This phrase connotes documenting the processes and then maintaining them as they evolve within the organization.

- Generic Goals 1 through 5: Establish processes that are performed, managed, defined, quantitatively managed, and optimizing

Six Sigma

The push of Six Sigma is to measure processes, and then to perhaps redefine them. As a rule, the program does not require you to document anything. However, the "define" part of the DMAIC life cycle does call for the definition of a project plan. This plan details the approach the team will follow when it undertakes its measurement, analyze, and improvement activities. The program also features steps in the control phase to define documentation that may be needed to redefine, monitor, and maintain improvements in the field.

- Promotes a documented project plan defining the measurement, analyze, and improvement approach
- Promotes use of control documentation that defines how improved process performance will be redefined, monitored, and maintained

Required Actions

ISO 9001:2000

Across its five main sections, ISO 9001 contains a series of requirements that the organization must meet in order to be seen as officially compliant with the Standard. The requirements are expressed as "shall" statements—for example, "The organization shall document a quality policy."

- Provides a series of requirements that must be realized for compliance
- Requirements are presented as "shall" statements

CMMI

The contents of the CMMI spec fall into three general categories: required, expected, and informative components. The only required components are the specific and generic goals described for each Process Area. The specific and generic practices that support the goals are expected components: you are generally expected to follow something similar to reach the goals. The rest of the material is informative in nature.

- Required components: specific goals and generic goals

Six Sigma

The program has no defined requirements. But Six Sigma does promote two methodologies, each with sequential steps. DMAIC is used to improve existing processes and includes the steps define, measure, analyze, improve/implement, and control. DMAVD (or Design for Six Sigma) is used to design new processes and includes the steps design, measure, analyze, validate, and deploy.

- No fixed requirements
- DMAIC methodology for existing processes
- DMAVD methodology for the design of new processes

Management Responsibility

ISO 9001:2000

Section 5 of the Standard deals with management responsibility, and the ISO places a strong emphasis on this responsibility. In general, management is responsible for three broad activities: designing the focus of the Quality Management System, defining and allocating the resources needed to run the system, and periodically reviewing the use of the system by the organization.

- Section 5, Management Responsibility
- Section 5.5, Responsibility, Authority, and Communications
- Section 5.6, Management Review

CMMI

Throughout CMMI, the model places emphasis on the involvement of senior management in the direction and use of the organization's process program. The Process Area Organizational Process Focus promotes the design of a strategic improvement plan. Process and Product Quality Assurance provides senior management with insight into quality and compliance issues. And GP 2.10 recommends that senior management periodically review the status of process components at play across projects.

- Process Area: Organizational Process Focus
- Process Area: Process and Product Quality Assurance
- Generic Practice 2.10, Involve Senior Management

Six Sigma

There are no direct management responsibilities defined for Six Sigma. However, there is broad recognition in the Six Sigma community that management's support of and involvement in Six Sigma projects is essential to program success.

- Management often represented as Six Sigma Champions

Organizational Oversight

ISO 9001:2000

Section 5.6 of the Standard calls for management to review the workings of the QMS on a regular basis. This typically covers measures of process performance, product quality, and customer satisfaction.

- Section 5.6, Management Reviews

CMMI

Two process areas in CMMI promote an organizational approach to the direction, design, and management of the process program. Organizational Process Focus establishes an organizational strategy for process improvement. Organizational Process Definition establishes an organizational repository of process assets for use by the organization's project teams.

- Process Area: Organizational Process Focus
- Process Area: Organizational Process Definition

Six Sigma

Six Sigma projects can take place at nearly any level within an organization. This being the case, the program does not define any requirements for organizational control. The role of the Champion does imply the need for organizational support, and in many organizations, Champions guide Six Sigma programs, but this at the discretion of the organization.

- No requirements for organizational control

Continuous Improvement

ISO 9001:2000

The ISO Standard devotes an entire section to continuous improvement.

- Section 8.5.1, Continuous Improvement

CMMI

At its core, CMMI is itself a model for continuous process improvement. One Process Area that addresses this directly is Organizational Innovation and Deployment. Here, practices are defined for identifying opportunities for process improvement, opportunities for process innovations, and methods for evaluating, piloting, and deploying process advancements. Additionally, Generic Practice 3.2 promotes the collection of improvement information, a support activity that can feed into OID.

- Process Area: Organizational Innovation and Deployment
- Generic Practice 3.2, Collect Improvement Information

Six Sigma

One philosophy of Six Sigma is that all processes should be open to analysis, that nothing should be immune from investigation and potential improvement. In this way, Six

Sigma supports continuous improvement. Additionally, the control phase of DMAIC promotes the periodic remeasurement of improved processes in the field.

- Continuous improvement through cyclical measurement and analysis of select processes

Resources

ISO 9001:2000

Section 6 of the Standard defines the resource requirements needed to properly run the QMS. This includes human resources, people skilled and trained in their job responsibilities; infrastructure resources, providing appropriate facilities; and work environment resources, the tools and equipment needed to run the system.

- Section 6.1, Provide Resources
- Section 6.2, Human Resources
- Section 6.3, Infrastructure
- Section 6.4, Work Environment

CMMI

When a managed process is implemented under CMMI, the model recommends that adequate resources be provided so that the process can be effectively practiced. Generic Practice 2.3 defines this practice. The term *adequate resources* includes the people, tools, equipment, and facilities needed to support the process.

- Generic Practice 2.3, Provide Adequate Resources
- Process Area: Organizational Environment for Integration

Six Sigma

Six Sigma does not stipulate resource requirements. However, the use of roles such as Master Black Belt, Black Belt, and Green Belt are promoted across various project design and execution activities.

- No fixed resource requirements
- Promotes appropriate use of Master Black Belt, Black Belt, and Green Belt roles

Training

ISO 9001:2000

Training for ISO 9001 is addressed under Section 6, Resources. The standard requires that the people assigned to manage the QMS are appropriately skilled to carry out their job duties. This includes assigning competent people, orienting them to the mission and reach of the QMS, and training them in their specific job responsibilities.

- Section 6.2.2, Competence, Awareness, and Training

CMMI

Training is an area that is continually supported under CMMI. The model devotes a Process Area to this domain, Organizational Training. Here the organization establishes an appropriate training capability and then delivers required training to its people. Additionally, Generic Practice 2.5 promotes training for those people who will be required to carry out the processes established for a project.

- Process Area: Organizational Training
- Generic Practice 2.5, Provide Training

Six Sigma

Recommendations for process training appear in the control phase of DMAIC. Control activities can include training people to properly use the new or improved processes. Outside of the program, the industry has developed a series of courses that support Six Sigma's potential to use sophisticated statistical process control techniques. These courses are built around Six Sigma belt designations: Master Black, Black, and Green.

- No specific program training stipulations; industry support for belt training
- Process training recommended in the control phase of DMAIC

Planning

ISO 9001:2000

Planning takes on a two-dimensional emphasis under ISO 9001. The first dimension is the planning of the Quality Management System. Management is responsible for ensuring that the systems objectives, policies, and process components are planned and then created. The second deals with product realization. Project plans are required to be established before product realization activities are begun.

- Section 5.4, Planning
- Section 7.1, Planning Product Realization

CMMI

Planning is a core theme that runs throughout all Process Areas in CMMI. In the model, planning is an essential act for sound management. The Process Area Organizational Process Focus helps the organization establish strategic plans for process management and improvement. Project Planning provides practices and guidelines for planning projects. Integrated Project Management extends PP by emphasizing the use of a standardized set of project processes. And GP 2.2 recommends that all activities embedded in a process be planned, monitored, and controlled.

- Process Area: Organizational Process Focus
- Process Area: Project Planning
- Process Area: Integrated Project Management
- Generic Practice 2.2, Plan the Process

Six Sigma

Planning activities are described in the define phase of DMAIC. Here, the Six Sigma team documents the approach the Six Sigma project will take. Planning is also suggested in the implement phase: plans for how to deploy the improved processes into the production environment.

- Planning is included in the define phase of DMAIC
- Plans for improvement rollout are often included in the implement phase

Requirements Management

ISO 9001:2000

Requirements management is customer-based under ISO 9001. Section 1 presents this focus as being threefold: work to understand the customer requirements, design and select processes to meet those requirements, and periodically confirm that the system is operating in such a way as to meet the requirements. (Related activities occur for configuration management.)

- Section 1.1, Understanding and Meeting Customer Requirements

CMMI

CMMI devotes two Process Areas to requirements management. Requirements Development presents practices for establishing customer and product requirements, and for validating these for completeness and appropriateness. Requirements Management presents practices for understanding the requirements, obtaining commitment to them, and tracking and controlling changes to the requirements.

- Process Area: Requirements Development
- Process Area: Requirements Management

Six Sigma

Requirements in Six Sigma are used as the basis for evaluating the performance and suitability of processes. Desired requirements are defined as Critical-to-Quality traits. Undesired traits are defined as defects. Both of these are used to shape the aim of the Six Sigma project and so are usually contained in the project plan and reflected in the project's scope and purpose.

- Emphasis on the definition of Critical-to-Quality issues
- Emphasis on the precise definitions of defects
- Requirements are bounded in the project purpose and scope

Configuration Management

ISO 9001:2000

Control is a major trait in the 9001 Quality Management System. Elements within the program and elements managed by the program are required to be controlled. Section 4 defines requirements for the version control of system documents and records. Section 7 deals with requirements for the configuration management of design and development changes, and for preserving audit trails of product components and establishing traceability of these components.

- Section 4.2.3, Control of Documents
- Section 4.2.4, Control of Records
- Section 7.3.7, Control of Design and Development Changes
- Section 7.5.5, Preservation of Product

CMMI

CMMI defines a Process Area for configuration management practices. Configuration Management promotes the establishment of product baselines, the management of changes to the baselines, and auditing baseline repositories to confirm ongoing integrity. Additionally, Generic Practice 2.6 promotes version or configuration control of important project work products that may emerge under process activity.

- Process Area: Configuration Management
- Generic Practice 2.6, Manage Configurations

Six Sigma

Configuration management is typically employed in Six Sigma during the measure and analyze phases of DMAIC. Data collection occurs in the measure phase. Here it is important that the integrity of the data be protected. This includes control over data access as well as data manipulation. In the analyze phase, the integrity of the data must be maintained in order to ensure the validity of the results that spring from statistical analyses.

- Data integrity is stressed in the measure and analyze phases of DMAIC

Design

ISO 9001:2000

Section 7 of the Standard deals with Product and Service Provision, and this includes requirements for product design. Here are contained the requirements for planning the design, for managing design inputs and outputs, for reviewing designs, and for verifying and validating design components.

- Section 7.3, Design and Development

CMMI

The Process Area Technical Solution presents practices for establishing proper technical solutions for a project, designing product components, designing component interfaces, validating these against customer needs, and then implementing the designs.

- Process Area: Technical Solution

Six Sigma

Design activities may encompass the most crucial step in the DMAIC process. They have the potential to address investigations that are simple or highly complex. The statistical guidelines in Design of Experiments are often called into play here. These are typically described in the definition phase and continued in the analyze phase. For new process development, the DMAVD methodology includes a distinct design phase.

- Design of Experiments is a technique to apply the appropriate statistical approach to a specific project or theory
- Design of new processes is also a key step in the DMAVD methodology

Verification and Inspections

ISO 9001:2000

Verification is covered under Section 7.3.5 of the Standard. The activities defined here are set into place to verify that the design components can be traced back to the customer requirements, that no requirements have been omitted, and that the represented set constitutes the proper system configuration.

- Section 7.3.5, Design and Development Verification

CMMI

The Process Area Verification covers two types of test and inspection activities under CMMI. Verification activities are conducted to verify that resulting products explicitly meet the requirements as defined for the project. Peer reviews are conducted to ensure that the iterative quality of products is maintained and controlled across selected phases of product development.

- Process Area: Verification
- Verification Goal: Conduct Peer Reviews

Six Sigma

The general purpose of the DMAIC methodology is to verify that improvements to a process will result in closer allegiance to customer needs. In this way, Six Sigma supports verification. This inspection point typically occurs during the analyze phase, when the performance data is examined and analytical results are interpreted to surmise the level of compliance with CTQs.

- The analyze phase of DMAIC is used to verify the process's goodness-of-fit to CTQs

Validation

ISO 9001:2000

Two sections in the Standard deal with validation. The first occurs under design activities. Here the product (service) designs are validated to ensure that they are appropriate for the operating environments. The next occurs later on in the production cycle. Elements of the product to be delivered are validated to ensure that they will operate properly in the intended production environments.

- Section 7.3.6, Design and Development Validation
- Section 7.5.2, Validation of Process and Product Service Provision

CMMI

Validation is a Process Area under CMMI that deals with ensuring that the products produced by the project teams will operate properly in the intended customer environments. Practices are defined to prepare for validation and to define specific validation activities, as well as to conduct these activities.

- Process Area: Validation

Six Sigma

The implement phase of Six Sigma precedes the control phase, and here the guidelines for process validation are typically established. These can describe tests to ensure the new or revised processes will work properly in the production environment.

- The implement phase can be used to define process deployment and validation rules

Defect Management

ISO 9001:2000

Defect management is addressed in Section 8 of ISO 9001. Section 8 deals with measuring and monitoring product and processes. If a product nonconformance is found—a defect—the Standard defines requirements for identifying, labeling, and managing the defect. If process or product defects are found, the Standard also describes requirements for taking corrective actions to remove the defect.

- Section 8.3, Control of Nonconforming Product
- Section 8.5.2, Corrective Actions

CMMI

Defect management under CMMI is mainly addressed through three Process Areas. Verification activities are defined to ensure that products fully meet customer requirements; and that results of verification activities (defects) are analyzed for follow-on actions. The same approach applies to Validation, although here the emphasis is on product performance in a production environment. Causal Analysis and Resolution deals with practices to identify and remove the root causes of defects in processes and products.

- Process Area: Verification
- Process Area: Validation
- Process Area: Causal Analysis and Resolution

Six Sigma

Early on in Six Sigma projects, defects are precisely defined. They are usually expressed as traits that detract from or impact Critical-to-Quality elements. Defects are typically defined in the define phase of DMAIC and then they are evaluated in the analyze phase and addressed in the improve/implement phase.

- Defects are defined in the define phase
- Defects are addressed in the analyze and improve phases

Root-Cause Analysis

ISO 9001:2000

The sections of the 9001 Standard that deal with defect correction are described in the previous section. The other side of this issue—prevention—enters here with root-cause analysis. Section 8.5.3 describes requirements to identify the root cause of process and product defects, and then work to remove those causes, thus preventing the defects from entering into the system.

- Section 8.5.3, Preventive Actions

CMMI

Causal Analysis and Resolution deals with finding the root causes of product and process issues and then taking action to remove these causes. CAR defines practices to identify opportunities for causal analysis, to initiate plans to address the causes, and then to implement these plans.

- Process Area: Causal Analysis and Resolution

Six Sigma

At its heart, Six Sigma is a root-cause analysis tool. Its purpose is to identify the root causes of problems in processes and to identify ways to remove or reduce them.

- Six Sigma is a root-cause analysis regimen

Measurement Activity

ISO 9001:2000

Section 8 of ISO 9001 is heavily focused on measurement and analysis. Here the Standard describes three basic areas where measurements should be taken: measurements of customer satisfaction, measurements of product quality, and measurements of process performance. These measures should then be analyzed to determine overall improvement opportunities.

- Section 8.2, Monitoring and Measurement
- Section 8.2.1, Monitoring and Measuring Customer Satisfaction
- Section 8.2.3, Monitoring and Measuring of Processes
- Section 8.2.4, Monitoring and Measuring of Product
- Section 8.4, Analysis of Data

CMMI

The Measurement and Analysis Process Area defines practices for establishing a measurement capability that is in line with business objectives. This PA also describes practices to define measurements, collection and storage procedures, analytic techniques, and reporting mechanisms.

(This area is complemented by the use of statistical process controls; see the following section.)

- Process Area: Measurement and Analysis

Six Sigma

Six Sigma is heavily based on the collection and analysis of measurements. The measure phase in DMAIC includes activities to collect process performance measures. This is extended in the analyze phase where the measures are analyzed and interpreted.

- Data is systematically collected during the measure phase of DMAIC and then interpreted in the analyze phase

Statistical Process Controls

ISO 9001:2000

ISO 9001 places strong emphasis on measuring process performance and product quality. But the Standard has no requirements for the use of statistical process controls or quantitative analysis.

- No requirements for statistical or quantitative analysis

CMMI

The use of statistical process controls is typically introduced at higher levels of sophistication under CMMI, the assumption being that an organization will need time to reach a stage where quantitative management can be employed. Quantitative Project Management defines practices for managing a project's quality and performance objectives quantitatively. Organizational Process Performance establishes practices for defining process performance baselines and models.

- Process Area: Quantitative Project Management

- Process Area: Organizational Process Performance

Six Sigma

More so than either ISO 9001 or CMMI, Six Sigma is able to rely on the full scope of statistical process controls as part of its approach to process improvement. In the define phase, the program establishes the range of measures and statistical techniques it will apply to the analysis of process performance. This is then carried out in the measure, analyze, and implement phases.

- Designs of Experiment along with measurement and analysis techniques are established in the design phase

- Data is systematically analyzed, evaluated, and interpreted during the analyze phase of DMAIC

Supplier Management

ISO 9001:2000

Section 7.4 of the Standard deals with requirements that center on the control of purchasing activities. These requirements define activities to ensure that suppliers are adequately qualified, that product selection is based on established criteria, and that supplier activities are monitored.

- Section 7.4, Purchasing

CMMI

Two Process Areas deal with managing suppliers. Supplier Agreement Management defines practices for selecting and working with qualified suppliers. Integrated Supplier Management defines practices for establishing ongoing and participatory working relationships with suppliers.

- Process Area: Supplier Agreement Management
- Process Area: Integrated Supplier Management

Six Sigma

Six Sigma makes no independent stipulations for dealing with suppliers.

- No stipulations for managing or evaluating suppliers.

Reporting

ISO 9001:2000

ISO requires that the organization produce 23 kinds of records in order to demonstrate adequate management of the Quality Management System.

- Documentation records
- Management review records
- Resource records
- Design records
- Product and service provision records
- Measurement and monitoring records

CMMI

CMMI does not require the kinds of system reporting that are found in ISO 9001. However, it does require that measurement activities and results be reported to the organization. It also requires that the results of compliance and quality audits be reported to management. And across the Process Areas in the model are practices for the general reporting of status and updates to management and stakeholders.

- Process Area: Measurement and Analysis
- Process Area: Process and Product Quality Assurance
- General status and update reporting recommendations throughout

Six Sigma

There are no fixed reporting requirements in Six Sigma, but they are implied in the analyze phase, as results of the Six Sigma efforts are typically reported to management to clear the way for implementing improvements.

- No fixed reporting requirements

Auditing and Oversight

ISO 9001:2000

ISO 9001 requires that the organization periodically audit the activities of its teams with the guidelines of the Quality Management System. Two areas are required to be audited. First, audit activities must be conducted against the processes of the QMS. Second, audits must be conducted to assess the quality of the products being produced under the QMS.

- Section 8.2.2, Internal Audit
- Section 8.2.3, Monitoring and Measuring of Processes
- Section 8.2.4, Monitoring and Measuring of Product

CMMI

Auditing under CMMI is similar to ISO 9001. The Process and Product Quality Assurance Process Area defines auditing and compliance reporting practices. Under this PA, process compliance is periodically audited, work product quality is assessed, noncompliance issues are resolved, and results are reported to senior management.

- Process Area: Process and Product Quality Assurance

Six Sigma

While there is no auditing feature embedded within Six Sigma, one can think of the program as an oversight capability in and of itself. Six Sigma is built as a tool to support data-driven decision making in pursuit of process improvement. It can be used to provide insight into performance and quality objectives at the executive level.

- Six Sigma itself can be thought of as performance oversight for an organization
- Activities in the control phase of DMAIC encourage periodic performance re-measures

Summary

- ISO 9001:2000, CMMI, and Six Sigma share many similar characteristics.
- The programs can be implemented independently or in tandem with one another.
- ISO 9001:2000 is a generic quality standard that can be implemented in any production environment.
- ISO 9001:2000 may be best used in organizations where the quality system required crosses many different types of functional areas.
- The Capability Maturity Model Integration is a process improvement model specifically designed for use in technology development environments.
- CMMI may be best used in IT shops that are charged with systems and software development.
- Six Sigma is a process improvement approach based in statistical analyses and geared toward shaping process to reflect the Voice of the Customer.
- Six Sigma may be best used in environments that are transaction intensive: those in which many similar actions are run through a set of stable processes.

G

Gartner Dataquest, Software Support Portfolio Review, 8
Gartner Group, Worldwide IT spending report of 2004, 8
General Electric, 22, 36, 74
Gentle Shepherds, 88
Goldman, Susan, 44
Grover, Shailesh, 44
guidelines, 54, 84

H

heavy versus light processes, 33
Hitachi and quality control, 129
Honda and quality control, 128
Honeywell, 22
Hughes Aircraft ROI, 25

I

Ichwantoro, Kricket, 107
IDEAL (Initiate, Diagnose, Establish, Act, and Learn), 50–52
IdeaMall, 66
implementation scheduling, 85
improvement opportunities, identifying, 60–65
industry, borrowing successes from, 48
Information Technology Management, 9
Initiate, Diagnose, Establish, Act, and Learn (IDEAL), 50–52
innovation and process, 40
inputs, 53
institutionalization, 85–92
    Assassins, 91
    Blind Victors, 86
    Drill Sergeants, 89
    Gentle Shepherds, 88
    Personal Trainers, 88
    Thankful Patrons, 87
International Electrotechnical Commission (IEC), 127
International Federation of the National Standardizing Associations (ISA), 127
International Organization for Standardization, 127, 254, 307
invisibility of technology industries, 6
iSix Sigma, 255
ISO 9000
    as a family of standards, 130
    history, 129
    ISO 9001, ISO 9002, ISO 9003, and ISO 9004, 130

ISO 9001, ownership, 133, 193
ISO 9001:2000, 7, 127–187
    adoption considerations
        adoption depth, 305
        application to IT, 304
        auditing and oversight, 326
        configuration management, 319
        continuous improvement, 316
        cultural shift, 306
        defect management, 322
        design, 320
        documented ROIs, 310
        focus on customer satisfaction, 312
        focus on quality, 313
        legislated support, 308
        long-term view, 309
        management responsibility, 315
        measurement activity, 323
        organizational oversight, 316
        planning, 318
        program documentation, 314
        program recognition, 307
        proven effectiveness, 310
        reporting, 325
        required actions, 314
        required knowledge and skills, 305
        requirements management, 319
        resource commitments, 306
        resources, 317
        root-cause analysis, 323
        short-term view, 309
        statistical process controls, 324
        supplier management, 324
        supported community, 308
        third-party recognition, 312
        training, 317
        validation, 321
        verification and inspections, 321
    common structure, 135
    five core directives, 131
        establish processes to meet the requirements, 132
        improve continuously based on the results, 133
        monitor, control, and measure the processes, 133
        provide resources to run the processes, 132
        understand the requirements, 131
    history of, 128, 130
    normative reference (Section 2), 138
    Quality Management System (QMS), 135
    required records, 135
    resources, 186
    scope (Section1), 137

James R. Persse is a nationally recognized technology and process management consultant. With over 20 years of industry experience, Dr. Persse is an SEI-authorized CMMI Instructor and a certified Six Sigma professional. His practice specializes in working with Fortune 500 technology organizations to select, design, and implement process improvement programs in the fields of development, integration, project management, systems engineering, and software engineering.

Dr. Persse is the author of *Implementing the Capability Maturity Model* (Wiley) and *Bit x Bit: Topics in Technology Management* (Little Hill).

He can be reached at *jpersse@AltairSol.com* or at *jrp@persse.com*.

COLOPHON

The cover image is an original photograph by Mike Kohnke. The cover fonts are Akzidenz Grotesk and Orator. The text font is Adobe's Meridien; the heading font is ITC Bailey.

Better than e-books

Buy *Process Improvement Essentials* and access
the digital edition FREE on Safari for 45 days.

Go to www.oreilly.com/go/safarienabled
and type in coupon code UNM5-NYLM-ALHR-53M3-FZAN

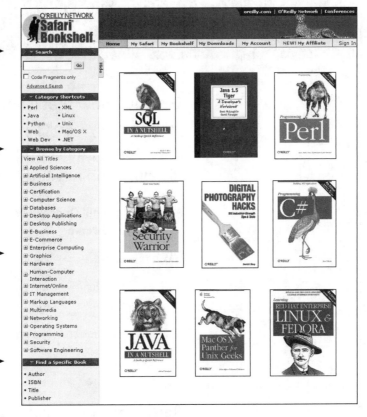

Search
thousands of
top tech books

Download
whole chapters

Cut and Paste
code examples

Find
answers fast

Search Safari! The premier electronic reference
library for programmers and IT professionals.